INSIDE
AL-SHABAAB

HARUN MARUF and DAN JOSEPH

INSIDE AL-SHABAAB

The Secret History of Al-Qaeda's Most Powerful Ally

Foreword by Christopher Anzalone

Indiana University Press

This book is a publication of

Indiana University Press
Office of Scholarly Publishing
Herman B Wells Library 350
1320 East 10th Street
Bloomington, Indiana 47405 USA

iupress.indiana.edu

Manufactured in the United States of America

Library of Congress
Cataloging-in-Publication Data

Names: Maruf, Harun, author. | Joseph, Dan
    (Journalist), author.
Title: Inside al-Shabaab : the secret history
    of al-Qaeda's most powerful ally / Harun
    Maruf and Dan Joseph ; Foreword by
    Christopher Anzalone.
Description: Bloomington, Indiana :
    Indiana University Press, 2018. | Includes
    bibliographical references and index. |
    Description based on print version record
    and CIP data provided by publisher;
    resource not viewed.
Identifiers: LCCN 2018019388 (print) | LCCN
    2018032045 (ebook) | ISBN 9780253037510
    (e-book) | ISBN 9780253037480 (cl : alk.
    paper) | ISBN 9780253037497 (pb : alk.
    paper)
Subjects: LCSH: Shabaab (Organization)|
    Terrorism—Somalia. | Insurgency—
    Somalia. | Islam and politics—Somalia. |
    Somalia—Politics and government—1991-
Classification: LCC HV6433.S582 (ebook) |
    LCC HV6433.S582 S53 2018 (print) | DDC
    303.625096773—dc23
LC record available at https://lccn.loc.gov/
    2018019388

1 2 3 4 5   23 22 21 20 19 18

CONTENTS

PART FOUR: RESURGENCE

FOREWORD

Christopher Anzalone

BEFORE THE RISE OF THE Islamic State and its pretensions as the new "caliphate," Al-Shabaab ran a multitiered governing administration over vast swaths of central and southern Somalia, threatening the very existence of Somalia's internationally recognized government. The militant organization recruited hundreds of foreign fighters from North America, Europe, the Middle East, and sub-Saharan Africa and established itself as a key regional ally and, later, affiliate of Al-Qaeda. Through its civil and political administrations, Al-Shabaab collected taxes and extorted "protection" money from locals, made alliances with businessmen engaged in the illegal charcoal trade, ran Sharia courts, and imposed a harsh form of law and order through its *Hisbah* police force. The United States, European Union, and Somalia's African neighbors had good reason to be alarmed.

Indeed, Al-Shabaab was a pioneer in jihadi-insurgent governance, building itself from the ashes of the Islamic Courts Union following the December 2006 Ethiopian invasion and ensuring its primacy over Somalia's insurgency through the ruthless use of coercion and outright violence. From its setup of a robust machinery for territorial control to its use of public events like communal prayers and outdoor executions, Al-Shabaab blazed a path for Sunni militants that would later be built on and scaled up massively by the Islamic State. The Somali jihadi group was also a trailblazer in the use of media, establishing a strong presence on Twitter and other social media platforms, and running a multilingual foreign propaganda campaign along with a domestic messaging operation aimed at Somalis. Most recently, Al-Shabaab deployed its media tools in the run-up to the 2017 Kenyan elections, releasing a string of propaganda videos in English, Swahili, Somali, Cushtic, and other regional languages.

Al-Shabaab represents a hybrid form of militant political Islam that is transnational in its ambitions while remaining, thus far, primarily local and regional in its core strategic operations. Although many analysts have predicted that the group's internal divisions and clashing personalities would result in an organizational split, Al-Shabaab has weathered leadership decapitation by US drone strikes and bouts of severe internal discord and infighting that claimed the lives or forced the flight of several of its founding leaders, as well as a sustained challenge from Islamic State. Despite suffering significant territorial, personnel, material, and financial losses since 2011, the group today remains a capable and resilient insurgent force. The presence of more than twenty thousand African Union troops in Somalia has not impeded the militants' ability to attack targets in that country or in Kenya, where Al-Shabaab has set up a network of cells and regularly conducts hit-and-run attacks on police and military targets.

Harun Maruf and Dan Joseph bring their years of experience in reporting on African politics and affairs for Voice of America to tell the story of the founding, rise, decline, and rebound of Al-Shabaab. Utilizing an array of sources, including interviews with Somali politicians and government officials, current and former insurgents, and Somali Islamists from Al-Shabaab, its predecessor Al-Itihad, and its onetime partner Hizbul Islam, Maruf and Joseph document in fascinating and extensive detail how the founding cadre of Al-Shabaab met and formed what would become one of the most formidable jihadi organizations in modern history, which would include the former ice cream server and US-educated university student Ibrahim al-Afghani, the rigid and slightly built Afghanistan-trained commander Aden Hashi Farah Ayrow, and the utterly ruthless emir of the group, Ahmed Godane.

Written with the flair and engaging prose of an action novel but with keen attention to sourcing and detail, the book documents Al-Shabaab's evolution from its days as the most radical faction within the military wing of the Islamic Courts Union to the bitter street fighting that wracked Mogadishu in

2009 and 2010, when it threatened the survival of Somalia's fledgling federal government. It also covers the transition back to asymmetric warfare following the group's loss of major urban centers such as Mogadishu, Baidoa, and Kismayo. Maruf and Joseph uncover new information about the organization's inner workings and divisions and take readers through key events in its history, such as the meeting in September 2014 to replace Godane after he was killed in a US drone missile strike and the group's heavy crackdown on Islamic State sympathizers and defectors.

The result is a gripping narrative account of the history and evolution of one of the deadliest and most successful jihadi organizations not only in Africa but in the world. The book, which is accessible to general readers while also containing new insights for scholars and other specialists, is a must-read for those interested in global affairs, contemporary conflicts, African politics, and political Islam.

CHRISTOPHER ANZALONE is a research fellow with the International Security Program at the Belfer Center for Science and International Affairs at Harvard University's John F. Kennedy School of Government and a PhD candidate (ABD) at McGill University. He has written extensively on political Islam, jihadist movements and organizations including Al-Shabaab, Shi'ite Islam, and Islamic visual cultures and new media.

SOURCES AND ACKNOWLEDGMENTS

WE WROTE THIS BOOK TO lift the veil on one of the most secretive, deadly militant organizations in the world. Several books and hundreds of articles have been written about Al-Shabaab or its role in Somalia's long-running cycle of violence. Many of these works are informative and insightful. But as reporters and editors who cover the events of the country on a daily basis, we felt uniquely well-positioned to write a detailed, comprehensive history of the group.

Gathering inside information about a US- and UN-designated terrorist group with a ruthless internal police force and a reputation for assassinating its critics is a difficult task but not an impossible one. We were able to interview more than a dozen former fighters and high-level officials who have defected from Al-Shabaab, most notably Mukhtar Robow Abu Mansour, the former deputy leader of Al-Shabaab, and Zakariye Ismail Hersi, the former Shabaab military intelligence officer, who gave us a small part of their vast knowledge about the group. We also interviewed dozens of people who fought against the group, including Somali government officials, military officers, and intelligence personnel, as well as many doctors, journalists, and ordinary civilians who were up-close witnesses to Al-Shabaab's violence. Their insights into Al-Shabaab and how the group has shaped or impacted people's lives were vitally important to telling this story.

xii | Sources and Acknowledgments

Special thanks goes to a few people who were especially generous with their time and help, including former Somali defense minister Abdihakim Mohamud Haji Fiqi, former intelligence officers Ahmed Moallim Fiqi and Abdi Hassan Hussein, and expert analysts Matt Bryden and Roland Marchal. We greatly appreciate them and their contributions to this book.

The majority of interview subjects agreed to be quoted by name. But because of the still-precarious security situation in Somalia and the sensitivity of the events being discussed, some people insisted on using an alias or speaking on condition of anonymity. To protect their safety we have honored their wishes.

A few of the interviews took place just in time. We spoke to the late commander of the Somali national army, General Abdikarim Yusuf Dhagabadan, who was killed in an Al-Shabaab attack on the Sahafi Hotel on November 1, 2015. May he rest in peace. We also spoke to Abdishakur Mire Aden, author of the book "Rise of Somalia Islamists," who gave us advice when we started researching for this book. Tragically, he was killed in the bombing of Mogadishu's Central Hotel on February 20, 2015. May he, too, rest in peace.

In addition to interviews, we spent countless hours reviewing news reports and analyses of Al-Shabaab's activities, as well as the group's own statements and videos, to locate and verify key information. The news reports came primarily from the Voice of America's Somali Service, CNN, major wire services (Reuters, Agence France-Presse, and the Associated Press), a handful of newspapers that closely covered the Somali conflict (*New York Times, Washington Post, Christian Science Monitor, Wall Street Journal, Guardian*) and Somali news organizations, particularly Shabelle News, Radio Horn Afrik, Mareeg News, Hiiran News, Garowe Online, and the Somaliland Times. As for Al-Shabaab's own material, most of it was accessed through websites such as YouTube, Jihadology, and SITE Intelligence.

Many more hours were spent poring over documents related to the group. Most of the documents come from one of four sources: US diplomatic cables released by WikiLeaks in what that organization calls the "Cablegate" leak; the indictments and trials of Al-Shabaab fighters, fund-raisers, and supporters by the US government; letters captured by US special forces from Osama bin Laden's compound in Pakistan and later released by the National Director of Intelligence; and the "Clinton emails"—the emails recovered from the private server that Hillary Clinton used while US secretary of state. Virtually all this material is available for viewing online, in its original form, if one takes the time to dig it out.

There are some people whose names do not appear in the text but who were immensely helpful "behind the pages" of this book. One is Elizabeth Arrott, a superb editor who looked over the early drafts of the manuscript, steered us toward punchier prose, and gave valuable input on the organization and flow of the chapters. She could do this book-editing thing full-time if she chose. Doug Alexander, a truly eagle-eyed editor, also provided an early and important copy edit.

Big thanks goes to Adam Omar, a keen observer of Somalia affairs, for his advice and for providing some of the photos. Also thanks to journalists Ismael Mukhtar Omar and Feisal Omar of Thomson Reuters who provided some previously unseen photos taken during the long battle for Mogadishu between pro-government forces and Al-Shabaab.

Last but not least, we thank our families who were patient with us as we spent long hours reporting, writing, rewriting, and editing in order to bring this project to fruition.

Harun Maruf and Dan Joseph
December 2017

INSIDE
AL-SHABAAB

BIRTH OF A MILITANT

A SLIM, CLEAN-SHAVEN YOUNG MAN sits on a rug, body hunched over a low-rise desk, eyes locked on the pages of a Quran. Sunshine pours in through tall, arched windows, beckoning him outside. But the teen stays focused on the text. His teachers at this *madrassa* have told him over and over: study hard, earn high marks, and you could win a scholarship to attend school abroad next year. The young man, a curious, inquisitive sort, likes that idea very much.

Dalha Ali has spent the past five years living and studying at al-Hidaya mosque in Mogadishu, learning the ways of the *Tabliq*, a sect of Sunni Islam known for peaceful and itinerant proselytizing. Overall, it's been a good experience. The mosque is in Wahara-Adde, a suburb in the Huriwa district with gentle hills and easy access to the beach, less than five kilometers away. The education has been first-rate, the accommodations decent, he's made friends, and he gets to go home every Friday and spend time with his family. But going to a university in a faraway country like Pakistan or Bangladesh ... That sounds like an adventure, not to mention an opportunity to advance his education. He can't wait to move on.

Then, off in the distance—the crackle of gunfire. The boom of artillery. Concentration broken, he raises his head and cocks an ear to the window. Are the sounds moving closer? No, but they aren't that far away. Must be the Isaley airstrip again, he thinks. The third battle there this month. The warlords don't want to give it up. But they'll have to, God willing. The mujahideen will take it from them.

With that thought, Ali's heart beats a little faster.

His heart is not alone. It is May 2006, and many residents of Somalia's capital are rooting for the mujahideen—the self-proclaimed fighters for Islam—to rout the warlords and their private armies who have dominated the city for the past fifteen years. It hasn't been so bad in Huriwa, which sits on Mogadishu's northeastern fringe. But for residents closer to the city center, life is a daily high-stakes gamble. Rich people are kidnapped and held for ransom. Rich and poor alike must pay fees to get by the warlords' roadblocks. Everyone is subject to a high risk of robbery, and too little cooperation with any of these crimes can lead to an early death, courtesy of a burst of bullets from an angry gunman. The people are sick of it, sick of suffering and dying, and are glad that *somebody* is finally attempting to restore order to their violent, lawless city. The warlords banded together and launched a joint attack against the emerging Islamist militias in February. But since then the Islamist side has won battle after battle.

Perhaps no one is more excited than young men in madrassas like eighteen-year-old Dalha Ali. Each night, after finishing their assignments and prayers, Ali and his fellow students gather to talk about the latest developments, gleaned from radio reports and hearsay. The news from the front lines is usually good; each week, it seems, the Islamists seize another base, another checkpoint, another key building. The students also trade news about the many friends and acquaintances who have dropped out of school or left home to join the fighting. Most have enlisted with the lead militant group in the battle, the Islamic Courts Union, or ICU. A mix of pressure and temptation to follow in their path fills the air. Ali has given thought to signing up himself; his older brother has already joined the Islamist forces. For the moment, though, he stays in school.

Then one day an especially exciting piece of news arrives. In a hugely symbolic victory, the ICU has captured the Daynile Compound, the headquarters of Mohamed Qanyare Afrah, one of the city's most powerful warlords. The compound was the same place where the warlords recently formed their coalition, the so-called Alliance for the Restoration of Peace and Counter-Terrorism. The ICU says it will set up Islamic courts in the space. Ali and his friends celebrate in their mosque.

But Ali's joy disappears when he learns a second piece of news. In the gun battle to capture the compound, his brother was killed near the Somali Defense Ministry.

That does it—he can no longer stay out of the fight.

One morning in mid-June, Ali and a friend sneak out of the mosque sometime after midnight, before dawn. Mogadishu has no streetlamps, but a near-full moon emits just enough light for them to make their way west, through streets lined with green overgrowth, piles of garbage, and an endless procession of one-, two-, and three-story buildings. Most are in sorry shape, the result of years of neglect or accumulated bomb hits and bullet holes inflicted since Somalia's 1990s civil war. The two students walk for hours, trekking through the districts of central Mogadishu—Yaqshid, Wardhigley, Hawlwadag—until they finally reach the edge of the Hodan district, where their families live. The boys split up. Ali goes to his parents' home. They are surprised to see him but he explains: I've been given time off from my studies.

Within a few hours, though, he's gone again. Later, Ali calls his family and announces that he is not going back to the mosque. He says he's going to join the youth fighters—the "Al-Shabaab" contingent of the ICU. He wants to make contact with Aden Ayrow, the man who is gaining fame as the lead commander of the Islamist forces and who recruited Ali's late brother.

That same day, he goes to a former complex of the Somali military. The ICU captured the building, the sprawling colonial-era Circolo Ufficiale, just weeks before. Ali walks in and volunteers his services. His offer is accepted, and within hours he is taken to the Oodweyne camp just outside Mogadishu. There he will begin training to become an Islamist militant fighter. He is one of thousands of young Somalis who enlist with the Islamist forces between that March and June, including a dozen from his own madrassa.

In many ways, the recruits are like all young men who join armies in time of war. Some, like Ali, are driven by personal reasons. Some desire to be part of a great victory they sense is coming. Some want to experience the risk and adrenaline rush of combat. And others are fighting for a cause—in this case, the cause of *jihad*, or holy war, to spread the rule of Islam in a land where they feel it should have ruled all along.

In an interview three years later, Ali looked back on this moment and spared no words about the mind-set he was in. "I was ready to die as a martyr," he said.[1]

It would be a much harder task than he anticipated.

PART ONE

ORIGINS AND RISE

ONE

JIHAD ARRIVES IN SOMALIA

THE SOMALI CAPITAL WAS ONCE a jewel. In the 1970s especially, Mogadishu boasted a mix of culture, history, and beauty to outshine almost any
city in Africa. Artifacts of Italian rule, such as the majestic Mogadishu Ca-
thedral, stood near monuments to Somali pride, such as the 770-year-old
Arab'a Rukun Mosque. Wide, tree-lined boulevards ran by thousand-year-
old neighborhoods with streets so narrow that two people couldn't walk
side by side. Women in short skirts and men in blue jeans shared the side-
walks with religious Muslims wearing hijabs and khamis. The overall vibe
was relaxed and cosmopolitan, and tourists from across East Africa came
to enjoy the cafés, hotels, and, above all, the beaches and warm, pure-blue
ocean waters. The crowning touch was the paint job—many buildings had
been whitewashed, giving the city's blend of Italian and Arab architecture
a look of cool, coastal elegance. Even before Somalia won independence in
1960, Mogadishu earned a nickname that a few decades later would sound
preposterous, but was 100 percent fitting at the time—the Pearl of the Indian Ocean.

Pearls don't form overnight. The map of modern-day Somalia was dot-
ted with port towns from ancient times, including Sarapion, a forerunner
of Mogadishu mentioned in Ptolemy's atlas circa AD 150. The future Somali capital emerged as a trading hub where merchants from East Africa,
the Arabian Peninsula, Persia, and even distant Asia converged. The Persian

influence was especially strong—the name Mogadishu derives from the Persian *Maq'adishah*, or "Seat of the Shah." Starting around 1100, the city experienced a golden age lasting hundreds of years. In 1331, traveler Ibn Battuta described it as a "very big town" with wealthy merchants, lots of camels and sheep, and a locally made fabric that was exported to Egypt. When explorer Vasco da Gama sailed by in 1499, a diarist noted that the city had buildings up to five stories high and numerous mosques topped with minarets. Another traveler, Duarte Barbosa, who visited in 1518, made Mogadishu sound like a giant horn of plenty. "Ships come there from the kingdom of Cambay [India] and from Aden [Yemen] with stuffs of all kinds, and spices," he wrote. "And they carry away from there much gold, ivory, beeswax and other things upon which they make a profit. In this town there is much meat, wheat, barley and horses, and much fruit; it is a very rich place."[1]

There was, perhaps inevitably, a long, slow decline, but in the mid-twentieth century, Mogadishu enjoyed a second golden age of sorts. Like the rest of Africa, Somalia had been overtaken by European powers: Italy seized control of lands along the Indian Ocean coast, while Britain took most of the northern lands along the Gulf of Aden. Both countries forcibly suppressed self-rule movements, most notably the Dervish state that lasted for some two decades in the interior. But while Britain left its territory poor and undeveloped, the Italians, starting in the mid-1920s, began to modernize urban areas, constructing roads, railroads, and factories and giving Mogadishu—or *Mogadiscio*, as they called it—a grid-like street plan, an airport, and a modern seaport. They also decorated the capital with elegant gardens, villas, hotels, and administrative buildings, the most famous being Villa Somalia, a spacious art deco residence for the local governor, built on high ground that offered a spectacular view of the ocean. Years later, the residence would be turned into Somalia's presidential palace.

The Italians' misadventures during World War II resulted in British forces seizing all their African territories. The developments worked out well for Somalia on two levels. First, the Italians' tendency to retreat and surrender spared Mogadishu and other Somali cities from real damage. Second, the postwar creation of a United Nations trusteeship administered by Italy paved the way for independence and prevented the type of bloody liberation war that scarred Kenya and other African countries. Fueled by UN development aid, the 1950–60 trusteeship period saw steady economic gains, declines in poverty and malnutrition, and a smooth transfer of power to Somali politicians. Corruption was a major problem from the start, but development and stability continued in the early years of independence as Somali voters ratified a constitution and the government proved able to keep the country safe and orderly. When President Aden Abdulle Osman—"Aden Adde"—lost the 1967 election, he relinquished his post to the victor, Abdirashid Ali Sharmarke. It was the first time an African head of state had voluntarily given up power to a democratically elected successor.

The United States respected the new Somali state and tried to keep it in the Western camp during the Cold War. In March 1968, President Lyndon Johnson held a state dinner for visiting Prime Minister Mohamed Ibrahim Egal and toasted both visitor and country: "You have helped to found a true democracy, where each man has a voice in his nation's future."[2]

Eighteen months later the democracy died, after President Sharmarke was shot and killed by one of his guards during a visit to the northern town of Los Anod. When parliament proved unable to choose a successor, army officers led by Major General Mohamed Siad Barre seized power. In a matter of months, Somalia became a military dictatorship with ties to the Soviet Union, nationalized banks, cooperative farming, and no democratic institutions.

Siad Barre—a man with a deep voice, outsized ego, and Hitler-style mustache—was able to win genuine popularity at first with successful campaigns to improve literacy and replace Italian with Somali as the country's national language. The army grew stronger, courtesy of Soviet tanks and advisers. Mogadishu was kept safe, clean, and growing, and the government showcased the capital when it hosted the summit of the Organization of African Unity—later known as the African Union (AU)—in July 1974. Future African presidents who attended the summit, such as South Africa's Thabo Mbeki, would look back fondly on that event. "This was the first and last time I visited Mogadishu," Mbeki wrote. "For many years afterward, Mogadishu and Somalia remained in our memories as African places of hope for us, a reliable rear base for the total liberation of Africa."[3]

Siad Barre's mix of nationalism and communism reached its popular peak in July 1977, when he acted on long-simmering dreams of a "Greater Somalia" and sent more than thirty-five thousand Somali troops into Ethiopia to take over the Ogaden region and its ethnic Somali majority. By November, the army controlled 90 percent of the territory. But the dream disintegrated when the Soviets, who enjoyed good relations with both Somalia and Ethiopia before the war, threw their full support to the latter. Ethiopian forces backed by Soviet weapons and thousands of Cuban troops drove out Somali forces in early 1978. It was a loss from which Siad Barre would never truly recover.[4] A group of government and military officials tried to overthrow him that April. The plot was instantly quashed, and the general later had seventeen alleged ringleaders executed by firing squad. But a handful of officials who escaped to Ethiopia formed the first of several anti–Siad Barre insurgent groups who would grow in strength in the following years.

The 1980s saw Somalia in an odd kind of limbo. On the surface, things in Mogadishu appeared fine. Videos posted to YouTube a quarter-century later—in tribute or in memoriam—show people walking and driving around an almost immaculate city.[5] Car traffic flows smoothly, markets are busy, buildings of all kinds look well-kept and freshly painted, and nary a gun nor soldier is in sight. Off-camera, however, the state was beginning to crumble as people grew angry with a sputtering economy, corrupt officials, and waves of killings and terror against communities believed to oppose Siad Barre. In one notorious incident, Siad Barre's elite Red Berets destroyed water reservoirs around the arid city of Galkayo; as a result, an estimated two thousand people died of thirst. Ethiopia sparked further unrest hosting rebel groups that battled the Somali army in the north and along the Somalia-Ethiopia border. The general clung to power but his grip grew weak, especially after a May 1986 car accident that confined him to bed for six months.

In May 1988, open warfare erupted when the insurgent group the Somali National Movement (SNM) seized control of the northern city of Hargeisa. Siad Barre's forces responded with weeks of aerial and artillery attacks that killed about five thousand people. The army retook the city, but Siad Barre's star had begun its final descent. By 1990, his government was fighting four different rebel groups—all secular—in various parts of the country and was losing ground to every one of them. The Red Berets developed itchy trigger fingers, killing forty-nine people following riots resulting from the assassination of the Roman Catholic bishop Salvatore Colombo on July 9. Demonstrations escalated and the government was accused of killing an estimated four hundred fifty more people eight days later when Muslim protesters demanded the release of jailed spiritual leaders. The US ambassador to Somalia, James Bishop, tried to encourage peace talks between the government and the rebel groups. At the same time, Bishop later recalled, he was preparing US embassy staff for the worst. "We conducted drills with increasing sophistication—e.g., mass casualty drills—so that the staff would be familiar with what it might have to do," he said.[6]

Amid all the shooting, no one noticed that an entirely different kind of opponent to Siad Barre had slipped into the country and had begun building the foundation for a very different type of insurgency.

In January 1990, as unrest moved the country toward civil war, a young Somali man returned to his homeland after spending nearly nine years abroad. For much of that time, he had lived in Washington, DC, where he'd been an ice cream server, a waiter, a taxi driver, and, at times, an economics student at the University of the District of Columbia. But the man born as Ibrahim Jama Me'aad did not return home planning to work in any of those fields. He had taken an executive position that came with heavy responsibilities, frequent travel, sky-high goals, and no perks of any kind. The job also had no real title, though if pressed for a description, Ibrahim could say he was in sales. His product was jihad, or holy war; his supplier was an Afghanistan-based outfit, just over a year old, that called itself Al-Qaeda.

Ibrahim's main sales tool was a series of videotapes glorifying the *mujahideen*, the Islamist insurgents who had fought to expel the Soviet army from Afghanistan. Soviet forces that once numbered more than one hundred thousand had left Afghanistan just eight months before, after nearly a decade of trying to prop up a pro-communist Afghan government. The tapes declared that the withdrawal was the result of mujahideen persistence and power, making little or no mention of the US funding and weapons that put the steel in their punch. Video clips focused on rifle-toting militants, draped in bullets and wearing Afghan *pakol* hats, launching assaults on airports and military bases. Other scenes showed the fighters in fierce battle with Soviet and Afghan government troops, with some using the shoulder-fired, US-supplied "Stinger" missiles renowned for shooting down enemy helicopters and planes. The VHS tapes were primitive compared with the slick, high-definition productions turned out by later radical Islamist groups like ISIS. But they effectively portrayed the war as the most heroic resistance a Muslim group had ever mounted against a modern power. Each time an 82- or 120-millimeter rocket was fired, voices off-screen exclaimed *"Allahu Akbar!"*—God is great.

Twenty years earlier, anti-Soviet propaganda like this would have been banned in Somalia. Now, with many Somalis still bitter at Moscow for having betrayed them during the Ogaden war, the tapes found a receptive audience. Supporters made hundreds of copies. Cinemas screened them. People bought them to watch in their homes. When someone shouted *"Allahu Akbar!"* in the video, those watching would often shout it back. And so in some small measure, the concept of jihad gained a foothold in Somalia.

Me'aad was no doubt highly pleased. He had fully committed himself to his new mission, going so far as to take on a new identity. He would be Ibrahim al-Afghani—Arabic for "Ibrahim the Afghan." Never mind that this "Afghan" was a native Somali, born in 1960 in the northern city of Hargeisa and raised in the same area, one of seven children (two boys and five girls) in a religious family. A childhood friend and schoolmate—who, like many associates of Al-Shabaab members, speaks on condition of anonymity for fear of reprisal—says Me'aad/Afghani showed a passion for Islam at a young age. "As early as grade eight he studied Islamic culture and was able to pass the knowledge to his peers. His Islamic knowledge was far ahead of his peers," says the friend.[7]

As a teenager attending Hargeisa's Farah Omaar High School, the future Afghani belonged to a group called *Al-Wahdat al-Shabaab al-Islam*, or Solidarity of Islamic Youth. The group promoted Salafism, the idea that Muslims must follow a purist interpretation of Sharia, or Islamic law. Al-Wahdat members believed that many Somalis were on the "wrong" side of the Quran and *sunna*, the way of life prescribed as normal through the teachings and practices of the prophet Muhammad, and they pushed for what they considered necessary changes to Somalia's laws and customs. However, the childhood friend does not describe the young Afghani as militant. Instead, he uses words such as friendly, ethical, modest, generous, and direct, as well as an "always concerned Muslim" and "hard to forget."[8]

Me'aad/Afghani left Somalia for the United States in 1981, apparently lured by the desire to work and study in a foreign land. He settled outside Washington, DC, the only American city at that time that had a significant

number of Somali natives. There, despite the US capital's mix of nationalities and cultures, his commitment to fundamentalist Islam deepened. A
view into this period comes from Mahdi A. Mohamed, a.k.a. Jamal Guddoomiye, a fellow student from Somalia who met Afghani in 1984. Guddoomiye became Afghani's roommate in the Summerfield Apartments, a
building in Silver Spring, Maryland, where a group of Salafist-minded Somalis had gathered, their rent subsidized by activist groups. "Twenty of us
lived in the same area. Six of us lived in the same apartment, myself and
Ibrahim included," Guddoomiye says.[9]

The future Afghani had an I-20 student visa, he recalls, but seemed to
spend the bulk of his time at the Islamic Center, in northwest Washington, one of the oldest and largest mosques on the US East Coast. "He liked
religion very much. He was very emotional and used to cry [about it]. He
was serious," Guddoomiye says. "There were academics who graduated
from Georgetown and Howard Universities who were more knowledgeable
[about Islam] than him, he could not take leadership [positions], but he was
more ambitious. He was taking Islamic studies and lectures all the time.
He was at the Islamic Center on Massachusetts Avenue twenty-four hours
a day. His goal was to spread religion and follow it strictly in life [in terms
of] personal features like clothing and beard and staying in mosques most
of the time."[10]

So stringent were the young Afghani's beliefs that he would almost never
allow his photo to be taken. "I don't have a picture of him because we hated
pictures, we believed pictures were *haram* [forbidden]. Unless government
forced us and necessitates, we would not take pictures," says Guddoomiye.[11]
Indeed, no confirmed photos of Afghani have publicly surfaced to this day.
His future aide in Al-Shabaab, Abu Ayan, says Afghani stood about 180 cen-
timeters tall—about five feet, ten inches—with a "strong, well-built body,
big legs, long nose, flat chest." He went bald as he grew older, but in Ayan's
evaluation "he was a handsome man."[12]

While he was in Washington, Afghani's interest in politics came to the
fore. "Sometimes he would surprise us and visit anti–Siad Barre rallies organized by the Somali National Movement [SNM]," Guddoomiye says.[13]
"For us Siad Barre and SNM were the same—two non-believers—but Ibrahim would attend." More broadly, Guddoomiye says he and Afghani hated

Egyptian leader Hosni Mubarak, who was suppressing the Muslim Brotherhood movement, and "we disliked America. We believed it was creating all the troubles for Somalia."

Dislike it or not, the future Afghani spent more than seven years in the United States, including a spell living in Culmore, a part of Falls Church, Virginia, with a small community of Somalis. It was also in the United States that his life took its central, fateful turn. According to a family member in Somalia—again, speaking on condition of anonymity—in 1987 or 1988 Afghani met and fell under the influence of Abdullah Azzam, one of the fathers of the then coalescing global jihadist movement.

Azzam was a Palestinian cleric and teacher in his late fifties known for his riveting speeches and striking two-tone beard: black down the middle, gray along the sides. As early as the late 1960s, he had envisioned a movement to spread strict Sharia to the entire Muslim world and beyond. He rose to prominence in the mid-1980s when he set up a network of guest houses and training camps for aspiring Islamist fighters along the Pakistan-Afghanistan border. By the time the Soviets pulled out of Afghanistan, the network had funneled thousands of foreign fighters into the ranks of the mujahideen.[14]

To keep his operation going, Azzam visited cities throughout the Middle East, Europe, and North America—including a reported fifty in the United States—to make speeches, raise money, and enlist fighters. Western governments didn't object; Azzam's group was battling the Soviets. It was on a visit to the Washington area that Azzam recruited Afghani.

On his travels, Azzam promoted several broader ideas. One was his interpretation of jihad itself. In its most basic sense, jihad refers to the obligation that Muslims have to maintain the religion. The obligation can take many forms, some entirely personal, spiritual, and peaceful. But since the earliest days of Islam, the term has also meant physical struggle against perceived enemies of the religion. Azzam pushed a very aggressive version of jihad, one that said governments in Muslim lands led by "unbelievers" must be overthrown and replaced by pure Islamic states. Al-Qaeda's very name— Arabic for "the base"—symbolized the group's drive to be the foundation for that sweeping change.

To advance his goal, Azzam advocated two strategies. One was that jihadist groups should cooperate across borders rather than operate as isolated religious or nationalist movements. The other was the primacy of the gun.

Azzam believed that the vast Islamic caliphates of centuries gone by could be restored only by holy war, unrestrained by notions of compromise and talk. "Jihad and the rifle alone!" was the slogan he preached. His teachings won him many followers and allies, most notably a young, wealthy Saudi named Osama bin Laden who helped finance the mujahideen camps.

Toward the end of 1988, Azzam's new disciple Afghani accepted an invitation to come to Afghanistan, where the war against the Soviets was in its final months. Guddoomiye says the end of his roommate's stay in the United States was hastened by the expiration of his visa. "There was no asylum or refugee openings for Somalis, so if you are a student and you are studying, you have to have other means to stay or you are deported," he says. "Some people gave him advice to marry a woman who has the permits here, so that he can get [legal] status. Ibrahim was so strict that he refused to enter a fake marriage just for getting legal status. He was given notice for deportation. That is one of the reasons he decided to go to Afghanistan, I believe. If he had status, I don't think he would have made the decision to go to Afghanistan lightly."[15]

The family member in Somalia says Afghani—still known at this point as Ibrahim Me'aad—traveled from Washington to Egypt, then flew to Pakistan and made his way to the city of Peshawar, near the Afghanistan border. There he spent a year or so under the tutelage of Azzam, Osama bin Laden, future Al-Qaeda chief Ayman al-Zawahiri, and others who were developing the concepts and strategies that Al-Qaeda would use to advance its vision of jihad. Afghani's teachers recognized their student's commitment to their goals, and they liked him, too, particularly Azzam and al-Zawahiri, according to the family member: "Azzam used to say to him, 'You're Me'aad, and we have a promise with Me'aad.'"[16] Me'aad/Afghani lost his patron when unknown assassins killed Azzam with a roadside bomb in Peshawar in November 1989. Just a few weeks later he returned to Somalia and adopted his new name, ready to fulfill his promise to build a state based on strict Islamic principles.

Even without Afghani, Somalia would have been a natural target for Al-Qaeda. Unlike many other African countries, Somalia's population was (and is) almost entirely Sunni Muslim, and many Somalis speak Arabic, the lingua franca of Al-Qaeda, in addition to Somali. Tactically, the long coastlines and porous borders with Kenya and Ethiopia make it easy to slip in and out of the country. From a distance, Siad Barre's Somalia looked like a good place to operate, offering remote spaces where Al-Qaeda could recruit young men and set up bases to train them as fighters.

But as a native Somali, Afghani likely knew that strict Sharia might be a hard sell. Somalia had virtually no experience with hard-line Islamic law of the kind promoted by Al-Qaeda or the Wahhabism found in nearby Saudi Arabia. If anything, Somalia had a reputation of moderation and tolerance. "You look at pictures of Mogadishu in the 1960s and 70s, there are women in miniskirts," says "Terry," a Westerner who spent considerable time in Mogadishu over the years and agreed to share impressions of the city. "They had the Italian influence. Ledo Beach is named after an island off Italy. It was bikini time."[17] Mogadishu also had a nightclub scene driven by locally flavored versions of American funk and disco. Somalis who wanted to drink alcohol or smoke cigarettes could freely do so. Many others chewed *khat*, a regionally grown narcotic leaf that when consumed gives the user a feeling of mild euphoria. Head-to-toe coverings like burkas were not a common sight.

In terms of religious practice, there were the purist Salafists, who belonged to Al-Wahdat in the north, and a similar group, Al Ahli, in the south. But they were outnumbered by those who practiced the mystical form of Islam known as Sufism. Sufis tend to seek connection with God through acts of self-sacrifice and inner purification; some make a point of revering deceased clerics and making their tombs into shrines. Control of the government and people's lives is not a priority for Sufis.

However, at the time of Afghani's return, his first goal—the toppling of Siad Barre—was already a work in progress. Throughout 1990, the strongest of the insurgent groups, the United Somali Congress (USC), seized control of towns and areas around the capital. The government's territory declined steadily until Siad Barre was known mockingly as the "mayor of Mogadishu." When US Ambassador Bishop met with Siad Barre at Villa Somalia five days before New Year's Day, 1991, he found the aging general to be alert but downcast and passive, saying "we don't know what's going to happen" and that whatever did happen was "up to God."[18] Insurgents entered the city three days later, and as fighting escalated in the streets, Siad Barre's men took to shelling the insurgents from the presidential palace, killing or wounding hundreds of civilians. Somehow, Siad Barre and a shrinking band of loyalists held out until January 26, 1991, when USC fighters penetrated the walls of Villa Somalia and he fled the capital. His government of more than twenty-one years—undemocratic and brutal, but still a government—dissolved into history.

A USC spokesman announced that the United Somali Congress would form a "broad-based democratic government."[19] But almost immediately the USC split in two and talks with other insurgent groups went nowhere. "One group had the airport, one group had the port, one group had the market area and there were already clashes," recalls longtime Voice of America reporter Scott Bobb, who arrived in Mogadishu five days after Siad Barre's fall. "They were all vying to control the airport, because they could charge people $100 to land, or for a visa at the port," he says.[20] Greater profits awaited those who could get a piece of the khat industry.

By mid-February, Somalia was engulfed in a multi-front civil war. No single group had enough strength to seize control. Further attempts to form a new government failed. The north broke away completely, declaring itself the independent republic of Somaliland. And most other parts of the country suddenly had no official administration, no one formally in charge.

Nobody knew it at the time, but Somalia's real problems had just begun.

⁓

The disputes that bedeviled efforts to build a new government could be described as political, financial, and territorial in nature, but they all really came down to one thing: power struggles between clans.

Clans are social units whose role in Somali society is so central, so deeply rooted, so part of the air that Somalis breathe, that it simply cannot be escaped. The clans are not based on ethnic, religious, national, class, or political ties; rather, the members of each clan are said to descend patrilineally from a common male ancestor who lived in the tenth or eleventh century. With their roots wrapped in legends and their lineages hopelessly intertwined, it's hard to say where one clan ends and another begins. But it's generally agreed that Somalia (including Somaliland) has five major clans: Darod, Dir, Hawiye, Isaaq, and Rahanweyn. Each one is divided into ten to twenty sub-clans, which in turn are divided into dozens of sub-sub-clans. In a country where virtually everyone shares the same religion, language, and ethnic ancestry, clan affiliation is the main trait that makes one person distinct from another. It's also the main thing that Somalis fight about when it comes to distribution of power.

In pre-independence days, the clan system posed few major problems. "In the countryside, clans lived for centuries and each clan lived separately from the other," explains former Somali army general Mohamed Ali Sharman, an official in governments from the 1950s to the 1980s. "But they had culture and tradition which they used to use to solve disputes over water and grazing. They used to give blood money; they used to solve their problems even when there was no government."[21] However, clan loyalties were like gum in the gears of the new government after independence. From the start, nearly all political parties were tied to clans. The bigger clans used their clout to get members appointed to top jobs in the cabinet and military. The appointees then funneled tax money back to their groups, even putting clan mates on the payroll for nonexistent jobs. Distrust and resentment grew by the year. "The modern government and clannism were incompatible," Sharman asserts.[22]

Siad Barre tried to stamp out clannism with no success. Instead, many Somalis complained publicly that he gave too many positions to people from his own sub-clan, the Marehan, and two other Darod groups. As the civil war started, some, though not all, of the insurgent groups were tied to clans: the USC was Hawiye, the Somali National Movement was Isaaq, and the Somali Democratic Movement was Rahanweyn.

More than one observer has suggested giving up on the idea of a central authority and letting clans run Somalia by their own customs and rules. What actually emerged was something called the "4.5 formula," first applied in 2000 at a government-building conference in Djibouti. The four major Somalia-based clans—Darod, Hawiye, Dir, and Rahanweyn—were each allotted sixty-one seats in a projected parliament, while "minor" clans split thirty-one seats. That government failed, but the same rigid formula would be used to build future parliaments and cabinets, leading to often-torturous negotiations that produced weak, brittle, short-lived administrations. The jihadists came in with a different idea: let Islam be the force that binds and guides the nation. Let everyone follow closely in the path of Allah, and peace will return to a troubled land.

With Siad Barre toppled, Afghani began to operate freely for the first time. In February 1991, he and fellow jihadists opened Somalia's first

Islamist militant training camp in the southern port town of Kismayo. They named it Camp Khalid ibn Walid after the seventh-century warrior who helped spread Islam across the Arabian Peninsula. Within a short time, using money provided by Afghan connections, the jihadists transformed a former paramilitary base into a place where fighters received not only basic weapons and soldier training but also instruction in military tactics, intelligence, and special operations. This was far more advanced than what other Somali armed groups were doing and a clear signal of the jihadists' long-term plans. Young Somalis were interested. When the camp opened, it had three hundred men. Two months later, it had one thousand. Encouraged, the jihadists opened several more training camps in other parts of central and southern Somalia.

Many of those flocking to the camps were members of Al-Itihad Al-Islam, or AIAI. The group's gravitation toward Afghani was no accident. AIAI arose in the early 1980s from the merger of two Salafist groups—Al-Wahdat, the northern-based group that Afghani belonged to as a teenager, and its southern counterpart, Al Ahli. The emir, or top leader, of AIAI was Sheikh Ali Warsame, who, like Afghani, was an Isaaq clan member from northern Somalia.

In the latter years of Siad Barre's rule, AIAI had thousands of members in the universities and mosques, and the government suppressed the group's activities. "They were being watched and followed," says former Somali army colonel Ibrahim Haji Mohamed. "Any member who was found out to be involved in extremist activities was being given six months in jail. It was an order that came from the national security committee."[23] The colonel says AIAI posed no threat to the Siad Barre regime, but in 1989 AIAI held a secret meeting in Mogadishu where they decided to form an armed wing of the organization comprising up to ten thousand militants. A former Somali air force colonel, Mohamud Issa, a.k.a. Abu Muhsin, was tasked with finding locations where such a force could be readied. Those plans never materialized, but the growth of the camps allowed AIAI to re-emerge with newfound strength.

That strength was quickly tested. By April 1991, warfare between the various rebel groups that had ousted Siad Barre was spreading across Somalia. A powerful USC contingent led by General Mohamed Farrah Aidid, a sworn enemy of Islamic militancy, advanced to the outskirts of Kismayo. AIAI was in a difficult position. Not truly ready to fight a battle, it faced the choice of vacating Kismayo or helping defend the city. Members debated whether to flee, fight, or try to stay neutral. A senior member of the group, Shiekh Abdulkadir Ga'amey, visited the camp and urged the militants to withdraw south to the town of Dhobley. But ultimately the group was swayed by the more firebrand leaders, including Afghani and one of AIAI's older figures, a long-faced militia chief and Ogaden clan member from the far south, Hassan Abdulahi Hersi, better known as "Hassan al-Turki." They would fight.

The battle with Aidid's forces—the very first between jihadist and secular forces in Somalia—was a disaster for AIAI.[24] Sixty of its fighters were killed, and another two hundred were wounded. The heaviest fighting took place in a jungle and farmland area north of Kismayo, around a bridge known as Arare. The spot is now a graveyard for slain AIAI members. Warsame blamed the loss on the commanders' mistaken belief that locals would rally to their side. "I was not consulted with about the fighting in Arare as well as [later] clashes in the northeast," he says. "They [the AIAI commanders] did not calculate the level of public support. That is what caused the failure."[25] In a double calamity, the jihadists lost control of their new camp to General Aidid, who destroyed it.

The events of early 1991 established a pattern for AIAI and its leaders. They would find a safe haven, assemble, establish training camps, build a stronghold, and then lose it all when they took on superior military forces. In 1992, the group gained a foothold in Somalia's Puntland region, where AIAI members were entrusted with running the lucrative port of Bosaso. Training sites in Qaw, east of the city, and in Galgala, to the south, attracted many new recruits. But an attempt to seize control of Puntland's cities that June was crushed by local clan fighters led by Abdullahi Yusuf Ahmed, a future president of Somalia and another sworn enemy of Islamic militancy. A few months later, AIAI militants began to gather again in the Gedo region, which borders Ethiopia. This time they built up some grassroots support by establishing Islamic courts and Muslim charities, and by helping restore law and order to the area. Within a year they had established an AIAI group in Ethiopia, which eventually tried to assassinate the country's transport minister and carried out at least two deadly hotel bombings. By late 1996, the Ethiopian government had seen enough and launched several large assaults, demolishing AIAI's bases in Somalia and Ethiopia, wiping out its courts and charities, and scattering its leaders.

AIAI made a greater impact when it helped engineer fatal attacks on American forces in Mogadishu. Thousands of US soldiers and UN peace-keepers were deployed to Somalia in late 1992 to protect aid workers trying to feed a population beset by the civil war, widespread lawlessness, drought, and famine. Until then, AIAI had avoided direct collaboration with Islamist militants abroad. That stance changed with the arrival of foreign troops. In early 1993, AIAI members including Afghani, Hassan al-Turki, and two other Somali militants known as "Ayatollah" (Abdullahi Ahmed Sahal) and "Abu Jabal" (Omar Dheere) helped weapons experts from Al-Qaeda slip into the country. Those experts—eight men in all, according to the 1998 US indictment of Osama bin Laden—provided training to local fighters and Al-Qaeda operatives who wanted to make the foreigners pay for setting foot on Somali soil.[26] The indictment also said that people trained by Al-Qaeda took part in attacks on US forces during the "Battle of Mogadishu," the fire-fight on October 3–4, 1993, that resulted in the deaths of eighteen American soldiers. Talking to reporters, bin Laden later hinted at his organization's involvement in that battle.[27]

Less clear is AIAI's role in land mine attacks that targeted the troops and peacekeepers. US officials blamed forces of General Aidid for the attacks, or voiced suspicion they were the work of outside groups like the Lebanese militant group Hezbollah. However, Abu Jabal later said on video that AIAI members trained by Ayatollah targeted US and UN vehicles with mines, and claimed credit for a blast that killed four Americans traveling by Hum-vee in Mogadishu's Medina on August 8, 1993. "For this attack we combined two land mines. We detonated and destroyed the car. Only metals were found," he said.[28]

A few more details on the AIAI–Al-Qaeda connection unexpectedly emerged years later in a 2017 Al-Shabaab propaganda video. Militant trainer Abu Hassan Saeeb, who was sent to Somalia in the 1990s, said the decision for Al-Qaeda to get involved in Somalia came from the top. "We were given the order by Osama bin Laden, who saw it was necessary [because] Somalia, which is a poor country, needed help with jihad," he said. Mahad Warsame Qaley, better known as Mahad Karate, said in the same video that Al-Qaeda conducted some of its training in Gaddoon Dhawe, a mountainous area in Somalia's Gedo region, in addition to private homes in Mogadishu.

What is certain is that the events of this period were an inspiration to Al-Qaeda and Al-Shabaab alike. Years later, top Shabaab leader Ahmed Abdi Godane said that Al-Qaeda's actions changed the course of the jihadist movement. "This was the start of the battle between Al-Qaeda and America," he said. "Sheikh Osama mentioned this in one of his speeches, saying 'That is when we found out the weakness of [the] American military.'"[29]

After years of ups and downs, victory followed by defeat, AIAI's top officials gathered in September 1997 to discuss the group's future. The leadership was divided on whether to give up violent jihad or to regroup and continue. One faction, including former emir Warsame, proposed issuing a religious edict—a *fatwa*—banning fighting and jihadism. Another faction led by Ibrahim al-Afghani and Hassan al-Turki strongly rejected that idea. They got support from AIAI's deputy leader, Hassan Dahir Aweys, a former Somali army colonel who had fought in the 1977 Ogaden war and who projected an unforgettable image, with large silver-toned glasses, a horseshoe-shaped mustache, and a long goatee, the tip of which he usually dyed bright orange. Hassan Dahir Aweys said that yes, he too was committed to holy war.

The meeting marked the effective end of AIAI. The group split into two factions. One faction, led by Warsame, formed *al-Itisam Wal-Kitab Wal Sunna*, a Salafist organization that rejected violence with the caveat that senior clerics were authorized to call for jihad if deemed necessary. The other faction—more of a movement than an organization—named itself Salafist Jadid, or the New Salafists. Its followers embraced the philosophy of Abdallah Azzam, with its emphasis on firepower and cooperation with foreign militants. Turki announced that his militia's training camps at Dhobley and Raskamboni in the south were open to those willing to continue on the jihadist path.

Al-Qaeda and future Al-Shabaab leaders looked back on this moment as an important turning point. In the aforementioned 2017 Shabaab video, Godane said, "When AIAI was disbanding, I met one of their men and he didn't understand it, he told me about how they blatantly destroyed jihad. He told me, 'We disbanded the Gedo camps, and said they will do it in the west [Ethiopia].'" According to Godane, he told the man: "The prophet said if someone leaves, others will come in their place. If we go bad, Allah will bring better ones. Allah will bring a new generation who will volunteer, who will come forward."

Al-Qaeda trainer and planner Abu Talha al-Sudani said in the same video: "The reason the Shabaab youth mobilized themselves was because AIAI confined itself to *da'wa* (preaching) and learning and were opposed to jihad. The youth rejected this; those who returned from Afghanistan were instrumental."

By "those who returned from Afghanistan," al-Sudani meant Somalis who had received training from Al-Qaeda in bin Laden's camps. Among the returnees were several future leaders of Al-Shabaab. One was Aden Ayrow, a protégé of Aweys who had sprung from El Hindi, one of the strongest Salafist mosques in Mogadishu. Slim and slightly buck-toothed, Ayrow hardly looked imposing but at age twenty-one was already a battle-hardened veteran, having fought in every significant AIAI battle since the first clash at Arare. He honed his fighting skills with Al-Qaeda in Afghanistan during the mid-1990s. "He was active, brave, decisive, and a tough cookie," says a former Islamist fighter who worked with him.[30] Ayrow was also unusually intelligent; his mother's nickname for him was "Polymath," and at seventeen he allegedly had been one of the AIAI members who worked with Al-Qaeda to plant the land mines that killed American troops.

Then there was Mukhtar Robow, a six-footer with a muscular build, a bushy beard, and an easy way with words. Born in 1969 in Abal, a village near the town of Huddur, Robow had entered AIAI circles in the early 1990s while working for the al-Haramain Foundation, a Saudi Arabia–based charity later accused by the United Nations of financing terrorism. He became a fighter for AIAI in 1991 and distinguished himself as a good organizer and a fierce fighter during battles against Ethiopian troops in and around the Gedo region. After Ethiopia crushed AIAI in 1996, he taught at an Islamic school in the town of Afgoye. A former student there says Robow used to carry a pistol all the time. "He was trained to carry it; he always kept it at his waist underneath his clothes."[31] By the late 1990s, he was preparing for active fighting again, linking up with al-Turki and then going to Afghanistan for training. Robow, in an exclusive interview for this book, says several other AIAI figures went to Afghanistan at approximately the same time, including Abu Jabal and Afghani.[32]

And on the fringe of the scene, there was the aforementioned Ahmed Abdi Godane, a highly intelligent and ardent Islamist with a university background. Godane lacked the combat experience that many of his fellow jihadists had; in fact, he had never been part of AIAI. What he did have was extensive instruction by Al-Qaeda, a mark of distinction in the jihadist world. While studying and training along the Pakistan-Afghanistan border during his school days, he had linked up with Afghani, with whom he shared a hometown, Hargeisa, and ties to the Isaaq clan. The two became good friends, and Godane became part of the Somali jihadist movement, if only from afar, after returning to his hometown in the late 1990s.

Afghani, the one-time ice cream seller, was by now a veteran militant approaching his fortieth birthday. Well-respected within the jihadist movement both within and outside of Somalia, he helped direct the Somali movement from behind the scenes, making decisions and dispensing advice as needed. He was also screening newly acquired jihadist videos. The old productions focused on the Afghan-Soviet war. The new ones promoted Al-Qaeda's ideology and plans for a regional Islamist regime as envisioned by bin Laden, who was emerging as the international jihadist movement's most recognizable and powerful leader. According to people who saw the videos, they outlined a road map for creating Al-Qaeda–controlled territories across the Arabian Peninsula and in the nearby "Land of the Two Migrations," Al-Qaeda's preferred term for Somalia. Bin Laden and other Al-Qaeda leaders appeared on camera, asserting that the goals were achievable and predicting that forces would "come to the aid" of Islam in both territories.

Somali jihadists could take inspiration from Afghanistan's Taliban movement, which seized effective control of that country in 1996. The country's new rulers openly provided safe haven for Al-Qaeda. They also enacted laws that, among other things, imposed strict codes on clothing and hair, banned the use of television and musical instruments, and forbade women from holding most jobs outside the home. Those found to violate Taliban codes could be imprisoned, be whipped, have their limbs amputated, or be executed. Many punishments took place inside a soccer stadium in the capital, Kabul; local legend holds that the stadium grass ceased to grow because the field was soaked in blood. Multiple observers of Al-Shabaab in the future would notice how many tactics the group borrowed from their Afghan counterparts; the *Guardian* newspaper would call them "Africa's own Taliban."

Starting in the late 1990s, the New Salafists took a series of bold steps to promote their agenda. With the help of Hassan al-Turki and Hassan Dahir Aweys, lawless Somalia became a sanctuary for a number of Al-Qaeda operatives from other countries. The most notable were Fazul Mohammed, Abu Talha al-Sudani, and Saleh Ali Saleh Nabhan—three men accused of playing key roles in the August 7, 1998, truck bombings of the US embassies in Dar es Salaam, Tanzania, and Nairobi, Kenya. The Dar es Salaam blast killed eleven people and injured seventy; the one in Nairobi killed two hundred twenty and injured more than four thousand others in the embassy and nearby buildings. Fazul, a native of the Comoro Islands, was considered the mastermind of the attacks, while al-Sudani was allegedly the financier. Nabhan, a Kenyan, was suspected of playing an unspecified role. The men's intermittent presence in Somalia would provoke US intelligence and military operations in the country for years to come.

Also in the late 1990s, the New Salafists began making inroads in another branch of the Muslim community. The Islamic courts were created in Mogadishu in the mid-1990s by clan elders and businessmen trying to reestablish at least partial order amid Somalia's anarchy and violence. Judges in the courts used interpretations of Islamic law to handle everything from property disputes to divorce cases to restitution claims for murders (in the latter case, often ordering the payment of "blood money" to the family of the victim). Over time, the clan-based courts gained influence and power and set up security forces to reduce crime. In 2000, they banded together as the Islamic Courts Union, or ICU, to better coordinate and mediate cross-clan affairs. In the absence of a working law enforcement or justice system in Somalia, the courts filled an important role. Their prominence, however, made the courts a natural target for infiltration by former AIAI members and Salafists. Using clan connections and financial influence, the jihadists gradually worked their way into the Islamic court system. Jihadist leaders who became court officials included Godane, Turki, Ayrow, and Robow, along with Aweys, who eventually rose to be the second-most-powerful figure in the ICU.

Most of this was taking place in plain sight but without any intervention from powers abroad. The United States had adopted a hands-off policy toward Somalia after withdrawing its troops in 1994. The United Nations had removed its peacekeepers the following year when it became clear they were doing nothing to stabilize the country. Neither the United States nor any other country sent diplomats to Somalia, because there was no real government for them to deal with. The UN and the East African bloc IGAD kept trying to fill the hole, spearheading five major and several minor attempts between 1991 and 2000 to establish a new central authority in Somalia. Time after time, leaders of various Somali militias and political factions gathered at conferences in Djibouti, Ethiopia, or Egypt. "The successive UN coordinators kept trying to get them to reach an agreement," says Voice of America's Scott Bobb. "They'd announce an agreement and it would collapse within weeks, it just didn't work. [The parties] weren't ready to, they didn't know how to, or they wanted all the beans in the pot."[33]

The streets of Mogadishu and other cities became ruled by the gun, with the people at the mercy of warlords—some clan-affiliated, some not—who could block roads, hijack cars, steal possessions, and kidnap people almost at will. Terry the Westerner recalls a city mired in total lawlessness. "It was very Mad Max. There were these things called green lines, where each section of the town was controlled by a different warlord. Everyone was carrying not just AK-47s, but 50 PKM [machine guns], very heavy guns. Pickup trucks, that's how we moved. The security situation was very uneven because of frequent clan fighting. It was pretty much all clan fighting at that period. Violence could happen at any minute, any second."[34]

For the average person in Somalia, this made life dangerous, even hellish. For the jihadists, though, the situation meant opportunity. No government meant no authorities. No authorities meant that perhaps the kind of Islamic state they envisioned could someday emerge. It was just a matter of building strength and biding time. Their day, they believed, was destined to come.

TWO

THE CIA, THE WARLORDS, AND ETHIOPIA

Mukhtar Robow had been in Afghanistan for about nine months when he got his first inkling that he might have to leave. At the time, Robow was living and training at Al-Qaeda's Al-Farouq camp, about 70 kilometers from the Afghan city of Kandahar. Men at Al-Qaeda camps usually had little to no contact with the outside world; "When you are in the camp, you are not allowed radio, computer, electronics, GPS. Only foods are allowed to come in," he says. But on or about September 1, 2001, according to Robow, the camp was visited by Osama bin Laden and his deputy, Ayman al-Zawahiri. Robow says the Al-Qaeda chief decided to share a secret with the group. "Bin Laden gave a talk and said to us, 'We will hit America in ten days. This hitting will change the course of history,'" Robow says. "But he did not say where. He also said that when that happens, the Americans will carry out indiscriminate bombing. He said we'll have to be relocated in those ten days. He said we'll have to be dispatched to different locations, and we'll have to change the positions that are known to others."

On September 9, Robow says, camp residents heard that prominent anti-Taliban leader Ahmed Shah Masoud had been assassinated. That was only the prelude. Two days later, as dusk fell over Afghanistan, camp leaders who had radios "came out of their positions, carrying their torches . . . shouting 'Allahu Akbar!'" Robow says. "That is how we learned what happened in New York."

What happened, of course, were the September 11 attacks on the United States. That morning, Al-Qaeda operatives hijacked four commercial airliners from East Coast airports, slamming two into the twin towers of New York City's World Trade Center and killing more than 2,600 people. Few if any images have stunned the world like those of the burning 110-story buildings collapsing to the ground. Television channels around the globe preempted all regular programming. Nations as far away as India put their forces on high alert. Sworn enemies of the United States like Libyan leader Moammar Gadhafi and Iran's supreme leader Ali Khamenei condemned the attacks. An isolated few expressed pleasure, mainly small groups of Palestinians and Iraqi leader Saddam Hussein.

And in Somalia—there, the response was practically nonexistent. Many Somalis followed the events on radio or television. But there were no known demonstrations for or against the attacks. No Islamist groups publicly congratulated Al-Qaeda. Somalia's nominal president Abdulkasim Salad Hassan sent a two-line condolence note to President George W. Bush.[1] With no Somalis among the hijackers or the victims, the catastrophe seemed, for a moment, to bypass the Horn of Africa.

Within months, however, the Western response to the attacks began to rattle Somalia's already unstable society. The US military offensive in Afghanistan that October not only ousted the Taliban from power but also sent the Somali jihadists there, including Robow, scurrying back to their home country. The influx drew the attention of the United States and its allies, who, after years of relative inaction, were suddenly determined to crush violent jihadist movements worldwide. US officials began to signal that Somalia was on their radar. "Somalia has been a place that has harbored Al-Qaeda and, to my knowledge, still is," US Defense Secretary Donald Rumsfeld told a news conference in November.[2] General Richard Myers, chairman of the US military's Joint Chiefs of Staff, went a step further a couple of weeks later: "Somalia is one potential country—there are others as well—a potential country where you might have diplomatic, law enforcement action or potentially military action. All the instruments of national power, not just one."[3]

However, Somalia posed a special problem for the United States, summed up in three infamous words: Black Hawk Down. On October 3, 1993, US special operations units had tried to capture two top advisers of Mohamed

Farrah Aidid, who led the dominant militia in Mogadishu at the time and whose force had clashed with the US soldiers and UN peacekeepers deployed to Somalia the year before. During the raid, Somali militia fighters shot down two UH-60 Black Hawk helicopters. The ensuing attempt by US soldiers to rescue the surviving crew members turned into a bloodbath, with American soldiers and aircraft fighting an all-night battle against mobs of Somali gunmen and civilians attempting to overrun the crash sites. When the sun rose and the smoke cleared, eighteen US soldiers were dead, along with hundreds of Somalis—anywhere from three hundred to fifteen hundred, depending on who was doing the estimating. Infuriated Somalis proceeded to drag the soldiers' burned, bloodied bodies through the streets of Mogadishu, images of which seared the American consciousness when they landed on front pages and television screens the next day.

Facing an intense public outcry, President Bill Clinton's administration scaled down the US humanitarian effort and withdrew the troops the following March. Ten years later, the incident had not been forgotten, kept alive in part by the popular 2001 Hollywood film that dramatized it. And the United States was left with no formal ties to Somalia or even informal allies inside the country.

But officials recognized that certain parties could be bought. Starting in late 2002, agents from the US Central Intelligence Agency began making surreptitious contact with the warlords whose fighters effectively controlled the streets of Mogadishu and other key cities.[4] Their goal was to recruit forces that would help the United States capture suspected terrorists traveling through or hiding in Somalia. The program, run out of the US embassy in Kenya, was headed by John Bennett, a CIA officer with more than two decades' experience who would later become head of the National Clandestine Service, a branch of the CIA intimately involved in spying and drone operations.

The first warlord the agency recruited was found through a Western security consultant; he had once helped the consultant secure the release of an aid worker who had been kidnapped in Somalia. A man we'll call "Cawsley" is a former aide to the warlord and is an educated Somali who speaks fluent English. He was present when the CIA made its pitch to the warlord at a hotel in the Kenyan capital, Nairobi.[5]

According to Cawsley, the CIA was represented by three male agents who said the US government was concerned about the presence in Somalia of Islamist militants and wanted terrorists, along with their potential for undermining peace efforts in the country. "Our objective is to intercept them and prevent them from getting a foothold here," one agent explained.[6] They asked the warlord to help the CIA hunt down particular suspects, including Fazul Mohammed, Abu Talha al-Sudani, and Saleh Nabhan—the three men wanted in connection with the 1998 East African embassy bombings. In return, the agents promised that the CIA would finance the operation and upgrade the warlord's military force.

Cawsley says his boss stated that he too was concerned about the rise of fanatics in Somalia but was not sure that the men the agents spoke of were in the country. The CIA agents said that the United States already had intelligence-gathering facilities in Somalia that were operational. "We have information, recorded messages, and intelligence to prove their presence," Cawsley remembers them saying.

"Then we have a mutual interest," the warlord responded.[7]

A short time later, the warlord received funds to strengthen his militia, refurbish a dusty airstrip, and set up a main base. Cawsley became a CIA informant. And the warlord's militia began to look for people on the CIA's wanted list.

In the following months, the CIA struck similar deals with more Somali warlords and militia leaders, the final total coming to eleven. One of those warlords—we'll call him "Warlord #4" because he was the fourth one to reach a deal—says the agents engaged in some indirect arm-twisting to win his cooperation. "The Americans came and said, 'The people who destroyed our embassies are in Mogadishu,'" he recalls.[8] "[They said] 'You will have to organize yourselves and kick them out of your country or hand them over.' Alternatively, they said 'we are going to use all means to fight them; we may bring the Ethiopians or come back ourselves.' We did not want the Ethiopians since they are the enemy of our people. Likewise, we did not want the Americans to come back. So we told them we'll fight them [the wanted men]."

Starting in early 2003, CIA operatives regularly flew into Mogadishu. Every two weeks or so they gave their allies new leads, updates, and guidance. No weapons or equipment were handed over, but the agents brought suitcases full of cash which they dispensed to the warlords. One of the warlords, Mohamed Qanyare Afrah, later told journalist Jeremy Scahill that the CIA gave him $100,000 to $150,000 per month for his services. By the time the operation was in full swing, all eleven warlords had significant forces, and five were using small airports around Mogadishu—at K-50, Isaley, Jazeera, Jowhar, and Daynile—where they could receive CIA operatives and hand over any suspects they captured. Significantly, the eleven entities had no coordination; each hunted the wanted suspects on their own.

Cawsley says the CIA agents were concerned with the embassy bombers—"They would come and say Nabhan was here, Fazul has been reported to be in the area, and he passed through this area, and so on."[9] But he says they sought other terrorist suspects as well, mostly Arabs and East Africans, along with Somalis suspected of collaborating with them.

The CIA operatives identified themselves using only one name, such as Chris, David, Paul, or Julian, says Cawsley. He says he never believed that they were giving their real name. He says he tried to ask one of them, David, about his family and background. The man said he was from Boston, but no other information was given. Cawsley did not believe he was telling the truth. "They were never going to disclose their identity," he says.[10]

Sometimes the agents would ask to be taken around Mogadishu, with the apparent goal of testing out tracking devices planted by persons unknown. "They picked up a signal and they wanted to check if the GPS takes them to the area," Cawsley says.[11] This being Mogadishu, getting around was no routine matter; the agents drove an SUV with tinted windows, while heavily armed gunmen provided by the warlords traveled in vehicles directly ahead and behind. "They never stepped out of the car," Cawsley says. "They carried their own weapon in the tinted car. They wanted to check if the telephone signal they picked up and the position match. But they never conducted a raid; they never carried out a strike." He also says most visits lasted only a matter of hours; on only three occasions did the agents stay overnight in volatile Mogadishu.

In March 2003 the operation captured its first significant target—Suleiman Abdallah, an alleged Al-Qaeda member from Tanzania, who was seized by gunmen working for warlord Mohamed Dhere while laid up in a northern Mogadishu hospital. Abdallah was taken to Djibouti, then Afghanistan, where according to a report by the United Nations Human Rights Council, he spent months at a time undergoing beatings, sleep deprivation, prolonged solitary confinement, and other forms of torture at the "Prison of Darkness" and the "Salt Pit"—two jails allegedly run by US intelligence agencies in the Kabul area. He was released after more than five years in custody.[12]

In June 2004 the operation also led to the capture of Mohammed Ali Isse, a Somali man accused of masterminding the killings of four foreign aid workers in Somaliland. Gunmen of warlord Mohamed Qanyare Afrah seized Isse from the home of an Islamist militant, shooting him in the process. According to a later *Chicago Tribune* report, he was treated and interrogated aboard a US Navy ship, underwent torture at an Ethiopian prison, and was then handed over to authorities in Somaliland, where he was sentenced to life in prison.

But it wasn't the warlords who reeled in the biggest Al-Qaeda–linked fish caught during this time. In March 2004 authorities in Djibouti arrested Somali national Gouled Hassan Ahmed and handed him over to US officials, who eventually—more than two years later—transferred him to the US prison for terrorist suspects in Guantanamo Bay, Cuba.[13] According to his 2008 detainee assessment sheet—obtained by Wikileaks and released through the *New York Times*—Ahmed admitted to being a member of both Al-Qaeda and AIAI and having facilitated operations for Abu Talha al-Sudani. He said he had received training from an Al-Qaeda camp in Khost, Afghanistan, and then he went to the Ogaden region, where he provided small arms training to AIAI members and fought the Ethiopian army. In 2003, he said, he surveyed the US military base in Djibouti, Camp Lemmonier, for a possible truck bomb attack, which he ultimately determined was unfeasible. As of this writing, Ahmed has spent more than a decade at Guantanamo and looks set to remain there, given that in September 2016 the camp's periodic review board turned down his request for release, saying he was still a "significant threat to the security of the United States."

Experts and human rights organizations believe the CIA-warlord operation captured between ten and twenty suspects in all. However, the embassy bombing suspects eluded the CIA's grasp. The main problem was that warlords' support for the United States was weak at best and based only on money and self-interest. Warlord #4 sounds like he deceived either the CIA or himself when it came to the three main Al-Qaeda suspects. "I knew the people they were looking for, but I did not think they were the wanted ones," he says. "I knew Fazul (Mohammed); he was staying at a farm in Lower

Shabelle. He was with a Somali farmer. I thought he was one of those foreign refugees who somehow live in the country."[14]

In some cases, warlords remained on friendly terms with their supposed enemies because of clan ties or established relationships. Warlord #4 says he was "close" to powerful ICU figure Hassan Dahir Aweys, who in November 2001 was designated as a "supporter of terrorists" by President Bush. He says the CIA agents knew about his connection and asked him to try to make Aweys cooperate: "I met Aweys; I told him that we should capture those men and hand them over. Aweys told me that it's *haram* [Arabic for "forbidden"] to listen to the infidels. He said that it was haram to hand over Muslims to infidels. He said to me that Somalia is a Muslim land and belongs to all Muslims. He said the blue [Somali national] flag is haram. He said to me I should repent and beg Allah for forgiveness."[15]

Once they realized the warlords were working with the CIA, New Salafist and pro-ICU figures launched a counter-operation to kill enemy warlords and their suspected collaborators. "They targeted anyone they thought was helping the Americans," says Cawsley.[16] The fighters were led by Aden Ayrow, who was gaining a reputation as a master trainer and strategist. Cawsley says one victim of the campaign was peace activist Abdulkadir Yahya, a former staff member at the US embassy, who was killed in July 2005 by masked men who invaded his Mogadishu home and fired several shots into his mouth and head.

One of the members of the killing unit was Mohamed Toora-Toorow. In an interview just a few days before he was killed in a hotel explosion in February 2015, Toora-Toorow provided details on how the unit operated.[17] Ayrow was the lead instructor, he said, but the team also received lessons from Ibrahim Afghani, former AIAI fighter Abdullahi Asparo, and a future top Al-Shabaab official, Fuad Shongole. He says the training took place at an animal market, a former Coca-Cola factory building, and a house in Mogadishu—an indication of how much the militants had penetrated the capital even before their later dominance there.

Toora-Toorow eventually became an aide to Ayrow, and the two would hunt down targets together. He recalled one such mission during the Ramadan holiday in 2005. "It was a man said to be an Ethiopian officer," he said. "We got the tip he traveled to the Lower Shabelle region," south of

Mogadishu. Trailing him, the two lost track of their target and split up, with Toora-Toorow driving down the coastline and Ayrow taking a road further inland. They thought the man was driving a Land Rover but instead saw him riding a bus halfway between the towns of Marka and Afgoye. What happened next? "We took him out of the car and handed him over to Bait Al-Amni," a jihadist intelligence house in Mogadishu. "He was interrogated; they used electric shocks on him. Eventually he was killed after the interrogation."[18]

Other men targeted by Ayrow's unit included warlord Mohamed Dhere, former army General Mohamed Abdi, and former intelligence officer Colonel Mohamed Osman Oon. Not every murder attempt was successful, but the attacks showed that the Salafists were not going away—and ratcheted up the tension in Mogadishu.

Cawsley says that, in retrospect, working with the CIA was a mistake. "The CIA agents were bounty hunters like us," he says. "We should have asked to meet the people behind them; government officials or people from the Congress, so that they (could) help us restore stability in our country."[19]

Instead, by 2005 fighting between the warlords and Islamist militants had become a several-times-weekly feature of life in the capital. The jihadists sparked international outrage that January when they seized a colonial-era Italian cemetery in the Huriwa district, destroyed the estimated six hundred to seven hundred gravestones, and used the land to establish a new training camp, their first in Mogadishu. A radio journalist who visited the site says this was no ordinary camp. "It was like the Villa Somalia of [jihadists]," he says. "It had a training campus, a mosque, a weapons store, a weapons repair section, an emergency clinic. It had a women's section where they used to prepare food for the trainees. And it had the black flag flying."[20] Godane was named leader of the camp, which was named Salahuddin Muaskar. There, Afghani screened videos that schooled new recruits on intelligence gathering, survival tactics, and the mujahideen rationale for martyrdom. Jihadist videos were also shown in many local mosques, schools, and madrassas. Little by little, despite—or perhaps because of—their violent nature, the jihadists were gaining ground in Somalia politically and militarily.

They had also gained a new name. Except for a few senior leaders like Aweys and Afghani, most of the Somali jihadists were in their teens and twenties, generally younger than the warlords and former army soldiers who opposed them. Instead of the generic New Salafists, the population began calling them "the youth," or more specifically, the Arabic form of the words—Al-Shabaab.[21]

~

By early 2006 the CIA operation was stalling; the warlords were no longer bringing in suspects, and all parties sensed that the Islamists were taking the upper hand in Mogadishu. In February, CIA operatives flew to the Somali capital and for the first time met with most of the warlords in a single gathering. They suggested the warlords would be more effective if they were a united force like the ICU. According to Cawsley, the agents proposed formation of an alliance similar to the Northern Alliance in Afghanistan, which had helped US forces topple the Taliban in 2001.[22] The idea was welcomed, and on February 18, 2006, ten warlords announced the creation of the Alliance for Peace and Counter-Terrorism. The name struck most Somalis as highly ironic, given the warlords' history of roadblocks, ransom, and robbery. But the alliance nevertheless issued a manifesto vowing to fight jihadist groups they accused of protecting foreign criminals and carrying out intolerable acts in the name of Islam. Fighting between the militia of Mohamed Qanyare Afrah and an ICU force began that same day.

In the absence of US diplomatic ties to Somalia, Somali affairs were watched by the US embassy in Nairobi. In a February 24 cable, classified as secret and sent to ten government agencies including the CIA, US Ambassador to Kenya William Bellamy warned that the Somali population would not rally to the warlords' side: "Islamists have definitely gained turf and may have won hearts and minds among a public tired of warlords and suspicious of foreign interference. Some contacts say the public perceives the Alliance members as having grossly overstepped their boundaries [and] having attacked all devout Muslims, not just violent Jihadi extremists."[23]

The warlords banding together was a fateful move, for it pushed the ICU and the "Shabaab" beyond mere association into a military alliance of their own. The Islamic courts, although they had their own militias, did not have the organization and strategic capability required for full-scale war. But the jihadists, after years of training, were ready to fill that role. Ayrow, Godane,

Robow, and a newer leader, Abdullahi Ali Nahar, a.k.a. "Abu Utayba," took charge of the front lines. And for weaponry, the ICU and Shabaab looked north to Somalia's near-neighbor Eritrea.

Eritrea and its authoritarian, secretive government play a small but important role in the history of Islamist movements in Somalia. From the 1990s onward, the government of president Isaias Afwerki gave quiet support to such movements—not due to a love for Islam or hatred for the Transitional Federal Government (TFG), but to cause worry for archrival Ethiopia. Eritrea was once part of its bigger neighbor but fought for decades to achieve independence, which was finally granted in 1991. Relations between Ethiopia and Eritrea remained tense afterward, flaring up into a 1998–2000 border war characterized by trench warfare and ghastly human wave assaults that killed an estimated seventy thousand people. Bitter feelings lingered for years afterward. Eritrea kept stirring the pot by helping Ethiopian rebel movements such as the OLF (Oromo Liberation Front) and ONLF (Ogaden National Liberation Front), and at some point officials realized that aiding Somali Islamist movements would provide yet another headache for Ethiopian leaders, who disliked the notion of Somalia being ruled by an aggressive Islamist regime that might make another push to seize the Ogaden region.

For years, the Eritrean government has denied providing weapons to Somali Islamist forces, an act that would violate the international arms embargo on the country imposed by the United Nations in 1992. Officials speaking to Western reporters usually denounce the allegations as "baseless" or "unfounded" and say they are the product of Ethiopian or US plots to defame the Eritrean government.[24]

The panel of experts that monitored the embargo, known as the UN Monitoring Group on Somalia and Eritrea, found otherwise. Former panel chief Matthew Bryden says that starting in 2006 Eritrea used the ONLF to direct arms and ammunition to the Islamic Courts Union and subsequently to Al-Shabaab. According to the Monitoring Group's periodic reports presented to the UN Security Council, senior ONLF members in Mogadishu made contact with the ICU and were then introduced to Shabaab leaders including Ayrow. Once arrangements were made, ONLF logistics personnel in Somalia's Puntland region organized the shipment of weapons—including rocket-propelled grenades, Kalashnikov rifles, BKM pistols, and the appropriate ammunition—through the central Somali town of Galkayo and down to Mogadishu. The monitors said Eritrea also sent trainers from its external intelligence service.

The monitors' conclusion that Eritrea was behind the arms supply, Bryden says, was backed by strong evidence and multiple witnesses. "I have spoken to ICU personnel who took part in those meetings, to translators who were there when Eritrean officials were present in those meetings, and to the ONLF people who organized those meetings and arranged for the transfer of weapons and ammunition," Bryden says. "So many people were involved that eventually, it was an open secret."[25]

Despite the Eritreans' contributions, by all accounts the CIA-funded warlords had more fighters, weapons, and money at the start of the fight in Mogadishu. However, they could not match the Islamists' organization and sense of purpose. Over three and a half months of often fierce gun battles that left hundreds dead, fighters from the Salahuddin camp defeated four major warlords—Bashir Rageh, Abdi Qeybdid, Muse Sudi, and Mohamed Qanyare Afrah—one by one. Ayrow received the lion's share of credit for the victory, though it should be noted that the fighting and tactics were fairly simple in nature. One of Ayrow's former fighters says his commander used what can only be called a Trojan horse strategy to defeat Bashir Rageh. Rageh's militiamen were stationed at Galgalato and the Elman port on the outskirts of Mogadishu. "Ayrow suggested we load men onto trucks and cover them with canvas to disguise them as commercial goods," says the fighter. He says when the trucks arrived at Rageh's first checkpoint, the driver paid the soldiers who collected "tax"—extortion money—from the vehicles using the road. "One vehicle after another went through until our militia was embedded in the area and started firing in their midst. It was a spectacular attack that killed so many militiamen."[26]

Osman Mohamed, a Somali who was a student in Mogadishu at the time, was among those surprised by the warlords' collapse. "The Islamic Courts (were) attacking each warlord's base, one at a time," he says. "On the day Mohamed Qanyare Afrah's base was seized (June 4) all the buses and transport in the northern half of the city stopped, but I walked from my house in Huriwa district all the way to Daynile district just to witness the base and what was going on. . . . I was walking with my school friends. We saw the base and the weapons they left behind. If you saw those weapons you would think, 'How could they have lost the battle to the less armed fighters?'"[27]

Although scattered fighting dragged on until July, Afrah was the last major warlord to fall. The ICU declared itself in control of Mogadishu on June 5, 2006. It had taken more than fifteen years of struggle, but Islamist forces ruled the Somali capital.

The people of Mogadishu mostly welcomed the takeover—although not necessarily for reasons the ICU and jihadists would have preferred. "People celebrated the victory of the Islamic courts not because they had particular love for the courts but they just wanted peace," says Abdi Aden, a longtime Mogadishu newspaper journalist. "They wanted roadblocks that divided the city removed; they wanted to be able to carry their mobile (phones) and jewelry freely in the streets."[28]

Cawsley, the former warlord aide, was not among the celebrants. The day before the ICU takeover, he got a call from David, his CIA contact. "It's up to you guys how you save yourselves; the only thing I can do is send an airplane to pick you up," he was told.[29] Some of the defeated warlords still had militias to protect them, while others fled to rural areas or Baidoa, the seat of Somalia's weak Transitional Federal Government. Cawsley seized his only realistic option; he traveled to the K-50 dusty airstrip outside Mogadishu, which was still controlled by clan militias, and caught a plane to Nairobi along with a colleague. He has not set foot in Mogadishu since that day.

At the time of the ICU's victory, the courts' leader, future Somali president Sheikh Sharif Sheikh Ahmed, hailed the defeat of what he called the "devil's alliance." "Thank God we have achieved one of the wishes of the Somali public. This is a great victory, let us be grateful to Allah for it and live in peace and togetherness in our country," he proclaimed.[30] Mogadishu's new rulers set out to restore order, and within a matter of weeks they had accomplished some positives—crime fell, roads and ports were reopened, and long absent, sorely needed services like trash collection began to operate.

But forces were quickly aligning against the ICU. US officials remained skeptical of its intentions. On June 2, three days before the ICU claimed full control of Mogadishu, US ambassador Bellamy sent a cable to Washington that said the United States should consider "nullifying" some of the figures who made the ICU victory possible. "Fazul, Nahan, el-Sudani, Abdi [Godane] and Ayrow must be removed from the Somali equation," he wrote. In a strategy not all that different from the CIA's, Bellamy suggested that the United States partner with local militias to forcibly "remove these five individuals from their positions in Mogadishu, from whence they are able to continue planning to strike US interests, including soft targets that could include private Americans."[31]

When the ICU sent a letter to Bellamy on June 12 saying it wanted to create a peaceful climate in Mogadishu and help establish a legitimate Somali government, diplomats drafted a response that cracked open the door to cooperation but was written with a plain air of distrust:

> The manner in which you address the foreign al Qaeda presence in Mogadishu will determine for us your intentions for Somalia and its relations with the outside world. If you turn over these individuals to face justice for the murders and other terrorist acts they have perpetrated and continue to plan, we will have a clear signal of your desire to contribute positively to the establishment of a peaceful, stable and responsible Somali state. If, however, these individuals are allowed to continue to find refuge within territories controlled by the UIC [sic], our conclusion will be that your Union is complicit with an entity that has taken the lives of innocent Kenyans, Tanzanians, Americans, and Somalis, and intends to do so again.[32]

Meanwhile, it quickly became clear that the ICU's key allies had something besides good governance in mind. The jihadists had never fully trusted the ICU leadership, who they believed did not adhere closely enough to fundamentalist Islamic beliefs. So when the ICU formed executive and *shura* (consultation) councils, jihadists made sure they got most of the key security and policy-setting roles. Godane was named secretary-general of the executive council; a transplant from Sweden, Fuad Shongole, became education secretary. Abu Utayba was appointed head of Mogadishu security, while the top two defense posts went to jihadists Yusuf Mohamed Siyad, better known as "Indo Adde," and Mukhtar Robow.

When it came to ruling ICU territory, jihadists issued a series of unilateral, controversial directives, such as banning movies and showings of the

2006 World Cup, prohibiting importation of khat, and enacting restrictions on haircut styles, clothing, and public interactions. Jihadist fighters were not shy about enforcing the rules. In one instance, gunmen shot and killed two people in the town of Dhusomareb who refused to leave a cinema showing a World Cup match. In another, they broke up a wedding reception because a band was playing and men and women were dancing together.

Some jihadists had bigger plans. Ahmed Mohamed Islan, known as "Ahmed Madobe"—an Islamist militant who would later become a Somali politician—says that soon after the takeover of Mogadishu, members of Godane's Salahuddin camp began agitating for the jihadists to break away from the ICU. "They would say, 'They are Sufis and philosophers, unoriginal people who lost touch with the true meaning of Islam,'" he recalls.[33] Apparently, the argument fell on receptive ears, because in mid-August 2006, about thirty representatives from four jihadist groups met at a house in the Yaqshid district of northern Mogadishu to form what they termed a new "umbrella" organization. According to Madobe and another participant, speaking on condition of anonymity, the four groups were Salahuddin, led by Godane; the Raskamboni Brigade, led by Hassan al-Turki and Madobe; and two of the more fundamentalist Islamic courts—El-garas from the Galgudud region and Yaqshid in Mogadishu.

The men chose to call the new organization *Harakat Al-Shabaab al-Mujahedeen*—HSM for short, although most people and media outlets simply referred to them as Al-Shabaab. This was the formal start of the organization that would fight for, dominate, transform, and terrorize Somalia for years to come.

As one of Al-Shabaab's first acts, the participants selected a former English teacher and AIAI member from the Salahuddin camp, Ismail Arale, as the group's emir.[34] Madobe was named deputy emir. Madobe says that after their selection, Godane coached them on how to cultivate an aura of mystery and leadership. "He brought us clothing, telling us to cover ourselves, to appear less in public and stay discreet. [He said], 'You'll look big and important, respected.'"[35]

Godane, incidentally, was not the only Shabaab leader to adopt such tactics. Afghani's former aide Abu Ayan recalls that when meeting with his boss, "It was very rare to see his face. He covered it partially with his brown scarf. . . . You can't see him. Only those top senior officials see his face."[36]

ICU leaders were not invited to the Yaqshid meeting. They heard about it later but said nothing, for fear of being targeted by Ayrow's killing operation.

Despite the friction, the Al-Shabaab/ICU forces continued to cooperate and seize territory. By September they had taken most of central and southern Somalia, except for the city of Baidoa, home of Somalia's Transitional Federal Government. The TFG, as it was commonly called, had existed in a precarious state since its creation in Kenya in 2004. It was the product of yet another United Nations attempt to form a central authority in Somalia. This one had at least gotten off the ground. But from the start, the TFG was a bloated, crippled creature, weighed down by internal rivalries, an ungovernable cabinet of eighty ministers, and a president, Abdullahi Yusuf, who many observers saw as lacking in political skills and mainly concerned with advancing the interests of his Darod clan. A former Somali army colonel, Yusuf could have posed a threat to Al-Shabaab—it was his forces who pushed AIAI out of Puntland in 1992. But he could do little in the present given the conflict within the TFG. In a single week in late July, two members of parliament were shot, thirty officials resigned, and Yusuf's prime minister, Ali Mohamed Gedi, barely survived a no-confidence vote in parliament.

About the only thing the TFG had going for it was the protection of Ethiopia, which grew increasingly concerned about the spread of Islamist forces next door. One week after the ICU claimed victory in Mogadishu, Ethiopian Prime Minister Meles Zenawi warned US diplomats in Addis Ababa that "if Baidoa was threatened, we will act."[37] He made good on his threat on July 20, when a force variously reported as several hundred or several thousand Ethiopian troops crossed the border and took up positions in and around Baidoa, forcing the ICU/Shabaab fighters to halt their advance about twenty-five kilometers from the town, although they continued to advance elsewhere.

Unable to mount a frontal assault on the TFG capital, the militants introduced a new tactic to Somali warfare. On September 18, 2006, a suicide car bomber crashed into the convoy of President Yusuf outside the parliament building in Baidoa. Yusuf was unharmed, but the blast destroyed several cars and killed at least five people, including the president's brother. The attack was the first known suicide bombing in Somalia's history. The second took place in late November at a government checkpoint outside the city, killing at least nine. Security experts opined that the wanted US embassy bombers—Fazul, al-Sudani, and Nabhan—were likely using their expertise to strengthen the Islamists and help them overcome the TFG and the Ethiopians.

To many outside observers, it seemed that the TFG was facing its final days. The situation came to a head in December, when the Islamists issued an ultimatum to the Ethiopian troops—depart Baidoa within one week or be attacked. The Ethiopians stayed. Fighting erupted in several nearby towns on December 19. In the first of two big battles, ICU fighters, many of them university students, clashed with Ethiopian troops in Daynunay, a former military base about twenty kilometers east of Baidoa. Initially, enthusiastic militias pushed to within eight kilometers of the TFG stronghold. But within four days the tide turned, as the Ethiopian regular army showed its superior training and military hardware. The ICU had nothing to counter artillery strikes on its front lines. When fighters tried to charge the Ethiopian lines, they were annihilated.

The second battle near the town of Idale was a different story. Here, the Ethiopians fought militias aligned with Al-Shabaab who had far better discipline and weapons. Mohamed Omer is a former militant commander who took part in the battle. He says Shabaab's top strategists and military leaders were on hand, including Fazul, al-Sudani, and Ayrow. "Al-Shabaab planned to fight in Idale to defend [the town of] Dinsor," he says. "They chose the area because it had forests and water reservoirs."[38] The clash began when Al-Shabaab enticed some Ethiopian troops outside Baidoa to leave their positions by deploying a unit to attack and then retreat. The Ethiopians gave chase and soon a large contingent of troops was moving toward Idale. They advanced right into an Al-Shabaab trap. Hundreds of Shabaab fighters attacked, setting off a fierce gun battle that bogged down the foreigners in unfamiliar territory with dusty, confusing roads.

The ensuing battle was one of the biggest Al-Shabaab ever fought. Guns and artillery roared for three days, from December 21 to December 23, with the sides pushing each other back and forth. Ethiopian troops dug trenches for themselves and their tanks. Al-Shabaab in turn massed recoilless rifles and bazookas in an effort to put the tanks out of action. After a short time, both sides made securing access to the two water reservoirs their top priority. "I witnessed the problem of having no water," says Omer. "You inhale gunpowder for hours, and the most important thing becomes getting a sip of water." He says the Ethiopians took control of the reservoirs, only for Al-Shabaab to snatch them back. The warring sides got closer and closer to each other and the lines were so fluid that each side was able to capture—and execute—many of the opponent's wounded. Omer says he saw a fellow Al-Shabaab commander, Abdalla Sudan, behead an Ethiopian soldier.[39]

On day three of the battle, both sides received reinforcements. Al-Shabaab got more weapons and men from Mogadishu, led by Afghan-trained Abu Uttayba. Ethiopian troops received more soldiers and tanks. But when another day's fighting resulted in no breakthroughs, the Ethiopians finally called in airpower. That made the difference. On the 24th, helicopter gun-ships began to rake the Al-Shabaab lines. On the 25th, Al-Shabaab forces grew noticeably weaker, and on the following day, they disintegrated alto-gether. "How do you know that your men are defeated?" says Omer. "Your men lose organization, different units are unaware of each other's position, you lose communication. I was nearly left there without a vehicle to escape [when] our forces fled."[40]

Al-Shabaab did not bother to defend Dinsor as they retreated; the hard-ware facing them was too powerful. The fighters headed straight to Buale and then proceeded to Kismayo, putting themselves temporarily out of the Ethiopians' reach. The ICU forces were also in full retreat, and by the 27th, astonishingly, Islamist forces had withdrawn from nearly all the terri-tory they had captured across Somalia earlier that year. That same day, they abandoned their bases in the capital. On December 28, 2006, Ethiopian and TFG forces entered the city unopposed. Islamic rule in Mogadishu was over after just six and a half months.

There has been considerable debate over how much the United States influenced Ethiopia's decision to invade, with critics saying Ethiopia acted at Washington's behest. However, a reading of US diplomatic cables be-tween October and December 2006 suggests strongly that Ethiopian Prime Minister Meles needed little encouragement. If anything, American visi-tors to Addis Ababa—including Ambassador Donald Yamamoto, Charge d'Affaires Vicki Huddleston, Senator Russell Feingold, and Assistant Secre-tary of State for African Affairs Jendayi Frazer—urged Meles and his aides to think twice before sending troops across the border.

In one early December meeting with General John Abizaid, the head of the US Central Command, Meles expressed his intention to deploy

Ethiopian forces in Somalia. According to a December 8 cable, "General Abizaid articulated that Meles had time on his side and that a rush into conflict would yield immediate victories against technicals [pickup trucks mounted with big guns], but not enhance security for Ethiopia."

In a particularly stark example, Feingold raised numerous questions about Ethiopia's plans after Meles said armed conflict was likely and that his forces aimed to strike "quick, painful blows" to the ICU, to show that Ethiopia would not allow "consolidation" of an extremist regime in Mogadishu.

> Sen. Feingold said he understood the GOE's [Government of Ethiopia's] concerns and recognized the difficulty of its situation, but said he was not enthusiastic about military action. . . . Sen. Feingold asked whether the GOE was concerned about the increasing military strength of the [ICU] and the difficult logistical challenges that Ethiopian forces would face operating in Somalia. If Ethiopia were unsuccessful in its offensive, wouldn't this embolden the Jihadists? . . . Feingold asked about the GOE's plans for stabilizing Somalia after military intervention, and wondered what kind of Somalia Meles hoped to see eventually. Would Ethiopia tolerate a unified Somalia? The application of Sharia Law?[41]

The United States finally signaled its acceptance of Ethiopia's plans in mid-December when Frazer publicly accused the ICU of having links to international terrorism. "The Council of Islamic Courts is now controlled by Al-Qaeda cell individuals, East Africa Al-Qaeda cell individuals," she told reporters. "The top layer of the courts are extremist to the core. They are terrorists and they are in control."[42]

The statement—based in truth, but an exaggeration of the reality—struck many Somalia watchers as a flat-out surprise. One of those shocked was the French analyst Roland Marchal, a respected writer and researcher on Africa, based at the Paris Institute of Political Studies, also known as Sciences Po. "I knew a couple of people who were involved in sensitive African issues [in Washington]," Marchal says, "and they were amazed by the shift in the US strategy, when Jendayi Frazer said the Islamic Courts Union is completely controlled by Al-Qaeda. They were saying, 'Where does this come from?' Then people said it came from Meles . . . and the American administration bought that version."[43]

Some Mogadishu residents rejoiced at the departure of Al-Shabaab and the ICU, thankful for an end to the restrictions on what they could watch, what they could wear, and how they could enjoy themselves. But the astute ones recognized that the conflict was far from over. As the Ethiopians closed in, Islamist militant leaders had issued calls via the internet and radio for Muslims to come to Somalia and help eject what they called "the invaders."[44] They said fighters were needed for an Afghan- or Iraq-style guerilla resistance. They knew many Somalis viewed Ethiopia as a mortal enemy and that Ethiopia did not want to keep its troops in hostile, war-ravaged Mogadishu forever.

If enough fighters and money could be raised, the jihadists believed they could still win control of Somalia. Then they could establish an Islamic state that, in their minds, would be the first step toward building a caliphate that would stretch across Somalia, and beyond.

THREE

"THE REAL JIHAD HAS JUST STARTED"

FOR ABOUT FORTY-EIGHT HOURS, MOGADISHU residents seemed not to mind—or were simply stunned—that thousands of well-armed troops from Somalia's historic enemy were taking over the capital. Initial reaction to the power shift was generally muted, with few people either cheering or jeering when they saw government and Ethiopian soldiers driving by. Some told journalists that they hoped the Transitional Federal Government (TFG) would finally establish stability. Others chewed khat in the streets in a clear rebuke to the departed Al-Shabaab and its hard-line rules.[1]

There was looting in some areas, gunfights over abandoned weapons in others, and warlords quickly tested the new rulers by setting up roadblocks. But TFG officials felt safe enough to enter the city starting on December 29, 2006, with Prime Minister Ali Mohammed Gedi being the first to arrive, in an Ethiopian helicopter. On New Year's Day, after meetings with clan elders, a confident Gedi moved to assert the government's authority, announcing three months of martial law and the immediate launch of a disarmament program. "All (weapon) owners, clan leaders, businessmen—all citizens of Mogadishu must hand over their weapons," he declared. If guns and explosive devices were not turned in within three days, he warned, the government would "collect the weapons by use of force."[2]

But the decree got a cold reception in the battle-scarred capital, especially from members of the Hawiye clan, who largely distrusted President

Abdullahi Yusuf, a Darod clan member. Only a handful of arms were surrendered. The TFG had made a miscalculation, the first of many to come.

Some observers think that even with the shrewdest judgment, the TFG was in a desperate, possibly hopeless situation. The bulk of Mogadishu's residents may have been glad to see Al-Shabaab depart, but they immediately missed the Islamic Courts Union. "For the six months they held Mogadishu—during that period it was fantastic," says Terry, the Westerner, who was in the city at the time. "There were no checkpoints, people were walking around freely, didn't fear being robbed, didn't fear being raped, didn't fear the lawlessness that had taken over for so long. People were happy the ICU had taken control of the security situation. . . . [They thought] 'If somebody gives us security, we give them support.'"[3]

Osman Abdullahi Gure was then director of Radio Shabelle, one of Mogadishu's top news outlets. He concurs that people were not happy to see the ICU shoved aside. "When the Ethiopian troops came, it was a time when the people were very pleased with the Islamic Courts," he says. "So immediately, from the beginning of the Ethiopian presence, people were angry for that reason alone."[4] But the Ethiopian presence itself would have been enough to provoke most Somalis. Tensions between Somalia and Ethiopia go back centuries, stemming from differences over religion, territory, resources, and regional power. Many Somalis had bitter feelings over losing the 1977 war and still felt that Ethiopia's Ogaden region, which is populated by people of ethnic Somali origin, should belong to Somalia. Despite Ethiopia's promise that its incursion was only temporary, many also believed Ethiopia was scheming to take over the entire country if it got the chance. Islamist figures like Hassan Dahir Aweys tried to play up those fears. "I call on the Somali people to fight these forces which want to change the map of Somalia itself," Aweys said in a June 2007 television interview. "In the offices of the provisional government, we found maps in which Ethiopia wiped out Somalia and annexed it to itself. It is common knowledge they have always wanted to do that."[5] Actually, it wasn't knowledge at all—but it was a fairly common belief, which made it easy for the militants to plant seeds of suspicion and distrust in the minds of Somalis.

French analyst Roland Marchal says Ethiopia made a "major blunder" by invading its neighbor and longtime rival. "If they were Nigerians, or the Ivory Coast army, there would have been a fight, but the fight would have been interpreted in a very different manner by the population," he says. "Most of the Ethiopian army contingent in Somalia, they were [ethnic] Somalis from Ethiopia [or] they were Oromos. So you could certainly say it was largely a Muslim army, made up of Muslim soldiers. . . . And yet, they were labeled as Christians by the population." That, Marchal says, was the "emotional dimension" of Somalis' reaction at work.[6]

Anger toward the Ethiopians began to build once the shock of their arrival wore off. Only a small spark was needed to turn the anger into action. Characteristically, the spark came from Ibrahim al-Afghani. Aden Ayrow's aide Mohamed Toora-Toorow, who was living in the Hamar Jadid neighborhood, said he received a phone call from Afghani just a few days after Al-Shabaab fled Mogadishu. Afghani told him to launch a new war against the Ethiopian and TFG forces and to fire the first shots. "He said, 'I'm ordering you to do whatever you can to fire upon them. The real jihad has just started.'"[7]

Toora-Toorow said that on the night of January 3, he and some colleagues planted a land mine near buildings known as the "Old Insurance Complex," located on October 21st Road in northern Mogadishu. Late that evening, the mine exploded under an Ethiopian military vehicle. No one died, but Al-Shabaab and other parties carried out additional attacks in the next few days. On the 7th, gunmen opened fire on Ethiopian soldiers driving past a hotel in the south of the city.[8] This time, a Somali government soldier and a thirteen-year-old girl caught in the crossfire were killed.

One battle for Somalia's future was over; a new, far deadlier one had begun.

⁓

From the minute the Islamists lost Mogadishu, Al-Shabaab's priorities changed. The group held fast to its goal of creating a strict Islamic state. But in terms of fund-raising, recruitment, and publicity, Al-Shabaab stressed a new top objective: driving out the Ethiopians. It did not take a genius to recognize that an appeal to Somalis' nationalism could hit home in ways that appeals to their religion might not. Soon, announcements of Al-Shabaab's attacks were ending with the tagline "Defeat the Ethiopian crusaders and their apostate brothers," a phrase designed to appeal to both patriots and

Islamist militants.[9] Messages to the public were laced with statements such as "We are after them wherever they are until they are forced to leave our country, not through negotiations and bargaining, but with machine guns and artillery."[10]

Al-Shabaab got a boost from Al-Qaeda's number-two leader Ayman al-Zawahiri, who released an audio message entitled "Rise Up and Support Your Brothers in Somalia," aimed squarely at an audience of jihadists and would-be martyrs. "Do not be affected by the first shock," he said. "The real battle will begin by launching your campaigns against the Ethiopian forces with God's help and might. The faithful groups in their pursuit of death for the sake of God will devour the Crusader invading Ethiopian Army."[11]

Defeating the invaders would not be easy. Unlike the warlords that Al-Shabaab and the ICU defeated the previous spring, the Ethiopian army was a real military force, made up of trained soldiers equipped with tanks, armored vehicles, and aircraft. Ethiopian officials consistently said that only four thousand troops had been deployed in Somalia, but Western diplomats stationed in Addis Ababa placed the number at ten thousand, and media reports put it as high as twenty thousand.[12] Whatever the number, the battle at Idale had just shown there was no way Al-Shabaab could win a toe-to-toe slugging match. Moreover, the militant group had just lost hundreds of fighters and used up large portions of their weapons and ammunition. A period to rest and rebuild was needed.

To complicate matters for Al-Shabaab, the African Union decided to implement a plan, originally proposed by East African nations, to deploy a peacekeeping force to help shield the fledgling TFG. The UN-authorized force would be known as the African Union Mission in Somalia, AMISOM. Uganda agreed to provide the first contingent of twelve hundred soldiers, scheduled to arrive in early March. The AU gave the force a strictly defensive mandate—protect the TFG and its key sites like the airport and presidential palace—but it would be one more obstacle and one more adversary for Al-Shabaab.

At the same time, Al-Shabaab leaders knew they enjoyed home-field advantage over their enemies. In Somalia, the Ethiopians and AU forces would be on unfamiliar turf. They would have long supply lines between Mogadishu and the Ethiopian border. And for reasons both political and financial, the Ethiopians in particular were unlikely to keep a long-term presence in the volatile Somali capital. If Al-Shabaab could not immediately defeat them, perhaps it could outlast them.

The home-field advantage grew stronger in early 2007 as Somalis both inside and outside the country began responding to Al-Shabaab's propaganda. It helped that Al-Shabaab was essentially the only insurgent group still standing. The ICU had shattered and scattered, and no purely nationalistic militias seemed to emerge. If a young Somali wanted to fight the Ethiopians, Al-Shabaab was his number-one option. According to the Center for Strategic and International Studies (CSIS), a Washington think tank, Al-Shabaab's membership jumped "from around four hundred into the thousands." CSIS noted that the vast majority of the recruits were "young, uneducated Somalis who wished to defend their families and reclaim their country."[13] Meanwhile, Somali immigrants in the United States, Europe, and the Middle East started raising money for the group. Legally speaking, the US fund-raising was in a gray area; the US government had designated some Al-Shabaab associates such as Aweys and Hassan al-Turki as terrorists but would not apply that tag to the group as a whole for another year.[14] However, certain Somalis in the United States didn't care. For them, sending money to Somali insurgents was just like defending the country against Ethiopia. The lines were not blurry.

The US government's prosecution of the fund-raisers opens a window into how Al-Shabaab raised money abroad. Amina Ali and Halima Hassan were Somali natives living in the Minneapolis area. The two women organized and hosted teleconferences, in which dozens, even hundreds, of potential donors heard a live appeal from an Al-Shabaab representative in Somalia. After the call, Ali and Hassan would take pledges from those listening and later collect the money.

US investigators recorded a number of the phone calls, including one aimed at women where the Al-Shabaab speaker, Hawo-Kiin Hassan Raage, urged her listeners to fund the men on the front lines:

> My dear sisters, who is the most important person? . . . It was narrated that the prophet said in the Hadith, "The most valuable person is the person who sacrifices his life for God." The most valuable person is the Mujahid. The person who provides supplies to the person who is going to jihad, and the one who takes care of his children, is like someone who went to jihad. So dear sisters,

let us help the Mujahid. . . . Let us stand up and feed the Mujahid. Let us stand up and take care of their wounds.

Al-Shabaab's true colors shone through in the run-up to the main pitch, when Raage focused not on the warriors, but on the importance of Islam.

We are saying that today is the day of jihad. Don't be distracted. Devote your-self to protecting the religion for the people, my dear sisters. Don't be preoc-cupied with other things. Protect the religion. It is the most important thing. What good can come out from simply feeding a person, if the person turns into an infidel?[15]

In time, Ali and Hassan would raise more than $8,500 for Al-Shabaab—fairly small change in American terms, but a significant amount of money in Somalia.

In California, four men led by a San Diego cabdriver, Basaaly Saeed Moa-lin, were raising funds by soliciting in mosques and among other cabdrivers. FBI agents listened in on numerous phone calls between Moalin and Aden Ayrow, talking under code names. In one call, in December 2007, Ayrow said he needed $3,000 for his forces in the Bay and Bakool regions. Moalin said he would "take care of the issue swiftly" and contacted his three con-spirators—Anaheim cabdriver Ahmed Nashir, San Diego imam Mohamed Khadar, and Issa Doreh, an employee of Shidaal Express, a money transfer firm that serviced Somalia. The money was quickly raised and sent to Soma-lia on January 1. Two days later, Moalin also gave Ayrow access to his house in Mogadishu. According to the prosecutors' later indictment:

Basaaly gave Ayrow detailed instructions to the house, and told Ayrow that "you can use it for anything you want—I mean—if you want to hide stuff in there." Basaaly told Ayrow that he could bury his "stuff" deep in the ground and then plant trees on top. Basaaly told Ayrow he would have trees brought over from a farm near Mogadishu for this purpose. Basaaly also told Ayrow that the house has an attic where he used to store documents and weapons. Basaaly stated that the house's only drawback was that it is "easily identifiable" and an "easy target" because of its location and trees. Ayrow shrugged off this concern, stating, "No one would know. How could anyone know, if the house is used only during the nights?"[16]

Moalin and his associates would raise more than $12,000 for Al-Shabaab before the FBI shut them down.

In Mogadishu, the new phase of fighting started slowly, with small-scale gun, grenade, and mortar attacks against Ethiopian soldiers and various Somali government targets. The international media did not take much notice at first, as Ethiopian and Somali government forces, with US intelligence and military help, were still chasing bands of Islamist militants. On January 7, 2007, a US AC-130 aircraft opened fire on a convoy of vehicles near Raskamboni a fishing village close to the Somalia-Kenya border. Pentagon spokesman Bryan Whitman said the attack was aimed at "principal Al-Qaeda leadership" in the area; subsequent news reports identified the main targets as Ayrow and Abu Taha al-Sudani and said that several people had been killed or wounded. Former Al-Shabaab commander Mohamed Omer confirms that Ayrow was in the convoy; he says he heard that Ayrow was wounded in the shoulder. Doubts lingered about Aryow's survival until March, when Koran Radio in Mogadishu broadcast a recorded message from him: "I am well. Whatever missile they fire, I will live until such time Allah allows me to die."[17]

On January 23, the United States launched another airstrike in the south, this one aimed at Al-Shabaab's deputy leader Ahmed Madobe. Madobe, badly wounded in the attack, was captured by US and Ethiopian forces six hours later. Eight others with him were killed. Madobe later told reporter Jeremy Scahill of the *Nation* and other reporters that he believed US intelligence tracked him through use of his satellite phone.[18]

But by February, the trend of insurgent attacks in the capital was escalating and becoming impossible to ignore. On the 16th, five mortar rounds were fired at the Mogadishu seaport. On the 18th, the city saw its first car bomb, a Toyota Corolla that exploded and killed four people.[19] Two days later, mortar attacks killed sixteen and injured more than forty others.[20] And the 21st brought the first targeted attacks on government officials. The commissioner for the city's Yaqshid district, Muhiyadin Hassan Haji, was hit by four bullets on his way home from work and died. A few minutes later, gunmen shot dead the deputy commissioner of the Wadajir district, Abdi Omar Googooye. Googooye was reportedly involved in efforts to set up a neighborhood guard system to keep insurgents from launching mortars.

Al-Shabaab was not the only faction carrying out the attacks. Clan militias and warlords were back on the streets, and a new "resistance," or

Muqawama movement, had been formed, led by the former deputy leader of the ICU, Abdulkadi Ali Omar. Al-Shabaab had broken with the ICU after the December 2006 fighting but formed a loose alliance with the new movement out of necessity. The rising violence caught the eye of United Nations Secretary-General Ban Ki-moon, whose organization was eager to see some hope emerge in lawless, conflict-ridden Somalia. In a report issued to the UN Security Council on February 28, Ban wrote, "I want to caution against any assumption that the fall of the [Islamic Courts Union] will automatically bring peace to Somalia. There are clear indications that a significant number of 'spoilers' remain active." Ban said he was "disturbed" by the violence in Mogadishu and emphasized that a "viable political process" was needed to help Somalis stabilize the country.[21]

Perhaps that is why the next day, President Yusuf announced that a grand Somali peace conference—a "National Reconciliation Congress"—would convene in mid-April.[22] But the idea was a fantasy driven by a delusion. Mogadishu wasn't safe, a fact made obvious on March 6 when a reported one hundred armed insurgents stormed a government base,[23] and again on the 9th when unidentified insurgents fired an RPG at an incoming plane carrying a half-dozen AU peacekeepers.[24]

The TFG nevertheless pushed ahead. On March 12, parliament members meeting in Baidoa voted to formally move the seat of government to Mogadishu.[25] President Yusuf moved into Villa Somalia the following day—just in time to be present for a mortar attack that didn't damage the compound but killed eight members of a family in a house nearby.[26]

~

These incidents were ripples in the water compared to the tsunami of violence that crashed over Mogadishu the morning of March 21, 2007. It had been an open secret that the Ethiopians wanted to seize the positions from which Al-Shabaab and the other insurgents were launching attacks. They planned a series of joint thrusts with the TFG to take control of five areas—Mogadishu Stadium, the al-Bakara, Florence and Sana'a road junctions, and Ayrow's base in the former Ifka Halane court complex, located in southern Mogadishu. The government cast the operation as a disarmament drive, and Interior Minister Mohamed Shieikh Mohamoud Guled warned civilians along a major thoroughfare, Industrial Road, to evacuate. "The security of the capital will be under control shortly," the minister assured a local radio station.[27]

The first drive, aimed at Ayrow's base, got started when Ethiopian tanks rolled out from the Somali Defense Ministry at 6:00 a.m. that day. But within a half-hour of hitting the streets, Ethiopian and TFG forces were ambushed in the Shirkole area by dozens of masked Al-Shabaab and Muqa-wama fighters armed with rocket-propelled grenades. A local Mogadishu University student who witnessed the fighting says he saw one Ethiopian truck destroyed near the university and another hit near Ifka Halane, killing seven soldiers.[28]

Then came a more horrific sight: the soldiers' bloodied corpses were pulled through the streets. "People including women and children were al-lowed to drag the bodies," says the student, speaking on condition of ano-nymity. "They were mutilating the bodies, poking them with knives and sticks." There were also photos of soldiers' bodies being stepped on, gawked at, and set afire. Not since the "Black Hawk Down" incident had Mogadi-shu's people acted with such venom.

The other TFG/Ethiopian thrusts ran into similar resistance. By day's end, media reports said at least sixteen people were killed and hospitals were treating more than one hundred wounded. An Ethiopian political official said his country's forces suffered thirty-four casualties without specify-ing how many had been killed.[29] Michael Ranneberger, who had replaced William Bellamy as the US ambassador to Kenya, sent a battle report to Washington in a cable that night: "According to local sources in Mogadishu, TFG forces initially seemed to have the upper hand, but insurgents were seen to be gaining by mid-afternoon. These sources reported that the TFG had not made any statements about the day's events, leaving the residents to wonder whether the insurgents might actually have defeated government forces."[30]

In follow-up cables over the next few days, Ranneberger noted that many Somalis saw the fighting as a clash between clans, or an Ethiopian effort to subdue branches of the Hawiye clan, which remained opposed to President Yusuf. "Although the radical Islamists have exploited and manipulated the current situation to the point of a breakdown in the reconciliation process, they do not seem to be driving the current clashes," he wrote.[31]

Mogadishu experienced two more days of fighting on March 22 and 23, highlighted by Al-Shabaab's claim that it brought down a Belarus-registered IL-76 departing from Mogadishu airport. Ranneberger characterized the incident as a "probable shoot down," accomplished with SA-18 missiles.[32] Hawiye clan elders then negotiated a shaky cease-fire with the Ethiopians, but Al-Shabaab broke the truce with a suicide car bombing on the 26th that caused heavy casualties and severe damage to an Ethiopian army base. Toora-Toorow said the bomber was his superior officer, Aden Okiyale. "We said goodbye to him near the Pasta Factory [an Al-Shabaab base]. He put mattresses on top of the car in order to disguise it as someone who is fleeing the city, and when he was driving alongside the Maslah barracks he turned the car into the base and detonated it." The Ethiopians moved out of the base the next evening. "When I visited I could still see the blood and bits of human flesh," Toora-Toorow recalled.[33]

Frustrated by the resistance and angered by the suicide bombing, Ethiopian forces began four days of heavy mortar and BM-21 rocket attacks on March 29. The attacks targeted areas around the stadium known to be insurgent strongholds—Hamar Jadid, Bar Ubah, and Towfiq. By many accounts, this phase of the early 2007 fighting was the most destructive of all, virtually wiping out entire neighborhoods. Witnesses described the Ethiopian shelling as indiscriminate and brutal on civilians. A Western journalist who was in Mogadishu at the time said Ethiopian forces fired from three main locations: the presidential palace, the Ministry of Defense building, and the abandoned Digfer hospital. "The shelling distances were two to five kilometers from origin to target area, and clearly there was little capacity to target specific buildings," he says. "In the Towfiq quarter, for example, all the houses, roofs and walls, were destroyed. It was clear there was just general targeting of the area."[34]

Al-Shabaab and the other insurgents responded to the Ethiopian barrage with mortars and rockets of their own, and for four days, Mogadishu residents endured the thunder of almost round-the-clock bombardment, accompanied by fighting on the ground and in the air. In one dramatic battle, watched by reporters on rooftops, an Ethiopian helicopter gunship fired on an insurgent stronghold only to be struck by a missile. The copter limped and sputtered back to the airport but crashed on the runway, killing two crew members.

"We used the SAM7 missile to bring down the helicopter," says Zakariye Ismail Hersi, Al-Shabaab's future chief of military intelligence. "It was one of several anti-aircraft missiles the Islamic court had received from Eritrea."[35]

Shortly before the missile strike, Hersi says, an old woman had come outside and prayed for the Ethiopians' defeat. When the missile struck its target, she began ululating in glee. "Everyone cried, it was emotional," he says.[36]

Sometimes, the fighting was reduced to a game of cat-and-mouse. Radio Shabelle's Osman Gure points to one incident that for him sums up the determination of Somali insurgents to defy the invaders. "An Ethiopian Ural (military truck) was burned down at Towfiq junction," he says. "A crowd dragged the body of an Ethiopian soldier to the animal livestock area in Huriwa district." When Ethiopian soldiers followed, trying to collect their fallen comrade, militants took the body to the Hawlwadag district, several kilometers away. Ethiopians continued to pursue in tanks. By now it was nighttime, he says, and one of the tanks got lost. Whether out of fear or frustration, the crew kept firing all night as they drove around the city, to the Black Sea area, to Bar Ubah, and finally to the Bakara Market.

"The Muqawama did not have anything to fire on the tank apart from an AK-47, which was ineffective," Gure says. "It showed how incapable the opposition were in comparison to Ethiopian troops. But on the other hand, it showed defiance, that with all the tanks the Ethiopians had, they could not recover their bodies."[37]

Fighting raged on until the sides arranged another cease-fire on April 2 to collect the growing number of corpses on the streets, rotting in the hot Mogadishu sun. Rights groups and clan elders estimated that between four hundred and one thousand Somali civilians had been killed along with an undetermined number of combatants.[38] While the cease-fire held, tens of thousands of residents fled Mogadishu. Conditions elsewhere were rough—the UN reported that in Afgoye, to the southwest, people were waiting twelve hours in line for water. But the residents' instincts were validated when more fighting broke out on April 18, triggered by another suicide bomb attack on an Ethiopian base. An additional 320 civilians were killed before Al-Shabaab and Muqawama fighters suddenly withdrew from most of their strongholds on April 26, allowing Ethiopian and TFG troops to claim control over several flattened neighborhoods.

By that point, an estimated 340,000 people, one-third of Mogadishu's population, had fled the city since the start of February.

The scope and savagery of the March-April fighting drew condemnation from Human Rights Watch, which said all sides in the conflict were showing "a wanton disregard for civilian life and property" and violating international humanitarian law. Speaking to the Voice of America that March, President Yusuf made no apologies for the Ethiopians' use of artillery against residential neighborhoods. "Why shouldn't we use it?" he said. "They [the insurgents] are within the civilian areas. The public should make them leave the civilian areas. When those guys leave the civilian areas, no harm will come to the civilians. We want the civilians to remove them, tell them to go away from our midst."[39]

—

Al-Shabaab did grant the president's request to leave Mogadishu—sort of—at the end of April. Because of the high number of casualties, the group moved many of its fighters and weapons to areas outside the capital. Commanders eschewed all-out war for a strategy of targeted attacks: assassination attempts on government figures and their perceived supporters, and shelling and suicide bombings of Ethiopian military bases. They also deployed units to attack the Ethiopians' main supply lines.

That was how in May 2007, nineteen-year-old Dalha Ali found himself positioned on the side of a highway northwest of Mogadishu, hands wrapped around an assault rifle, awaiting the order to open fire. The former Tabliq member and would-be Islamic scholar was now a full-time, battle-tested fighter for Al-Shabaab. His unit had been assigned to ambush enemy soldiers traveling a highway between Baidoa and the town of Afgoye. Lookouts farther up the road would call when an Ethiopian or Somali government convoy was coming their way. The Al-Shabaab fighters would get into position. One of them would initiate a countdown: three kilometers away, two kilometers; one thousand meters away, five hundred, one hundred. "By this time you are just seconds away from firing," Ali would later explain.[40] "My heart was booming; (I was) nervous, sweaty. But when the bullets fly, all the nerves go away. I never liked them to count the kilometers. I just wanted fighting to begin."

A lot had happened in the year since the night Ali slipped away from the Tabliq mosque and joined the Islamist forces. For one thing, he had a new name. Islamist militants often re-brand themselves to demonstrate their commitment to jihad, their fighting prowess, or other point of pride. Ali joined the trend and became Asad Yare—a combination of Somali and Arabic for "little lion." He was not a tall or especially strong man but regardless of their size, lions can fight, something that Ali/Yare felt increasingly able to do. During 2006, he had received extensive instruction at Al-Shabaab camps at Oodweyne outside Mogadishu and the Dafeed-Leego area in the southwest. He was now well trained in a variety of tasks, such as handling roadside bombs, firing mortars and recoilless rifles, and driving "technicals," the pickup trucks mounted with machine guns and anti-aircraft guns that are often used by non-state armies. He was also indoctrinated into the Al-Shabaab way of thinking. Aden Ayrow had lectured the recruits during training. You will be battling infidels and their henchmen, he told them. You are going to liberate Baidoa from the infidels of Ethiopia. One day, you will defend a vast Islamic emirate.

That was before the ICU and Al-Shabaab suffered such heavy losses in December. But Ali and hundreds of fighters like him did not lose heart, and he eagerly met up with Ayrow and Al-Shabaab fighters who regrouped in Mogadishu in early 2007. Within weeks, he was taking part in attacks on Ethiopian troops, first in the northern suburbs, then on the highway. Oddly, he would only acknowledge indirectly that he was killing people. "I was firing bullets, (and) people must have been in the direction I was aiming at," he later said.

Every two months, Ali would rotate to his second assignment: being an operative for Al-Shabaab's security force, the Amniyat, in Mogadishu's sprawling, outdoor Bakara Market. Both logistically and emotionally, this was a very different task. Instead of targeting mostly foreign soldiers, Ali was expected to shoot Somali civilians believed to be collaborating with the Ethiopians and the TFG. Targets included government officials, civil servants, political activists, journalists, and people suspected of working for foreign nongovernmental organizations. Sometimes, Al-Shabaab went after individuals who simply visited government offices, in order to scare the populace into avoiding all contact with officials.

Ali considered this part of his job to be the "dirty war," as compared with the "clean war" being fought against the Ethiopians outside the capital. "I did not like operating in Bakara," he said. "If your emir . . . had an issue with someone he would simply ask you to '*soo toosi*,' a jargon word for 'get rid of him.' I liked fighting in the ambushes; I wanted to be a martyr fighting the Ethiopian troops."

Martyrdom remained at the forefront of his mind at this time. Three of his former classmates were in his unit, until one was killed in action one day. The following night Ali met the young man in his dreams. "He told me to hurry up," Ali said. "He was telling me to join him, to get my martyrdom quickly."

But through some combination of luck, good training, and instinct for self-preservation, Ali stayed alive. Al-Shabaab and, presumably, God were not finished with him. He still had lots of fighting left to do.

FOUR

GODANE

SOON AFTER THE HEAVY FIGHTING of March and April 2007, Al-Shabaab encountered its first major internal crisis. The group's emir, Ismail Arale, was arrested on May 31 in tiny Djibouti while traveling to Eritrea's capital, Asmara. Within days, he was transferred to the local US military base, Camp Lemonnier, and then flown 7,800 miles (12,550 km) away to the American prison camp in Guantanamo Bay, Cuba.[1] Al-Shabaab was without an official leader.

Angry hard-liners in Al-Shabaab, including Godane and Ayrow, said the absent Arale had been trying to "defect" to the group's former ally, the Islamic Courts Union. Some ICU leaders had recently reestablished themselves in Eritrea and called on Al-Shabaab to join them and form a Somali government-in-exile. Al-Shabaab leaders were divided on the issue, but according to his Guantanamo prison record, published by Wikileaks in 2011, the emir had accepted an ICU invitation to attend a conference in Asmara, with his travel paid for by the Eritrean government. The plans were disrupted because Arale was traveling under an alias and was arrested by Djiboutian officials for passport fraud. Another Al-Shabaab commander traveling with him, Muhiyadin Ilka'Ase, was detained but released. He later told friends he was released because officials didn't know who he was.

Al-Shabaab replaced Arale on a temporary basis with Hassan Afgoye, the group's chief of finance, then set about to choose a new emir. The crisis came at a delicate time for the group. It had shown that it could effectively fight the Ethiopians and had emerged as the primary opponent of Somalia's Transitional Federal Government. At the same time, it was clear Al-Shabaab did not have the strength to seize power or drive the Ethiopians out of the country. The next leader would have to increase the group's resources and come up with a new strategy to defeat the TFG and its allies. That task had become even more difficult with the arrival, between March and July, of more African Union peacekeepers from Uganda and Burundi. The AMISOM force now numbered 3,500 soldiers and was patrolling the streets around the key TFG sites and Maka al-Mukarama Road, which connected the presidential palace and the airport. They also safeguarded President Yusuf's "National Reconciliation Congress"—although that event produced no results once it finally got going in July, thanks in part to Al-Shabaab's threats to bomb the conference venue and shoot anyone trying to attend.

Al-Shabaab's leaders gathered in August 2007 to choose the next emir.[2] Among those present at the meeting was Zakariye Hersi, the group's future chief of military intelligence. In a few years, the United States would offer a $3 million reward for information leading to Hersi's capture.[3] At this point, Hersi was twenty-five years old, unknown to the public, and fairly new to Al-Shabaab's leadership, having entered the inner circle through the now-deposed Arale, who had been his friend at the International Islamic University in Islamabad, or IIUI, where Hersi studied economics and Arale studied English literature.[4]

According to Hersi, Al-Shabaab leaders met for two days in the Kurtunwarey district, south of Mogadishu. He says there were eighteen leaders at the meeting, including Ahmed Abdi Godane, Ibrahim al-Afghani, Mukhtar Robow, Hassan al-Turki, along with several less prominent figures such as Ahmed Iskudhuuq, Hussein Dayniile, Mukhtar Abu Muslim, and Daud Abu Suhayb. Hersi says it was agreed that the new emir's main task was to prepare Al-Shabaab for a fight against Ethiopia. "The view was that the fighting was getting intense, the operations (were) complex, and it was thought someone who could pull everyone together was needed," he says. After a period of debate, "Godane became the unanimous choice."[5]

Unanimity would be unusual among this group, given the strong-willed nature of many Al-Shabaab leaders. But then, Ahmed Abdi Godane himself was unusual. Hersi calls Godane "a genius."[6]

The background of Al-Shabaab's best-known, longest-reigning, and most powerful emir has long been clouded in mystery, lost behind conflicting information about his birth date, real name, and other details. His exact year of birth remains unknown. An Al-Shabaab video that presented a short biography of Godane gave it as 1969, while a family member interviewed for this book, who asked not be named, said it was 1971. Godane's profile on the US "Rewards for Justice" website said he was born July 10, 1977—the least probable date of all, given that he was attending universities in Pakistan in the early 1990s. What seems most likely is that Godane was in his mid-to-late thirties when he ascended to the top position in Al-Shabaab.

Many articles and analyses referred to him as "Abu Zubeyr"—a real alias for the Al-Shabaab emir, but not his real name. The *New York Times* was further off when it referred to him in a 2009 article as Mohamed Mukhtar Abirahman. The "Rewards for Justice" site got it mostly right, missing only the final name in his complete appellation, which was Ahmed Abdi Aw-Mohamud Godane.

The air of secrecy extends to Godane's appearance; he usually covered his face when traveling and there seem to be very few pictures or videos of him. The ones that exist show a man standing about five feet, eight inches tall, with a lean build, a short, neatly trimmed beard, and watchful brown eyes that suggest high intelligence.

This much is certain: He was born in Hargeisa, the future capital of Somaliland, and hailed from the Isaaq clan, the dominant clan in the area. His father was in the military during Mohamed Siad Barre's rule. He was raised in Hargeisa and attended a madrassa as a youngster before being enrolled at a secular high school. A few other nuggets known about Godane's past suggest a gifted man: he reportedly won a scholarship to study the Quran in Sudan as a boy; as an adult, he liked to both write and recite poetry; and he could speak Arabic and English in addition to Somali.

Things come into clearer focus starting in 1988, when Godane was a teenager. The situation in Hargeisa changed drastically that year when the heavily armed and Ethiopian-backed Somali National Movement attacked government bases in the north, igniting a civil war in the region. Hundreds of thousands fled across the border, mostly to Ethiopia. Godane, however, went to smaller, safer Djibouti. From there, the bright young student obtained backing from a Saudi philanthropist to attend Jama'at Abubakar Islamiya, a university in Karachi, Pakistan, that was popular with many African and East Asian students. He left for Pakistan in November 1989.

His adventure got off to a rough start when he arrived at the Karachi airport, as authorities put him in quarantine because he could not produce a card showing he had received the required vaccinations and health exams. Friends traveling on the same plane went to the university and told Somali community leaders of Godane's plight. A well-known Somali scholar at the school, Sheikh Bashir Ahmed Salat, drove out to the detention center to see what he could do. Immigration officials told him Godane would be held for six days while receiving medical treatment, but they allowed him to speak with the undoubtedly upset student. To speak to the quarantined, "you don't make contact with them, you speak to them through a barrier," Salat remembers.[7] He says he left the detention center but asked his family members to deliver food to Godane for the next six days. They did, and teacher and student forged a relationship that would last for years.

After he was released, Godane went to live with friends. He was admitted to the university and decided initially to focus on Arabic and Islamic studies. "He was brainy, good at education; it was an easy thing to him," says Salat.[8] He describes Godane as a quiet person who didn't mingle with others a lot. At this time, Godane apparently did not show signs of being a jihadist, although Salat notes that during the summer, he traveled north to the cities of Islamabad and Peshawar where radical Islamist movements were active. This was not unique behavior, he says; many students from Islamic countries did the same.

In August 1990, after almost a year in Karachi, Godane was admitted to the International Islamic University of Islamabad (IIUI). There, he switched his focus to economics and became friends with a fellow Somali, Abdulkadir Askar. The two would be study partners for the next six years. "He was a brilliant student. He always passed with an A or A-plus in every field of study," Askar says.[9] Askar noticed that Godane did not have the financial backing that some other students enjoyed and would have to appeal to charities and wealthy Saudis to pay his tuition. But the money was found, and Godane graduated from IIUI in 1996 with a bachelor's degree in economics and a master's degree in finance and Islamic banking.

However, the move to Islamabad proved fateful for Godane in other ways. "That is where he met the Islamic Jihad," says a former IIUI acquaintance of Godane, speaking on condition of anonymity. The men the acquaintance refers to were actually leaders of Egyptian Islamic Jihad (EIJ), an Al-Qaeda–affiliated group led by Osama bin Laden's close ally Ayman Al-Zawahiri. According to the acquaintance, EIJ recognized Godane's potential as a leader and took him to their bases in Peshawar and Afghanistan, where he was brought into the circle of Al-Qaeda itself. "They trusted him very much," the acquaintance says. "They taught him on leadership and the ideology that the only way to restore the dignity of Islam is jihad."[10]

Peshawar in particular was a hub for Arab jihadists, many of them exiled Egyptians, whose goal was to radicalize and train Muslim university students. Godane encountered several high-level Al-Qaeda leaders, including al-Zawahiri, Abu Xafsi al-Misry (the father of bin Laden's son-in-law), and the top Al-Qaeda man in Africa at the time, Abu Ubaidah al-Banshiri. "Whoever goes in that zone was almost certain to be recruited," says Salat. "They were the holders of jihadist ideology, in particular the Egyptians."[11]

In Peshawar, Godane also met Somalis who advanced his drift toward jihadist thinking. One was the ever-present Ibrahim al-Afghani. "When it comes to Somalis, he was the one who influenced [Godane]. He was his mentor," says Askar, who says al-Afghani would stay at the university hostel as Godane's guest on trips to and from Afghanistan.[12] Two other Somalis, Aden Jihad and Mohamed Abdi Farah, were influential as well. All four had come from northern Somalia and were from various parts of the Isaaq clan, helping to cement their bond and solidifying their desire to fight for Islamic rule back home.

According to former Al-Shabaab insiders, during this time Godane was given access to what is widely known as the "Al-Qaeda Manual." The jihadist handbook, written in Arabic, was discovered in a computer file by police in Manchester, England, during a search of a suspect's home in 2000. The 179-page book lays out Al-Qaeda's belief system and extensive guidelines for carrying out terrorist attacks. The unidentified author or authors preach that armed force is the only way to destroy secular governments and replace them with Islamic states. "Islam does not coincide or make a truce with unbelief, but rather confronts it," says a passage in the introduction. "The confrontation that Islam calls for with these godless and apostate regimes does not know Socratic debates, Platonic ideals or Aristotelian diplomacy. But it knows the dialogue of bullets, the ideals of assassination, bombing and destruction and the diplomacy of the cannon and machine gun."[13]

The rest of the book gives detailed how-to instructions on topics such as obtaining weapons, carrying out espionage, and conducting covert communications. "It contains the ideology, training, organization, time for training, time for wakeup, sleep, administration, intelligence apparatus, operational issues, dealing with tribes, clans, challenges," says Salat. However, he adds, the system outlined in the manual has a key weakness. "It's very centrally controlled; it empowers top leadership who run tightly and narrowly run groups," he says.[14] Perhaps that is why one day Godane would be accused of being rigid and authoritarian.

In Pakistan, Godane also heard and absorbed Al-Qaeda's worldview— literally, that jihad is a worldwide enterprise, aimed at spreading Islam everywhere, not just select countries or a region. When asked to give reasons for Al-Shabaab's existence in a 2011 interview with the group's own Radio Andalus, Godane voiced an outlook that put global priorities front and center, above those of Somalia. "Application of Sharia and restoration of caliphate are the prime principles," he said. After that, "confronting invasion of the Christians in general and in particular the invasion of the Habesha [Ethiopians]; creation of a society who are true followers of Islam; confronting tyrants and secularists, unification of Islamic people under the Sharia; and freeing Muslims from jails." He acknowledged Al-Shabaab's connection to Somalia and compared the group to Somali anti-colonial movements of the past, like the one led by Ahmed Gurey against Ethiopia in the 1500s. But significantly, he put those movements in a jihadist context. "These were holy wars," he said. "The basic foundation of Ahmed Gurey's jihad was defending Allah's religion and the unification of Islamic people."[15]

Askar says that by 1995, he was seeing big changes in his friend. The two would argue over matters of war and religion, with Godane voicing the sentiments of an aggressive-minded radical jihadist. "[H]e would say it's permitted to kill people in the name of applying Sharia. He would say it's permitted to even fight against other Muslims in the name of Islam. I would push him and say, 'So you want everyone killed?'" Godane apparently didn't call for that, but Askar remembers him saying that waiting for Islam to dominate the world is a "waste of time."[16]

Clearly, Godane had decided he wasn't going to wait. He would do everything in his power to make the world a place where Islam reigned supreme.

~

The IIUI acquaintance has this take on the future Shabaab chief's personality: "He is a good-mannered person, respectful, has soft personality, very pleasant, polished, not impulsive, who likes to listen but does not engage in one-on-one debates. The hallmark of his character is he knows what he wants and he is committed to getting [it]."[17]

That last quality started coming to the forefront after the radicalized Godane left Pakistan and returned to his hometown of Hargeisa sometime in 1997. Godane now had to support himself and took a job at the Somaliland Ministry of Resettlement as a case officer dealing with refugees returning from Ethiopia. Six months later, he landed a more high-profile job as a salesman with al-Barakaat, a large, international Somali money transfer firm. But all along, Godane was taking part in religious debates about Salafism, and he started criticizing the Somaliland administration, accusing them of being un-Islamic. According to Abdirahman Janaqow, a former Somali justice minister who knew Godane, the young militant tried to set up his own jihadist organization in Somaliland, but the environment was "too hostile."[18]

In 2002, Godane and Ibrahim al-Afghani relocated to Ethiopia's Ogaden region, hoping to set up a new jihadist group to liberate what they regarded as "occupied territory." But the sojourn turned out to be more about money than militancy. One night, a group of armed men attacked a convoy of drug dealers traveling from Somaliland to Ethiopia. Godane was one of the attackers. "These were khat vehicles that bring the narcotic to Somaliland but carry lots of cash on their return to Ethiopia," says a person familiar with the incident. "The vehicles were attacked between Wajale town and Jigjiga on the Ethiopia side of the border. People got killed and the money was taken." Ethiopian and Somaliland intelligence quickly arrested two of the attackers, but several others, including Godane, escaped. Officials have never confirmed the amount of money stolen but people familiar with the theft say it was equivalent to about $1 million. According to jiahdists, this money is *ghanima*, wealth dispossessed from non-believers.

After only a few months in the Ogaden, Godane and al-Afghani moved on to southern Somalia, where the absence of a working government was more conducive to their plans. Janaqow, who was a leader within the Islamic Courts Union, remembers his first meeting with Godane in Mogadishu. He says the young militant approached the ICU with the same proposal for a jihadist group he had tried to establish in Somaliland. "They came with an idea to set up an Islamist organization, which when they presented we rejected, because it was an agenda based on violence, targeted assassinations, typically what they ended up doing later on."[19] He says that after the rejection, Godane and al-Afghani quietly infiltrated the Islamic courts using the wealth they obtained from the khat heist.

By late 2002 Godane was regularly associating with the other men who would form Al-Shabaab. The next few years saw him establish his credentials as a jihadist leader. He was accused of being involved in the murders of several foreign aid workers in Somaliland, including Italian national Annalena Tonelli in 2003, and sentenced in absentia to twenty-five years in prison for terrorism-related offenses.[20] He became a close ally of Ayrow and took command of the Salahuddin Muaskar training camp in 2005. As mentioned, Godane and his fighters played a central role in the ICU's defeating the warlords and taking control of Mogadishu in 2006. And shortly thereafter, he was named the secretary-general of the ICU's executive council. By the time Al-Shabaab was formed later that year, he was one of the dominant figures in the Somali jihadist movement.

So Godane's rise to the top spot in Al-Shabaab—publicly announced on December 22, 2007[21]—was a shock to no one. Nor was the quickening pace of attacks against Ethiopian and TFG targets in Mogadishu in the last few months of the year. More surprising to some were developments which showed that under Godane, Al-Shabaab was going to carve out its own path and not be part of a larger insurgent movement. In September 2007, members of the Islamic Courts Union, Somali diaspora, and secular Somali leaders gathered in Eritrea's capital and formed a new group, the Alliance for the Re-Liberation of Somalia, or ARS. The stated goal of the ARS was to resist the Ethiopians—Eritrea's chief enemy, not incidentally. But Al-Shabaab swiftly rejected the new alliance, accusing it of "selling short" the larger goal of jihad. The group maintained its stance even as other insurgents in Somalia—the Muqawama groups—gradually aligned themselves with the ARS. The loose Shabaab/Muqawama military alliance grew strained, especially after June 2008, when the United Nations opened a dialogue with the ARS in an attempt to bring it together with the Somali government.

Alongside the political wrangling, Al-Shabaab continued to fight, both inflicting and taking serious casualties. Shabaab fighters focused on the Ethiopian troops, targeting them with ambushes, IEDs, and suicide bombings. It was not uncommon for fifty to one hundred people to be killed any given week in the Mogadishu area. "What we did was attack them daily," says Zakariye Hersi. "It was impossible to take over the bases, but attacks were relentless. . . . Whenever they leave the stadium and are going to the Pasta Factory, they were being ambushed. Our strategy was to cut one base from another and attack if they attempt to reinforce each other, and it was to make sure they don't stay in their bases peacefully."[22]

Radio Shabelle's Osman Gure says violence could erupt any time at any place. "One day you may see Al-Shabaab firing rockets from inside the Bakara Market and then in comes a heavy response and shelling from the other side," he recalls. "On another day you may be caught at a checkpoint where people are being arrested summarily. There is an Ethiopian truck standing by and people are being loaded off. But then someone may throw a hand grenade at the soldiers and the troops open fire indiscriminately and people get killed. It happened to me one day just outside Abu Hurayra mosque where I was arrested as I came out. As I was arrested someone threw a grenade. Ethiopians and government troops responded with heavy gunfire. Twenty people were killed."[23]

Terry, the Westerner, who visited Mogadishu during this period, believes the Ethiopians for the most part were simply reacting on gut instinct. "A lot of these guys are not well trained—better trained than most East African soldiers I guess, but still jumpy as hell," Terry says. "They shot out of fright. I don't think they wanted to kill Somalis. They just opened fire because they were scared."[24]

Longtime Voice of America correspondent Pete Heinlein, who was based in Ethiopia's capital Addis Ababa during this period, thinks Ethiopian troops were more frustrated than anything. "They didn't have the capability to fight a guerilla war," he says. "Their one strength was that [they] were feared by Al-Shabaab because they didn't care about the rules of fighting. A lot of the stories about massacres are true. They had no qualms about going in and killing everybody. . . . It was a terrible, terrible war."[25]

Gure says the TFG and President Yusuf kept tensions high with indiscriminate nighttime shelling of pro-insurgent neighborhoods. Most of the shots, he says, came from the presidential palace compound. "So you would have the president go to bed late at night but before that he may order the firing of several salvos into the neighborhoods overlooking the palace. People used to call these shells 'Abdullahi Yusuf's bedtime music.'"[26]

But amid the carnage, Al-Shabaab's losses were being offset by some very tangible gains that were giving the group new strength by the day. The increase in manpower and popular support during 2007 allowed Al-Shabaab to launch more attacks, capture Ethiopian weapons, and take advantage of the vast, lawless spaces where neither the Ethiopians nor AMISOM nor the TFG were present. New training camps were opened without interference. Small towns were seized and put under Al-Shabaab rule. Al-Shabaab had to fight or co-exist with warlords and ICU/ARS forces in some areas, but by early 2008, the group controlled chunks of the Somali countryside and had established footholds in some major cities, most notably Kismayo, with its busy, revenue-generating Indian Ocean port.

In the strongest sign yet that the group had become a major force, on February 26, 2008, the United States designated Al-Shabaab as a terrorist organization. Such declarations are not symbolic; from that day on, it was illegal for any US citizen to provide the group with material or financial support. In a news release, the State Department said, "Al-Shabaab (The Youth) is a violent and brutal extremist group with a number of individuals affiliated with al-Qaida. . . . Al-Shabaab has used intimidation and violence to undermine the Somali government and threatened civil society activists working to bring about peace through political dialogue and reconciliation. . . . Given the threat that Al-Shabaab poses, the designation will raise awareness of Al-Shabaab's activities and help undercut the group's ability to threaten targets in and destabilize the Horn of Africa region." [27]

The release contained one major error—it named Ayrow, not Godane, as the group's leader. But otherwise, the State Department was right on target. Al-Shabaab was violent, it was extremist, and it posed a threat not just to Somalia, but to the entire Horn of Africa. In a short time, the extent of that threat would become very clear.

FIVE

AL-SHABAAB AMERICANS

AHMED ALI OMAR WANTED TO be a doctor. After graduating from Thomas Edison High School in Minneapolis in 2004, he enrolled at a nursing school in neighboring St. Paul, thinking that would be a good way to acquire a basic medical education. His mother fully supported his aspirations. "I paid $7,000 and a second installment of $3,000 for him to study eighteen months," says Fadumo Hussein. "He learned (about) taking blood samples; he completed the course in time and got a job."[1] The wages from that job came in handy; Ahmed was the oldest boy in a Somali-American family of thirteen siblings—four boys and nine girls—and had become de facto head of the family in high school after his parents divorced and his father largely faded away from their lives.

His mother says Ahmed was a good young man and helped to raise his brothers and sisters. "He never drank alcohol, never smoked cigarettes, and he was always nice to me," she says. "He was receptive, used to buy diapers, do the shopping, and help the younger siblings with their homework." When he relaxed, Ahmed liked to do so in typically American ways, like watching NBA games or hanging out with his brothers at the Mall of America in Bloomington; he'd buy them chips and ice cream if he had the money. But Hussein thought his mind was fixed on being a doctor. "He was ambitious," she says.

So it was shocking and perplexing when Ahmed Ali Omar boarded a Northwest Airlines flight to Amsterdam in December 2007 and then disappeared.[2] He had told his mother he was going on the Hajj, the pilgrimage to Islam's holiest city, Mecca, undertaken by some two million Muslims from around the world each year. But he never returned, and Hussein says she has not had any contact with her son since then. "I don't know what to say to you," she says. "He has been away since, and I don't know whether he is dead or alive."

She does know where he went, because nearly two years later, in August 2009, Omar was one of five young men indicted by a US federal grand jury for fighting in Somalia on behalf of Al-Shabaab.[3] Prosecutors accused Omar of helping persuade at least four fellow Somali-Americans to go to Somalia for terrorist training. The group allegedly funded their travel by soliciting at local malls and apartment buildings, falsely claiming the money would be used to build a mosque or assist with Somali relief efforts. Once they arrived in Somalia, prosecutors said, the young men learned how to fire AK-47s, helped to construct an Al-Shabaab training camp, met with Saleh Nabhan and Mukhtar Robow, took part in an ambush of Ethiopian troops, and filmed propaganda videos. All five were charged with conspiring to provide material support to a terrorist group, conspiring to kill, kidnap, maim, and injure people outside the United States, and discharging a firearm in a crime of violence.

Asked why her oldest son left the United States and joined Al-Shabaab, Hussein simply shuts down. "Just leave him," she says several times, unable to answer the question. The most she will do is speculate. She believes her son may have been homesick and wanted to see Somalia. The family lived there until he was seven, and then they spent three years in Somali refugee camps in northern Kenya before coming to the United States. She thinks that when Omar and the others went to Somalia, they were recruited by Al-Shabaab and joined the group—a fact that would have made it impossible for them to return to their adopted home.

"Most of the children did not go to harm anyone," she says. "I don't think they will give him a bye now. May Allah keep him safe wherever he is."

According to sources in Somalia, Omar was still alive as of 2017 and was very much involved in Al-Shabaab. He was reportedly a junior officer in the group and married to the daughter of a top militant.

~

Ahmed Ali Omar was not an isolated case among the Twin Cities' Somali-American community. Between October 2007 and October 2009, more than twenty young men left the area with little or no warning, for the purpose of taking up jihad. Some were high school or college students who parents and teachers believed to have bright futures. Others had made a living stocking shelves or delivering packages. At least two were involved in gangs. But nearly all of them had a few things in common. They were born in Somalia and had come to America as kids. They were known to be active at local mosques. And a short time after their disappearance, they turned up back in Somalia, either training with or fighting for Al-Shabaab.

Concerned parents and watchful US officials knew what was going on: Al-Shabaab was reaching out to Somali-American youth through the internet and local sympathizers, urging them to forsake Western society and become fighters for radical Islam. Al-Shabaab's recruiters concentrated on the Twin Cities area because it was home to one of the world's largest Somali communities outside the Horn of Africa, with at least twenty-five thousand Somali refugees and immigrants by most counts.[4] The US government initially assigned Somali refugees to the area in the early 1990s—a seemingly odd choice, given the stark difference between Somalia's year-round equatorial heat and Minnesota's North Pole–like winters. But the transplanted Somalis decided to stay, in part because of welcoming volunteer groups like Lutheran Social Services, Catholic Charities, and World Relief Minnesota who helped the immigrants adjust to a new country. Once they adapted to the climate, some of the immigrants thrived, finding jobs, launching businesses, and enjoying life without the prospect of gunfire around every corner.

However, more than a few Somalis found the transition difficult. Some were still tormented by the violence they had seen and/or experienced at home. Others were ill at ease with the vast differences between Somalia's traditional Islamic culture and America's liberalized, freewheeling society. For many, barriers of language, race, and culture made it hard to earn a living.

Kids, who tend to adapt to new environments more easily than adults, were not immune to these struggles, says Dr. Ahmed Mohamed Yusuf, a psychotherapist who has worked with many Somali-Americans in Minneapolis. "Children sometimes will remember where they come from," he says. "If they experienced war and lots of killings, bombings, they can develop post-traumatic stress disorder." As for kids not scarred by war, they sometimes dealt with more existential issues, Yusuf says. "If a child comes here, then they could develop identity issues when they get older unless you intervene. Someone without identity, the question comes in when they are seventeen, eighteen, nineteen—who am I? I don't know this country called Somalia and I'm living here, my parents are different, from the outside, so who am I? What is my identity? That is a big thing. That is the downside of coming to this country. A great country, the most advanced country in the world, [but] then you have this, both immigrants and refugees who when they get older, they don't really have any idea what is going on with their lives."[5]

Former police officer Bob Fletcher has seen such Somali-American teens, first in his role as sheriff of Ramsey County, Minnesota, and now as head of the Center for Somali Studies, which aims to keep youngsters off the paths of crime and Islamic radicalism. The kids who listened to Al-Shabaab's propaganda, he says, tended to feel "an internal sense of disenfranchisement" from society. "There were kids not doing well educationally and who were searching for some sense of belonging and self-esteem. Those are desperate kids, and those kids sometimes go to gangs, sometimes to extremes. . . . On the other end there were kids doing fine academically, starting college, who had not been in trouble with the law. But those kids had a common denominator—they did not necessarily feel that they fit in perfectly with American life, and that is the dilemma."[6]

Crafty Al-Shabaab recruiters played on that confusion and resentment as they worked the community for new fighters and money. In 2007 and 2008, their job was made easier by the fact that many Somalis in the diaspora were infuriated by the Ethiopian invasion of their homeland. Osman Ahmed is the uncle of a seventeen-year-old boy, Burhan Hassan, a quiet, straight-A student who abruptly left for Somalia in November 2008 during his senior year at Minneapolis's Theodore Roosevelt High School. "Of course it all started with the arrival of the Ethiopians, which split the Somalis," he said at a VOA panel discussion on Al-Shabaab recruiting. "Some said the Ethiopians intervened at the invitation of a legitimate Somali government, and others said it was aggression by an enemy state, therefore should be resisted. That is where the justification started—that the country was occupied, and it is obligatory to defend it."[7]

One who apparently bought the "defense" argument was another Roosevelt High alumnus, Mohamed Abdullahi Hassan, a.k.a. "Miski," who left Minneapolis to join Al-Shabaab in August 2008. "The Ethiopians came and invaded Somalia. I came to help the Muslims and people of Somalia so they may be free one day, without control of the Ethiopians," explained Miski, speaking to VOA by phone in December 2015.[8] By that point, he was in a Mogadishu jail cell, a month after surrendering to Somali authorities, and was wanted by US law enforcement on terrorism charges.

Abdurrahman Mohamed Abdalla, who lives in the United Kingdom, saw his son also lured in by Al-Shabaab propaganda, although the boy was captured in Kenya before linking up with the group. "The problem is they try to target and diminish the role of the parents and the role of knowledgeable scholars in those situations," he said at the discussion on Shabaab recruiting. "They spread smear campaigns against moderate scholars who know about their bad interpretation of the religion. They also try to take advantage of the cultures and the way of life in Europe and in America. For instance, they exploit the notion that says anyone is free when they are eighteen years of age, that one is free in his/her thinking and free to do whatever he/she wishes to do."[9]

A prime example of that angle is a video made by Salman al-Mujahir, a Kenyan-born Shabaab operative, shortly before he carried out a suicide bombing in Uganda's capital, Kampala, in July 2010. The soon-to-be-bomber —looking young, healthy, and happy—sits under a tree and talks to the camera while nestling an AK-47–style rifle. Speaking in Swahili, but given English subtitles, he describes his motivations, singling out alleged oppression of Muslims in Uganda and Uganda's role in the AMISOM force fighting Al-Shabaab in Mogadishu. The pitch to teenagers comes near the end. "My coming to Somalia is not a show of my weakness or because I lived a poverty-stricken life," he says. "Not at all! I have left behind my beloved parents, friends, and even wealth, all for the sake of Allah. My dear Muslim brothers, let not your family or parents hold you back from going forth to jihad." The video ends with him firing his rifle into the distance as a jihadist chant plays.[10]

Al-Shabaab targeted Somali communities in Canada, Scandinavia, and other parts of the world as well. Sweden was a particular focus, as Somalis there had experienced low assimilation and high unemployment. A Swedish foreign affairs official said in July 2009 that some Somali parents would rather see their sons "fighting for Al-Shabaab and the homeland than drinking beer in the metro."[11] By that point, at least twenty Swedish citizens were in Somalia fighting for the militants, including top Shabaab official Fuad Shongole.[12]

In its outreach, Al-Shabaab took full advantage of the new technologies and social media that were rapidly shrinking the world. In the 1980s, the mujahideen in Afghanistan faced barriers of time, distance, and cost to spread their message. Fund-raisers had to travel to meet with distant donors; pamphlets and videos had to be copied, then mailed or distributed by hand. In contrast, by 2008 Al-Shabaab could reach people worldwide at little expense by sending out short messages on Twitter, longer ones on Facebook, or posting a video to YouTube. When media companies shut down its accounts, the group could fall back on pro-jihadist bloggers and websites to broadcast its words. To talk with individuals, the group could use the phone, texts, or email; to address groups of supporters, it could organize an international conference call. In all, it had become much, much harder for officials in the United States or anywhere else to block Islamic radical propaganda, and the results showed in Minnesota.

One of the Minneapolis recruits, Kamal Said Hassan, gave details on how he was lured in during the 2012 trial of Mahamud Said Omar, a Somali-American man who was eventually convicted of helping fighters travel to Somalia. Hassan said a key moment was a conference call where a group of young men sat cross-legged in a circle around a speakerphone, listening to a Shabaab member in Somalia. "He was on the phone saying they were doing a great job against the Ethiopian troops," Hassan said. "Basically he was advertising for us what was going on there." The call lasted no more than fifteen minutes, he said, but afterward the would-be recruits were hooked and wanted to join the fighting.[13]

Hassan said another recruiter, Omer Abdi Mohamed, made appeals to his nationalism and exploited his poor understanding of Islam. "I didn't have much knowledge about the Quran or the Hadith, and when he was interpreting verses, I believed what he was saying. . . . I thought that I was being a good Muslim and Somalian by joining these men and going over there," he said.[14]

Once a recruit decided to join Al-Shabaab, he had to get to Somalia, a process complicated by the lack of international flights to the dangerous country. But if the recruit had access to enough money, which could be provided by Shabaab sympathizers such as Omer, the process was not truly difficult. Malik Jones, a Baltimore man who joined Al-Shabaab in August 2011, outlined his journey to US investigators after his arrest. Jones started by traveling to New York, where he caught a commercial flight to Casablanca, Morocco. After a six-day wait, he took another commercial flight to the United Arab Emirates, then another from the UAE to Nairobi. Once in the Kenyan capital, he used taxis and bus rides to cross the border and reach an Al-Shabaab controlled part of Somalia, where he was quickly put into a three-month training program.

Other Shabaab recruits took equally roundabout travel routes meant to throw off any suspicious FBI agents. While the itinerary varied from recruit to recruit, the last step, the crossing of the border by bus or taxi, "is a common travel route for foreign fighters who are traveling to Somalia in order to join Al-Shabaab," said an FBI agent who testified in the indictment of Jones.[15]

Oddly enough, Al-Shabaab's most prominent American recruiter came not from Minnesota but from a state with virtually no Somali community at all. Omar Shafik Hammami wasn't even Somali. His father was a Syrian Muslim immigrant who came to Alabama in 1972 and married a local Christian girl. Hammami, born in 1984, grew up in the small Gulf coast town of Daphne and, despite his Middle Eastern heritage, had little trouble making friends in the conservative area. He went to church with his mother and sister, was elected president of his high school sophomore class, and dated a girl that a *New York Times* profile of Hammami described as a "luminous blonde." Classmates recall him as being intelligent and charismatic.[16]

But when he was about sixteen, friends and family began to see his personality shift. He became focused on Islam, more serious in general, and argued with teachers and other students who disagreed with his opinions.

Thanks to high grades, he was able to skip his last year of high school and go to the University of South Alabama, where he fell under the influence of a Salafist preacher at an off-campus mosque. By multiple accounts, Hammami gradually became more dogmatic, refusing to listen to music or be photographed, and chastising himself for looking at women. He also studied Arabic and began to closely follow world events, especially US military operations in Iraq and Afghanistan.

Traveling with a friend who was also a convert to Islam, Hammami went to Toronto, where he married a Somali girl, and then to Alexandria, Egypt, where his wife gave birth to a daughter. But he never seemed to find a place of belonging until, without telling his wife, he went to Somalia in November 2006. There he stayed, even after his wife refused to join him and went back to Toronto with their child. By the end of the year, he linked up with Al-Shabaab, drawn by its promise of a strict Islamic state in Somalia. He provided some insight into his thinking during a September 2013 phone interview with VOA's Somali Service. "As long as the Somali government is standing against Sharia, it's going to be permissible and it's going to be obligatory to fight against them, until they change that," he said. When reminded that parliament had made Sharia the basis for the law in Somalia, Hammami was unmoved. "It doesn't matter if it's the basis; if even one word of the Sharia has changed then it doesn't adhere," he said. "It's like being pregnant, you either are or you're not. So you're either going to follow all of Sharia or you're not a Muslim anymore."[17]

It took several months, but Al-Shabaab leaders were in turn drawn to Hammami. It didn't take great imagination to see that an America-born-and-raised jihadist with a strong personality and who spoke American English (albeit with a faint southern accent) could be deployed to great effect on the recruiting front. In October 2007, Hammami made his first public appearance in an Al Jazeera television report on Al-Shabaab. He wore camouflage, carried a rifle, spoke from behind a green scarf that covered most of his face, and was referred to as Abu Mansoor Al-Amriki, which translates roughly as "the victorious American." Al-Jazeera let him deliver a short pitch for the group: "O Muslims of America, take into deep consideration the example of Somalia," he said. "After fifteen years of chaos and oppressive rule by the American-backed warlords, your brothers stood up in order to establish peace and justice in this land."[18]

Despite the scarf, friends and relatives in America recognized him immediately. So did US counterterrorism agents. On December 13, the US district court in southern Alabama issued a warrant for Hammami's arrest on charges that he had provided material support, resources, and his services to a terrorist group.[19]

Over the next few years, Hammami provided one of the most unusual, sometimes head-scratching aspects of the Al-Shabaab story. Before going to Somalia, Hammami had never received any military training. Yet by the summer of 2008, he was leading attacks on Ethiopian troops—or at least that was the way it was portrayed in an Al-Shabaab video, titled "Ambush at Bardale," later posted to YouTube. The video, said to be taken on July 15, 2008, features Hammami speaking to the camera, reality-TV–style, while crouched in a wooded field. "What we're doing now is camping maybe one hundred meters from the main road between Baidoa and Luq," he whispers to the camera. "We are waiting for the enemy to come. Their numbers are close to a thousand or more. So what we're planning is an ambush, to try to blow up as many of their vehicles as we can, try to kill as many of them as we can, and take everything they've got, *in'shallah*." He grins. Moments later, the sound of rapid gunfire crackles through the woods, kicking up dust and shaking tree branches, although who is shooting whom, if anyone, cannot be seen.

Other videos released over the next few years showed Hammami reading from the Quran, lecturing to his fellow soldiers (and by extension, the viewers), or delivering messages aimed at American Muslims or Americans in general. One half-hour video plays almost as a tribute to Hammami, showing him leading a line of fighters in a run, glorified by slow-motion effects. But the aspect of the videos that got the most attention—and ridicule— was Hammami's vocal stylings. In many of the videos, he delivers rhymed couplets spelling out threats and promises of destruction to Al-Shabaab's enemies, intoned and presumably written by the star of the videos himself. "Land by land, war by war, only gonna make our black flag soar," went one. "Bomb by bomb, blast by blast, only gonna bring back the glorious past." In their periodic mentions of the videos, US media tended to describe these as raps or "rap songs," although in truth they were more like stoned chanting, enhanced with a touch of reverb.[20]

Despite their oddities, the videos caught the eye of would-be militants, racking up tens of thousands of views on YouTube, and helping to inspire more young men to follow Hammami's path. Along with the Minnesota recruits, Baltimore's Malik Jones and two men from Seattle traveled to Somalia to join Al-Shabaab, while others from Chicago, Brooklyn, New Jersey, and Virginia were caught en route. Those who made it into Al-Shabaab's ranks sometimes popped up in Hammami's videos or other Shabaab productions. When Hammami's July 2008 video surfaced online the following March, US intelligence officials said one of the militants in the background was Shirwa Ahmed, one of the very first Minnesota Somalis to join Al-Shabaab. By that point, Ahmed was dead, having driven a Toyota pickup packed with explosives into an office of the Puntland Intelligence Service in Bossaso.[21] The attack on October 29, 2008, was one of multiple suicide attacks that day that killed twenty-eight people.

Ahmed was believed to be the first US citizen to become a suicide bomber. The second was another Minneapolis man, Farah Mohamed Beledi, who traveled to Somalia in October 2009, a year after getting out of prison for a nonfatal stabbing. Beledi died on May 30, 2011, while attacking a military checkpoint in Mogadishu; African Union peacekeepers said he was shot before detonating his bomb, although another attacker close by set off a blast that killed three soldiers.[22] The FBI identified Beledi through his fingerprints.

Other Americans who joined Al-Shabaab were killed, wounded, or fell off the radar. Some, like Kamal Hassan, eventually returned to America, where they were met with terrorism charges and prison. Malik Jones was wounded in battle, recovered, and was arrested by Somali government authorities in 2015 while trying to escape an Al-Shabaab purge of fighters who wanted the group to switch its allegiance from Al-Qaeda to Islamic State. He was brought back to New York and pled guilty to terrorism-related charges in September 2017.

In perhaps the saddest case, Burhan Hassan, the boy who left Minneapolis during his senior year of high school, was dead by the following June, still short of his eighteenth birthday. Family members told local media that he was killed by Al-Shabaab members for trying to escape. He was later shown, smiling, in an Al-Shabaab video that honored him as a martyr.

"My nephew was a delightful boy who completed learning the Quran by heart," said his uncle Osman Ahmed. "Whenever he came back from school he liked to take his book bag and head to the mosque to do his homework, where he used to chat with his friends after completing the work. . . . But other forces were in play in the same mosque. They [the students] were attacked from the religious angle with misguided ideas and teachings. That is where the problem lies."[23] Ahmed is now an advocate for families whose youth have traveled to Somalia.

The American recruits had only a small effect on Al-Shabaab's fortunes. But Hammami's and Shabaab's recruiting efforts were a propaganda coup—evidence that the group could reach into the enemy's heartland and find people willing to support its cause. Another jihadist group, ISIS, would attempt and accomplish the same feat several years later. By then, Al-Shabaab's war against the Ethiopians would be just a memory, succeeded by fights for the soul of Somalia itself.

SIX

RADICAL ORGANIZATION

ALTHOUGH AL-SHABAAB'S IMPACT WAS GROWING, Aden Ayrow would not be around to see it. At about 3 a.m. on May 1, 2008, residents of Dhusamareb, a town in central Somalia, were jolted awake by loud explosions. By morning light they had figured out what happened—an airstrike had destroyed the house where Ayrow was staying, killing him, an assistant, another Al-Shabaab official, and a number of bodyguards. "Three missiles hit it in a samosa (triangular) shape," says a neighbor who asked not to be identified. "It was leveled to the ground, making a big hole. No one in the house survived; only pieces of human flesh were found in the morning."[1] American officials said the missiles were Tomahawks fired from a US Navy ship somewhere off the Horn of Africa; it was later revealed that US intelligence agents had been closely tracking Ayrow's communications and movements for months.[2]

Ayrow had clan links in the Dhusamareb area and recently had gone there to set up an Al-Shabaab administration—only to be rejected by the local clan leaders because of his ruthlessness and ties to Al-Qaeda. Godane later said that Ayrow's death hit him hard. In his 2011 interview with Shabaab's Radio Andalus, he said: "I was on the phone with him that night. He said to me, 'We'll speak in the morning; I have a lot to discuss with you.' I heard the news just before the sunrise prayers, that missiles are raining on his home. I was telling myself that he will be away from home, that he will survive the strikes—until the morning when it became clear that the house was destroyed and he martyred there. It was one of the deaths that affected me so much." Godane then urged members of Ayrow's clan to avenge his death and attack "Christians and the Americans and munafiqs (hypocrites) who participated in his killing."[3]

US and Somali officials portrayed Ayrow's death as a relief to the Somali people. "This will definitely weaken the Shabaab," said Mohamed Aden, the consul at Somalia's embassy in Kenya. "This will help with reconciliation. You can't imagine how many Somalis are saying, 'Yes, this is the one.' The reaction is so good."[4]

But in reality, the effect of Ayrow's loss on Al-Shabaab was virtually nil. By the time of his death, the group had gained too many new fighters and followers for the loss of one man, however important, to halt its momentum. 2008 was the year Shabaab began to swallow up big sections of southern and central Somalia and impose its own harsh brand of Islamic law on the populace. For the first time, an Islamist militant group was growing on Somali soil without any crippling setbacks. The United Nations and various international observers sounded alarms, but none of Shabaab's opponents on the ground—Ethiopia, the African Union mission, or the Transitional Federal Government—had the strength or initiative to stop its advance. US missiles and the counterterror efforts hindered the group's progress but couldn't halt it either. The ARS and the various clan militias still operating became less of a factor as the year went on. Pro-government forces held onto the big prize, Mogadishu, but even there Shabaab forces were making incremental advances and forcing the government into an enclave that grew smaller and smaller.

Some of the Shabaab takeovers were military victories, with the group attacking and overwhelming weaker opponents. On August 20, 2008, Al-Shabaab and the Raskamboni Brigades, led by Hassan al-Turki, launched an offensive to capture the southern port city of Kismayo from militias loyal to former defense minister Barre Aden Shire, better known as "Hirale." Three days of heavy fighting ensued, in which nearly ninety people were killed and more than two hundred injured.[5] But on August 22, after an especially heavy day of gun battles, the pro-government fighters withdrew, and Shabaab moved in. The port would soon generate roughly $1 million per month for Al-Shabaab's coffers.[6]

Other conquests were accomplished more quietly, with fighters simply marching into places that lacked strong local rulers or a TFG/Ethiopian force. On November 16, 2008, TFG soldiers abandoned Barawe, a coastal town 280 kilometers north of Kismayo. Within hours, Al-Shabaab gunmen arrived in force, taking over the police station, the port, and the main administration building.[7] After that, according to one Barawe resident, "They told people to gather and through loudspeakers told (us) that Harakat Al-Shabaab Mujahideen has taken over and that the town will be under the shade of Allah's law. They gathered the elders separately and told them they need to work with the Harakat."[8]

By this time, the group the elders were told to "work with" was becoming something of a well-oiled jihadist machine—at least as much as conditions in chaotic Somalia would permit. Al-Shabaab was never a ragtag rebel group, but the university-educated Godane, with his economics degree, installed a level of organization that set it apart from most militant groups of any stripe, and certainly apart from the thieving warlords and the corrupt or powerless government officials that Somalis were used to. "It was Godane who set up the structure of the administration, and he is the one who created the *maktabs* (departments) of Al-Shabaab," says Zakariye Hersi.[9]

A word like "administration" obscures the nature of Godane and Al-Shabaab itself, who would always remain jihadist and committed to imposing a harsh, punitive version of Islamic law. But unlike many insurgent groups who succeed in capturing territory, such as M23 in eastern Congo and Nigeria's Boko Haram, Al-Shabaab did attempt to govern the areas it captured, and there was unquestionably a method to its madness.[10]

One thing its leaders made clear as a cloudless day: Al-Shabaab was not a democracy. In his Radio Andalus interview, Godane said the group took its concept of government from the Quran, *sunna*, and the legacy of traditional Islamic governments from the prophet Muhammad's time, as well as the caliphates of Rashidun, Umawiyah, Abbassiyah, and Uthmaniya, which ruled various parts of the Muslim world for centuries. He disdained the numerous "reconciliation conferences" for Somali politicians that failed again and again to give the country a stable or functioning government. "Our concept of government is not being derived from infidel conferences," he said. "It is one based on Islamic history and principles of religion. It's not a blind mimicking of the West or the East."[11]

In a January 2009 interview with Al Jazeera television, Mukhtar Robow stated that establishing caliphates was Shabaab's main goal. "We want to bring that system back and govern the world with God's law," he said.[12]

Godane was smart enough to recognize that clans were the basic building blocks of power in Somalia, and Al-Shabaab worked to win and maintain their material, financial, and political support. But Godane saw them not as true allies but as a means to an end. At times, he would try to play the clans against each other. "Some clans deserve more [praise] than others in rushing to come to the aid of the mujahideen and jihad," he said in one speech. "To those who first come to the aid of the jihad I say, 'Do not get tired, don't be complacent.' Others should rush to the *khayr* (the good) because someone who came late may overtake those ahead of them."[13]

In line with Al-Qaeda teachings, Al-Shabaab had (and still has) a top-down structure, with decisions flowing from a small group of leaders. Under Godane, the group set up *Shura* (consultative) and *Tanfid* (executive) councils to set policies. According to Hersi, the Shura council numbered from thirty-eight to forty members, the Tanfid somewhat less. The Shura Council's job was advisory; it could recommend action but did not make actual decisions. That was the task of the Tanfid, who members included Al-Shabaab's most influential clan, militia, and religious leaders. Al-Shabaab has never had anything like a constitution, though it did set down some organizational guidelines. Insiders say the guidelines are written on a packet of about ten A4-size pages that is distributed to only a few individuals. The guidelines state the powers of the emir, deputy emirs, the councils, and regional governors, as well as the process for appointing and firing governors and other officials. It was and still is an internal document, not to interfere with Sharia.

When the leaders made a decision, its implementation was tasked to a maktab. These were Al-Shabaab's equivalent of government agencies. The number of departments ranged from seven to eleven, depending on shifts in Shabaab politics and policies. At minimum, the organization always included the maktabs of Da'wa (preaching), Zakat (taxation), Wilayat (regional administration), Amniyat (security), Jabhat (the army), Garsoor (judgement and justice), and less powerful departments dealing with general finances, health, and humanitarian affairs. Each maktab had a chief, accountable to the emir. According to insiders, the maktab heads were replaced or moved around frequently to prevent any one person from gaining too much power. Also, Al-Shabaab's culture emphasized obedience; once a decision was made, it was expected to be passed down the chain of command and put into place with little questioning or resistance.

At the core of Al-Shabaab's mission sat the maktab of Da'wa. The Da'wa department was established to spread Shabaab's form of Islam and ensure the people maintained a strong, fervent belief in it. To that end, Da'wa officials reprogrammed mosques, libraries, media outlets, and other public institutions to reflect the group's fundamentalist point of view. Barawe is historically known as a hub for the leaders of moderate Sufi Islam, the form of Islam practiced by most Somalis. When Al-Shabaab seized control of the town in 2008, it took immediate steps to detach residents from their religious roots. First, Da'wa officials hid books and texts written or studied by Sufi scholars and replaced them with the teachings of preferred Shabaab theologian Ibn Taymiyyah, or other Salafist material. They also made the controversial decision to destroy the tombs of Sufi scholars in the town, including Sheikh Qasim Barawe, one of the most well-known Sufi leaders in all of Somalia.[14] The rationale was that the tombs were leading to idolization and were undermining belief in Allah.

Finally, Da'wa officials directed the townspeople to attend classes about *tawhid*, Al-Shabaab's sanctioned mode of Islamic thought. Tawhid asserts that other modes are inferior because they allegedly doubt the oneness of Allah in their worship and their application of ungodly rules. According to one Barawe resident who is close to Sufi leaders, "They registered the businessmen, tailors, shopkeepers, and even the Sufi scholars and ordered them to attend lectures on tawhid in mosques where they brought in their own scholars. . . . They even told my (imam) to join in to rediscover his Islam-ness."[15]

The lectures were given by carefully selected speakers who could be trusted to toe the Al-Shabaab line. Sometimes, the Da'wa would play audio and video messages from well-known Salafi scholars, like al-Afghani's mentor Abdallah Azzam and Shiekh Mohanmed Al-Maqdishi of Jordan. There was no escaping the lectures, even in remote areas or the army. "They (would) send preachers to villages and embed some of them within the Jabhat units in the front lines to give them sermons," says a former Al-Shabaab official, speaking under an alias, "Quulle."[16]

The Da'wa maktab was also put in charge of Al-Shabaab's education system, which placed Islam smack in the center of the curriculum. In lower grades, children learned basic skills like reading and writing but also practiced reciting the Quran by heart. Starting at age eleven, male students attended special madrassas set up by Shabaab. These were boarding schools, most of them built outside the towns, where boys were kept five and a half days a week, released only on late Thursdays and Fridays. Students would spend two years at these schools, being force-fed an intensive Islamic education. Once they finished, about eighty-five percent of the students were recruited into the ranks of Al-Shabaab, according to Quulle. He says the remainder found excuses to continue their education up to the university level or were whisked away by their parents to another region. But students were officially released only on a case-by-case basis and only with Al-Shabaab's approval.

The brightest and toughest boys were molded by Shabaab into young militant leaders. By age twenty many were either jihadist preachers or operatives in Shabaab's intelligence and special operations units. Some were promoted to decision-making positions as commanders or district officials. Quulle says the Bay and Bakool regions produced the most Al-Shabaab recruits. "These are regions where Al-Shabaab was involved in schools and training for a long time and the local clans have been receptive," he says.[17]

Given that not everyone was so receptive to its preaching and teachings, Al-Shabaab had the *Hisbah*, its version of a police force. Hisbah members had two primary tasks: to keep public order and to enforce the strict Islamic code. Like police anywhere, they wore uniforms, carried small arms or sticks, and patrolled the streets. Part of their job was regular crime-busting: catching thieves, breaking up street fights. What made them distinct to Al-Shabaab was their second role. It was Hisbah officers who ordered people into mosques for mandatory prayer. It was they who told shop owners to shut their doors until prayers were over. They arrested women for not wearing a *hijab* or, in some areas, a burka, and forced haircuts on men whose hair was deemed to be overly long. Smoking cigarettes, watching movies, playing Western music, and chewing the mild drug khat—the last a very common habit in Somalia—were all crimes for which Hisbah officers stayed on perpetual watch.

Each town that came under Shabaab control was given a Hisbah force: fifteen men for a small town like El-Garas, up to eighty for a city like Kismayo, with each force operating under its own emir. The members of the force—all native Somalis—got paid about $100 per month, with more money set aside for two—sometimes three—meals per day at the local police station. By most accounts, Hisbah police succeeded in reducing the rampant theft and violent crime that had plagued Somali towns for years. But many people found the price for that security too high. Not only did Al-Shabaab's rules expunge much of the joy from life, but also those arrested faced brutal penalties. In the eyes of Godane and many fellow jihadists, Islamic texts called for specific, agonizing punishments for certain crimes. So thieves could be sentenced to lose a hand. Adulterers could be sentenced to death by stoning. Ten to one hundred lashes with a whip could be the penalty for any number of offenses. And the police would often carry out these punishments in public, to display their power and to dissuade others from committing what Al-Shabaab viewed as crimes against God.

The actual sentences were determined by the *Garsoor*, the justice system, and the *qaalli*, the judge of Al-Shabaab's court. The Al-Shabaab justice system was simple. When the group captured a town, it set up a local court consisting of one to three judges and a clerk that would hear both civil and criminal cases. Court rules allowed for neither juries nor lawyers, empowering judges to both collect evidence and issue verdicts. In theory, the system might have been fair if the accused had some basic rights. But in practice, defendants in criminal cases were at a severe disadvantage. The accused had to appear in person before the judge, while the accuser was given the option of either appearing or sending an agent. Not only were defendants denied legal counsel, but they also faced judges who sometimes didn't bother to hear their side of the story. And the chance for a successful appeal was limited. "The accused has one chance to say he doesn't agree with the ruling—only after the lower court makes a decision," says a former local-level Al-Shabaab judge. "You can't say the same when the upper court makes a decision."[18]

The upper regional court had the power to overturn a verdict, but lower court judges often consulted with their superiors before issuing important or controversial decisions, reducing the chance they would be overruled.

Several people involved with the courts say they grew harsher as time went on. Initially, they say, Al-Shabaab appointed local religious scholars to the courts to gain public support. But eventually, the group kicked them out in favor of ideologues trained by Shabaab itself. The strict rules applied to judges, too. In 2009, a judge in the Shabaab-ruled town of Bulabarde was caught chewing khat in the home of a woman who was selling the green narcotic leaves. He was immediately replaced.

In perhaps the most notorious case involving Al-Shabaab courts, a court in Kismayo convicted Asha Ibrahim Dhuhulow of adultery in October 2008 and sentenced her to death by stoning. Judges said Dhuhulow was twenty-three years old. But a few days later, the Voice of America's Somali Service tracked down her father in Kenya's Dadaab refugee camp. He said his daughter was just thirteen and that she was arrested after she went to Al-Shabaab authorities in Kismayo to report that a member of the group had raped her.

On the morning of October 27, militants announced over loudspeakers that a woman would be stoned to death that day. Hundreds flocked to a Kismayo stadium to get a glimpse of the victim, who turned out to be Dhuhulow. "She was brought in a pickup truck together with a white sheet and stretcher to carry her body after death," recalls one person who witnessed the scene. "She was blindfolded and was being escorted by three women. She was crying, saying 'I didn't do it.'"[19]

Workmen had dug a narrow, deep hole in the stadium grounds. Dhuhulow threw herself down on the grass and kicked and screamed as her three escorts tried to push her into it. When the women couldn't do it, men took over and forced her in. Others shoveled in dirt and buried Dhuhulow up her neck. Nearby were sacks of stones lined up in advance and a group of men ready to start throwing. Once Dhuhulow was immobilized, they did.

"Three times they checked her pulse whether she died," said the witness. "They kept on hurling stones at her head until she was dead."[20] No one in the crowd could help Dhuhulow, as the militants had formed a ring around the execution area. Earlier, when large numbers of people tried to get close to the hole, the militants had opened fire to push them back, killing an eight-year-old boy and wounding another spectator.

~

Al-Shabaab could get away with these kinds of deeds because behind its brutality lay some genuine military power. The tide of money and eager recruits that began during 2007 had swelled the group's size and allowed the development of distinct units to handle different tasks, much like a regular army. Foreign fighters with Al-Qaeda training played a prominent role in developing these units. Chief among them was Saleh Ali Nabhan, by now one of the most wanted men in the world, with the United States offering $5 million for information leading to his capture.[21] Other battle-hardened instructors and fighters came from Afghanistan and Chechnya. The foreigners passed along highly sophisticated skills about military strategy, making explosives, constructing IEDs, and carrying out suicide missions and special operations. The recruits were trained at Al-Shabaab's network of camps in southern and central Somalia, each one named after a famous jihadist. Abdullah Azzam had several named after him, the biggest one near the town of Balad. When Aden Ayrow was killed, a camp was named after him near the town of Jilib.

The recruits were put through an arduous regimen designed to hammer their bodies, minds, and souls into ideal jihadist shape. Mohamed Jama, who was one of the first recruits to join Al-Shabaab in 2006, describes the schedule: "In the first half of the day it's military training. Second half—religion, Islamic law, lectures. You only sleep four hours at night. You're working all day with no breaks."[22]

Depending on their skills, recruits were placed in one of the two main components of Shabaab's military wing: the *Jabhat*, the army, or the *Amniyat*, the security force. Jabhat members were the foot soldiers of Al-Shabaab, tasked with fighting frontline battles against the Ethiopians, AMISOM, and the Somali government. Their mandate was to seize and defend territory for the group. They lacked the heavy weapons of a state army, but their assault rifles, grenades, mortars, and machine guns often, though not always, sufficed for Somali warfare. Al-Shabaab never acquired tanks, so soldiers mainly drove "battlewagons," also known as technicals—pickup trucks with anti-aircraft guns mounted on their backs. A Jabhat division consisted of three hundred men, which included subunits of one hundred (a *saryo*), thirty (a *safila*), and ten (a *majmu'a*). The troops had their own commanders and bases. According to one former commander, the divisions were spread across Shabaab's territories but were moved around and concentrated depending on the volatility and importance of a given area. In time, the Jabhat would become the largest force in Al-Shabaab, numbering about five thousand men, some of them foreigners who had sneaked into Somalia after hearing Shabaab's call to fight for jihad.

If a recruit was unusually skilled or showed a knack for strategic thinking, he became a candidate for the Amniyat, the most organized, well-equipped, and feared force in all of Al-Shabaab. More than any other part of the group, Amniyat members ensured Shabaab would be labeled a terrorist organization. It was they who carried out the "special operations"—the suicide bombings, assassination attempts, and attacks on the centers of government power. The Amniyat was also Al-Shabaab's spy agency, in charge of collecting intelligence and catching suspected enemy collaborators. Amniyat members tended to be the most hard-core militants of the group, known for their complete commitment to jihad, their hatred of foreign troops, and not incidentally, their loyalty to Godane. Perhaps because of the Ethiopians' presence, the majority of Amniyat members from the start were Somalis, many of whom seemed to believe jihadist theology that those who sacrifice their lives to kill so-called infidels will be rewarded in heaven with praise and young women. Their extremism made them stand out even in an extremist group.

One Al-Shabaab commander who later defected to the TFG sums them up this way: "Amniyat are recruited from within the locals, they conduct their missions in secrecy, and they are not people you can understand."[23]

The Amniyat were organized into several units. *Jugta Ulus* was the commando or "quick reaction" force. The unit would occasionally fight alongside the Jabhat in emergency situations. But their main task was to carry out attacks to tip a battle in Al-Shabaab's favor. According to Hersi, they were armed with shoulder-fired missiles, recoilless rifles, bazookas, and heavy machine guns. They also had the training and weapons to bring down enemy helicopters and airplanes. In 2007, for instance, they succeeded in bringing down a Russian plane meant to deliver supplies to African Union forces.

Another unit was the *Mukhabarad*, the intelligence service, responsible for surveillance and collecting information used to carry out the group's plots. Shabaab leaders were and still are known for studying targets for months prior to an attack. The Mukhabarad furthered that goal by planting spies who collected classified information in the presidential palace, AMISOM headquarters, and in TFG institutions, among other places. It's never been confirmed, but it's widely believed that the unit also infiltrated the TFG's National Intelligence and Security Agency. One technique the Mukhabarad allegedly used was to target certain officials with death threats. With the TFG so ill-equipped to protect its own people, the official would often turn over classified information to stay alive.

The third major branch in the Amniyat was the *Mutafajirad*. This was the unit specializing in suicide missions. The unit had two subgroups. One, known as *Amaliya Istishhad*, carried out "traditional" suicide bombings, the kind where one or two people get close to a designated target and set off explosives strapped to their body or car. The other group, *Amaliya Inqimas*, handled larger, more complex types of operations that could be described as suicide assaults. Inqimas units were sent to attack a target with orders not to come back alive. They consisted of between four and ten men, one of whom was usually a suicide car bomber, with the rest being commandos who attacked the target with guns and grenades following the bomb blast. The attackers all wore suicide belts and were supposed to blow themselves up when they ran out of ammunition. The tactic was first used in Afghanistan by the Taliban. As the years went on, it became Al-Shabaab's favored method of attack, used to assail important targets such as parliament, the local UN headquarters, and the presidential palace. The group also used it to carry out savage, headline-grabbing assaults in Kenya, like the 2015 rampage at Garissa University College that killed 148 people.

According to Al-Shabaab insiders, Amaliya Inqimas members were chosen carefully and then given rigorous training in weapons, explosives, personal defense, and combat. During that time, they were camped and indoctrinated separately from other units. Just before an operation, Shabaab would assign them bodyguards to give them a feeling of importance. They were also given money and women—and told that even more women would be available in the eternal life that followed once they carried out their lethal mission. The incentives and psychological training were so extreme that in some cases, members of the unit competed with each other for the right to carry out suicide missions. Those who were chosen were congratulated by the others.

The Amniyat's extremism was also on display in its handling of poor souls suspected of spying for or collaborating with Al-Shabaab's enemies. "When (those) people are detained, some are kept in solitary jails. Amniyat says don't touch their cases," says the former local-level Shabaab judge.[24] From the start, these suspects were often tortured and ran a fairly high risk of execution unless other powerful individuals intervened. A former Al-Shabaab media official says that in 2011, he and some friends saved the life of a clan mate who was accused of passing information to a government army general. "They called us to listen to (a recorded) audio conversation, but we argued the information was general and nothing specific and does not amount to the death penalty," he says. The result? "They detained him for eight months, tortured him, and then released him."[25]

Along with secret jails, the Amniyat ran courts where suspected spies and collaborators were given show trials. Sometimes, suspects learned what they were charged with only minutes before their execution. In those cases, judges would simply announce the accused had confessed to spying, giving the doomed defendant no chance to speak. Desperate people facing death pleaded for help. Another former Al-Shabaab judge says there was a case in October 2009 when two young men were sentenced to death for spying. Just before a firing squad pulled the trigger, he says, one of the men yelled that he did not confess to the crime. "He screamed 'I'm not a spy!'" says the ex-judge.[26] He was shot anyway. A similar situation unfolded a year later in Beledweyne when Al-Shabaab executed two young girls on spying charges. As people gathered to watch the execution, the girls rejected the accusations against them and tried to communicate with the judge. But relatives who spoke to the media said the girls' plea fell on deaf ears.

Over time, cases like these raised suspicions and resentment toward Al-Shabaab and ate up much of the goodwill the group had gained from fighting the Ethiopians.

—

Preoccupied as it was with war, enforcing Islamic law, and advancing the cause of jihad, Al-Shabaab actually did devote some energy to day-to-day governing. It had to, as by late 2008 more than a million Somalis were living in Shabaab's virtual state-within-a-state. Each of the ten Somali regions where Shabaab eventually captured territory had an appointed *waali*, or governor. The governor oversaw all civil services in Shabaab-controlled areas, including welfare, road maintenance, and the regional offices of the Da'wa, Hisbah, and other departments, though not the army and security forces. The ten governors reported to the *waali of wilayat*, the governor of governors, who was the regions' main link to Al-Shabaab's emir. These political appointments were not afterthoughts; the waali of wilayat was considered the most influential of the maktab chiefs, and when Al-Shabaab gradually lost most of its territory in the early 2010s, it maintained the governor positions so that it would be ready to reassert authority in case its fortunes turned upward again.

At times, Al-Shabaab's authoritarian governing style could have some positive effects. Bulabarde is a T-shaped town divided by the Shabelle River. Two rival clans that reside on opposite sides of the river have clashed for years over water use and farmlands. Upon taking over the town, Shabaab officials told the clan elders they would not tolerate hostilities. "They took over the three main water wells including one which has water that tastes like rain water," recalls a journalist who lived in the town at the time. "They run the wells themselves and there was no further argument." He says Shabaab settled a similar dispute over mango farms along the riverbanks. "Some families were claiming they inherited (the farms) from forefathers but lost them to powerful clans during the civil war. Al-Shabaab told them to stop fighting and that since they did not have documents to prove who owned (each farm) they said whoever controlled the farms pre-1991 when the government collapsed will keep it."[27]

But a big part of governing is tax collection, and Al-Shabaab proved quite adept at this. From the time they began taking over towns, the group imposed fees and taxes on all kinds of economic activity in order to finance its greater goals. The *Zakat* maktab mostly ran the taxation system. The department was—and as of 2017 still is—led by Sheikh Suldan Mohamed, better known as Aala Mohamed. Somewhat counterintuitively for a tax chief, Mohamed often stepped forward as Al-Shabaab's humanitarian figure, raising money for the poor, orphans, and those left hungry by Somalia's periodic droughts. Unlike many other Al-Shabaab leaders, he never covered his face, and he gave interviews to Al-Shabaab media outlets, although he rarely mentioned operations or internal politics. His media presence partially diverted attention from the fact that most of the tax revenue was being used to buy tools of war. "This money is used for buying ammunition and weapons; some is spent on operations," says a former Al-Shabaab commander.[28]

Truckers were one of the main targets of Shabaab's tax regime. Even in a country as dangerous as Somalia, trucks still traveled the roads, carrying commercial goods around the country and to neighboring Kenya and Ethiopia. To get through Al-Shabaab territory they had to pay a fee—$500 for small trucks, up to $1,200 for a large trailer, of which $300 was the tax on the truck and $900 was for the cargo. Vehicles working for well-funded international aid agencies were a particular target. The United Nations' World Food Program suspended its operations in southern Somalia in 2009 after it learned Somali subcontractors had paid several million dollars to Al-Shabaab. Shabaab also imposed a $120 tax on the construction of new homes, per-bag fees on farmers selling their crops, and duties on charcoal exports and imports of food and fuel coming through Shabaab-controlled ports like Kismayo. The group made additional money by renting out farms technically owned by the government or foreigners such as former Italian residents from the colonial days. These included big farms in the Lower Shabelle region between Bula Marer and the Golweyn and Janale area—the nation's breadbasket. If a farm owner chose to sell his land, he had to pay a 20 percent tax on the sale price.

Another big source of revenue came through *Zakat al-Mal*—taxes collected on wealth such as livestock when the herd grows to a certain size. Livestock is the primary economic pillar in Somalia; the country has some of the largest numbers of sheep, goats, and camels in the world. Thus, herders were given the option of paying Al-Shabaab with animals instead of cash. For goat and sheep, the tax was roughly one animal for every one hundred in the herd. For camels, the tax was one young male for every twenty-five a herder owned, and two young females for every one hundred. Herders who owned fewer than twenty-five camels could pay their taxes in goats and sheep. Once the yearly collections were completed, some animals were given to the governor of the region, who redistributed them to the poorest of the poor. In the Burdhubo district, for example, the Zakat office often made donations of about a dozen camels and some 270 goats or sheep, according to a former Al-Shabaab official who served as the local emir. However, he says, this is a small number of livestock compared with the total collected. "The rest of the livestock, 85 percent, is taken to the markets in different regions and are sold and cashed. The cash goes into the Zakat cashier," he says.[29]

And finally, Al-Shabaab made money off high-seas piracy. Between 2007 and 2012, bands of young Somali men armed with guns and stolen fishing boats took advantage of the country's lawlessness to hijack ships traveling in the Gulf of Aden and the western Indian Ocean. The pirates, basing themselves in the coastal towns of Hobyo, Haradhere, and Eyl, seized more than forty ships per year, generating hundreds of millions of dollars in ransom payments for the vessels, their cargo, and their crews.[30] For a time, the threat of Somali piracy was considered as big or bigger than the one posed by Somalia-based terrorism, especially when the pirates began seizing oil tankers and taking in payoffs of up to $7 million.

Al-Shabaab generally held the pirates at arm's length; the group had its hands full on land, and open robbery clashed with the strict code of Sharia that Shabaab was trying to enforce. But given the huge sums of money involved, and facing the demands of running an army and quasi-government, Shabaab officials grew comfortable with strong-arming the pirates into giving up a slice of the profits. A former Shabaab media official in Haradhere says the group looked at the pirates as infidels and dealt with them discreetly, but adds: "Pirate money is not considered *haram* [forbidden]. The only way *ghanima* [spoils of war] from the field could be haram is if the person who obtains it uses it in an un-Islamic way, or spends it on acts such as alcohol, adultery, gambling, or other unlawful activities."[31]

A former pirate describes the typical agreement: "You identify who you are attacking and where, then you inform them and say 'we are going there.' Once you execute the operation you inform Al-Shabaab and say 'we succeeded or we failed.'"[32] If the pirates succeeded in collecting a ransom, they would often hand over five- and six-figure sums to keep peace with the more powerful militants. A 2011 Reuters report, based on interviews with pirates, Shabaab officials, and residents in the town of Haradhere, found six payments of $66,000 or larger during the first half of the year. In the biggest transaction, Al-Shabaab reaped a $600,000 windfall after the owners of the German freighter *Beluga Nomination* paid over $5 million to free their ship. Such payments dried up only when international naval patrols and increased security on the ships brought a halt to the hijackings.

Between all the revenue streams, it's hard to pinpoint what Shabaab's total income was in any given year. The UN monitoring group estimated that at its peak, the group took in $70 to $100 million annually—certainly a plausible figure, given the number of ports and the size of the territories Al-Shabaab once controlled and the group's ability to fund conventional-style warfare. Monitoring chief Matthew Bryden says the estimate was based on very detailed research into Shabaab's tax checkpoints and the exports (mainly charcoal) going through the ports.[33]

French analyst Marchal believes that number is too high, but it's worth noting that former Shabaab official Hersi says that the group used to take in more than $2 million per month—or at least $25 million per year—from the regional administrations alone. Add in port revenue, contributions from Eritrea, money from foreign fund-raisers, and ransom from the occasional kidnapping, and $70–100 million does not seem a far-fetched figure.

The overall effect of Al-Shabaab's organization was to give the group a strength and resilience that few other insurgent groups anywhere could match—certainly none in Somalia, including the Eritrean-backed ARS. And as Al-Shabaab's influence and power grew during 2008, the Ethiopians began making noise about pulling out their troops. In an interview that April with the US magazine *Newsweek*, Ethiopian Prime Minister Meles Zenawi said hundreds of Ethiopian soldiers had been killed or injured in Somalia and that the invasion was costing his country "substantial amounts" in money terms. He said the invasion had been necessary to stop Islamic radicals from taking over Somalia but made it clear that his troops would not stay forever. "We were told by the African Union and others that in our withdrawal we shouldn't create a vacuum, at which point we indicated we could wait a bit longer, so long as the African Union was in a position to replace our troops. That has taken an inordinate amount of time," he said. Asked whether Ethiopia might withdraw without AU peacekeepers in place, he said, "Well, that's an option. It's an option we will not take lightly. But it's an option."[34]

At the same time, Ethiopia was coming under international pressure to change tactics in Somalia. Its troops had often carried out extrajudicial killings and turned their artillery on residential neighborhoods, destroying hundreds of homes. Groups like Human Rights Watch likened the measures to those Ethiopia had used to crush insurgents in its Ogaden region. The Ethiopians couldn't hide the attacks, because they were reported on Somali radio stations or news websites almost as soon as they happened. Later on, Ethiopian officials would admit they did not know how to handle the Somali media.

Those same rights groups condemned Al-Shabaab for its own violations and atrocities, but Godane and the other leaders didn't care. They were winning—slowly, at a high cost—but undeniably taking the upper hand. A strict Islamic state was becoming a possibility in Somalia. The next step was to get the infidels and apostates out of Mogadishu.

PART TWO

THE BATTLE FOR MOGADISHU

SEVEN

"TFG IN GRAVE JEOPARDY"

IN EARLY 2008, YOUNG DALHA ALI was given more responsibilities on the bristling front lines of Mogadishu. Along with carrying out ambushes and assassinations, Al-Shabaab now tasked him with driving weapons between battle sites in the capital. At any given moment, the car they gave him might be packed with mortars, bomb material, guns, and ammunition—making it a candidate for spontaneous explosion if he hit a bad bump in the road or if a random bullet pierced the trunk.

There was no longer any time away from the war for this would-be Islamic scholar. In a single day, he might plant IEDs along a road, deliver bullets to an active battle zone, and shoot someone. It was not the life expected for a young man who had studied in the peaceful Tabliq tradition. But Ali carried on with his duties, seemingly without complaint or question.

Then one day, Ali and a colleague were ordered to "get rid of" a target, a Somali man who regularly visited the compound of the presidential palace, Villa Somalia. The Amniyat suspected that the man was a collaborator with the Transitional Federal Government—an apostate, to Shabaab's way of thinking—and they had tracked his movements, including the routes he traveled, the places he frequented, and the mosque where he prayed. Ali was assigned to carry out the killing.

After the fact, Ali said he and his fellow operative followed the man into his mosque for midday prayer. They knelt down and prayed next to him without giving away their intentions. Finally the man exited the mosque. Ali and his colleague followed him outside and pushed him into a narrow alley between two buildings. However, Ali chose not to kill him right away. Instead, he asked, "Why do you visit the palace every day?"

The man's response shocked Ali. He said his son, an Al-Shabaab operative, was being held at a detention center inside the palace compound. The boy had been arrested in Bar Ubah for throwing a bomb and carrying a pistol, he said; he was just bringing the boy some breakfast each day so that his son wouldn't starve.

Ali had been given an order, but the man's story was compelling enough for him and his colleague to make an independent decision. They stepped aside and told the man to go. When Ali reported back to his supervisor, he admitted to aborting the mission. "He is the father of one of us ... the man is a Muslim," Ali recalled saying.[1] He said he had decided to question the man, rather than kill him, after seeing him enter the mosque. It was hard to understand how an "apostate" would pray; apostates and infidels don't pray, he told the supervisor. Surprisingly, the supervisor let the matter drop, and the man survived.

Ali remained with Al-Shabaab for a while after the incident, but the man's story lingered with him and weakened his loyalty to the group. He could not suppress his feeling, reinforced by what he saw and was told to do each day, that Al-Shabaab was senselessly murdering innocent people. Not everyone was as lucky as Ali's intended target. Not everyone who prayed in a mosque survived. In fact, Al-Shabaab was now threatening Islamic scholars and imams who objected to the group's actions.

Unbeknownst to Ali, those threatened included Sheikh Bashir Ahmed Salat, the old university teacher of Al-Shabaab's emir, Ahmed Godane. Salat had returned to Somalia in 2006, and he even saw Godane one day outside a mosque. "We greeted each other briefly. That was the last time I saw him," Salat says.[2] But in 2009 Salat—by then the chairman of an influential Islamic council—faced the wrath of Al-Shabaab after he issued a fatwa which declared that fighting the Transitional Federal Government was "unreligious." He immediately received death threats from Shabaab, and soon thereafter gunmen killed two of his scholar associates, Sheikh Abdulkadir Ga'amey and Ahmed Ali Dahir.

The "dirty war"—Ali's term for killings between Somalis in Mogadishu—was becoming a more prominent part of the conflict. It was dawning on him, and many other Somalis, that no one was safe from Al-Shabaab.

~

As 2008 wound down, Somalia's political situation took a radical but not entirely unexpected turn. After months of stop-and-start talks, the Transitional Federal Government and a faction of the Alliance for Re-liberation of Somalia (ARS)—now repositioned as a "moderate" Islamist group—signed political agreements in Djibouti. The two entities would share power in a new TFG with a hugely expanded parliament of 550 members. Soon after, Ethiopia announced it would withdraw its troops from Somalia by the end of January. For the first time, Islamists were going to play a role in a United Nations–backed Somali government—although they weren't the kind of Islamists that Al-Shabaab considered legitimate.

If there was any hope that Al-Shabaab would be mollified by the agreement, it was shot down instantly. Muktar Robow, serving as Al-Shabaab's spokesman, told reporters, "We have already rejected the [peace] conference and the agreements. We are now saying again that we will not accept them." In fact, the prospect of Ethiopia's withdrawal—which Al-Shabaab had promoted as its goal—only seemed to whet the group's appetite for more battle. When Al Jazeera television aired a report about Al-Shabaab that December, Shabaab members spoke in sweeping terms about exporting jihad. "We are fighting to lift the burden of oppression and colonialism from our country," said Robow. "Once we are successful with that, we will fight on and finish oppression elsewhere on Earth."[3] An Al-Shabaab fighter in Marka, Ibrahim Almaqdis, was even more aggressive. "We wish to tell [President] Bush and our opponents our real intentions," he said. "We will establish Islamic rule from Alaska and Chile to South Africa, Japan, Russia, the Solomon Islands, and all the way to Iceland. Be warned, we are coming."[4]

While the threats to distant lands could be dismissed as crazy talk, Al-Shabaab's rejection of the peace accord could not. For years, the United Nations had monitored a mostly unsuccessful arms embargo on Somalia, first imposed during the civil war, and assessed the strength of the clashing parties. A report from the UN monitors in November 2008 made it clear that the TFG, in either its old form or the new, was in no shape to fight off an insurgent assault. The report said that the TFG had up to twenty thousand security personnel on paper but warned that many of them were "phantoms" whose pay was "diverted"—that is, taken or redirected—by senior commanders.[5] It noted the Ethiopians had trained seventeen thousand Somalis to be TFG soldiers over the previous two years but said that four-fifths of them had defected or deserted—effectively putting more armed opponents on the streets. The authors said the TFG forces that actually existed were "disorganized and undisciplined" and were largely structured along clan lines that usually reflected their commanders' affiliation. They also warned, disconcertingly, that Al-Shabaab was purchasing weapons from TFG and Ethiopian soldiers, using money raised for the group abroad. The TFG was being sold out from within.

The disorder in the TFG military forces was mirrored by disarray on the political side, where the government's top leaders could barely speak to each other. The US embassy in neighboring Kenya handled US affairs regarding Somalia at this time. In a diplomatic cable to Washington on December 11, 2008, classified as secret, Ambassador to Kenya Michael Ranneberger said that the relationship between the Somali president Abdullahi Yusuf and the prime minister Nur Hassan Hussein had become so dysfunctional that until a consultation four days earlier, "the two had not met face to face in months."[6] He said Yusuf also habitually rebuffed the prime minister's calls. Ranneberger said the feud was mainly due to clan rivalry—Yusuf was Darod, Hussein was Hawiye—and that the infighting undermined nearly everything the TFG tried, including efforts to reorganize the army, to set up local governments, and even to guard the TFG's top leaders. TFG officials who still have security, Ranneberger said, "are protected by the armed militias they personally feed and pay."

With the Ethiopians set to leave, the only stable pro-government force seemed to be the African Union mission, AMISOM, which continued to protect the airport, the seaport, the presidential palace, and the crucial Maka al-Mukarama Road. But the force still had only 3,500 soldiers and a mandate to defend, not attack; many observers feared AMISOM would not be able to handle Al-Shabaab once the Ethiopians went home. Many Somalis didn't trust the AU troops either. According to Terry, the Westerner who was in Mogadishu at the time, "The local population was sort of looking forward to having AU troops come in, but they were extremely wary, because Somalis don't like any foreigners coming in. They feel like they're being taken over. They ask, 'Is this a ploy by Uganda or the US or proxies to try to control us?'"[7]

With the situation seemingly tipped in their favor, Al-Shabaab and smaller Islamist groups intensified their attacks on pro-government forces as the Ethiopian withdrawal and the new TFG's debut drew near. "We used to attack every Ethiopian base in Mogadishu three times a day," boasts one former Al-Shabaab fighter.[8] The attacks weren't limited to the capital; starting in September, Shabaab forces laid siege to Baidoa, regularly striking at police, TFG, and Ethiopian targets. And two days after the TFG and ARS signed their final deal in October, suicide bombers attacked the United Nations compound in Hargeisa and four other locations in Somaliland and Puntland, killing at least twenty-eight people. Al-Shabaab did not claim direct responsibility but posted a "last testament" video from one of the bombers online, and Somaliland authorities blamed the group for the attacks.

The heaviest fighting, as always, took place in the capital, where Shabaab fighters were now trading shells and gunfire two or three times a day with Ethiopian, TFG, or AMISOM troops. "This was not one or two incidents," says Abdulkadir Aden, a dentist who ran a clinic in Mogadishu. "I used to travel to the Baraka Market in the morning and no day passed without me seeing dead or wounded people along the way." Aden says that between August 2008 and March 2009 alone, he had three close calls with incoming shells—one outside the Abu Hurayura mosque, another while walking on street 2 of the Bakara Market, and the last at the KPP junction while driving to work. The mosque incident might have been the scariest. "It was midday prayers," Aden says. "The shell landed at the entrance of the mosque near the ablution and the bathrooms. The area [where] the shell hit is concrete, so every piece of shell became hundreds of small shrapnel. I was just eighteen meters [sixty feet] away when it landed."[9] After each of the attacks, dozens of people lay wounded, and Aden stopped to help them. The incidents inspired the dentist to find partners and start a new ambulance service for Mogadishu in October 2008. Over the next few years, the service would transport thousands of wounded people to local hospitals, saving many lives.

Events moved quickly as the year turned. Somalis and the international community had grown fed up with the ineffective and inflexible Yusuf; he resigned on December 29. As promised, the Ethiopians left Mogadishu on January 15 and withdrew from Somalia entirely by January 25—in some cases abandoning major bases, which either the clans or the militants quickly occupied. And on January 31, the new parliament elected former ICU leader Sheikh Sharif Sheikh Ahmed as Somalia's president. Sheikh Sharif, as he was usually called, was forty-five years old, a member of a Hawiye sub-clan, the Abgaal, and had a degree in Islamic law from a Libyan university. He was known to be a friend of Hassan Dahir Aweys and Aden Ayrow, and like Al-Shabaab he had opposed the warlords and the former version of the TFG. The hope was that he would have enough stature and credibility with the militants to get them to lay down their arms and start negotiating.

The new president took office knowing there would be no honeymoon period. Five days earlier, right after the Ethiopian pullout, Al-Shabaab had taken control of Baidoa, the only big city besides Mogadishu that was still under TFG control.[10] The TFG's entire territory was now down to about two-thirds of Mogadishu. Little wonder that parliament's vote and President Shiekh Sharif's swearing-in were held in Djibouti, not Somalia, ostensibly so that foreign diplomats could safely attend.

Besides AMISOM, perhaps the only thing saving the TFG at this point was the fact that there were divisions on the insurgent side, too. With the Ethiopians gone and a former ICU figure installed as president, some Islamists turned against Al-Shabaab's radicalism. A moderate militia named Ahlu Sunna Walj Jama'a emerged as a thorn in Al-Shabaab's side, seizing the towns of Guri-El and Dhusamureb in central Somalia.[11] These developments carried a warning for Al-Shabaab—in both towns, locals said Shabaab fighters had established law and order, but they had angered people by trampling on their religious customs.

In early February, a potentially more serious challenge appeared when four other Islamist organizations—Raskamboni Muaskar, Anole Muaskar, Jabhat al-Islam, and an ARS splinter group—combined to form a new movement. They called it Hizbul Islam, or the Islamic Party. Somalia suddenly had two significant jihadist groups, similar in their nature and goals, though many observers viewed the leaders of Hizbul Islam as being more interested in power than religion. All the group's leaders were former AIAI or Al-Shabaab figures whose loyalties and interests had taken them elsewhere. The most notable were two older leaders—Hassan al-Turki and the always-colorful Aweys. Aweys, who had spent two years in exile in Eritrea, made a dramatic return to Mogadishu on April 23, 2009, landing at the K50 airstrip outside the capital on a chartered plane that had taken off from Asmara at 3:30 a.m. According to a later report by the UN monitors, "Aweys left Asmara in possession of an estimated $200,000, which he subsequently distributed to various Hizbul Islam leaders."[12] Within days, he had convinced Hizbul Islam's first emir Omar Imaan to step aside, assumed control of the group, and announced a war against the TFG and AMISOM.

"This group, it was a kind of recycling of the old militia system," says French analyst Marchal. "To a certain extent, you had a number of people who were clan fighters, who survived the clan fighting of the 1990s and then became Islamists because that was the new fashion. . . . Ideologically, they could pray five, six times a day, but at the end of the day they want to smoke a cigarette and they want to chew khat. They want a young lady serving tea. . . . Which is very different than Shabaab."[13]

Some Somalis were still trying to prevent the country from sliding back into another round of pointless, bloody civil war altogether. Leading Islamic scholars met in early 2009 and formed the Ulema Council of Somalia. Among them, ironically, were Aweys' own brother Ahmed and Sheikh Bashir Ahmed Salad, the leader of AIAI's peaceful offshoot Al-Itisam Wal-Kitab Wal Sunna. Such councils had played roles in building peace and stability in Somalia in the past, cajoling political leaders to compromise. In this case, the scholars took a direct and detailed approach, issuing a fatwa that denounced waging war in Mogadishu and called for negotiations between the government and opposition groups, including Al-Shabaab and Hizbul Islam. They also demanded the pullout of AMISOM troops within 120 days from March 1 and called on the new government to adopt Sharia as the country's law within ninety days.[14]

According to former Shabaab military intelligence chief Hersi, Al-Shabaab actually held a meeting with the Ulema Council. "The Muslim scholars sent a committee of five men to us, to mediate between us and Shiekh Sharif," he says. "They proposed the cease-fire and the withdrawal of AMISOM troops. I was one of those who attended on behalf of Al-Shabaab. But in the end Godane refused. Me, Abu Mansur [Mukhtar Robow], and Abdullahi Yare were for it; Godane, Afghani, and [Mahad] Karate were against it. They were saying the scholars were not sincere, they can't implement it, the government can't guarantee. . . . Our argument was, let's try them, we just came out of two years of war, we cannot continue it, let's give them a chance for six months. But the decision was ultimately his [Godane's]. He decided we should not attend meetings anymore."[15]

Hersi believes the group made a mistake by turning down the proposal. "That was like turning away from achieving our political goals for our fighting," he says. "Any fighting should have a political end. We would have turned our success on the battleground into political achievement."[16]

The new president wasn't done trying yet. In March, he proposed a motion to make Sharia the basis of the country's laws. In early April, parliament approved it on a unanimous vote. Even though the motion was largely symbolic, its passage forced Al-Shabaab to alter its recruiting and fund-raising pitch. More than a few Somalis wondered why the group kept fighting if the Ethiopians had gone home and Sharia was now the law of the land.

Al-Shabaab's answer was AMISOM. The group argued that the presence of the AU troops constituted another foreign occupation. The transcript of an April 2009 fund-raising call, organized by loyal Minnesota fund-raiser Amina Ali and featuring Shabaab official Moallin Burhan, captures the change in the atmosphere.[17]

> ALI: People are wondering—people are questioning the jihad itself and want to know the purpose of the current jihad. . . . They are saying the jihad was waged against the Ethiopians and the Ethiopians left. They said, "Why wage jihad against Sharif's government? The goal was to adopt Islamic law and they adopted the Islamic law."

> BURHAN: . . . The reason is: Ugandan troops and Burundian troops are still in the country. They are Christians. They are carrying the cross. They invaded our country. They did not come here through our consent. That means, they are considered to be infidels, who are aggressors, and the action to be taken against infidel aggressors is war. God says, "Will you not fight the people who violate their oaths, plotted to expel the messenger and took aggression by being the first to assault you? Do you fear them? Nay, it is God you should fear, if you believe!"

For good measure, Burhan went on to accuse Ugandan troops of killing civilians, spreading AIDS, and impregnating Somali girls.

—

On March 19, 2009, jihadist websites posted a new audiotape from Osama bin Laden. By this time, seven and a half years after 9/11, the world did not screech to a halt every time one of the Al-Qaeda chief's missives appeared. But this one caught the ear of Somalis. For the first time, the Al-Qaeda leader focused specifically on their country. The message was addressed to "champions of Somalia" and called on Islamists to overthrow the Transitional Federal Government. "This Sheikh Sharif . . . must be fought and toppled," bin Laden said. He compared Sheikh Sharif to "presidents who are in the pay of our enemies"—a likely reference to the heads of Ethiopia, Uganda, and Burundi—and implored Muslims to support the Somali jihad. "The victory of the Mujahideen in Somalia is a matter of extreme importance, and not backing them nor taking their hand is extremely dangerous, because if the limbs are eaten, it is easy for the enemy to devour the heart of the Islamic world," he said.[18]

Al-Shabaab hardly needed bin Laden's encouragement, welcome as no doubt it was. That April, the group's leaders began to plan for a large-scale offensive against the TFG. They offered no public explanation why, but the reasons were obvious: with the Ethiopians gone, AMISOM limited to defense, and the TFG an unholy mess, this would be their best chance to seize Mogadishu and take power. To accomplish that, they would need to capture neighborhoods held by pro-government forces, then push into the TFG's main stronghold. That area, protected by AMISOM, was just a few square miles in central Mogadishu, spread out in a thin, irregularly shaped enclave along the Indian Ocean coast. The enclave's location and shape would allow attacks on multiple fronts—but the sea and a shortage of manpower meant Al-Shabaab couldn't impose a siege. The militants would have to find a way to overrun the key government positions, with Villa Somalia, the presidential palace, being the top prize.

Ahead of the push, Al-Shabaab leaders mended fences with Hassan Dahir Aweys and struck an alliance with Hizbul Islam, though it was clear Al-Shabaab was the senior partner. Aweys had been able to keep control of Hizbul Islam only because Al-Shabaab fighters helped his men win two battles against an internal challenger, militia leader Indho Adde.

Final preparations for the push began the first week of May. On the 4th, Al-Shabaab started bringing huge amounts of weapons and ammunition into Mogadishu, along with a number of "battlewagons"—pickup trucks with anti-aircraft guns or machine guns mounted on the back. On May 6, Radio Garowe in Somalia's Puntland region reported that insurgents were "pouring" munitions into the city, putting some in the Daynile district and spreading the rest to other "opposition" strongholds. The militants boosted their numbers as well. Al-Shabaab forces based in Marka, Kismayo, and Baidoa converged on the capital, while Hizbul Islam mobilized militias in Balad and the capital itself.[19] When all assembled, the combined force stood between six thousand and seven thousand fighters, armed with an array of assault rifles, mortars, grenades, and machine guns. The power assembled was impressive by Somali standards, especially so for insurgents. However, Shabaab forces similar to this had taken on the Ethiopians in December 2006 and March-April 2007 and lost both times. Al-Shabaab was now larger, better organized, and better equipped than before: could it defeat a professional army?

Of course, the TFG forces barely qualified as professional, and AMISOM, while made up of full-time soldiers, was not as large or cohesive as the Ethiopian force had been. But AMISOM had a few factors in its favor. The force had recently been bolstered by the arrival of another 850 soldiers from Uganda, bringing troop strength up to 4,350.[20] The troops were fairly well armed and disciplined, and they had the advantage of tanks if needed. As for the government, it seemed to have no advantages. On the eve of battle, the TFG forces still amounted to a mishmash of soldiers, police, and militia groups bound together by political expediency. A US estimate put their number at four thousand, which combined with AMISOM gave pro-government forces the numerical upper hand. But the TFG forces remained less organized than any group on the battlefield.

A leader of Ahlu Sunna Wal Jama'a outlined the situation to US diplomats in Addis Ababa, who summarized his views in a cable to Washington: "The problem with the TFG, he said, was that the parts of their security forces refused to work together or support each other. He said the former TFG forces, police forces and the former Islamic Courts militias did not trust each other and wouldn't come to each other's aid. He thought Sheikh Sharif was too weak to be able to force the different groups to work together."[21]

The various units were also simply outgunned, says Somali General Abdullahi Anod, who was the head of forces at Villa Somalia. "At the beginning, Al-Shabaab was better armed than us," he says. "Each of their units had small arms, machine guns and bazookas, and technicals. We did not have that in each unit."[22]

If the assemblage had one thing going for them, it was desperation. There was nowhere for soldiers in the TFG enclave to retreat, unless they knew how to swim.

Al-Shabaab and Hizbul Islam launched their offensive on May 7, with fighters from both groups attacking a familiar target—Mogadishu Stadium, in the city's Wardhigley district. There, they traded gunfire with a pro-government militia for two days while clashes spread, first to other parts of Wardhigley and then next door in the Yaqshid district, where Hizbul Islam fighters battled the government for control of the main police station. Casualties were sadly normal by Mogadishu standards—fifteen reported fatalities on May 8, seven the following day—so the fighting didn't spark unusual comment from journalists and Somali officials. Residents of the city, for the most part, stayed put.[23]

It was on May 10 that observers realized this was not just another flare-up in the capital's endless firefight. That day, the militants began pushing pro-government forces southward, toward the TFG enclave, in heavy fighting that injured dozens of people. A senior Shabaab official, Mohamed Ibrahim Bilal, boasted that "Now, north Mogadishu is under our control."[24] The militants had taken five key positions, he declared, including the stadium and the Somali Defense Ministry. A photo posted online showed Shabaab hoisting its black flag over the stadium. But the capture of the Defense Ministry was the real coup. The brick four-story building is one of the tallest in Mogadishu and overlooks most of the city. Within a short time, the militants turned it into a command center and mounted artillery and anti-aircraft guns on the roof to blast away at their foes. Meanwhile, at least fourteen people were killed when a mortar shell, its origin undetermined, hit the entrance to a mosque.[25] Thousands of people began streaming from the battle zone to other neighborhoods or displaced-persons camps in the "Afgoye corridor," a strip of land southwest of the city that by the following year would become the world's largest concentration of internally displaced people.

In public, President Sheikh Sharif and other Somali officials tried to project calm; the president gave a news conference on May 11 where he restated his commitment to dialogue and said his government's top priority was to avoid civilian casualties. "The government is committed to holding free elections and to avoid taking power by the gun," he said. But a few hours later, shells fell inside the presidential palace compound.

In a series of cables sent that week to Secretary of State Hillary Clinton and the military's Africa Command, among others, US Ambassador to Kenya Michael Ranneberger tried to hammer home the message that the TFG was in deep trouble. "The government has lost control of the important Industrial Road area of Mogadishu," he wrote on May 11. "TFG soldiers and police are holding defensive positions along Soddonka Road in the Hal-Wadag and Wardhigley neighborhoods. The Prime Minister [Omar Sharmarke] told us the TFG will require more arms and ammunition in the days ahead, and asked us and the wider international community for help."[26]

After a relative lull on the 12th, fighting erupted again on the 13th, with Al-Shabaab taking aim at the TFG lines. Ranneberger cabled that day that Prime Minister Sharmarke sounded "audibly more nervous" in a phone conversation but had assured him that TFG forces were holding their positions along Soddonka Road.[27] The ambassador was told that a late-morning push had been repulsed near Suq Ba'aad Market, roughly one and one-quarter miles from the presidential palace. He also noted that AMISOM soldiers had not come under concerted assault and remained in their camps—possibly so that they would not interfere with TFG plans, or possibly because their mandate allowed them to only defend, not attack.

Behind the front lines, the two sides were vying for the support of the clans, who everyone sensed could make or break the Islamists' offensive. The tug-of-war centered on sub-clans of the Hawiye. Hassan Dahir Aweys had the support of the Habr Gedr and Ayr, and in the opening days of the battle, most TFG fighters with ties to either clan switched sides to join the Islamists—a perfect example of how clan loyalties could trump almost any other factor in Somali affairs. Backers of the TFG then lobbied President Sheikh Sharif's sub-clan, the Abgaal, to make sure they didn't defect, too.[28]

Another drama involving militia chief Indho Adde highlights the instability of the situation. Adde had joined forces with the TFG in April after losing the fight for control of Hizbul Islam to Aweys. On May 11, he and his fighters surprised the TFG by rejoining the militants and handing over their heavy weapons. But just three days later, Adde opened negotiations with the TFG to switch sides yet again. On May 17, he did. Ranneberger said that according to "rumors," it was either because he didn't like the way Hizbul

Islam treated him or because the TFG offered more money.[29] Adde would soon assume a prominent defense position in the government.

Meanwhile, a propaganda war raged on Somali radio stations. One US contact reported hearing an Al-Shabaab spokesman say, "We are at war with evil. We urge the people to stand and support us. We are nearing victory to create a true Islamic government."[30] US, UN, African Union, and Somali officials countered by spreading the message that Shabaab and Hizbul Islam were power-hungry and didn't care about the civilians whose homes and livelihoods were being destroyed. They also pointed out that Al-Shabaab had between two hundred and three hundred foreign jihadists in its ranks. Somalis, they hoped, would hate these outsiders in the same way they abhorred the Ethiopians. Shabaab official Hussein Ali Fidow tried to spin the foreigners' presence as a positive. "Jihadists from all corners of the world have been here with us since we confronted the infamous warlords in Mogadishu three years ago," he told reporters. "They have been coming to Somalia to fight the enemy of Allah. . . . Ugandans and Burundians, who are here illegally, should be called aliens, not the international jihadists."[31]

The 13th was the day journalists, officials, and analysts began to warn the world that President Sheikh Sharif's government could fall.[32] "STRATFOR sources in the area say [Sharif] could be toppled in a matter of days," said a report from the US-based global analysis firm, which added that Somali businessmen attuned to power shifts were putting their money and support behind Al-Shabaab. An expert from another analysis firm, the International Crisis Group, stated ominously, "This is looking like the final assault." A BBC report was only somewhat more circumspect: "Military and intelligence sources say it is by no means certain the fragile Western-backed interim government can defend itself. . . . If not, Somali becomes the West's worst nightmare: A strategically placed country under the control of Islamic militants with links to Al-Qaida." And a *Christian Science Monitor* correspondent reported that pro-government forces controlled only twenty-five city blocks in Mogadishu. The headline on the article read, "Somali Government Encircled by Hardline Islamists."

In actuality, Al-Shabaab and Hizbul Islam had neither surrounded nor penetrated the government's enclave. But with reporters and officials unable to walk the streets—too many bullets were flying—concrete information was hard to come by.

The 13th was also the day President Sheikh Sharif signed the bill that made Sharia the law of the land across Somalia. At a ceremony, the president said now that Somalia was under Islamic law, he saw no reason the fighting should continue. The militants obviously disagreed; Godane released an audio message saying that the TFG planned to "introduce democracy and Jewish theories," and shells fell again on Villa Somalia mid-afternoon.[33]

Those shells marked the beginning of what would be the battle's climactic phase. After the attack, which caused no casualties, the US embassy in Nairobi contacted the Somali security minister, Omar Hashi. Besides giving a military update, Hashi passed along a new and disturbing report. Three top militant leaders—Godane, Hassan al-Turki, and Muhktar Robow—had arrived in Mogadishu, he said.[34] Hashi said they had come "to encourage their fighters," but it wasn't hard to imagine that they were positioning themselves close to Villa Somalia in case the TFG crumbled.

Ranneberger's cable that day described what happened next: "We asked Hashi his assessment of the strategic situation. He responded, laughing, 'We cannot be scared of monkeys. These are monkeys. We have the upper hand.'"[35]

Despite Hashi's bravado, it remained far from clear who had the momentum as the morning of May 14 dawned. A French Press Agency (AFP) report that day said Somalia's president was "holed up in his compound" as residents fled the city and that "hardline Islamist insurgents prepared their bid to seize power."[36] In a phone interview, Aweys called on the president to resign. "I am calling on Sheikh Sharif Sheikh Ahmed to abandon his self-proclaimed presidential job in order to spare the lives of Somalis," he said.[37] If he heard the call, Sheikh Sharif paid it no attention.

Meanwhile, TFG security officers, voicing rare pride in their forces, vowed that the militants would be driven back. Fighting thundered throughout the day across multiple districts—in Wardhigley, not far from the palace; in the Sinaay and Afarta Jardino areas of northern Mogadishu; and in the Yaqshid district.[38] The gun battles grew so heavy in Yaqshid that aid group Medicins Sans Frontieres (Doctors Without Borders) was forced to shut down one of the city's few operating health clinics, leaving local shell and gunshot victims nowhere to turn. MSF, the Red Cross, and the UN humanitarian office all demanded that the fighters show respect for civilian safety—pleas that went unheeded amid the gunfire. By the end of the day, at least ten more people were dead and another thirty wounded. The fatalities included Ab-diqani Aden, brother of the dentist who had set up a Mogadishu ambulance service the year before. Abdulkadir Aden says his brother, a truck driver, was on Street 2 of the Bakara Market, waiting for his cargo to be unloaded, when a shell landed. "The shell destroyed the truck," Abdulkadir says. "He was thirty-nine years old. He left seven children."[39]

At 1020 UTC, 1:20 p.m. in Somalia, Ranneberger transmitted a cable, clas-sified as secret, to Secretary of State Clinton and other officials. He gave it a screaming headline worthy of page one in any newspaper—TFG IN GRAVE JEOPARDY AS FIGHTING RAGES—and said in the de facto lead that "very urgent action is required" to help the government resist the Al-Shabaab on-slaught.[40] In phone calls that day, Prime Minister Sharmarke and Minister of Security Omar Hashi had asked for funds to pay the TFG's fighters, plus more weapons and more ammunition, he explained. "We need Washington approval to send 500,000 dollars immediately to the TFG, with authority to send another 500,000 . . . as needed." Ranneberger said AMISOM had agreed to provide some ammunition and suggested that international part-ners be approached for the weapons.[41]

As if a warning was needed, he added: "Collapse of the TFG would be a major setback for US interests. An Al-Shabaab government and/or a return to total chaos and warlordism, or some such combination, would substan-tially increase the already strong terrorist threat emanating from Somalia." Three and a half hours later, Ranneberger sent another cable to Clinton, say-ing President Sheikh Sharif sounded "subdued" in a phone call but had ex-pressed confidence the TFG could reverse its losses if its troops were prop-erly paid and supplied.[42]

The secretary of state acted. The TFG got its money,[43] and that night Clinton sent a letter to the United Nations' Somali Sanctions Committee asking for a waiver to the UN arms embargo on Somalia.[44] In late June, a senior State Department official told reporters that the United States had shipped "in the neighborhood of forty tons worth of arms and munitions into Somalia in support of the TFG."[45] However, a State Department letter several months later detailed a more modest donation, consisting of seven-teen tons of ammunition and no weapons. The letter to US Senator Russell Feingold said the Ugandan government and AMISOM made the ammuni-tion available to the TFG on an "as-needed basis," with the understanding that the United States would replenish Uganda's stocks. "We established this procedure to ensure that the TFG did not possess weapons or ammunition in excess of its needs or capacity for use, hence reducing the risk of these items being lost to the opposition," the letter said.[46]

On the ground in Mogadishu, the situation grew worse as Thursday dragged on, with the militants creeping closer to Villa Somalia. One Somali news outlet, Hiiraan Online, reported "heavy fighting" at a spot on the Wardanha Road just three-tenths of a mile from the palace. Perhaps that is why at midday, President Sheikh Sharif fired his military chief, General Said Dhere. For his replacement, the president tapped Yusuf Hussein Dhumaal. The appointment said a lot about Somali government dysfunction—Dhumaal was deputy commander of the Somali police force, not a soldier. (Ranneberger said Hashi should be the chief.) But Dhumaal took over and the fight went on.

Late on the 14th, United Nations aid agencies announced that after eight days of fighting, more than thirty-four thousand Mogadishu residents had fled their homes. Casualties by that point had mounted to 135 dead and more than 500 wounded—easily the worst week Mogadishu had experienced in many months. Heavy rain made conditions even more miserable, especially for those trying to escape the constant shelling and gunfire. When there were lulls in the fighting, minibus drivers loaded up packs of Mogadishu residents and drove them to the Afgoye corridor. Once they got there, however, the internal refugees found only overcrowded camps that had no place to put them. "Almost all the new arrivals are staying under trees with nothing to shelter from the rains," said Ahmed Dini of Peaceline, a civil society group.[47]

And yet, behind all the misery and dire headlines, there was a surprising fact—the TFG was holding on. Al-Shabaab and Hizbul Islam had not overrun the presidential palace, the airport, or any other key government installation. Sheikh Sharif was still president and still at Villa Somalia. And apparently, Al-Shabaab and Hizbul Islam were exhausted, for on the morning of May 15, Mogadishu was calm. No cease-fire had been declared, and reporters noted that Islamist fighters maintained positions less than a mile from the palace. But the air of Mogadishu was blessedly free of gunfire, and there were no new attacks on the TFG lines.

For the time being, the TFG had won.

EIGHT

"SEND TROOPS . . . WITHIN 24 HOURS"

IN ACTION MOVIES, THERE'S OFTEN a scene about halfway through where the protagonists—it can be the heroes or the villains, the drug dealers or the cops—assemble in one room to talk, vent, argue, and strategize. Two such scenes unfolded on May 15, 2009, after the guns of Mogadishu fell silent for the first time in over a week.

Scene I happened at the State Department in Washington, in the office of the new US Assistant Secretary of State, Johnnie Carson. Carson, a soft-spoken, goateed diplomat who had served in a half-dozen African countries over a nearly forty-year career, had become chief of the Bureau of African Affairs just eight days before, the same day Al-Shabaab and Hizbul Islam launched their attack. Now, he listened as his visitor, TFG Foreign Minister Mohamed Omaar, gave a face-to-face plea for help. The Islamists are in a strong position, Omaar asserted. They have hundreds of foreign fighters from Afghanistan, Bosnia, Chechnya, Yemen, and elsewhere in their ranks. Eritrea supplied them with three planeloads of weapons right before the offensive. Hassan Dahir Aweys has pulled the Haber Gedr sub-clan to his side. And all the Somali radio stations are controlled by ex-warlords and other critics of the TFG. Nevertheless, Omaar said, the government is confident it can hold Mogadishu—if it receives sufficient money, equipment, and political backing. The Arabic-language service of Al Jazeera television is sympathetic to Hizbul Islam, he added. Maybe the United States could per-suade CNN to show "other perspectives" of the Somali crisis to the world? Carson made no promises about CNN, but he assured Omaar of robust US support.[1]

Scene II was unfolding some 7,800 miles away at what could rightly be called a Somali jihadist summit. Most of Al Shabaab's and Hizbul Islam's top leaders had gathered at a secret location about thirty kilometers from Mogadishu, near Afgoye, to plot their next steps against the TFG. Ahmed Godane, Mukhtar Robow, Ibrahim al-Afghani, Fuad Shongole, Hassan al-Turki, and Hassan Dahir Aweys were among those present, according to accounts the United States received. The leaders discussed strategy for the next offensive in Mogadishu, but it was not an altogether smooth meeting. One snag came when the Al-Shabaab leaders demanded that Aweys disavow a comment reported in Somali media that was critical of Osama bin Laden. (He did.) And according to Foreign Minister Omaar, Al-Shabaab rejected a proposal from Turki to form a joint, equal partnership with Hizbul Islam. Instead, Godane and al-Afghani said other groups must become part of Al-Shabaab and fully accept its leadership.

A few days later, the *Somaliland Times* newspaper carried a report that said Dahir Aweys was so incensed by Godane's "pretensions" to be head of the insurgency that he "threatened to strike with an iron hand the young northerner."[2]

Despite the ruffled feathers, the parties moved on and prepared them-selves for more battle. Fighting in the city entered a lull while clashes con-tinued elsewhere. On May 15, Al-Shabaab began fierce battles with Ahlu Sunna Wal Jama'a in locations north and west of the capital. On the 17th, the militants captured the town of Jowhar after TFG-allied militias abandoned their positions.[3] This setback was compounded when Shabaab fighters raid-ed a UN warehouse in Jowhar and took food meant for tens of thousands of local children. Al-Shabaab also seized the nearby town of Mahaday, a sym-bolic prize because it was the birthplace of President Sheikh Sharif.

On the political front, the TFG worked frantically to find the support it needed to survive. In diplomatic terms, the international community was willing. In mid-May, the UN Security Council affirmed that it saw the TFG as "the legitimate authority in Somalia" and passed a resolution that asked the African Union to "maintain and enhance" AMISOM's deployment.[4] The AU and the East African bloc IGAD both called for sanctions on Eritrea, which they accused of arming the militants, and called for imposition of a blockade and no-fly zone over Somalia to prevent the entry of foreign fighters and weapons. The Security Council would in fact impose an arms embargo on Eritrea and travel sanctions on the country's leaders in December, despite protests from the Eritrean ambassador, who called the measures "shameful" and based on "fabricated lies mainly concocted by the Ethiopian regime and the US administration."[5]

When talk turned to money and military matters, however, promises of aid to the TFG seemed to evaporate. In April, international donors meeting in Brussels had pledged $213 million to help the Somali government and AMISOM improve security. But less than a third of the money was actually delivered, according to a UN report six months later.[6] Nor did any outside force impose a blockade or no-fly zone on Somali territory. At a June 2 meeting with US diplomats in Nairobi, the Somali prime minister, Sharmarke, complained about other unfulfilled promises. Libya pledged $2 million but gave the money to a private foundation in Dubai, he said. Iraq pledged $5 million but had not released the money at all. Djibouti had donated ammunition, but some of it was incompatible with TFG weapons. And Kenya had been no help, he said; Somalia's neighbor could not even be induced to stop Islamist militants from crossing its borders.

"The international community, including ourselves, is just watching. The African Union and UN representatives just make noise about foreign fighters," admitted a high-ranking official of South Africa's Department of International Relations and Cooperation on May 20. Speaking to a US visitor, the official expressed concern that the TFG would not survive past June.[7]

US support was more reliable but didn't come with a blank check. The United States gave the TFG another half-million dollars at the start of June, but only after Somali officials gave a detailed account of how they spent the first $500,000 and promised to hand over a list of military officers and other figures whose salaries needed to be paid.[8] Meanwhile, UN monitors reported that during this period Eritrea was funneling $40,000 to $60,000 per month to figures in both Al-Shabaab and Hizbul Islam, allowing the groups to purchase weapons that were freely available on the Mogadishu streets.[9]

The government's continued impotence was laid bare by two incidents in early June. On June 6, Radio Shabelle director Mukhtar Mohamed Hirabe was murdered in the Bakara Market. Gunmen ambushed him, firing multiple shots into his head and severely wounding one of his colleagues, Ahmed Hashi.[10] It had become apparent by this time that Shabaab was targeting Somali journalists for what the group considered unfavorable coverage. Hirabe was the third Radio Shabelle employee and the fifth Somali journalist killed in 2009 alone. Six years later, it was revealed that this shooting and those of at least five other journalists were arranged by Hassan Hanafi, a Mogadishu radio reporter who had been radicalized and turned into an Al-Shabaab collaborator.[11] A military court in Mogadishu found him guilty of murder, and he was executed by firing squad on April 11, 2016.

The other incident involved Hassan Dahir Aweys. On the 7th, rumors raced through the capital that the Hizbul Islam chief had been killed or badly wounded during a battle in Wabho, a town in Somalia's Galgadud region.[12] The rumors turned out to be false; Aweys turned up in the capital on the 8th and proclaimed himself to be "healthy and fit." What's notable is that he chose to declare his well-being at a press conference in the Yaqshid district, only three miles from the presidential palace. Flanked by several bodyguards, the Hizbul Islam leader spoke and took questions from reporters for more than an hour, with no apparent concern that TFG and AMISOM forces would come to arrest or kill him.[13] He unreservedly told the crowd that fighting would continue until Islamic law was implemented nationwide and AU troops had left the country.

Despite these incidents, and the obvious fragility of the TFG's situation, President Sheikh Sharif struck an optimistic, even upbeat tone in a phone conversation with Ranneberger on the evening of Sunday, June 14. "President Sharif began the conversation by stating 'All is well,'" the ambassador reported in a cable the next day.[14] He said Sheikh Sharif went on to claim that recent fighting had severely damaged the militant groups and that the TFG was planning an offensive to capitalize on the situation. If the international community immediately honors its pledges for help, Sheikh Sharif said, "We can quickly conclude the war." Ranneberger said nothing quite so hopeful in his response, but like other US officials he assured the president of continued support, both in money and military supplies. When their talk was done, Sheikh Sharif asked the ambassador to convey to Secretary of State Clinton his greeting and his appreciation for US support. "We will not lose this opportunity," he said in conclusion. "We are adamant that we will succeed in our efforts."

~

The president's words were put to the test two days later, when Al-Shabaab attacked Galgalato, a village on the eastern outskirts of the capital, in the Karan district.[15] TFG forces fell back briefly but reclaimed the lost ground. The TFG offensive got underway Wednesday morning, when government forces attacked Shabaab and Hizbul Islam positions in the central Hodan district. The initial results were everything Sheikh Sharif could have hoped for; within a couple of hours the TFG had taken several locations from the insurgents, including a police station, a former army hospital, and a pair of spots known as the Milk Factory and the African Village. Just as quickly, though, the gains evaporated, as TFG personnel retreated under strong jihadist counterattacks. By day's end, the gunfire and shelling had wounded more than seventy-five civilians and killed at least eighteen. The TFG had also suffered dozens of casualties, including the death of Colonel Ali Said, Mogadishu's police chief and a key government commander.[16]

News reports that day tended to focus on the loss of the police chief or the tragic deaths of five children who were killed by a mortar shell while taking cover under a balcony. (Local media blamed AMISOM for the attack.) Nearly overlooked in the mayhem was the fact that during its counterattacks, Al-Shabaab assaulted a spot on Maka al-Mukarama Road, one of the most critical positions held by the TFG and AMISOM troops.[17] Ranneberger sent a cable the next day saying the attack targeted the Dabka road junction and "caught TFG troops completely by surprise." He said TFG forces suffered high casualties and that Al-Shabaab briefly seized control of the junction before retreating in the face of AMISOM mortar attacks.

Ranneberger didn't have to explain the road's importance to his superiors; Maka al-Mukarama connects Somalia's presidential palace to Aden Adde International Airport. Losing it would cost the TFG the biggest road under its control, the main supply route for its enclave, and its primary escape route in case the government collapsed. The fact that Al-Shabaab could seize part of it, even temporarily, was a troubling sign for the government.

Ranneberger's cable noted that top TFG officials did not share the president's view that Al-Shabaab was near defeat. He said Somali police chief Abdi Qeybdid "told us that 'extremist militia are battle hardened, stronger, show extreme endurance and are better trained' than the government forces.... The Prime Minister [Sharmarke] admitted being surprised by the strength and organization of the opposition, and asked for urgent provision of ammunition and weapons."[18] Sharmarke also said the death of Ali Said had "dampened" the spirit of the TFG troops.

If the 17th dampened the TFG's spirit, the next few days found it swamped under a deluge of bad news. On the 18th, the setback came from Beledweyne, a city near the Somalia-Ethiopia border. Beledweyne was the hometown of Minister of National Security Omar Hashi. Hashi, one of the TFG's more experienced and able figures, had gone there a few days earlier to meet with members of his sub-clan and organize a local offensive against Al-Shabaab. At about 10 a.m. he stepped out the front door of the Hotel Medina—and right into the path of an oncoming Toyota packed with explosives. The ensuing blast killed Hashi and nearly thirty others, including his security guards and a former Somali ambassador to Ethiopia, Abdikarim Farah Laqanyo, who the United States and Ethiopia considered one of Somalia's most promising and peace-minded politicians.[19]

The driver of the car was a slim seventeen-year-old, Mohamed Derow Sheikh Aden. In a video shot in the car, just minutes before the attack, he looked baby-faced and happy. The Al-Shabaab cameraman asked him why he was smiling. "I'm smiling because I'm going to meet seventy-two virgins tonight," he said.[20]

In Minneapolis, Al-Shabaab's loyal fund-raiser Halima Hassan called her colleague Amina Ali to share news of the attack:

HASSAN: Omar Hashi is gone.

ALI: Did he die?

HASSAN: He is dead.

ALI: May God protect the people from him. Go on.

HASSAN: The hotel he was staying in, with hundreds of other.... I think
the Ethiopians were there also ... all the Hawadle clan elders, and

Laqanyo, the foul-mouthed one, who was the former Somali ambassador to Ethiopia . . .

ALI: Go on.

HASSAN: All the officials, they are still counting the dead.

ALI: Wonderful!

HASSAN: His maternal cousin—his own maternal cousin, who is a member of Al-Shabaab, was the guy who went inside with it.

ALI: He went inside with it and blew it up?

HASSAN: Yes.

ALI: Wonderful![21]

In the inevitable cable to Washington after the attack, Ranneberger wrote that Hashi's death "has further demoralized the TFG" and "strikes a powerful blow to the struggling government."[22]

More blows fell the following day. By this time, Al-Shabaab had taken over Galgalato, then moved into a nearby area, Keysaney. That set the stage for a militant thrust on the afternoon of the 19th. For two decades the Karan district had largely escaped the violence and destruction that had devastated other parts of Mogadishu. This day, its lucky streak ended, as gunfire and mortars rained down on its western neighborhoods.[23] Thousands of Karan residents ran for their lives, fleeing by car, truck, donkey cart, and foot. In a matter of hours, Al-Shabaab captured the entire district, an area covering twenty square kilometers. Again, the Islamist radicals had closed to within two miles of Villa Somalia, this time from a completely different direction.

There was a huge discrepancy between media reports on the day's clashes and accounts behind the scenes. News agencies reported fierce fighting in Karan between TFG forces and Al-Shabaab. TFG officials, talking to US diplomats in Nairobi, spoke of rapid retreat and a greater loss of ground than most observers realized. Ranneberger cabled the details to Washington:

In dozens of frantic telephone calls from Mogadishu during the June 19 fighting, a clearly unnerved TFG described its security forces as fleeing without a fight as Al-Shabaab troops advanced into Karan District. By early evening, Al-Shabaab troops had surged past the Global Hotel, the "safe" home for TFG parliamentarians at the Karan-Shibis [District] border. A key TFG figure told us that at one point escape routes to the seaport and the airport from Villa

Somalia had been completely cut off. One prominent MP, Mohammed Hussein "Engineer" Addow, was killed while fighting and, according to the Prime Minister and others, beheaded by Al-Shabaab forces.[24]

Addow was the third well-known TFG official killed in three days.

Shabaab fighters pushed closer still to the palace when fighting resumed on the 20th. A Mogadishu resident reported seeing "heavily armed Islamist fighters" advancing into the Hamar Weyne district, just south of Villa Somalia, and exchanging fire with government troops. "It seems they are close to taking control of the area," the man said. Shabaab also launched early morning attacks in the Yaqshid district and Sana'a Junction.[25]

At this point, with the TFG facing a threat to its existence, AMISOM finally stepped into the fray, directing mortar fire at the Shabaab frontlines. The backing helped and no doubt encouraged pro-TFG forces, who repelled the Shabaab attacks and then counterattacked, pushing Al-Shabaab out of the Shibis District and retaking the bulk of Karan. The latter development was especially welcome on the government side, as Karan has elevated areas from which the militants could fire on the palace and the seaport.

With the TFG's future still highly in doubt, cabinet ministers gathered at Villa Somalia on the 20th for an urgent meeting. It did not take long for them to agree on extraordinary measures. Somalia was declared to be under a state of emergency, and president Sheikh Sharif was given special powers—though it was not clear what the powers were or how they would change the TFG's plight.

Right after the session, Information Minister Farhan Ali Mohamed spoke to Voice of America's Somali Service.[26] The minister called on Somalis to "save their national flag." But his main appeal was to powers abroad, for them to give the TFG immediate help and, in his words, save it from Al-Qaeda. The appeal was directed at the United Nations, the African Union, the East African bloc IGAD, and any other party that could assist the TFG.

When asked if the government would accept help from Ethiopia, he said, "We want anyone."[27]

Parliament Speaker Aden Mohamed Nur put the appeal in even starker terms when he addressed fellow lawmakers. "The government is weakened by the rebel forces," he said. "We are asking neighboring countries—Kenya, Djibouti, Ethiopia, and Yemen—to send troops to Somalia within twenty-four hours." Nearby governments must protect Somalia, he said. "Otherwise the trouble caused by these foreign fighters will spill to all the corners of the region."[28]

Lest Somalis reject the proposed new influx of soldiers, President Sheikh Sharif said, "The troops we are demanding are not coming to harm the people, but they are coming to save the people and work [for] the order of the government."[29]

Al-Shabaab was quick with its response. Spokesman Ali Dhere condemned the call for foreign troops and said it amounted to a plea to the devil. "If they have appealed to the Satan and the infidels and their messiah Ethiopia, we are appealing to Allah to come to our aid," he said. Then he issued a graphic warning to those who might help the TFG: "[A]ny country that wants to have their troops returned in body bags or see the dead bodies of their sons eaten by dogs, cats, and hyenas, then send it. The mujahideen have sold their life to Allah and are in waiting."[30]

No troops from Somalia's neighbors came rolling across the borders on June 21. In fact, Ethiopia appeared to reject the TFG's appeal, saying an intervention would require an international mandate.[31] (Some Somalis noted Ethiopia did not wait for a mandate when it invaded in 2006.) The TFG could have used help in that day's fighting, as Al-Shabaab retook some of the ground it had lost the day before in the Karan district. But according to Ranneberger, the militants suffered a setback when AMISOM forces—acting on a TFG tipoff—shelled the Sana'a Junction, killing a number of Shabaab combatants.[32] It wasn't the first time government and African Union forces had cooperated, but it was notable that the ensuing artillery strike hit enemy fighters, not civilians. That hadn't happened very often.

And then suddenly the fighting stopped. Monday, June 22, dawned with no gunfire in the streets and no artillery shells flying overhead. No one declared victory or defeat, but it became apparent that once again, the Islamists had exhausted their resources and the TFG had survived the blitz.

President Sheikh Sharif held a news conference that day in which he confirmed the state of emergency and renewed his government's appeal for help from abroad. Leaders of the African Union and the Organization of the Islamic Conference voiced support for aiding the TFG—but none of their members stepped forward with the needed tanks and troops. The only tangible help that materialized came from within, as the TFG signed a cooperation agreement with Ahlu Sunna Wal Jama'a, the anti-extremist militia that had begun fighting Al-Shabaab a couple of months earlier. The United States had encouraged the sides to work together. However, US diplomats who attended the signing ceremony in Nairobi noted a certain lack of excitement on the part of Ahlu Sunna. According to a US cable, the ASWJ representative who signed for the group "noted unenthusiastically in his remarks that 'any government is better than no government at all.'"[33]

In Mogadishu, Al-Shabaab was demonstrating the consequences of having no real government in charge. The group held the area known as Suqa Holaha in northern Mogadishu. On the morning of the 22nd, the same day the fighting stopped, Al-Shabaab fighters assembled several hundred people at a local parade ground. There, the crowd was forced to witness an impromptu Shabaab court, policed by rifle-toting, masked fighters in green fatigues. Four young men in their late teens and early twenties were brought out to face the judge, Sheikh Abdallah Haq. The judge held up two pistols and three mobile phones for the crowd to see. These men, he declared, were guilty of stealing these items. "The defendants have admitted the charges against them and were sentenced accordingly," Haq announced. Their sentence? Each would lose one hand and one foot in a public amputation. The accused were not given a chance to deny the charges or defend themselves.[34]

Al-Shabaab did not carry out the sentence immediately, allegedly because of that day's heat. Amnesty International issued an appeal to the militants—don't go through with the "cruel, degrading, inhumane" punishments.[35] But the plea fell on deaf ears. The four accused men were brought back to the same parade ground three days later. One by one, each man was made to lie down on a plastic mattress. Hooded Shabaab members held down their limbs. As another audience of hundreds watched, a masked militant used a long, curved-blade knife normally used for slaughtering camels to slice off the right hand and left foot of each man. The victims screamed in agony or passed out. Onlookers vomited and cried. But the knife man kept cutting, finishing the job within a matter of minutes.[36]

Before the amputations, medics had applied tourniquets to the affected limbs, keeping bleeding to a minimum and enabling the men to survive. However, one victim, Ismael Abdulle, reported that two weeks later, Fuad Shongole arrived at the house where he remained in detention. The knife man had not taken enough of his leg, Shongole ruled. Another inch was required. This time, the cutting tool was a plumber's saw.[37]

Amnesty International denounced the amputations as a form of torture, one that amounted to a war crime. But Al-Shabaab spokesmen were defiant. "We have carried out this sentence under the Islamic religion, and we will punish like this everyone who carries out these acts," said Ali Mohamud Fidow, Shabaab's governor for Mogadishu.[38]

The amputations underscored the new realities of life in the Somali capital. The TFG still stood. AMISOM was there to protect it. But in much of Mogadishu, Al-Shabaab and its version of the law was firmly in charge.

NINE

ZENITH AND STALEMATE

IMAGINE A WORLD WHERE WELL-ARMED insurgents have taken over most of Washington, DC. They effectively rule three-fourths of the capital, with the remainder best described as a no-man's land. The US government continues to operate; it controls the White House, a few adjacent buildings, and the highway down to Reagan National Airport. But the insurgents are never far away. Drive toward the airport and you run the risk of sniper fire and roadside bombs. Walk through the Ellipse and you become a target for gunmen atop nearby office buildings. Every so often, the insurgents fire mortar shells toward the White House. They aren't good shots, and rarely do they hit anything meaningful. But everyone is aware that it takes just one projectile to do something cataclysmic, like kill the president, which would likely trigger the breakup of the government and leave Americans in the hands of a rigid, fanatical theocracy.

That was Somalia's capital on June 22, 2009.

If there was ever a moment when Al-Shabaab looked set to take power in Somalia, when AMISOM's presence seemed futile and the TFG's collapse appeared imminent, that Monday might have been it. News organizations reported that President Sheikh Sharif was "clinging to power by his fingertips"[1] and that Ethiopian troops would return to "back up a fast-failing Somali government."[2] (In truth, the Ethiopians deployed only along the border.) In Nairobi, Kenyan prime minister, Raila Odinga, said the consequences would be "very grave" if Al-Shabaab took over Somalia—but not a single Kenyan tank or soldier crossed the border to prevent it from happening.[3] And in a cable to Washington, US ambassador Ranneberger said the TFG had experienced a "near rout" and "near disappearance" during the weekend fighting. Most likely, he said, it survived only because of AMISOM's intervention.[4]

Ranneberger's colleague, US ambassador to Ethiopia Donald Yamamoto, went so far as to say the United States should develop a "Plan B" to protect American interests in case the TFG fell. "[W]e have no guarantees that it will survive, let alone succeed, to establish a viable national government. As a result, we cannot afford to wait to see what happens," he wrote in a cable to Washington that week.[5] Yamamoto said the United States should step up intelligence gathering against the militants, boost counterterrorism support to Somalia's neighbors, and also give support to the Somaliland and Puntland regions, which he predicted would be the "next targets" of Al-Shabaab if the TFG collapsed. He also suggested that the United States prepare an evacuation plan for the AMISOM troops, in case the force "found itself in Mogadishu without a TFG to support."

The despair permeated the streets of Mogadishu, where the average person was just trying to stay alive. All necessities were in short supply, especially food. The city's largest health-care facility, Medina Hospital, reported on the 22nd that most of its patients were going hungry. People were usually fed by relatives, said hospital official Dahir Mohamed, "but now the relatives are either in hospital themselves or have fled the city to safer areas."[6] The UN World Food Program normally ran sixteen feeding sites around the city, making hot meals for some eighty thousand people per day, but had shut the sites down two days earlier after gunmen occupied the headquarters of its Somali partner organization. The sites wouldn't reopen for more than a month.

Those wanting to escape this dystopia were free to board one of the minibuses carrying people to Afgoye—if they could scrounge up the money. Drivers were charging up to $50 for a one-way, thirty-mile drive, or hundreds to go to more remote regions. Some found ways to pay it, while others began a long, arduous walk through scorching summer heat. By the end of

June, more than two hundred thousand Mogadishu residents had fled their homes in the previous eight weeks.[7]

In perhaps the most telling sign, officials acknowledged that a majority of Somalia's 550 parliament members were currently outside the country. Many had taken or re-taken up residence in Nairobi, where Reuters noted that Somali MPs were often seen sipping tea and talking politics in the city's cafes. "I cannot be a member of a government that cannot protect me," said one of them, Abdallah Haji Ali. "In Somalia, nobody is safe."[8]

No one in Somali, US, or African officialdom could argue otherwise. What many failed to understand was that, to paraphrase Mark Twain, reports of the TFG's demise were exaggerated—not greatly perhaps, but definitely exaggerated.

The fact was that both Al-Shabaab and Hizbul Islam had been weakened by the May and June fighting. No casualty totals are available, but it seems clear that hundreds of Islamist militant fighters were killed or injured during the offensives. The losses were not permanent, as Shabaab in particular was still recruiting and training new fighters. But neither group had bottomless reserves. Veteran Al-Shabaab military officer Mohamed Jama says manpower was always a problem during long periods of combat. "As the fighting continued we could not sustain supplying new men into the front lines because the fighters were weary, wounded, or killed."[9] He says other fighters were sent back to their home regions to replenish Shabaab units that had been "emptied" for the battles in Mogadishu. The circumstances left Al-Shabaab and Hizbul Islam short of the strength needed to finish off the TFG.

Villa Somalia remained a focus of concern for US and Somali officials. The militants had guns trained on the palace; their fighters held ground just a short run from the compound gates. Who wouldn't expect an all-out attack? But Al-Shabaab and Hizbul Islam held back. A successful assault on the palace would likely require more than one thousand fighters to push aside AMISOM, topple the TFG, and then hold the position in the face of counterattacks. The price in blood and steel would be high, possibly more than the groups could bear. "We understood the size and sacrifice it would require to raid the palace," says former Hizbul Islam official Hassan Mahdi. "As long as AMISOM was there, we knew that taking it over would be costly."[10]

Mahdi says the groups discussed ways of getting inside the compound that might minimize losses. "There were secret plans that came from Shabaab to enter the palace," he says.[11] "One of the plans was to dig a tunnel that goes right under [it]. The second plan was to attack the palace from the sea side. So taking over the palace was not out of the question." But, he says, the groups never developed these plans because of "mistrust over the war and strategy." Mistrust within the Islamist militant camp would be a major problem in the months to come.

With a large-scale assault on the palace unfeasible, Al-Shabaab tried other approaches to force a TFG collapse. Taking a page from bin Laden's playbook, the group released an audio message to Somali radio stations on July 5. The normally reclusive Godane voiced the twelve-minute tape, asserting the TFG was near collapse and Somalis should prepare for the creation of a true Islamic government. He gave TFG forces five days to surrender their weapons to Al-Shabaab. After that, he said, its leaders would be tried in an Islamic court, on charges of killing civilians and encouraging foreign armies to reoccupy Somalia.[12] Had Al-Shabaab broadcast that message on a day when government forces were in retreat, the TFG conceivably might have disintegrated. Instead, State Minister of Defense Indho Adde dismissed the threat out of hand and said that Godane was so afraid of being seen, he wore women's clothing as a disguise (an often rumored but never proven allegation.)

Shabaab also tried to hollow out its foes by inducing soldiers to sell their weapons—a practice the TFG and AMISOM were never able to stamp out entirely—and swindling the government out of money. Abdihakim Mohamud Fiqi, who would later be a two-time Somali defense minister, describes the typical scam: "Shabaab members would contact officials in the government whom they've known through previous acquaintance or clan lineages. One would say he has decided to defect to the government side [with fellow fighters] because the group is not giving them bullets, food, supplies, and salary. They would pretend to be in desperate need." Officials would tell the Shabaab men to set up a time and place to cross the front line—but the would-be defectors would say they needed money first to pay bills or fuel up their vehicles. "They would sometimes ask for as much as $5,000 or as little as $500," Fiqi says. "We sent money to some of them just to get them to come, but we never heard back from them."[13]

Fiqi admits the TFG fell for similar swindles where Shabaab members offered to sell heavy machine guns or supposed intelligence on the location of insurgent leaders. "They speak in a persuasive way," Fiqi says. "They made the war a business venture. The defection was never true; they never gave reliable information. [After] we spent money on them several times, we closed the line."[14]

In the midst of the scheming, Al-Shabaab and Hizbul Islam continued to press their agenda through firepower. "Our focus of the fighting was to cripple the government's revenue sources like the seaport and Bakara Market and the administration institutions like Villa Somalia," says Shabaab's Mohamed Jama.[15] So fighters near the port would fire on workers unloading cargo ships; snipers atop buildings near Villa Somalia would fire at people inside the compound walls. When AU Peace and Security Council chief Ramtane Lamamra visited Villa Somalia in early 2010, the president's chief of staff warned him to stay away from windows; otherwise you might get shot, Lamamra was told.[16]

The insurgents also kept baiting AMISOM into shelling Bakara by launching mortars from the market. Besides sparking condemnation from human rights activists, the shelling played into Shabaab's propaganda that the AU troops were occupiers and killers, not peacekeepers. "Instead of AMISOM remaining calm and rational about [insurgent attacks], they were just like the Ethiopians—they became trigger happy, fired indiscriminately, and all hell broke loose," says Terry, the Westerner in Mogadishu. "So people said, 'See, they're not here to help us, they're here to kill us, so we're going to help Shabaab.' That's what happened."[17]

However, one of those artillery exchanges triggered or at least hastened a development that, in the long run, would have huge consequences for Al-Shabaab and the course of the war. For weeks, African Union leaders had talked about rewriting AMISOM's mandate so the troops could be more proactive. Somali officials had pushed for it, knowing the TFG could not drive back the insurgents alone. The policy was still under discussion when on July 11, as part of fighting in Mogadishu's Shibis district, Al-Shabaab fired four mortar rounds into the grounds of Villa Somalia. The attack killed three Ugandan AMISOM soldiers and wounded eight.

The next day, with no announcement or fanfare, AMISOM tanks and troops left their bases and advanced with TFG soldiers into insurgent-controlled parts of Mogadishu. No honest observer could label the operation as defensive. The AU force had effectively tossed aside its mandate.

The US deputy chief of mission in Kenya, Pamela Slutz, described the attack in a cable to Washington, saying it involved eight to ten AMISOM tanks and armored personnel carriers—and that Shabaab fighters ran when they saw the force rumbling toward them.

> The TFG re-took the Abdi-Aziz and Shibis districts, including key landmarks the Global Hotel and Old Seaport, according to government contacts. The TFG also drove into the Karan district. In Karan, President Sheikh Sharif and State Minister Indho Adde conducted a press conference from Keysaney Hospital, well inside former Al-Shabaab–held neighborhoods. . . . By the end of July 12, the TFG forces had pushed their attack a kilometer or more into extremist neighborhoods to the north and east of Villa Somalia. A TFG spokesman announced they had killed forty Al-Shabaab or Hizbul Islam fighters.[18]

Voice of America reported that at one point on that Sunday, AMISOM forces were active eight kilometers north of Villa Somalia. A spokesman for AMISOM's Ugandan contingent announced a de facto change in policy: "We are not just peacekeepers at the seaport, airport, and Villa Somalia. We are supposed to be in the whole country. And so, anywhere where we think there is danger, anything we think we can assist, we will do that."[19]

The gains began to evaporate the next day, when AMISOM armor stayed inside its bases, and Al-Shabaab retook parts of Karan. But the lesson seemed clear—working together, going on the offensive, AMISOM and the TFG could push back insurgent forces.

However, there was no follow-up attack and no planning at that time for a coordinated campaign. The TFG was simply too dysfunctional on too many levels. TFG armed forces commander Yusuf Dhumaal discussed the problems with US diplomats in Nairobi that month, as he recovered from a gunshot wound. Relations with AMISOM were "excellent," he said, but he added that poor discipline and communication among his forces often meant they couldn't take advantage of AMISOM artillery strikes. He also said that AU troops were not always willing to provide backup to their less able TFG partners.[20] Tensions grew two weeks later when the TFG accused AMISOM of supplying less ammunition than it had promised. US diplomats soon learned the reason: AMISOM feared that government soldiers would sell their extra bullets to the insurgents.

Instead of seeing a breakthrough, Mogadishu remained the arena for a bloody, destructive, disheartening stalemate.

⁓

One very experienced Al-Shabaab operative did manage to get inside the presidential compound. But Dalha Ali wasn't working for the group anymore. After becoming disillusioned with Al-Shabaab—and what he considered its senseless, indiscriminate violence—he had switched sides in the early part of 2009, joining the security detail of TFG Interior and Security Minister Abdulkadir Ali Omar. The two first met during the ICU days, when Omar was chief judge of a court at Circulo Officiale, the building where Ali signed up to become an Islamist fighter.[21]

Omar needed good security. He was never a member of Al-Shabaab, but the group saw him as a traitor of sorts, as he had fought against President Yusuf's TFG as a leader of the Muqawama groups. In March 2009, the minister was lucky to survive an IED explosion, near his house in Mogadishu, that killed two others. Dalha Ali, with his knowledge of urban combat, weapons, explosives, and Al-Shabaab itself, was an ideal choice to provide protection.

The job gave Ali access to the Villa Somalia compound, where Omar had his office. Each day he passed through the wrought-iron gates controlled by TFG guards, followed by three other checkpoints manned by AMISOM troops. The only people who get through these checkpoints are those with security clearance. Ali might not seem like a candidate to win such clearance, given his three years' fighting and killing for Al-Shabaab. But over a period of months he gained the trust of Omar, who needed his skills and expertise. The TFG wanted Islamist militants to cross lines anyway. If a young man had some blood on his hands from fighting for the wrong side—well, that could be overlooked. It had to be. How else would the country ever move forward?

The job was certainly a more comfortable fit for Ali than his bomb-planting and assassination duties in Al-Shabaab. But according to a friend in Somalia, speaking on condition of anonymity, Ali remained very discontented. A few years earlier, he had been an aspiring religious scholar set to attend school overseas, away from Somalia's chaos. Now, he was locked into a life of violence, where even in his new, defensive role, he would still have to shoot and kill people, maybe even former buddies he knew from Al-Shabaab.

"He was young, bright, ambitious in life," the friend says. "He dreamed of going abroad; he was curious about life abroad. He would ask people if they can bring him a smartphone. But he was unable to get out of the life that he was trapped in. He was not happy with his past; he was given orders and assignments he did not want, and he felt he was being used."[22]

The friend says Ali's frustration "may have pushed him to the wall," emotionally speaking. He essentially let his job with Omar drift away while he focused on other priorities, including long-awaited trips to other countries—one to Kenya, one to South Africa. After a while, he ceased to be a guard for anyone or a visitor to Villa Somalia. He would return one day, but for a markedly different purpose.

⁓

On August 6, the United States gave Sheikh Sharif and the TFG an unprecedented vote of confidence. Secretary of State Hillary Clinton, swinging through Kenya on a seven-nation tour of Africa, held a private discussion with the Somali leader in Nairobi, and then she appeared with him at a joint news conference. Yes, the Somali government is fragile and needs significant help, she told reporters. But she commended Somali officials for fighting Al-Shabaab, allowing accounting firm Price Waterhouse to monitor their books, and striving to provide basic services to the Somali people. Clinton made it clear that the Obama administration was 100 percent behind Sheikh Sharif. "We believe that his government is the best hope we've had in quite some time for a return to stability and the possibility of progress in Somalia," she said.[23]

Luckily for her, no one asked Clinton how much governing the TFG was actually doing, because the correct answer would have been "none." In fact, events over the previous month suggested that if any organization was exerting authority on the ground in Somalia, it was Al-Shabaab.

- On July 14, pro-Islamist gunmen kidnapped French intelligence agents Marc Aubriere and Denis Allex from a Mogadishu hotel. The kidnappers quickly turned over the hostages to Hizbul Islam. But upon hearing of the abduction, Al-Shabaab demanded custody of the men. Witnesses said dozens of Shabaab fighters surrounded the house of Hassan Dahir Aweys and threatened to storm it unless their demands were met. Hizbul Islam gave in and let Al-Shabaab take Al-lex. Aubriere won his freedom in late August—reports are conflicting on whether he escaped or was let go for ransom—while Allex would remain in Shabaab hands more than eighteen months before the group executed him in January 2013, after a failed French rescue operation.

- On July 20, Al-Shabaab established an Office for the Supervision of the Affairs of Foreign Agencies. The new department immediately demanded that the UN shut down its offices for development, political affairs, and security in Somalia, which Shabaab accused of supporting the TFG. The same day, Shabaab gunmen raided UN compounds in Baidoa and the nearby town of Wajid, stealing vehicles and radio equipment. No one attempted to block them or recover the stolen goods. The UN could do little but suspend operations in Baidoa and appeal to Al-Shabaab to lift the ban. Shabaab said no, and UN operations across much of the country were reduced to life-saving activities like food distribution.

- On June 28, Al-Shabaab stoned a man to death in the town of Wanalaweyn, after one of its courts convicted him of rape and murder. On July 10, Shabaab beheaded seven people in Baidoa whom they accused of renouncing Islam or spying for the government. And in early August, Shabaab administrators in the town of Merka began forcibly pulling out people's gold and silver teeth—with unsterilized tools—because the militants viewed the teeth as a sign of vanity that contradicted Islam. It was unclear what happened to the gold and silver after it was extracted.

Together, the incidents paint a picture of an extremist movement at the height of its power, one that has shoved aside the official government to become the country's true ruler, similar to the Taliban in Afghanistan, Hezbollah in Lebanon, or ISIS in parts of Syria and Iraq. In territorial terms, Shabaab had indeed reached a new peak. By mid-2009, the Shabaab-Hizbul Islam alliance controlled about 80 percent of Somalia south of the Puntland region. The remainder was ruled not by the government but by militia group Ahlu Sunna Wal Jama'a or local clans. At least three million Somalis were living under Islamist extremist rule. In Mogadishu, the lines changed slightly day to day, but most observers saw the insurgents exerting full or partial control over ten of the capital's sixteen districts, including Yaqshid, Wardhigley, Hodan, Hawl Wadag, Karan, Abdi Aziz, Huriwa, Daynile, Shibis, and Dharkenley.

That picture is deceptive, however. The fact was that at its moment of zenith, Al-Shabaab was starting to lose the support that had powered its rise.

The population that had generally backed Al-Shabaab when it fought the Ethiopians and restored order to towns and villages was slowly but surely growing fed up with the strict rules imposed on their lives and the violence Shabaab used to enforce them. A Human Rights Watch report compiled during 2009 quoted dozens of Somalis complaining about Shabaab fighters beating and flogging people for things such as listening to music, playing board games, wearing "un-Islamic" attire and hairstyles, and breaking the group's rules about men and women being together in public.[24] A nineteen-year-old woman from Kismayo told the group that she was jailed overnight for sitting outside her house and chatting with a male neighbor. "They said, 'You are a woman, you are not allowed to sit close to a man in public.' I said, 'We have the right to associate with whom we please.' They shouted at me and threatened me all the way to the station house."

One Mogadishu woman said she was arrested for failing to wear the thick, full-body *abaya* mandated by a local Shabaab official and was thrown into a shipping container being used as a makeshift jail cell.

> My husband was then asked, "Are you going to take the ten lashes normally prescribed for women who are supposed to wear the abaya?" He refused and they said, "Okay, then your wife will take it." A young man gave me ten lashes with the whip. He beat me so much that I felt heat and pain throughout my body. He was raising his hand back and counting, "One, two, three, four, five . . ." It felt so painful that if I had a gun I would have killed that man.

Though some Somalis continued to support the militants for restoring order to their towns, many others fled to areas not under Shabaab control, including Puntland and Somaliland. Occasionally, the dissension would break into open revolt, such as the time in December 2008 when protesters in the southern town of El Wak dared to pelt Al-Shabaab fighters with stones. The fighters responded by opening fire, killing eight demonstrators.[25]

Ahlu Sunna Wal Jama'a, representing the more moderate strain of Islam, began to present Shabaab and Hizbul Islam their first real military challenge outside Mogadishu since the Ethiopians left. As fighting raged in the capital, the sides fought a series of almost-daily battles in central Somalia, mostly in the Hiiran, Middle Shabelle, and Galgadud regions. The see-saw battles for control of various towns could grow huge at times; a battle in Galgadud's Wabho district on June 5, 2009, killed more than 120 people, about half of them noncombatants. Eventually, Ahlu Sunna gained control of most of Galgadud and parts of other regions, giving the government a friend if not a true ally in a few areas outside the TFG enclave.

Tensions in Al-Shabaab's alliance with Hizbul Islam were beginning to surface as well, as evidenced by the dispute over the French agents. From the start, Shabaab had considered itself top dog in the relationship. Its disregard for its partner became even clearer during a power struggle over the port city of Kismayo. The two groups had agreed to share control of the city and the tax revenue generated by the port; some reports said the plan called for them to rotate management of the city every six months. But in September 2009, Al-Shabaab created a new governing council for Kismayo that excluded the Raskamboni Brigade and Anole, two of the main factions that made up Hizbul Islam. When local Al-Shabaab leaders wouldn't back down, both Hizbul Islam and Al-Shabaab rushed hundreds of fighters to the city. Shooting erupted on the morning of October 1, leaving twelve people dead. The gun battle ended with Al-Shabaab in firm control of the city and the militant alliance under severe strain.

Somehow, the groups patched up their differences and stayed together. But many in Hizbul Islam suspected Al-Shabaab didn't want a partner at all. "There was a secret agenda by Al-Shabaab that they exist only and to make Hizbul Islam disappear," says Hassan Mahdi.[26]

Hizbul Islam wasn't always the best partner to have. In mid-August, both groups announced they would launch attacks during the Ramadan holiday. To jihadists' way of thinking, Ramadan was and is an appropriate, even ideal time to confront apostates and infidels. However, Hizbul Islam spokesman Mohammed Osman Aruus was very specific, saying the offensive would start on the first day of the month-long holiday—August 20 that year—with attacks on AMISOM bases in Mogadishu. Without the element of surprise, the offensive ran into trouble immediately. TFG and Ahlu Sunna Wal Jama'a fighters actually put Al-Shabaab on defense that first day with an attack in the town of Bulobarde, north of Mogadishu. Twelve hours of battle climaxed with a shootout on a bridge over the Shabelle River. Local residents counted the bodies afterward: at least twenty dead, most of them combatants.

Al-Shabaab managed to keep its grip on the town and also recaptured the town of Bula Hawa, near the Kenyan border, from Ahlu Sunna fighters who had taken it three days earlier. Things didn't go as well in Mogadishu. When militants attacked an AMISOM base at the K4 junction with a barrage of mortars and gunfire, the forewarned AU soldiers responded with an equal or greater barrage of their own.[27] The ensuing battle lasted most of the day and spread to three other districts of the city, killing at least twenty-four people and wounding over one hundred, most of them civilians. But AMISOM held on to the base.

On the 21st, Al-Shabaab and Hizbul Islam launched sustained attacks on two TFG strongholds—the Mogadishu intersection known as "Ex-Control Afgoye" and Maka al-Mukarama Road.[28] The clashes grew especially intense and perilous for the TFG around the intersection. "AMISOM troops in nearby Siyad academy had to intervene to repel extremist fighters, reportedly causing them severe casualties," Ranneberger reported. On the 22nd, President Sheikh Sharif appealed to the militants to agree to a Ramadan cease-fire. Both Al-Shabaab and Hizbul Islam dismissed the president's request, with Hassan Dahir Aweys crowing: "We will not accept that cease-fire call. This holy month will be a triumphant time for mujahideen, and we will fight the enemy."[29]

However, US diplomats did not send any cables to Washington during this period warning of the TFG's imminent demise.

In fact, Shabaab suffered a major loss during this Ramadan with the death of Saleh Ali Nabhan. Nabhan, one of Al-Shabaab's key links to Al-Qaeda and one of its most able instructors, was in a two-truck convoy driving south toward the town of Barawe on September 14 when four American AH-6 "Little Bird" helicopters swooped down from the sky, guns blazing. Nabhan and nine men traveling with him, including six non-Somalis, were killed.[30] A US Navy SEAL team quickly landed, retrieved Nabhan's body, and then flew to an offshore vessel. It was later revealed that American intelligence had been closely tracking Nabhan, waiting for a moment when he was away from civilians. Al-Shabaab could not disguise the seriousness of the blow. "We are very, very upset," said a Shabaab official from nearby Marka.[31]

The response came three days later. On the 17th, a group of Somali security officials and AMISOM officers gathered for talks at the main AU base, located on the grounds of the airport. Guards let two white United Nations vehicles driven by English speakers pass through the gates, thinking the passengers had come for the meeting. Their mistake became evident minutes later when two deafening explosions ripped through the base. Seventeen people were killed, including AMISOM's deputy commander, Burundian major-general Juvenile Niyogyunguriza. Another ten were wounded, among them AMISOM's top commander, Ugandan general Nathan Mugisha. In a single stroke, Al-Shabaab had nearly decapitated its most powerful foe. "We have got our revenge for our brother Nabhan," said Shabaab spokesman Ali Dhere.[32]

The group tried beheading the TFG as well. Twice in October, Shabaab fired on the airport when President Sheikh Sharif was present; both times he escaped unharmed.[33] A Sheikh Sharif aide dismissed the attacks as militants "guessing at the arrival of the president." But in reality, the string of attacks strongly suggested that Shabaab had informants inside the TFG and/or AMISOM. "I'm surprised by the level of intelligence of Al-Shabaab—highly sophisticated," says former defense minister Fiqi. "They do not have the same capacity as the government but bigger and better. . . . They had people among us who gave them correct information. We did not have the same penetration among them."[34]

But still, Shabaab could not land a knockout punch. Perhaps that is why the group selected a much softer target for its next major attack.

December 3, 2009, started out as a rare festive occasion within the violence of the Somali capital. Benadir University was holding a graduation ceremony for forty-three medical, engineering, and computer science students who had persisted with their studies amid Mogadishu's violence and completed the school's six-year course. Hundreds of people, including a number of TFG ministers, crowded into a ballroom of the Hotel Shamo, an upscale, five-story hotel located in the K-4 neighborhood—nominally a government-controlled area. Videos taken that day depict an utterly normal graduation scene, with students wearing black robes and tasseled hats, officials in suits giving speeches, people sharing hugs and taking photos, and audience members fanning themselves as they wait out the speeches in the hot, stuffy room. Armed guards were present too, but not around the stage. The mood was upbeat and cheerful.

It was during remarks by Professor Osman Mohamed Dufle that the ceremony abruptly ended. A single loud blast ripped through the room, leaving broken chairs and bloodied bodies everywhere.[35] The explosion killed twenty-five people, including nine graduates, two journalists, and three TFG officials—Health Minister Qamar Adan Ali, Education Minister Ahmed Abdullahi Wayel, and Higher Education Minister Ibrahim Hassan Adow. Another official, Sports Minister Suleyman Olad Roble, was badly wounded. He would die two months later.

Initial reports said the bomber had sneaked into the room dressed as a woman in a black abaya and veil. But footage that emerged later shows a young man dressed in a white shirt, standing near the stage, recording the event with his camera. According to a friend who later spoke to the British newspaper the *Guardian*, this man, "Abdi," was the bomber. He said Abdi was an ethnic Somali who had been raised in Denmark and was recruited by Shabaab to come fight in Somalia.

Instantly, the bombing triggered a wave of disgust toward Al-Shabaab.[36] The United States, the United Nations, the League of Arab States, and other entities issued a joint statement with unusually strong language, condemning the attack as cold-blooded, cowardly, and the sign of a "complete disregard for human life."[37] More remarkably, ordinary Somalis felt emboldened to speak out as well. In blogs, newspapers, and radio call-in shows, people expressed a common thought—how could Al-Shabaab slay young, innocent students whose skills could have helped rebuild this shattered country? The anger was enough to generate Mogadishu's first open protest against the militant group on December 7. Hundreds of people took part, chanting "Down with Al-Shabaab" and "We don't need violence." They also took the daring step of setting fire to the group's black flag before police told them to disperse.

Sensing the backlash, Shabaab spokesman Ali Dhere denied that the group was responsible, saying the blast was the result of a government plot or rivalries within the TFG. There is no evidence that anyone believed him.

The bombing also exposed divisions within Al-Shabaab itself. Many of the group's members could not see the point of the attack, especially given what it cost Al-Shabaab in terms of public support. Two weeks after the bombing, Somali media outlets began reporting a split in the group. One faction led by Ahmed Godane wanted to intensify jihad, the reports said, while another faction led by Mukhtar Robow was said to be open to "ideological changes" so that the group could open talks with "rival parties"—an ambiguous phrase that some interpreted to mean the government.[38]

US contacts in Somalia reported similar friction. Ambassador Ranneberger provided more details in a cable dispatched to Washington on Christmas Eve.

> Godane reportedly condones suicide bombings, is seeking a closer relationship with foreign fighters, and wants to now announce an Islamic caliphate in Somalia. . . . Several other Al-Shabaab leaders reportedly think the December 3 suicide bombing represented a bridge too far, are uncomfortable with the influence of foreign fighters in their midst, and think the time is not right to proclaim an Islamic caliphate. Our contacts tell us that Al-Shabaab factions loyal to Mukhtar Robow and Al-Shabaab spokesman Ali Dhere think Al-Shabaab is being hijacked by a foreign agenda and told Godane they need to gain greater popular support before announcing a caliphate. Some contacts tell us Robow and Dhere may be even further apart from Godane than their statements indicate but that the Al-Shabaab leaders fear assassination by Godane if they do not continue to proclaim their intention to move toward a caliphate.[39]

As always, Ranneberger reported, clan politics lay just below the surface.

> Contacts within the Hawiye and Rahanweyn clans tell us Al-Shabaab leaders from those clans are feeling stepped up clan pressure after the December 3 suicide bombing in Mogadishu. A well placed Hawiye/Habr Gedir/Ayr contact told us Al-Shabaab leaders are being shamed by the clan because many Hawiye and Rahanweyn, constituting much of the population of Mogadishu, suffered as a result of the December 3 attacks. (Note: Godane would probably not face clan pressure in Mogadishu because he is from the northern Isaaq clan.)[40]

Ranneberger added that the time was right for the TFG to try to lure away Al-Shabaab's rank-and-file, though he acknowledged that hard-liners like Godane "are unlikely to be co-opted." Leaders like these, he suggested, should be "military targets."

The TFG apparently did not act on the ambassador's advice, as both Godane and Robow remained part of Al-Shabaab and the group as a whole remained intact. But government officials saw weakness in their enemy. When Prime Minister Sharmarke met with US embassy staffers in Nairobi on December 30, he told them the TFG planned to launch a new offensive in mid-January.[41] This one will would push the insurgents back, he promised. He predicted that by mid-February, when the current TFG celebrate its first anniversary, large parts of Mogadishu would be in the government's hands.

TEN

THE RAMADAN OFFENSIVE

MILITARY OFFENSIVES ARE EASY TO declare but hard to carry out. Sharmarke wasn't lying to the United States; the TFG really was making plans and gathering resources for an attack. But Al-Shabaab spies had already detected that something was afoot. On January 7, the group acted, targeting new TFG military chief Mohamed Gele Kahiye with a roadside bomb as his vehicle drove through Mogadishu's Hodan district. "We got information indicating that the apostate government is planning an offensive against the holy warriors, but with the help of Allah we will destroy their intentions," said a Shabaab commander. Kahiye escaped, but one of his security guards was killed.[1]

On February 5, 2010, the TFG deployed two thousand troops at four locations around the capital, apparently ready to attack.[2] Officials told US diplomats that their goal was to form a "defensive cordon" around Mogadishu. But Al-Shabaab knew what was coming and attacked first, firing on government and AMISOM bases that same day. The ensuing battles killed nineteen people. Two days later, the Associated Press ran a story on "delays" of the offensive caused by a lack of equipment and low morale among the troops—one of whom had said that he and fellow soldiers hadn't been paid and were being fed just two meals a day.[3] The sides exchanged mortar fire for the next week, killing dozens of civilians. But the offensive never got off the ground, and Shabaab spokesman Ali Dhere mocked the TFG's failure to move: "They always vow to wage final war against us and it never happens."[4]

The absence of the offensive—or of any tangible progress toward making Somalia a stable, functioning country—fueled a rising frustration among the countries involved with AMISOM. The tensions nearly boiled over at periodic meetings of regional foreign and defense ministers held in Addis Ababa around this time.[5] Uganda and the African Union said Somalis needed to do more to secure their own country; the Somalis said they would do it if the AU and European Union provided the funds to pay TFG troops. AMISOM and the EU said Somali soldiers needed more training; the Somalis, backed by the Ugandans, said training did little good unless the troops were paid and properly equipped. And AMISOM commander Mugisha repeatedly demanded more equipment and firepower, including but not limited to radar, ships, and attack helicopters. Burundi's Minister of Defense Germain Niyoyankana warned that the rancor was allowing Somalia to sink further into chaos. "We say the same things at every meeting. We make resolutions, yet nothing changes," he said.[6]

Voice of America correspondent Pete Heinlein, who was posted to Addis at this time, says that for all their talk, the countries and blocs helping AMISOM were leery of wading deeper into the Somali morass. Heinlein and other reporters would sometimes get off-the-record briefings with a top official in the African Union Peace and Security Council. "He was telling us the troop-contributing countries were promising they would help, the political people were saying they would get the money from the US and the EU—but the countries are afraid of getting thrown into this, [because] it looks like a losing proposition," Heinlein says.[7] "While the Security Council kept saying all these countries are committing troops, those commitments would never come through. And behind the scenes, our friend was saying, 'This isn't happening'—even though the EU and the Americans were talking a big game."

In the eyes of many observers, the only reason Uganda and Burundi kept their troops in Somalia was for the financial rewards it brought. Both countries reaped benefits by putting their men on the line and letting others pay the bills. A January 2010 US diplomatic cable outlined how the money flow worked, at least when things went smoothly.[8] The African Union, using money supplied by the United States or the European Union, was to pay each soldier in AMISOM a gross salary of $750 per month. But instead of paying the soldiers directly, the AU transferred money for the wages to the governments of Uganda and Burundi. In Burundi's case, the government deducted a $100 tax from each soldier's paycheck. The cable didn't spell it out, but basic math suggests that the tax gave Burundi, which had two thousand soldiers in Somalia at the time, an extra $200,000 per month to use or distribute as it saw fit—significant money in East African terms. Burundi also benefited by letting the United States pay for its soldiers' uniforms, including armored vests. The result was a stronger, battle-tested army for Burundi, built primarily on other countries' cash.

Not everything ran smoothly, of course. The same cable noted complaints from Burundi that the AU had not paid the AMISOM soldiers in six months at that point. It also noted that Burundian soldiers were getting disgruntled, not only because they hadn't been paid, but also because they had learned that salaries for United Nations peacekeepers in Sudan's Darfur region were 25 percent higher.

With no TFG offensive in sight, Al-Shabaab and Hizbul Islam resumed their efforts to take power and enact their strict forms of Sharia. In late February, Shabaab made one of its boldest moves yet, outlawing the World Food Program. The group's declaration minced no words: "Effective as of today, all of WFP's operations inside Somalia are terminated and the organization has been completely banned. All Somali persons, businessmen, and truck drivers who are currently contracted to or working with WFP are hereby instructed to terminate their contracts immediately."[9] The militants had harassed the food agency for months, raiding its offices (as discussed in Chapter 9), extorting money from its drivers, and accusing it of giving out expired food. But this went beyond mere harassment—this was Shabaab asserting itself as a national governmental authority. The WFP vowed to keep feeding people in need, but Shabaab had the power to make the ban stick in most of the areas it controlled.

Hizbul Islam flexed its own muscles the first week in April, declaring that Mogadishu radio stations were to stop playing music. Raising voices and instruments in song was un-Islamic, the group decreed. The move angered many Somalis, who relied on pop tunes to ease the strain of their lives. But out of the capital's sixteen stations, all but two complied with the ban.[10]

Some weeks it appeared the TFG might do Shabaab a favor and collapse on its own. For years, Somali politics has been plagued by a thorny question: who holds ultimate power, the president or the prime minister? Governments built through long negotiations have collapsed due to disputes between the two officeholders and their allies in parliament. President Sheikh Sharif's administration was no different, and never was the resulting chaos more on display than on May 16, 2010. That Sunday marked the first time all year parliament had met; until then, violence, feuds among MPs, and the sheer number of lawmakers living abroad had kept the house from assembling a quorum. When MPs finally gathered, speaker Aden Madobe, an ally of the president, tried to organize a vote of no-confidence in Prime Minister Sharmarke. After a short, chaotic session comprised mainly of shouting and finger pointing, Madobe declared that the motion had passed and told reporters he had asked the president to form a new government. But parliament's senior lawmaker, Haji Shugri, told the media a different story—he said lawmakers had in fact voted to fire the speaker. "I ask anyone who wants to be the next speaker to bring their CV and application," he said.[11]

As he talked, reporters could hear explosions in the distance. Al-Shabaab was launching mortars at the building while parliament was in session. Their aim was haphazard as ever, and they scored no direct hits. But elsewhere in the city, at least sixteen people died.

Terry, the Westerner in Mogadishu, said many people in Somalia considered politicians, not Al-Shabaab, to be the main obstacle to peace in the country. "The problem wasn't Shabaab. The TFG itself was imploding. That's what I felt most keenly. It's not the external threat, it's the internal threat that was going to tear it apart. There was so much backstabbing and bickering and BS going on within that government that people were fed up and were like, 'Get your crap together, because we're not going to have a government left.' And Shabaab was almost a kind of sidebar at that point, because people were like, 'Can this government survive their inner bickering and conflicts?'"[12]

Somehow it did, and the great standoff of Mogadishu went on. The government made another attempt to push Al-Shabaab away from Villa Somalia in May. "I led a Somali force from the palace with three hundred new troops trained in Sudan. My mission was to capture the Bakara Market," says General Abdullahi Anod, the head of government forces at Villa Somalia.[13] But it took his force three days to even reach the edge of the market, just two miles north of the palace. The drive amounted to nothing, and TFG casualties were steep: fifteen killed, sixty wounded, according to Anod. Among those killed was his deputy, Colonel Ahmed Doha, shot in the head by an Al-Shabaab sniper.

The frustration, or perhaps desperation, led the TFG and Sheikh Sharif to make some decisions that most outsiders would regard as dangerous, if not utterly foolish. On July 1, Sheikh Sharif visited a frontline area in northern Mogadishu to meet with the troops and, hopefully, inspire them to fight. The president came dressed for action, wearing brown military fatigues, a black flak jacket, and at one point, a strapped-on AK-47 rifle. Tempting fate, he climbed on top of an AMISOM tank, though he was cautious enough not to take part in actual fighting. He returned to the palace unharmed.[14]

Encouraged, TFG generals sent him out again the following month, this time in hopes of forcing AMISOM soldiers to move beyond their bases and the TFG sites they shielded. "We told the president that since AMISOM is mandated to protect him, he should go to the front lines," says General Anod.[15] By "go," Anod means "stay"—he wanted the president to base himself near the action. So Sheikh Sharif allowed himself to be placed in a bunker underneath the Jubba Hotel, a bombed-out, five-story structure located about a mile east of the palace, in the Shangani district. According to Anod, the strategy worked—Ugandan AU soldiers followed the president and helped the army clear out Islamist fighters from several nearby locations, including the former Police Transport Building.

But the tactic nearly backfired. In mid-August, Al-Shabaab launched a heavy attack on the hotel. This time, according to former defense minister Fiqi, Sheikh Sharif took part in the fighting and was riding in a tank that fell into one of Al-Shabaab's tank-swallowing trenches. "He was very close to being killed," Fiqi says.[16] The president survived, Fiqi says, only because the army rushed more tanks to the scene and evacuated him before he was shot or taken captive.

Such was the life of Somalia's president in 2010. It was not Sheikh Sharif's first brush with death by enemy means, and it would not be his last.

~

The incident that would trigger the end of the stalemate happened not on the front lines or the palace, nor any of the Somali towns and villages where Al-Shabaab was tirelessly imposing its harsh version of Sharia. It occurred in Uganda's capital, Kampala, on a hot July day where most people were focused on an event more than a thousand miles away from the wreckage of Somalia's endless war.

July 11, 2010, marked the first World Cup final played on the African continent. More than eighty-four thousand fans packed Soccer City stadium in Johannesburg for the match between Spain and the Netherlands. Around the world, a record TV audience estimated at 910 million viewers tuned in. Many of those watching were in soccer-crazed Africa, where the match unfolded in prime-time evening hours. In Kampala, Uganda, as elsewhere, bars, restaurants, and other establishments showing the game did brisk business. Even without an African team in the final, fans were in a festive mood, revved up by the action on large-screen TVs, the specials on beer and alcohol that many places offered, and raucous crowds including both men and women. It was everything a young soccer fan could love—and everything that Al-Shabaab despised, in a country whose soldiers were at war with Shabaab every day.

The first suicide bomber blew himself up at the Ethiopian Village, a popular Kampala restaurant, during halftime of the match. Fifteen people were killed. An hour later, at the ninetieth minute of the match, another suicide bomber and an IED exploded at the Kyadondo rugby club, which was hosting a World Cup party. Another sixty people died, with dozens more wounded.

Investigations by Ugandan police eventually revealed a complex plot involving Al-Shabaab members operating out of Somalia, Kenya, and Uganda. The mastermind, a thirty-three-year-old Ugandan, Issa Ahmed Luyima, had gone to Somalia the year before, joined Al-Shabaab, and taken part in combat missions against AU forces in Mogadishu. By his own accounts—offered in court and in a news conference organized by the police—Luyima recruited the bombers, smuggled in suicide vests from Somalia, and scouted potential targets with the help of his brother. The plan was carried out after he had sneaked into Kenya, where he was arrested a few days after the blasts.

A Ugandan court would eventually sentence Luyima and four accomplices to life in prison.

Suspicion had fallen immediately on Al-Shabaab, and the group put any doubts to rest on July 12 when Ali Dhere spoke to reporters in Mogadishu. "We warned Uganda not to deploy troops to Somalia; they ignored us," he said. "We warned them to stop massacring our people, and they ignored that. The explosions in Kampala were only a minor message to them. . . . We will target them everywhere if Uganda does not withdraw from our land."[17]

Godane released a rare audio message a few days later casting the attack as retaliation for the many times AU troops had launched mortars into Mogadishu neighborhoods. "What happened in Kampala is just the beginning," he said. "We are telling all Muslims and particularly the people of Mogadishu that those martyred in AMISOM shelling will be avenged."[18]

From Shabaab's militant perspective, the attack may have made a kind of sense—you kill Muslim civilians, we retaliate. An eye for eye, a tooth for a tooth. Get out unless you want us to spill more blood. What Shabaab leaders seemed not to consider was the possibility that Uganda might react by doubling down on its fight in Somalia. President Yoweri Museveni was facing a reelection campaign, trying to extend his twenty-four years in power. His human rights record was under assault by groups like Amnesty International, but the United States and other Western nations gave him tacit support because he was a reliable ally in the "war on terror." He had every reason to keep his troops in the heart of Mogadishu.

"The day he decides to pull his troops because of deaths in Kampala, then Museveni is very weak," says analyst Roland Marchal. "Internally, that would have become a political issue. And the Americans—he got protected because of his role in countering terrorism. So if he gives that up, who is he? An old chap, a dictator who doesn't want to leave power, who uses a hammer to get rid of opposition."[19] Disposable, in other words.

In late 2009, Ugandan officials had threatened to remove their troops unless the TFG started to stabilize the country. But after the attacks, Museveni sounded a much more determined note. "We were just in Mogadishu to guard the port, the airport, and the State House," he said four days after the blasts. "Now they have mobilized us to look for them. We are going to go on the offensive [against] all those who did this."[20]

~

What Museveni likely didn't know was that his foes in Somalia would launch their own offensive first.

On the morning of August 23, the twelfth day of Ramadan, Mogadishu residents listening to their radios heard the strident voice of Al-Shabaab spokesman Ali Dhere come over the air. He was not reading out a press statement. Instead, he issued a call to arms, a fiery declaration of war against AMISOM and the TFG—or as Dhere referred to them, the Christians and the apostates. He argued these parties had violated Somalia's territory and dignity and were "massacring our children and women every day." Dhere said the new offensive was named *Nihayat Al-Mu'tadin*, or "The End of the Aggressors," and asserted that it would finish the war over Mogadishu once and for all.

In his Mogadishu home, Mohamed Olad Hassan listened with professional interest.[21] Hassan, a then thirty-three-year-old native Somali, was the local correspondent for the Associated Press and the BBC. He had covered Somalia's incessant conflict since 2003, staying in the country despite repeated threats to his life, a 2007 shrapnel wound from an explosion near his house, and a searingly close brush with death in Al-Shabaab's 2009 suicide bombing at the Shamo Hotel. He survived the latter event by pure luck. Like other reporters, Hassan was in the hotel ballroom that day to cover the graduation of Mogadishu medical students. Mid-ceremony, he left his seat for a moment to move his recorder closer to the podium. When he got back, he found that a Radio Shabelle reporter had taken his chair. Unperturbed, Hassan simply claimed the seat to the left. Less than five minutes later, the bomber set off his explosives. Hassan was knocked unconscious by flying debris but woke up a few minutes later. The reporter who had taken his seat, Mohamed Amin, was killed instantly, one of twenty-five fatalities in the room.

Hassan says Al-Shabaab used intimidation to get Dhere's speech on the majority of Mogadishu radio outlets. "There were radio stations that pretended they were independent, but they worked with Al-Shabaab," he says.[22] Speaking over this ad hoc jihadist network, Dhere cast the offensive as a national duty, to be supported not only by Al-Shabaab's frontline fighters but

Somalis everywhere, of every age, economic status, and clan. "I tell all the Muslim people, you have been called upon to this offensive," he said. "Come and join, all of you, so that later on, no one group can claim success on its own, so that it belongs to all those who took part. You can participate with wealth, life, experience, and opinion, whatever you have. . . . I urge you to follow these words and rally around us in order to keep Allah's word high." It was almost as if Dhere was giving a nationwide address, trying to unify Somalia under an umbrella of jihad and violence.

The announcement was not a total surprise. The militants had been flexing their muscles again: in mid-August Al-Shabaab banned three international aid agencies[23] on charges that they tried to spread Christianity, while Hizbul Islam rounded up one hundred men in Mogadishu who failed to shave their mustaches and grow beards in line with the group's latest edict.[24] Then there was the blast that leveled a house in the Bar Ubah neighborhood on the night of August 20. It turned out to be a premature car bomb explosion inside an Al-Shabaab "factory." According to the government, ten Al-Shabaab operatives were killed, seven of them foreigners—three Pakistanis, two Indians, an Afghan, and an Algerian.[25]

But the basic decision to attack, to launch another arduous, expensive, bloody assault in hopes of taking down the government—that struck many observers as unwise. The military situation in Mogadishu had not changed. The TFG was still weak and internally divided, but AMISOM remained firmly in control of the sites that mattered—the palace, the airport, the seaport, and Maka al-Mukarama Road. In fact, AMISOM's hand grew stronger a few days before the offensive as several hundred new Ugandan soldiers began to arrive, boosting the AU force's troop strength to 6,100.[26] More would arrive the first week in September, giving AMISOM a force of seven thousand.

Al-Shabaab had built huge new stocks of guns and ammunition for the offensive—some bought from arms dealers in the Bakara Market, some purchased from unpaid TFG soldiers who were still willing to give up bullets that could slay them in exchange for money that allowed them to eat. But the group continued to lack the vehicles and firepower to match AMISOM's tanks and armored personnel carriers. Mukhtar Robow says Al-Shabaab sent letters to Al-Qaeda seeking help in this department, for "something that makes a hole in the tank." He says Al-Qaeda wrote back "but Godane did not show us their response."

On the manpower front, Al-Shabaab was still receiving a steady supply of fighters from its training camps, but observers noted that an increasing number of them were boys between the ages of eleven and seventeen—child soldiers, illegal under international law. Some enlisted for upfront payments, usually in the $200 to $250 range, while others were coerced into joining or simply whisked away against their will. One woman explained to Human Rights Watch how Al-Shabaab seized her twelve-year-old son and fourteen-year-old nephew: "One day [my son] did not come home from the madrassa. I went to the school and asked for him. Then my son called me. He said, 'Mom, I am in Kismayo. I was taken by Al-Shabaab to be recruited to fight. Please pray for my release.' I have not heard from him since. I do not know if he is alive or dead. My brother's young son was taken as well. My brother went to find them. I was told Al-Shabaab hanged him because he was looking for the boys."[27]

In some cases, children were pressed into Al-Shabaab *by* their families. As one woman explained: "My husband was in Al-Shabaab. He came and said to my eldest son [age ten], 'You must also join. He overpowered me and took my son. Later I heard my son died in the war. I went to where my husband was, Horera mosque. . . . He said, 'I am pleased to inform you that our son died a martyr. He went straight to paradise. He showed me footage he took of my son being killed in the war. His blood. His body."[28]

In terms of military strength, the use of child soldiers was somewhat counterbalanced by the hundreds of experienced foreign fighters working with Al-Shabaab. But the presence of these men turned off not only Somali civilians but also exacerbated tensions among Shabaab members, many of whom felt the foreigners should not play such a prominent role in Somali affairs. "It's an ongoing problem in those kind of organizations," says analyst Roland Marchal. "You have foreign fighters but as soon as they become numerous enough, they want to get a share in the authority, in the leadership, and this can't be allowed. Because if you are not a global jihadi you say, 'This is my country, and I'm going to fight for it. I'm going to make the decision. I'm not going to argue with a Lebanese, a Saudi, or a Kenyan.'"[29]

Robow says that shortly before the offensive, he met with two representatives of Godane—Farhan Kahiye and Bashir Mohamed Mohamud, better known as Qorgab—and counseled caution. "I advised them that if you want to enter war," says Robow, "we have to unite Shabaab, Hizbul Islam and other scholars, intellectuals, businessmen and others who are on the outside. . . . We need that agreement, then we will be a force and we may not need go into a big war." He says the Godane camp disagreed. "They said, 'We are at the gates of the palace, one office cannot take a letter to another'"— meaning that government officials risked being shot even moving within the walls of Villa Somalia. All Al-Shabaab had to do was climb the hill to the palace, they argued. Robow says he remained unconvinced.[30] Ultimately, though, he agreed to take part in the offensive.

AMISOM said it was ready for whatever Al-Shabaab had in store. It was no accident that on the same day Dhere announced the offensive, AMISOM's deputy political chief Wafula Wamunyinyi exuded confidence at a news conference in Nairobi. "We are going to expand and move the insurgents out of Mogadishu," he said. "We will make major, major strides."[31]

Declarations made, the battle commenced within a few hours of Dhere's speech. Shells began raining down on the Bakara Market around 3 p.m., terrifying shoppers who were buying food to break the daily Ramadan fast. Simultaneously, Shabaab fighters seized control of a Mogadishu radio station, Radio Holy Quran, and attacked military barracks in the capital's Hodan, Hawlwadag, and Bondhere districts. Ambulances were soon racing to pick up dozens of dead and wounded, dodging incoming shells and raging gun battles on the streets.[32] Mogadishu had experienced years of gruesome violence, but never anything like this. In Mohamed Olad Hassan's estimation, the intensity of the fighting topped even that of the Ethiopian-Shabaab clashes in March 2007, which destroyed entire neighborhoods. The AMISOM troops, he says, drew motivation from their belief that no one would attempt to rescue them should they lose the battle. "The African Union soldiers—they were desperate to defend themselves, not just defend the government. They had nowhere to run. They could not retreat or evacuate. If they backed up, where would they go?"[33]

"There is not one area of the capital that is safe today," a local civil society worker told a reporter. "We are getting reports of dead bodies on most of the major roads of the city. They are determined to kill what is left of [Mogadishu]. Who will they rule if we are all dead? Whoever wins will rule corpses."[34]

A local journalist reported: "It is extremely dangerous to go out or even stay in. It feels as if the whole city is on fire."[35]

The next day, August 24, was worse. The Muna Hotel was a popular spot for officials living in or visiting Mogadishu. The old building had crumbling walls and a garish aqua-green paint job but was inexpensive, within TFG territory, and employed its own security guards. A pair of guards were stationed at the entrance when two men in TFG fatigues approached at about 11 a.m. According to a witness, they were bragging of having beaten some rebels. The security guards smiled and asked to hear more—only to receive a hail of bullets from the "soldiers," who were actually trained Shabaab Amniyat fighters. The gunmen charged inside and opened fire in the small lobby, killing four and wounding others. Then they climbed the stairs and began moving from room to room, shooting at anyone they found. Some guests jumped off second- and third-floor balconies to escape; others fought back with their own guns. Real TFG soldiers soon arrived, adding to the volume of flying bullets. The shootout finally ended after about an hour, when the attackers ran out of ammunition. Cornered on an upper floor, the men detonated suicide vests and blew themselves up.

Stunned police and rescuers spent the rest of the day tramping through pools of blood, sifting through piles of debris and fallen plaster, tallying up the casualties. The death toll of thirty-three was a shock in itself. But the TFG had also lost six members of parliament and five security personnel, in addition to the twenty-two civilians killed. Never had the militants wiped out so many members of the government in a single stroke. Al-Shabaab quickly claimed responsibility, saying the assault was the work of "special forces." One of the assailants turned out to be a sixteen-year-old boy who had worked as a bodyguard for Mukhtar Robow.[36]

The hotel assault, deadly as it was, was only a body blow to the TFG. That night, Al-Shabaab went for the neck, making a new attempt to cut off Muka al-Mukarama Road. Hassan says that around 7 p.m., soon after dark, more than seven hundred Shabaab soldiers launched an attack aimed at seizing a section of road about two-thirds of a mile from the presidential palace. Opposing them, holding the position, were hundreds of Ugandan AMISOM troops and a smaller number of TFG fighters, some of them army troops, others part of pro-government militias. The resulting battle was possibly the bloodiest in Mogadishu history.

Hassan says Shabaab fighters unleashed all available weapons on the AMISOM line—"machine guns, rocket-propelled grenades, bombs, everything they could find." The AMISOM/TFG troops took cover behind concrete barriers and struck back with their own guns, tanks, and artillery. Fierce, close-range fighting took place in small streets and alleyways that branched off the main road. "One of [the Shabaab fighters] told me at that time that in an alley six meters (about 19½ feet) wide, there could be three hundred or four hundred soldiers fighting," Hassan says. "That could be the cause of the large number of deaths. They were packed into a small space."[37]

The exchanges intensified throughout the evening and into the early hours of Wednesday, August 25. Shabaab forces, moving north to south, crept closer to the road, and at some point during the night AMISOM troops retreated—though not very far. Sheikh Osman, a pro-government militia commander, described the retreat as "military tactics." Hassan elaborates: "Shabaab got within fifty meters [about 165 feet] of the road. AMISOM got a suspicion they would be trapped in the road. They went to the other side, so they would be clear [have a clear view] of whatever is coming. But they were still facing them. They retreated, but they did not give up control of the road."[38]

In an interview not long before he was killed in October 2015, Somali army chief General Abdirkarim Dhagabadan described the retreat as less organized. "No one knew where to go or hide," he said. "It was fire and explosions. They brought in lots of men from Bakara Market; we were facing new fighters every minute, and they pushed us back."[39]

Al-Shabaab commanders saw the developments as a victory, and in the early hours of the 25th, Abdiaziz Abu-Mus'ab, the group's military operations spokesman, proclaimed it as such. "Thanks to Allah, we have killed many soldiers and the mujahideen fighters are now in full control of their last strongholds," he said in a statement released to Somali media. "The apostate government and its Christian masters were controlling only one of the four main roads in Mogadishu and with the assistance of Allah's power, our fighters cut off that road today and the enemy cannot move between their positions."[40]

But his claim, iffy at best during the nighttime battle, crumbled completely at dawn. Fresh AMISOM and TFG troops reinforced their colleagues, bringing in more tanks. The sides blasted away at each other for another two hours before the Shabaab units—fatigued, thinned-out by casualties, and ultimately outgunned—fell back around 8 a.m., leaving Maka al-Mukarama Road in government hands.

No one could have known it at the time, but Al-Shabaab, despite many future attacks on the road and the presidential palace, would never come so close to overrunning the Somali government again.

AMISOM and TFG soldiers knew the battle could have turned out differently. "They came close tonight," army officer Issa Ali told a reporter, "but behind us are AMISOM tanks and at last we drove them away."[41]

Hassan says he went to the site of the clash later that day and found "huge destruction"—bullet holes everywhere, fallen trees, knocked-down telephone poles, and a burning building pumping out smoke that covered the area like an early morning fog. There weren't many people around, but there were plenty of dogs, chewing on the remains of the dead. Hassan took note of where the corpses were located: "on the north side of the road, where the militants were coming from." He says he personally counted about sixty bodies; friends and colleagues told him that more were strewn across the streets of nearby neighborhoods.

Neither Al-Shabaab nor AMISOM ever released casualty figures from the battle, but Hassan says he heard estimates from officials: seventy soldiers killed on the AMISOM side and some 250 deaths for Al-Shabaab.

Al-Shabaab's strength was not exhausted, and the next few days were marked by intense, seesaw clashes around the city. On the twenty-seventh, Al-Shabaab seized an Ahlu Sunna Wal Jama'a base in the Hodan district in heavy fighting. TFG forces recaptured it two days later. On the morning of the twenty-eighth, Shabaab fighters briefly succeeded in taking Dabka Junction. "We are getting weaker and weaker every day," a TFG commander lamented to a *Washington Post* reporter.[42] But within three hours, AMISOM forces arrived in armored personnel carriers affixed with large machine guns. The soldiers blasted away at the Shabaab fighters until they retreated and then took up positions at the intersection behind quickly erected concrete barriers.

At the height of the battles, Al-Shabaab was publicly lauded by a fellow jihadist group based in Iraq, though few paid attention.[43] Islamic State would loom much larger on Al-Shabaab's horizon five years in the future.

Still another threat to the TFG had materialized on August 25, when Shabaab fighters took over an E-shaped, three-story secondary school in the Wardhigley District. The 15 May school wasn't a military target per se, but its location begged capture. One arm of the school was located a mere 150 feet—less than half a football field—from the edge of the Villa Somalia compound. The distance from the school to the actual presidential palace was just 850 feet. In other words, Al-Shabaab had seized an elevated building within shooting range of the TFG's headquarters—and the TFG was in trouble like never before.

Al-Shabaab wasted no time in taking advantage of its new position at the school. "They mounted a heavy machine gun called a DSHK, a Soviet-made weapon, on top of it, and snipers fired and targeted people in the presidential palace," says General Abdullahi Anod. The TFG's immediate response was to call in AMISOM, which positioned a Ugandan tank outside the palace walls to fire at the school. Each time the Shabaab force on the roof began shooting, Anod says, the tank would fire salvos in return until the attacks came to a halt. It wasn't a perfect solution, as the tank's straight gun turret could only hit targets on the edge of the roof. But it was enough to keep the shooting down to a manageable level.

On August 30, Al-Shabaab fired mortar shells at Villa Somalia, missing the president but killing four Ugandan AMISOM soldiers. Shiekh Sharif sent out a new appeal for help, although its tone was odd, almost as if the president was speaking about a country other than his own. "It is quite impractical to expect Somalia alone to contain the evil Al-Qaeda/Al-Shabaab alliance, as Somalia is emerging from twenty years of destruction and chaotic political environment," he said. "Since terrorism has become a borderless threat, the Somali government is renewing its plea for urgent international support."

Despite the calm tenor, the TFG was clearly in peril again. According to General Anod, it was around this time that Sheikh Sharif received an offer from Yoweri Museveni which could have ended the battle in Mogadishu for good. "The Ugandan commander [Mugisha] brought a message to the president from the Ugandan president," Anod recalls, "saying that he is ready to evacuate him, the prime minister, and the speaker of parliament to Kampala."[44] In short, he was ready to help them flee Somalia—and prepared to let the TFG collapse.

For a short time, says Anod, Sheikh Sharif and his military chiefs discussed the idea. "The president consulted with us," he says. "I told him he will be just like Mohamed Siad Barre—if he leaves Villa Somalia, that will be the end of his reign. I told him if he accepts, Al-Shabaab will take over the palace, the clan militias will disperse, the politicians will flee, and people from the diaspora who are working with the government will flee the country. Other commanders told him the same. They told him if Uganda wants to do something for him, they should defend him here in the palace."

Sheikh Sharif agreed with the military men. "He was not going to accept [the offer]; he turned it down," Anod says.[45]

Hassan says he heard a similar story from a government spokesman named Abdullahi. "He told me that they were thinking about moving out of the presidential palace, but they didn't get the last order from the president. He insisted on staying in the position."[46]

In a brief, testy phone interview in 2015, Sheikh Sharif denied that he considered fleeing the palace. "That is not true," he said. AMISOM officials declined to be interviewed for this book.[47]

What is certain is that Sheikh Sharif continued to have a dangerous existence, living and working inside the palace compound while combat raged around its walls. He would live this way for months to come, knowing he could be felled at any minute by a random shell, a sniper's bullet, or attacks from other, unexpected sources.

～

Political tension, not military carnage, held center stage as evening fell in the Somali capital on September 20, 2010. A power struggle between President Sheikh Sharif and Prime Minister Sharmarke over a proposed new constitution had reached the breaking point, and Sharmarke was preparing to resign the next day. Some Somalis thought that Sheikh Sharif should go too: twenty months into his presidency, conditions in Somalia had not improved in the slightest. His government remained bloated, corrupt, and dysfunctional; Al-Shabaab and Hizbul Islam still controlled most of Somalia south of Puntland; there were still no basic government services; and soldiers were still only occasionally paid.

Maybe it was talk of the political situation that caused soldiers posted at Villa Somalia's main gate that night to let down their guard. Maybe it was a bribe, the money making up for all the missing paychecks. Perhaps the soldiers had been chewing khat and just didn't care. In any case, when a convoy carrying AMISOM troops passed through the wrought iron gate, the soldiers did nothing to stop a slim young man carrying an AK-style assault rifle from jumping on the back of one of the trucks.

Protocol called for the truck to stop at three checkpoints inside the walls, each manned by AMISOM troops. The stowaway made it through at least one, possibly two, for reasons that were never explained. By the third, either because of detection or by his own choice, he made his presence known. He dashed off the truck, running into an open area of the compound between the offices of the president, the prime minister, and the interior and security minister. He fired off shots from his rifle, wounding two guards. He threw a hand grenade, causing an explosion but no damage or casualties.

And then he was shot. One bullet struck the right side of his head. Within a few minutes, he was dead.

Officials rushed over to examine the gunman's body. It didn't take long to recognize him—it was Dalha Ali, a.k.a. Asad Yare, the former Shabaab fighter turned bodyguard for Interior Minister Omar. Had he come back to kill Omar? The president? The soon to be ex-prime minister? There was no way to know. Officials recognized that the damage could have been much worse—they found him wearing a suicide vest that had not exploded.

A Somali news site posted a photo of Ali's body online the next day. The picture, taken at close range, shows his body lying faceup on the brown patterned tiles of a floor. Blood from the wound near his right temple has trickled across his cheek and forehead, forming lines that look like bright-red tiger stripes. More blood has pooled on the floor behind him. His right eye, mostly closed, looks down and off to the right, while his left eye remains wide open, gazing straight ahead. If not for all the blood, a casual viewer might conclude the subject is alive and staring defiantly at the camera, in a manner that says, "You looking at me?"

But he wasn't alive. He was dead at age twenty-two, four years and five months after jumping into the life of an Islamist militant.

One could argue that Ali had achieved what he declared himself "ready" to do in 2006, to become a martyr. But that came before so many things happened . . . before his days of prayer and study became a distant memory . . .

before his enemy evolved from warlords to Ethiopians to fellow Somalis . . . before he went from being a mere foot soldier to a trained assassin . . . before he viewed Al-Shabaab as killing people for arbitrary, baseless reasons . . . before he felt so bad about himself . . . before he felt imprisoned in his own life.

If given the chance to go back, to choose a different path, it's possible this bright young man wouldn't have been so ready to die.

ELEVEN

WITHDRAWAL

DALHA ALI'S ATTACK ON THE presidential palace symbolized the Ramadan Offensive for Al-Shabaab: grand plans, audacious strikes, but in the
end, no results. The pushes to capture Maka al-Mukarama Road and TFG/
AMISOM bases came to naught. A suicide attack at the airport September
9 killed a few soldiers and civilians but accomplished nothing strategically. An attempted truck bombing at the seaport two days later fizzled when
guards shot out the vehicle's tires. Day after day of gun battles and artillery
exchanges left scores of people dead, but brought no gains in terms of territory, arms, or popular support. On September 17, the government declared
that TFG and AMISOM forces had "successfully repulsed" the offensive.[1]
Although Ali attacked the palace three days later, and fighting continued in
Mogadishu as always, Al-Shabaab's spokesmen did not reject or laugh off
the government's claim. It was essentially true.

The failure of the offensive provoked the biggest leadership crisis yet in
Al-Shabaab and its partner, Hizbul Islam. Leaders in both groups questioned the decision making of Godane, none more so than Shabaab's deputy leader, Mukhtar Robow. The two men had rarely—if ever—been on the
same page strategically. Robow believed in working with the clans; Godane
talked down to them. Robow wanted Shabaab to have good ties with Al-
Qaeda; Godane pushed for the groups to formally merge. Tension between

them first became public in May 2009, when Godane ousted Robow as Al-Shabaab's spokesman and replaced him with Ali Dhere. The strain had grown in the sixteen months since, as Robow—a moderate by Al-Shabaab standards—voiced objections to the Hotel Shamo bombing, the bans on foreign aid agencies, and the group's general direction.[2]

But it was the Ramadan Offensive that made Robow take a stand. Al-Shabaab and Hizbul Islam suffered heavy losses in the campaign—five hundred to seven hundred dead, according to multiple sources—and a hefty portion of those killed were fighters from southern Somalia affiliated with Robow and his Rahanweyn clan. Their deaths said a lot about Al-Shabaab's internal politics and priorities. Observers noted that Robow's fighters had manned the front lines during most of the campaign, while foreigners and Somalis from other regions kept a safe distance. ("When we are fighting here, the foreigners are a bit in the rear," one Ugandan Shabaab commander told CNN.[3]) There were also reports that at the height of the offensive, Shabaab's Amniyat force deliberately shot wounded fighters, including some commanders, ostensibly so they would die and achieve martyrdom. Reporter Mohamed Olad Hassan says he believes the Amniyat killed the fighters so they wouldn't be captured and hand over secrets. But many suspected that in actuality, the Amniyat was settling scores for Godane. Among the not-quite-voluntary martyrs was one of Robow's top aides, Sheikh Ayub.

For Robow, these deaths were the last straw. On or about October 1, he pulled his thousand-plus men from Mogadishu and sent them home to the Bay and Bakool regions. The loss of manpower was quickly noticed. "Residents say whip-wielding militants are no longer patrolling through the city's biggest market," one news agency reported.[4]

For the next week, Al-Shabaab appeared on the verge of a split and a military collapse. Robow reportedly demanded major changes in Al-Shabaab, including the resignation of Godane as emir, the disbanding of the Amniyat, and an end to the ban on foreign aid agencies. Face-to-face negotiations between Godane and Robow failed to resolve the impasse. Ibrahim al-Afghani, who supported Godane, was quoted as saying, "Mukhtar Robow is a transgressor. He is a tribalist. He is nothing. Let him leave." Robow apparently considered doing just that, holding talks with Hassan Dahir Aweys about forming a new militant group to oppose Al-Shabaab. TFG and AMISOM forces, meanwhile, flipped to the offensive and captured new positions in Mogadishu, including a hotel and a former military hospital near the Bakara Market. The TFG's information minister, Abdurrahman Osman, sensing an opportunity, called on fighters in Al-Shabaab and Hizbul Islam to switch sides. "We are ready to work with our brothers in these groups provided they renounce the use of violence," he said.[5]

Somehow, Al-Shabaab leaders papered over their differences, with Godane remaining as emir, and Robow sent his men back to the capital, stabilizing the military situation. Robow also went on a PR tour of sorts, speaking at two Mogadishu mosques to deny the reports of a rift in the Islamist militant camp. "We are telling our leader, Sheikh Osama bin Laden, that your students in Somalia are still united," he declared. "There is no split among them, contrary to what was propagated by the TFG and the enemies of Somalia."[6]

But his words left few convinced. The discontent and divisions within the militant ranks could not be swept under the rug.

The date is unclear, but at some point in the second half of 2010, Robow lost his influence in Al-Shabaab's military operations. The change affected Al-Shabaab's relationship with the clans and was a big blow to both troop morale and military capacity, says Mohamed Jama. "That's when the supplies diminished and the enthusiasm decreased," he says. Jama says Robow was close to certain foreigners, in particular Khattab Al-Masry and Omar Hammami, two men he says led a quick reaction force that would bolster the front lines. Without Robow, the unit didn't function, and "the lack of this unit was a big setback in the fighting."[7]

Meanwhile, relations between Al-Shabaab and Hizbul Islam were getting worse. Trust between the two supposed allies was so low that they could not fight side by side against their common enemy.

"One day at around 2 p.m. on a Friday, just after Friday prayers, we agreed to attack the government jointly," says Hizbul Islam's Hassan Mahdi. He says the group launched a heavy assault from the Sana'a district and reached Bayhani junction and a cinema near Karan junction. Only one problem— Al-Shabaab never joined the fighting. The Hizbul Islam fighters were pushed back. "The next morning we met Al-Shabaab and asked them why they didn't show up," Mahdi says. Shabaab didn't explain why but said they were ready to fight that day. "So we launched another massive attack and took over Hotel Global. [But] late in that afternoon we were again driven back to Sana'a."[8]

Mahdi says Shabaab leaders were never happy to see another Islamist force in Somalia and repeatedly tried to persuade or coerce their Hizbul Islam counterparts into merging the two groups under Al-Shabaab's banner. Hizbul Islam leaders were not totally opposed. "We were discussing unity. We even said to them, 'Take the chairman of the new unity organization,'" Mahdi says. "We discussed with them the possibility of taking the name Hizbul Islam or another name, but they refused because they want to be the only one to exist. That was the base of the differences. They planned that they will be the only power. We met about five times and every time they were trying to take over our soldiers and our weapons."[9] He says one set of talks in August 2010 fell apart when Shabaab, acting unilaterally, launched the *Nihayat Al-Mu'tadin*.

Al-Qaeda encouraged Al-Shabaab to be flexible. Senior Al-Qaeda leader Atiyah Abd Al-Rahman wrote to Godane: "Perhaps there is no objection for you to give up on changing the name, for example, changing the name of Harakat Al-Shabaab al-Mujahidin and they can keep their name; however a new name would be selected for the union. If you would somewhat yield in the matter of their involvement in the administration, the leadership would be your responsibility in its entirety." He added, "[Even] if all negotiations were to fail with them, do not cut a helping thread. If they were not on your side, the least you could do is to ensure they won't turn against you."[10]

Eventually, Al-Shabaab got what it wanted through politicking and force. As 2010 went on, Shabaab leaders persuaded various components of Hizbul Islam to switch their allegiance, including key Raskamboni Brigade commanders Hassan al-Turki and "Dulyadeyn," a man who would become prominent in Al-Shabaab's war against Kenya. Late in the year, Shabaab fighters attacked their erstwhile allies in Luq and Afgoye. Hizbul Islam fighters began to abandon their posts or pledge loyalty to Al-Shabaab. In mid-December Hassan Dahir Aweys finally bowed to the inevitable and agreed to a "merger" of his organization with Al-Shabaab, though most analysts correctly portrayed the development as the senior group swallowing its junior partner.

Aweys put the best possible face on the development, endorsing the merger at a public rally in Afgoye attended by Shabaab spokesman Ali Dhere and propaganda chief Fuad Shongole. "I am pleased to witness the unity of Al-Shabaab and Hizbul Islam. I urge all Islamist fighters and all Muslims to join the war," Aweys said.[11]

Mahdi, who remained active in the insurgency, says only about 10 percent of Hizbul Islam's personnel joined Al-Shabaab "for real." But Godane and his allies in Al-Shabaab now had what they wanted—unchallenged leadership of the jihadist movement in Somalia. Now they could turn their full attention to overthrowing the TFG. However, they would not be facing the same TFG as before.

—

For four years, both Al-Shabaab and the TFG had used the specter of foreigners influencing, dominating, abusing, and killing Somalis to paint the other side as a tool of wicked international interests. How ironic then that when President Sheikh Sharif needed a new prime minister in September 2010, he turned to a citizen of another country, a man living more than 7,700 miles away, who had roots in Somalia but had been gone so long that in many ways, he was alien to the land he was picked to lead.

At the time of his nomination, Mohamed Abdullahi Mohammed—better known by his nickname, Farmajo—resided in the northern US city of Buffalo and worked as a commissioner for equal employment at the New York State Department of Transportation. Farmajo was a native Somali, who was born in Mogadishu in 1962 and grew up in the southwestern Gedo region as part of the Marehan, a sub-clan of the Darod. But he had lived full-time in the United States since 1985, when he worked for the Somali foreign ministry and was posted to the Somali embassy in Washington. After four years there, Farmajo decided to steer clear of the growing upheaval back home and enrolled at the University of Buffalo. He went on to plant deep roots in the cold Rust Belt city, earning a history degree, gaining US citizenship, getting married, raising four children, and working for a succession of local governments. In time, he became a recognized leader of the Buffalo Somali community, which consisted of about three thousand immigrants and refugees, along with their children. He also wrote a dissertation on Somali politics and stayed in touch with friends back home, some of whom were part of the TFG and arranged for him to talk with Sheikh Sharif when the Somali president came to New York City in September 2010 to address the annual United Nations General Assembly.[12]

How any of this qualified him to be prime minister of war-ravaged, clan-riven Somalia was never well explained. But after a brief delay parliament approved him, and from the time he took office, Farmajo distinguished himself by forcing through reforms designed to give Somalis a government that worked. He named a cabinet of only eighteen ministers, down from thirty-nine in the previous government, and gave most of the posts to technocrats who had at least a general idea of what they were doing. He also limited foreign travel by officials, outlined a federal budget, and took other steps to reduce waste and corruption. The moves endeared him to Somalia's donors and to many ordinary Somalis, who were beyond fed up with governments that distinguished themselves only through robbery and ineptitude.

One of Farmajo's new appointees was a former diplomat in Washington, Abdihakim Mohamud Fiqi, as defense minister. Fiqi had no military experience. However, his diplomatic work put him a step up on his predecessor, a former peace activist nicknamed "Gandhi," who before entering politics had been an anthropologist and professor of geology. Upon assuming office in mid-November 2010, Fiqi quickly realized he was captain of an empty vessel. He had accepted the job knowing that Al-Shabaab occupied the Ministry of Defense in northwest Mogadishu and was using it as a logistics and command center. What he didn't know was that the TFG's "interim" ministry was useless as well. "The ministry had two rooms in the [privately owned] Jirda Hussein building. It had no Internet and no electricity," Fiqi says.[13] In addition, he learned, Al-Shabaab snipers targeted anyone who tried to go inside.

For Fiqi, this complicated the transfer of power. "I wanted the handover ceremony to take place at the ministry, but my predecessor said he never went there for security reasons. He said, 'Let's meet in the palace.' So we went to the palace and we held the ceremony in the living room of the Somali armed forces commander." Ceremony might be too strong a word for what actually took place. "We just shook hands," Fiqi says. "The minister said to me there is no document, there is no other property or wealth to hand over, there's no references, no transport, and there was nothing functional, and there you go—good luck!"[14]

The new administration's most urgent need was to strengthen the army. TFG soldiers had earned fresh disdain from AMISOM during the Ramadan fighting, when hundreds of them abandoned their positions during battles—sometimes because they ran out of ammunition, sometimes because they chose to flee rather than fight. There were multiple issues at play, including poor training, clan and political rivalries, and weak coordination between units. But Fiqi learned that the biggest problems remained pay and food, or the lack thereof. "I was called by the AMISOM commander Nathan Mugisha, who told me something heartbreaking," he says. "He said to me, 'I'm troubled by the situation of Somali forces who do not get a salary, who are not getting food. When my soldiers are having their lunches next to them, they're staring at them with needy eyes. [My soldiers] have to offer to share their lunch.' I was touched by this very deeply. The sacrifice Somali soldiers were making was great, and on the other hand, they don't get lunch, they don't have uniforms, they don't have boots, they don't have food or medicine, and even then they were ready to die in the front line."[15]

At the time Farmajo took office, most TFG soldiers had not been paid in four to six months, in part because of government corruption and bungling, and in part because the United States and Italy had withheld money meant for salaries rather than see it slide into the wrong pockets. The TFG managed to untangle the situation enough to get the funds flowing again, and troops began receiving paychecks in December 2010. The government then took additional steps to raise morale, such as arranging for the men to get medical care at private hospitals and paying soldiers' $100 monthly salaries to their families if they were killed. They also offered the troops a very African incentive plan. "We agreed to slaughter animals for them to eat when they make advances," Fiqi says.[16]

How to get those advances became the government's next order of business. Farmajo, Fiqi, and company came into office with one advantage over their predecessors, in that the TFG was no longer quite so close to death. Even before the Ramadan Offensive, AMISOM had begun using its increased manpower to set up several new bases around Mogadishu, including one near the busy K4 intersection and another on a hilltop that militants had previously used to fire on Villa Somalia. The failure of the Ramadan Offensive slowed down the fighting and allowed AMISOM troops to take effective control of a few more areas. Al-Shabaab could still target almost any part of the city with artillery or hit-and-run attacks, but the new AU bases hindered its movements and made it harder for the group to organize the kind of large-scale attacks that had put the TFG in jeopardy so many times.

In February 2011, AMISOM and TFG leaders held a strategy meeting in the parliament building. Those in attendance included TFG deputy army chief General Dhagabadan, AMISOM commander Mugisha, and Ugandan contingent commander Paul Lokech, who Fiqi calls "a brave man who was not afraid of going to the front lines." The sides initially had different ideas on how to recapture the city from Al-Shabaab. "Our commanders wanted to take large areas and large territory," says Fiqi. "AMISOM was against it, they suggested gradual advance and seizing areas we can control." After hours of discussion, the sides agreed to move in stages. "They were right because seizing an area you can't control is problematic," Fiqi says. "So we took baby steps. It would have been devastating [for morale] to occupy big areas and then lose [them]."[17]

Dhagabadan said the leaders also decided that TFG and AMISOM would need to attack from new directions. "Fighting them in the heart of the Hawlwadag and Bakara area was costing a lot of men and time," the general said.[18] He said the parties agreed on a new strategy of attacking Shabaab positions from both east and west of the capital, pushing toward the militants' main bases at Mogadishu Stadium and the Ministry of Defense.

It would not be easy. Al-Shabaab had lost some of its punch, but by employing unconventional tactics, the militants made it hard for their foes to advance. The system of tunnels and trenches the group had been constructing since 2007 was exploited to the fullest. "Al-Shabaab's best tactic was to get our attention fixed on the troops fighting above the ground while others beneath us came [up] to ambush us," says Fiqi.[19] In one attack from below, Shabaab nearly killed General Dhagabadan. Fighters shot out the tires of his vehicle and continued shooting as he scrambled for another car. The general survived, but several others around him were killed. Other times, AU and government troops found Al-Shabaab fighters to be active in areas that supposedly had been liberated. The fighters hadn't sneaked past checkpoints; they came up from holes in the ground.

General Anod says hidden trenches continued to devour AMISOM vehicles as well. Using their digging prowess, Shabaab would hollow out the ground beneath the street, he says; troops could walk over the road with no effect, but once heavy equipment like tanks rolled over, entire streets collapsed. "Tanks fall into the trench, the gun breaks off, everyone inside dies," he says.[20]

But as 2010 wound down and the new year began, AMISOM and the TFG gradually gained the upper hand over their foes. The combination of regularly paid TFG troops and the arrival of another one thousand Ugandan and Burundian soldiers finally gave the pro-government side a clear advantage in manpower. Morale improved, and AMISOM and the TFG were also exhibiting better coordination. "We asked the Ugandans to use snipers and target Al-Shabaab men who are reinforcing the front lines," says Anod. "They did that effectively. For instance, near Aden Adde [Road], when we attacked them from the ground, AMISOM snipers targeted them from high-rises."[21]

Keen observers saw the changes. A February 2011 analysis by the International Crisis Group noted that AMISOM had expanded its positions in Mogadishu. It said, "There are indications of an impending major military campaign to retake the city and then fan out to areas in southern and central Somalia." But the report downplayed prospects of success and held out little hope for the TFG, dismissing Farmajo's leaner cabinet as "impressive on paper" but unlikely to deliver on objectives like stabilizing the country or passing a new constitution. It suggested donors instead throw their support to local administrations that could govern better than the TFG. The report also contained a strong recommendation for AMISOM: "Do not attempt a major offensive unless an appropriate accompanying political strategy has been developed."[22]

For better or for worse, the TFG and AMISOM weren't listening. For more than a year, the government had been promising an offensive to oust Al-Shabaab from the parts of Mogadishu it controlled. D-Day finally arrived on Saturday, February 19, 2011, when AMISOM troops launched an attack on a mile-long stretch of Shabaab's tunnel-and-trench system in the Hawlwadag district. To hear AMISOM tell it, they hadn't known about the underground passages before this day. ("The discovery and closure of this tunnel is a major step forward in the stabilization effort in the city," said spokesman Barigye Ba-Hoku.[23]) In any case, the AU soldiers attempted to neutralize the system, firing heavily into the passages and destroying parts of it with armored bulldozers. Al-Shabaab fought back, and by the end of the weekend more than twenty people lay dead, the majority of them civilians. But suddenly Al-Shabaab's ability to move fighters and supplies around Mogadishu was severely hampered.

For the first time, AMISOM and the TFG exploited their momentum. Troops dislodged Shabaab fighters from the high school next to the palace, removing the threat of sniper attacks to those inside the compound. February 23 brought the breakthrough the TFG had been waiting for. In heavy fighting, TFG and Burundian troops advanced block-by-block up Industrial Road in northwest Mogadishu. By the end of the day they had captured three major bases from Al-Shabaab: the old Milk Factory, the former Officers Club, and the Defense Ministry.[24] For the government, the Defense Ministry compound was the biggest prize of all. Al-Shabaab was now denied one of its central command centers and staging areas for attacks. The guns on the roof could now be turned on Shabaab militants fighting in the front lines of Bakara Market and Villa Somalia.

The Burundians spearheaded the attack. Al-Shabaab estimated that seven hundred Burundian soldiers assaulted the Defense Ministry alone; Fiqi said fifty were killed. "They fought bravely and sacrificed their lives," he says.[25]

Shabaab officer Mohamed Jama remembers exactly where he was that day. "At around 7 a.m., I was in a seminar in Lafweyn Hotel. An officer walked in and said, 'We will continue the seminar another [day], there is fighting at the Defense Ministry. They broke the defenses.'"[26] In his role as military coordinator, Jama funneled men and weapons to the front line but says the Burundians kept fighting their way past trenches Al-Shabaab had dug into the road.

Jane's Terrorism and Security Monitor gave one of the few detailed descriptions of the battle: "Unable to use armored vehicles [because of the trenches], the Burundians carried out an infantry assault supported by artillery. Advancing from the southwest, they breached the compound and cleared the [Defense Ministry] building-by-building, during a day of intense fighting in which both sides suffered heavy casualties."[27] Afterward, according to Jane's, Shabaab forces still surrounded the ministry, but AMISOM forces broke the cordon after three days and armored personnel carriers brought supplies to the Burundians in the compound.

Hizbul Islam's Hassan Mahdi thinks the assault could have been prevented if at any time beforehand, Al-Shabaab had attacked the Jalle Siyad Military Academy, a complex on October 21st Road that the Burundians were using as a base. The academy was the reported launching pad for the operation. "Had we captured this base from them, we would have attacked Ex-Control [checkpoint], Kabka Factory, and it would have been difficult for them to attack the Defense Ministry," he says.[28] Why Al-Shabaab refused to attack the academy is not clear; it may have been another strategic blunder or simply an indication of the mistrust between Shabaab and Hizbul Islam.

The loss of the bases was a huge, almost fatal blow to Al-Shabaab's war strategy. Shabaab's leaders considered trying to retake the Defense Ministry, Mahdi says, but concluded the odds of success were low. "It was realized [a counterattack] would need two thousand men if seven hundred Burundians were defending the ministry," he says. "When you are on the offensive you need three times more men to attack one person in a defensive position. We did not have heavy weapons to destroy it completely."[29]

As February turned into March, suspicion spread like a virus in the Shabaab ranks as the group continued to lose key areas, such as Florence Junction in the Wardhigley district. Some commanders suspected their battle strategies were being leaked to the government. General Anod says that for some time, Shabaab leadership had been fearful of keeping the same fighters in one front line for more than a few hours. "Their militias would fight in three or four different lines in one day," he says.[30] The idea was to make sure the fighters did not set up regular contact with government military commanders, which could lead them to defect and surrender the position.

But unity and cohesion within the group were indeed breaking down, according to Jama. "It was the first time Al-Shabaab leaders suspected some among them were giving out information to the government," he says. "It was the first time Al-Shabaab set up prisons for people who were suspected of being spies, and Al-Shabaab mainly suspected [former] Hizbul Islam fighters. They were pointing fingers at them, especially the officials."[31]

The arrival of more AMISOM troops enabled another pro-TFG offensive beginning May 12, this one aimed at retaking the sprawling Bakara Market, a key source of tax revenue for the militants. Al-Shabaab lost its commander for the market on day three of the fighting and its commander for the Hawlwadag district on day four. On the 22nd, AMISOM seized the Wadnaha Road on the market's southern edge. The next day, another top commander, Abu Hubeyda, was killed as AMISOM seized the African Village area. When the offensive finally petered out a week later, the militants still held the market itself but most of the traders had closed their shops and fled the fighting, shutting off the flow of tax dollars to Al-Shabaab.

Al-Shabaab was further crippled at this time by a phenomenon that hit Somalis of every clan and political affiliation. 2010 had been a good year for Somalia in terms of rain, easing the country's seemingly perpetual food crisis. But 2011 developed into one of the hottest, driest years Somalia and the Horn of Africa had ever known. As early as February, humanitarian agencies began warning of a failed harvest; by June, food had grown so scarce that Somalis in rural areas were fleeing their villages en masse, herding into the cities or crossing the borders into eastern Ethiopia and northern Kenya. Stories of families abandoning stick-thin, dying children by the side of the road as they trudged toward refugee camps caught the world's attention and sparked a sizeable but late international aid campaign. Eventually, the United Nations declared a famine across six regions of Somalia and a humanitarian emergency in many others.

Al-Shabaab, as the preeminent authority in most of south-central Somalia, had the power to make the situation better for millions of Somalis. By all accounts, they made it worse. Distrust of foreign aid agencies was the key factor. "They were accusing the aid agencies of being spies; some were accused of working with the government," says an aid worker for a well-known Western relief organization.[32] As a result, the big agencies best equipped to help people, like CARE International and the UN World Food Program, were banned from distributing food and water. Smaller agencies allowed to operate had to fight their way through red tape. "You go to an office at 9 a.m. to get permission [to distribute food] and you do not get clearance," says the aid worker. In addition, at the height of the drought Al-Shabaab continued to demand that people pay zakat—taxes—on their livestock and farm produce. Then they spent the money on war or self-preservation instead of helping the population cope with the drought.

A study of the famine by the Feinstein Center at Tufts University contains accounts of people seemingly blocked from receiving aid by Al-Shabaab at every turn.[33] A livestock herder from the Bakool region reported:

> When we feel livelihood stress, we normally start charcoal burning which is not normally affected by either drought or rains. . . . But Al-Shabaab taxed charcoal production and we could not pay. . . . If we pay tax and increase the price, buyers will go to where there is no Al-Shabaab. . . . By May 2011, almost all of the livestock were dead and we first moved to Rabdhure town. Then we moved to Wajid in June. We received assistance from ACF [an aid organization], but it was later chased by Al-Shabaab.

A woman displaced from the Bay region:

> We moved to Dollo refugee camp because there was no aid coming because of Al-Shabaab. Only Al-Shabaab or those working for them were able to survive because they could access resources through taxation and intimidation. There were some Islamic organizations bringing some food and they handed it over to Al-Shabaab [who] take it for themselves.

And a farmer trying to reach Mogadishu:

> We jumped on a lorry. No one bothered us until we reached Shalambod, near Marka, where we were stopped by Al-Shabaab. They lectured us saying that it was [a] bad idea to take the children to a place where there were many Ugandan, Burundians, and other infidels. . . . Most of the people were afraid and didn't say anything but some people talked back to them, saying that they had nothing to eat and no one was coming to this area to help, so they had to take their children to where they can get help or else they will all die. . . . Others said that they sold everything they had, including their land and homes, and had no place to return to and asked, 'Where will we return to?' Al-Shabaab's reply was that this drought was brought upon us by God and he will take it away and help us.

Eventually, an estimated 260,000 Somalis died due to the drought and famine.

A new fissure opened among the Shabaab leadership as pressure mounted for the group to lift its bans on outside aid. The split fell along predictable lines: hard-liners like Godane insisted the bans stay in place, while relative moderates like Robow, whose home Bay region was hit extremely hard by the drought, wanted to let aid agencies do their job. The tug-of-war played out in statements from spokesman Ali Dhere. On July 6, Dhere announced the ban had been lifted and said aid groups should contact a special Shabaab committee set up to deal with the drought. But on the 21st, Dhere told a very different story, saying the ban was still in place. He also minimized the reports of catastrophe. "Yes, there is drought but conditions are not as bad as they say," he declared.[34]

Even in its weakened state, Al-Shabaab continued to carry out raids and suicide attacks. Some of these damaged the TFG—the group shot and killed airport official Omar Qaldaan on June 8, and killed Interior Minister Abdi Shakur Sheikh Hassan on June 10 with a suicide bomb blast inside his home. But assassinations could not replace the offensives of the past. The first week in June alone, AMISOM forces seized Mogadishu's Tarabunka Road, the entire Bondhere district, the Damanyo army camp, and neighborhoods in Wardhigley and Yaqshid. Ugandan Colonel Paul Lokech was bold enough to announce the militants had been pushed back from Villa Somalia and no longer posed a threat to the government seat. Looking back, General Dhagabadan didn't go that far but said fear was growing among Al-Shabaab fighters that their window to escape the city was closing. "This eased the pressure on the palace and Maka Al-Mukarama," he said.

Militarily, Al-Shabaab was growing more desperate. Somali media outlets reported throughout the spring that the group was resorting to more and more forced conscription of teenage or even younger boys to fill out its ranks. Shabaab even put out a call for elders to take up arms. Some actually did, leading to the spectacle of a few dozen old men, mostly in their sixties and seventies, marching through the town of Beledweyne with small arms that included spears, daggers, and bows and arrows. Two of the would-be soldiers were photographed mid-parade, both lugging assault rifles on shoulder straps while carrying large, black Al-Shabaab flags. The image might have been imposing, even fearsome, had it not been for the stoop in the men's shoulders, the age in their faces, or the fact that each man had dyed his beard flaming orange in an obvious effort to hide its true color—gray, or perhaps white.

On the evening on August 5, 2011, Mohamed Jama was commanding a unit on the front lines of the Yaqshid district, one of the parts of Mogadishu still largely under Al-Shabaab's control. The night started out like any other in the Somali capital. It was warm, in line with the equatorial heat; dark, due to the erratic power supply; and tense, with the potential for combat in the air. The potential turned to reality when Jama received an order for his men to push forward against a TFG position. They did, launching what Jama describes as a massive attack "with bullets flying everywhere."

The attack had barely ended when the night turned highly atypical. Jama's unit received a new order: abandon your positions.

"We were called and told to leave our bases and walk to a certain location," he recalls. "Previously we used to take vehicles to the front line and back. [This night] we were told to leave our bases and go to Suqa Xolaha or others, like myself, to Daynile camp."[35]

Jama was puzzled, but he and his men followed orders. As they walked, the fighters saw or heard about other Shabaab units who had received the same instructions and were now trekking through the streets to locations on the outskirts of Mogadishu. The men realized, to their astonishment, that it was a general retreat. Within a matter of hours, the areas that Al-Shabaab had fought so hard to capture and defend, at the cost of thousands of casualties, were given up. The remaining Shabaab bases in the city at Ifka Halane, Shirkole, the Pasta Factory, Maslah, Bakara Market, Taleh, KPP Junction, Ali Kamin, Black Sea, Hamar Bile, Hamar Jadid, and along Industrial Road . . . all vacated.

Jama and his unit spent the night walking to Daynile. In the morning, they met residents from the neighborhoods who gathered around them, seeking answers as to what was going on. "They asked if we were leaving them," Jama recalls. "We didn't know what to say to them—we were surprised too. We didn't know what was happening. We were in the middle of a project run by others."[36]

The "others" were Godane and his supporters, who had decided the costs of maintaining Al-Shabaab's strongholds in the capital were too great.

Before the pullout, Al-Shabaab still controlled about a third of Mogadishu. The group made sure to portray its move as a military decision rather than a retreat. "The mujahideen have completely vacated Mogadishu for tactical purposes," said spokesman Dhere. He said the group would change its "fighting strategy to hit-and-run attacks, where the mujahideen will attack on the spot wherever government and African Union forces are based."[37] Guerilla warfare, in other words. But Dhere mentioned nothing about plans or hopes to retake the city from the TFG and AMISOM. Al-Shabaab's ambition to take control of the Somali capital had been set aside.

It was a stunning turnaround. Government and AU forces could not believe that Al-Shabaab had pulled out. Soldiers took days to move into the abandoned bases, fearing they were booby trapped, or that the entire withdrawal was a setup for a massive counterattack.

But for Al-Shabaab insiders, the retreat was not much of a surprise.

"There were dead and wounded fighters every day, and [the battle] was difficult to sustain," says Zakariye Hersi. "Godane accepted that we [needed to] withdraw from Mogadishu. The military officials discussed it for about two weeks, and he took the final decision."[38]

"Military weakness was the reason," says Hassan Mahdi. He traces the defeat back to the loss of the Defense Ministry. "It forced [Al-Shabaab] to save their weapons and men after they lost the Defense Ministry, because their front lines were ambushed from behind and were caught in the middle of two government units."[39]

Mahdi also admits that eroding morale also played a part. "Morale failure comes when you do not advance from one position for almost a year to two years," he says. "The soldiers become tired. If you cannot realize your goals, you get disappointed; people start to question your objectives and what you're fighting for."

Talking to the media, Hassan Dahir Aweys said Al-Shabaab was simply outgunned: "We don't have tanks, and it's wrong to have face-to-face fighting with troops armed with tanks."[40]

For many ordinary citizens, the withdrawal was a huge relief. Says one Mogadishu media commentator, speaking on condition of anonymity, "Some of the residents listened to Ali Dhere saying it was a tactical withdrawal, but other people thought Al-Shabaab did not have the same power as two years earlier and there was lots of pressure on the leadership. Some even suggested the killing of bin Laden [in May 2011] morally affected their fighters. I was happy to see them leave the city and take their fighting outside."[41]

The chairman of a Muslim scholars' council, Sheikh Bashir Ahmed Salad, felt the same. "I urge them to leave other areas in the country they still occupy," he told the local media on the day of the withdrawal. "I welcome their withdrawal from Mogadishu. I think it will reduce the bloodshed, killings, displacement; it will bring back and public services."

Perhaps no one felt more relieved than one emergency medical worker who lived in the Hodan district in 2011. With Shabaab in the city, violence and stress never stopped, he says. "I was busy helping people and offering health care to the injured; my phone was ringing day and night. I never had the chance to see my children for days because of the size of the problem." His anxiety extended to the nighttime hours, when he insisted on what one might call defensive sleeping arrangements: "I never let my children sleep under one roof in fear of a shell landing on the house, killing all of them at once."

"When they announced the withdrawal, we got relief, less pressure, less time in dealing with emergency situations," he adds. "It was possible for me to have lunch with my kids and the family in one place, watching TV together."

"It was [a] very stressed life. I never felt happy, not one day. When they left, to me it was like when the Ethiopians withdrew from the city."[42]

Like the Ethiopian withdrawal, Al-Shabaab's pullout would not bring permanent peace to Mogadishu. But the sense of permanent war was gone too. For now at least, the fighting had moved to the outskirts of the city, to other regions of Somalia—and to within Al-Shabaab itself.

The remains of a bombed-out car found after the fighting for Qooryole, March 2014. *Gabe Joselow*

A boy holds the remains of an AK-47 rifle in Mogadishu, August 2011. Many Mogadishu children have grown up in a world defined by guns, bombs, and violent death. *Adam A. Omar*

Longtime Al-Shabaab emir Ahmed Abdi Godane (*left*) looks at a weapon with his chief bomb maker, Abdullahi Ali, better known as Ante Ante. Screenshot from Al-Shabaab video

Fuad Shongole (*right*) rose to the top echelons of Al-Shabaab in 2008 and remained through the purges of emir Ahmed Godane and the transition to the new leadership. *Screenshot from Al-Shabaab video*

Mahad Karate, who became Al-Shabaab's number-two leader in 2014 after the death of Godane. *Screenshot from Al-Shabaab video*

The ruins of Nasiib Buundo Road in Mogadishu's Shibis district. Al-Shabaab fighters reached this area during the 2010 Ramadan Offensive. This photo was taken August 12, 2011, a few days after Shabaab fighters pulled out of the city. *Adam A. Omar*

The ruins of the Ministry of Education's Department of Examinations, located on Jubba Road in the Shibis district. Photo taken August 12, 2011. *Adam A. Omar*

Close-up shot of Omar Hammami, a.k.a. Abu Mansoor al-Amriki, the Alabama native who went to Somalia in 2006, joined Al-Shabaab and became its main voice to the English-speaking world. *Screenshot from Al-Shabaab video*

Omar Hammami. *Screenshot from Al-Shabaab video*

Kenyan soldiers order journalists to move back as Al-Shabaab's assault of the Westgate Mall unfolds in Nairobi, September 2013. *Gabe Joselow*

Journalists react to the sound of gunfire inside
Westgate Mall, September 2013. *Gabe Joselow*

Al-Shabaab co-founder Mukhtar Robow
confers with Omar Hammami in the field,
2008. *Screenshot from Al-Shabaab video*

The blue waters of the Indian Ocean meet the Somali coastline.
This photo was taken in a helicopter above the town of
Merka in 2014. *Gabe Joselow*

A scene from a Shabaab propaganda video: a four- or five-
year-old boy holding an assault rifle supposedly dreams of his
equally well-armed father. *Screenshot from Al-Shabaab video*

PART THREE

ON THE RUN

TWELVE

DIVISIONS AND PURGE

EVEN AT THE HEIGHT OF Al-Shabaab's power, there were personal and strategic differences among its leaders. According to Zakariye Hersi, the arguments started as early as 2009 when Ethiopian troops left Somalia. "The differences were 'What are we going to do now that Ethiopia has been defeated?'" he says. "Are we going to reach out to the government? Are we going to give the cause and the struggle back to the people and the clans who were involved? Or are we going to take a completely different road?"[1]

At the time, the top leaders were in agreement that Shabaab should continue the war against the TFG, says Hersi. When the Ethiopians left, Mukhtar Robow made a statement that there was actually no difference between President Sheikh Sharif and his predecessor Abdullahi Yusuf Ahmed. "The only difference is the hat," he said, referring to Sheikh Sharif's trademark white kufi cap.

But the failure of the 2010 Ramadan Offensive and the ensuing setbacks opened new rifts between Al-Shabaab leaders and brought old ones to the surface. The power struggle between Godane and Robow was the most prominent divide. There were also deeper ideological debates, such as whether the group should slightly relax its hard-line laws and halt suicide attacks that killed civilians, like the Hotel Shamo bombing, in order to win greater public support. "One thing the West did not want to see is that Shabaab is a bit decentralized," says French analyst Roland Marchal. "You have people in Shabaab who actually can talk, who believe it's not impossible to have a discussion. You have others who are completely hard on everything. The way they react in front of the population is so tough, unilateral, and authoritarian. But others are ready to discuss."[2]

Godane unquestionably fell into the authoritarian camp. In his first two years as emir, Al-Shabaab's Tanfid (executive) and Shura (consultative) councils were able to blunt Godane's autocratic tendencies. "Until 2010, all decisions were run through the Tanfid and Shura," says Hersi. "No key political decisions were made without the two councils becoming aware of it." However, by the latter part of that year, "only two to three people made key decisions" as Godane consolidated power. Hersi says that when Godane was challenged about his "small circle consultations," he would "simply give a philosophical answer like, 'I thought that was the consensus decision.'"[3] Godane could get away with his power play largely because of the ever-loyal Amniyat and its willingness to jail, torture, or execute Godane's internal opponents. The shooting of wounded fighters allied to Robow during the offensive was a blazing red flag that no one failed to see.

Still, Godane's critics refused to shut up and passively accept his rule. Speaking at the Bakara Market mosque in December 2010, Da'wa head Fuad Shongole questioned whether Godane was fit to be emir, noting the leader's reclusiveness and reluctance to show his face in public. A week later, he gave another speech urging Shabaab police to stop flogging and jailing people for trivial offenses. "If we are stronger than the public, we should remember that Allah is also stronger than us. . . . We need to fairly treat the people if we are to succeed," he was quoted as saying.[4]

Other senior Shabaab leaders, including Robow, Ibrahim al-Afghani, and Hassan Dahir Aweys, voiced similar positions. Even Osama bin Laden came down on their side. In an August 2010 letter to a contact in Somalia— one of thousands seized by US forces when they killed bin Laden at his Abbottabad, Pakistan, hideout—the Al-Qaeda chief wrote, "Please remind the brothers in Somalia to be compassionate with the people and remind them of the Hadiths (Mohammed's reported sayings) on this. . . . Please talk to the Somali brothers about reducing the harm to Muslims at Bakara Market as result of attacking the headquarters of the African forces."[5] Senior Al-Qaeda leader Atiyah Abd al-Rahman concurred in a letter to Godane in December

2010: "You are a state and should demonstrate justice and forgiveness and be kind to people as much as you can."[6]

In the face of mounting criticism, Godane showed some willingness to listen and negotiate. In February 2011, he informally rescinded his earlier policies by calling a meeting of the Tanfid and Shura Councils, held at a secret spot in the Lower Shabelle region. Seventeen Shura members and a number of Tanfid reportedly attended. Most prominent among them were Afghani, Amniyat chief Mahad Karate, internal affairs head Hussein Ali Fidow, former Mogadishu governor Ali Jabal, Shura Council head Moallim Burhan, and media chief Abdullahi Yare. Robow wasn't there. Godane's camp said Robow refused to come, but when others talked to him later on, Robow said he was never told about the meeting.

At the meeting, Godane's critics called on him to quit. Those familiar with the meeting say Afghani told Godane that he was a failure as a leader. He gave the emir a list of ill-considered practices, ranging from indiscriminate violence to failure to consult with others. "He told him the project needs a new face," one militant said.

Godane's critics were running out of patience. "We tried to replace him at least on two occasions," says a former commander, speaking on condition of anonymity.[7] This was one of them.

But Godane withstood the challenge, asking for and receiving political support from the assembled leaders. As a concession, he agreed to the formation of a "tribunal" to decide how the group's internal struggles should be resolved. An arbitration committee was formed, consisting of Burhan, Jabal, spokesman Ali Dhere, former Raskamboni commander Mohamed Dulyadeyn top judge Abdul Haq, former Amniyat member Ismail Samatar, and chairman Zubayr al-Muhajir, a British jihadist of Ivorian descent who had joined the Islamic Courts Union in 2006.

On paper, the committee looked balanced, as it included people from both the pro- and anti-Godane camps, and from both the Tanfid and Shura Councils. However, the panel's ruling, issued on June 23, 2011, amounted to a repudiation of Godane and a push to reallocate power in Al-Shabaab. The nine-page ruling, obtained for this book, referred some of the most contentious issues to the Shura Council. But in a victory for the anti-Godane camp, it ruled that Al-Shabaab must set up special courts where people with grievances against the group could submit complaints. It also banned assassinations within Al-Shabaab, said Hizbul Islam members should be appointed to positions in the organization, and barred the recruitment of child soldiers, the latter a demand by Robow. The one place the committee agreed with Godane was a ruling instructing all Al-Shabaab members to inform the emir when communication with Al-Qaeda.

As a final signal to Godane, the committee said Godane would only serve as emir for another six months, at which time Al-Shabab would choose a new leader.

What happened next is a matter of dispute. Al-Shabaab insiders say Godane accepted the ruling and said he needed a three-month transitional period. His close supporters say he asked for three months to take corrective measures. What is agreed is none of the rulings were implemented.

Godane held fast to his position as emir and within days took steps to signal that he would accept no one's ruling or recommendations. First, he ordered Al-Shabaab's withdrawal from Mogadishu, reportedly on the advice of Al-Qaeda commander Abu Yahya al-Libi, a man he admired and learned from while in Afghanistan. Godane's opponents criticized the move, which did little to improve the group's fortunes, but Hersi thought the move was at least partly a political maneuver. "There were internal conflicts, but Godane was clever," says Hersi. "He used the withdrawal to quell the conflict, to turn focus away from him and others and on to the withdrawal, and to make his opponents lose balance and create a new political debate, to cover the old one that was taking place."[8]

Later in August, Godane fired both Afghani and Robow as his official deputies, replacing them with a sole second-in-command, longtime ally and Amniyat chief Mahad Karate. Afghani would remain a loyal member of Al-Shabaab. After another year, Robow would walk away from the group, resettling in his home Bakool region under the protection of his Rahanweyn clan. The United States would maintain a bounty on his head for years, but Robow was essentially retired from Al-Shabaab after 2012.

With Mogadishu lost and the internal turmoil still raging, Al-Shabaab could have descended into chaos or a bloodbath at this point. However, a couple of deadly attacks showed that the group, and Godane, was still a fearsome force. On the morning of October 4, scores of Somali students were lined up outside a compound housing the Ministry of Education, preparing to register for scholarships for study abroad being offered by Turkey. A Shabaab suicide bomber picked that moment to explode a truck filled with fuel drums at the compound's main entrance. More than seventy people were killed, 150 others wounded. The bombing reinforced Al-Shabaab's image as a cruel, pitiless terrorist force. But it did signal to AMISOM and the government that the war in Mogadishu was far from over.

The second attack showed that Shabaab had not lost its shrewdness. On October 20, about three hundred Burundian AU soldiers marched on foot into the Daynile district, an area on the northwestern fringe of Mogadishu that Al-Shabaab had not abandoned. According to witnesses, Shabaab fighters retreated at first and the Burundians advanced with little resistance. But the soldiers had actually walked into a trap. Shabaab fighters cut off their escape route and opened fire from all sides, killing more than sixty Burundians within a matter of minutes. TFG General Anod says the Burundians erred by not sending small surveillance units into the area ahead of the main force.[9] The general led a force of three hundred Somalis that helped to extract the Burundians before they were annihilated.

Following the Daynile attack, words of congratulations poured in from international jihadists, shoring up Godane's position. In December, speaking to Al-Shabaab's Radio Andalus, Godane hit back at those who wanted a greater role in decision making, casting them as self-centered individuals who were harming jihad:

> We take our principles from the Sharia. We all share Islam, and everyone has a role to play, everyone is required to contribute. We all have to sacrifice with self and wealth and share the burden. But it will be a shame to Muslims if one stands aside and complains of lack of consultations even though it's possible he may not have contributed. You should not stand behind anyone to contribute. It's not about privileges and positions and being invited to contribute. Everyone should reach out and contribute in parity with others.[10]

Of course, what Godane neglected to add was that if all Somalis contributed equally to jihad, he, as emir of the top jihadist group, would stand first among equals, making him de facto ruler of Somalia.

—

If there was one thing that kept the leaders of Al-Shabaab under the same tent, it was their admiration for Al-Qaeda and Osama bin Laden. Many of them had personal dealings with bin Laden at one point or another and looked up to him as a spiritual mentor and jihadist visionary. That didn't mean they took orders from him. For years, the ties between Al-Qaeda and Al-Shabaab were strong but informal. Bin Laden and his deputy Ayman al-Zawahiri encouraged Al-Shabaab in letters and audio messages, and Al-Qaeda–linked militants in Somalia shared expertise in bomb making and war tactics. But the relationship went no further. Al-Shabaab and Al-Qaeda remained separate groups, and the leaders of Al-Shabaab made strategic decisions independently.

Godane wanted more. He wanted the two groups to be one, for Al-Shabaab to be Al-Qaeda's official branch in Somalia, in the manner of Al-Qaeda in the Islamic Maghreb (AQIM) or Al-Qaeda in the Arabian Peninsula (AQAP). Such a merger would fit into the jihadists' dream of a worldwide caliphate and might generate greater respect for Al-Shabaab—and not incidentally, Godane himself. Godane proposed the idea in a letter to bin Laden in 2010. In his response, however, the Al-Qaeda chief stopped short of approving it. If anything, bin Laden seemed interested in constructing what US politicos call "plausible deniability."

> Now, in relation to the issue of unity, I see that this obligation should be carried out legitimately and through unannounced secret messaging, by spreading this matter among the people of Somalia, without any official declaration by any officers on our side or your side, that the unity has taken place. But there remains the situation of the brothers on your side and their talking about their relationship with Al-Qaeda, if asked. It would be better for them to say that there is a relationship with Al-Qaeda which is simply a brotherly Islamic connection and nothing more, which would neither deny nor prove.
>
> And for the above matter, there are two reasons. The first: If the matter becomes declared and out in the open, it would have the enemies escalate their anger and mobilize against you; this is what happened to the brothers in Iraq or Algeria. It is true that the enemies will find out inevitably; this matter cannot be hidden, especially when people go around and spread this news. However, an official declaration remains to be the master for all proof. . . .
>
> The second: The matter is that some Muslims in Somalia are suffering from immense poverty and malnutrition, because of the continuity of wars in their country. I have a determined plan of action, using one of my sermons to press the merchants in the countries of the Arabian Peninsula to support pro-active and important developmental projects which are not expensive; we happened to have tried these in Sudan. Therefore, by not having the mujahideen openly

allied with Al-Qaeda, it would strengthen those merchants who are willing to help the brothers in Somalia, and would keep people with the mujahideen.[11]

By early 2012, though, bin Laden was dead—courtesy of the June 2011 US Navy SEAL raid on his Pakistani hideout—and al-Zawahiri was in charge. Bin Laden's former deputy had always been closer to Godane than the Al-Qaeda supremo himself. On February 9, 2012, Godane and al-Zawahiri released videos announcing a formal merger between their groups. Specifically, Al-Shabaab entered into a *bay'ah*, or contract, with Al-Qaeda. The merger made worldwide news, though analysts correctly noted that it would have little practical effect, as the groups had been cooperating for years.

In the upper echelons of Al-Shabaab, there was no real opposition to the merger itself, but Godane's critics saw it as yet another example of him acting unilaterally. Those feelings multiplied a hundredfold weeks later when Godane issued a memo that effectively said his contract with Al-Qaeda is transferrable into a *bay'ah* between himself and the Somali people. In other words, he was the emir of Somalia, and all the country's people were subject to his rule. It was a staggering display of egotism that left his opponents shaking their heads, wondering what could be done.

The new discord broke onto the international stage in March when Shabaab's best-known figure in the West, Abu Mansour al-Amriki—Alabama's own Omar Hammami—publicly spoke about the internal divisions for the first time. In a one-minute video posted to YouTube, he said he and Shabaab's leaders disagreed on matters of Islamic law and strategy, and because of this, his life was in danger.[12] Somewhat incongruously, he spoke in front of a large Al-Shabaab flag hung on the wall, with an AK-47 perched against the flag. Al-Shabaab denied Hammami's allegations on its Twitter account two days later:

> HSM is surprised by the video of Abu Mansoor #AlAmriki that surfaced on the internet recently claiming that his life is "endangered by HSM."
> We assure our Muslim brothers that #AlAmriki is not endangered by the Mujahideen & our brother still enjoys all the privileges of brotherhood.[13]

Hammami was not mollified. In a second video, apparently recorded at the same time as the one in March but not released until October, Hammami spoke of friction between global jihadists and Somali members of

Al-Shabaab. The video, entitled "An Urgent Message," called on the "commanders of jihad and honorable scholars" to intervene.

Later that month, criticism of Godane reached a new level when Hassan Dahir Aweys lent his voice to the chorus of detractors. Unlike Hammami, Aweys chose to deliver his remarks live, at a pre-planned speech at a mosque in Marka. Al-Shabaab, he said, was claiming to be the only true Islamic organization in Somalia, but he had no right to assert such a monopoly. "Whether it is Harakat Al-Shabaab, Harakat I'tisam, or Muslim Brotherhood, they are all part of Islamic groups," he said, "To say we are the only Islamic organization, therefore we have the right to shed blood of those who disagree with us, and to justify killing people . . . that is not right to say, it's not the right thing."[14]

Aweys compared Godane's strong-arm tactics to those employed by Mohamed Siad Barre. "It did not work for Barre, it won't work now," he said. He urged Shabaab to show compassion to the people. "To make threats and to say to people 'I am going to kill you' or make such threats is [a tactic] long gone; the world has moved on. I hope we are going to review these."[15]

One idea floating through the leadership ranks was to allow Al-Qaeda to mediate the disputes. Burhan, Hammami, and Afghani all openly advocated for this option, not least because Afghani had many allies in Al-Qaeda, even with bin Laden gone. Godane and his allies demurred and suggested they seek mediation from Somali scholars sympathetic to jihad. The Godane camp proposed Sheikh Hassaan Hussein, a.k.a. Abu Salman, a hardline Somali-Kenyan cleric known for being pro-Shabaab and not hiding his views. Salman hated Somali scholars who he considered to be half-hearted in their attitude toward jihad. He also despised Hammami, who had criticized some of his sermons.

The situation remained unresolved, and with Shabaab's energies focused inward, the group's fortunes continued a gradual downward slide. The war against the TFG and AMISOM was turning into a debacle. With support from the United Nations Security Council, the African Union had gradually expanded the size of AMISOM and persuaded new countries, primarily Kenya and Ethiopia, to contribute troops. With more than fifteen thousand men now at their disposal, AMISOM and the TFG launched a general offensive in late 2011 to retake major Somali population centers. The overmatched Shabaab fighters lost control of Beledweyne on December 31,

Baidoa on February 22, Afgoye on May 25, Afmadow on May 31, and Balad on June 26. Many of these losses took place with little or no fighting; Shabaab units sometimes fled when they learned enemy forces were approaching. Al-Shabaab insisted the retreats were tactical maneuvers, intended to let its forces regroup. The withdrawals did prevent the loss of men and military equipment. But no one could fail to see the overall trend.

The heaviest blow fell in September 2012. Al-Shabaab leaders had known for months that their foes were gunning for Kismayo, the coastal city whose port generated, at minimum, several million dollars per year for Al-Shabaab through taxes and fees. Shabaab set up checkpoints and trenches around the city to halt any advance. But in an apparent failure of intelligence, the group made no preparations for an attack by sea. At around 3 a.m. on September 28, Kenyan Navy ships deposited hundreds of troops on a beach a few miles north of Kismayo. The Kenyans then launched "Operation Sledge Hammer," a three-pronged assault that involved bombing runs by Kenyan K-5 jets, shelling by Kenyan naval vessels, and a ground advance by Kenyan and Somali government troops.[16] The Shabaab contingent in the city fought back at first and tried to rally locals to their side over the radio. But just one day later, they abandoned Kismayo, four years, one month, and seven days after seizing the city. Shabaab again portrayed the withdrawal as tactical and warned over its Twitter feed that it would turn Kismayo from "a peaceful city governed by Sharia into a battle zone."[17] The threat turned out to be hollow—after some scattered IED blasts, Kenyan and Somali forces ran the city with little trouble, and Shabaab lost its number-one source of funding.

The setbacks intensified Al-Shabaab's internal power struggle, which observers could increasingly watch blow-by-blow over social media and the Internet. During 2012, Hammami lashed out repeatedly at Godane and his allies via his videos and on Twitter, accusing them of corruption, murder, and ignoring global jihad. Al-Shabaab took to mocking him on its own Twitter account, deriding his "narcissistic pursuit of fame."[18] In January 2013, Hammami tweeted that the group had given him fifteen days to surrender or be hunted down and killed. He chose to flee to the bush, cementing his status as a marked man.

The next escalation came in mid-February, when a leading Salafist scholar, Sheikh Abdulkadir Nur Farah Ga'amey, was killed while praying at a mosque in the city of Garowe. Ga'amey was a former AIAI member who had rejected Al-Shabaab and denounced the group's killing of fellow Muslims. Al-Shabaab did not claim responsibility, but Godane's opponents pinned the blame on the emir and the Amniyat. Aweys took to the airwaves, denouncing Ga'amey's death in a phone call to a Somali television station. A journalist asked him if Al-Shabaab was responsible. Aweys gave a half-denial that hinted at the split within the group. "We are not involved in any act that is maiming the community, we deny it," the old jihadist said. "Shame on whoever did it, whether from outside or inside."[19]

Two months later, in April, Hammami posted another message on Twitter, saying he had barely survived an assassination attempt by Al-Shabaab. Afghani, Burhan, and Aweys, among others, signed a letter condemning the attempt that was published on jihadi websites. And in April, several websites published one of at least three letters sent by Ibrahim al-Afghani to Ayman al-Zawahiri. The letter was among a collection of documents the Associated Press found after French and African forces ousted Al-Qaeda in the Islamic Maghreb and other Islamist groups from power in northern Mali. In the fifteen-page letter, entitled "An Open Letter to Our Emir Sheikh Ayman al-Zawahiri," al-Afghani said he felt compelled to write on behalf of the "silent majority" of al-Shabaab fighters.

"He [Godane] is expecting blind obedience; he failed to consult with us, and is placing personal desires above the requisites of Sharia," Afghani wrote. He also said Godane was "sowing conflict among the leaders by lavishing his supporters with largesse, and depriving his critics of the basics of survival and starving them; mistreating foreign jihadists; marginalizing Al-Shabaab scholars; inciting young jihadists against scholars and leaders by issuing threats of liquidation; preventing certain scholars from publishing, teaching."

"The fruits of jihad in Somalia are in danger of being lost, just as in Algeria in the 1990s," Afghani wrote. He mentioned that Godane had sabotaged the decisions of the special court set up to address the discord among Shabaab leaders. And Afghani urged al-Zawahiri to intervene.[20]

The letter may have been the last straw in the Godane-Afghani relationship. Godane was already incensed by the increasing number of Somali and foreign jihadists using Twitter to disparage him and his decisions. Except for Hammami, the people behind the tweets were using fake names, although most of them were members of Al-Shabaab. Godane suspected the media-savvy Afghani of encouraging the criticism.

In Godane's mind, the time to eliminate his opponents had arrived. Amid all the sniping online, the emir gathered political support from important Shabaab figures and religious backing from pro-jihad scholars. According to a former Tanfid member, members of the Godane camp included deputy emir Mahad Karate, financial chief Hassan Afgoye, intelligence chief Abdishakur Tahil, judge Dahir Ga'amey, deputy defense chief Daud Abu Suhayba, and the governor of the Bay and Bakool regions, Ahmed Diriye. The key religious backing came from Abu Salman, the Somali-Kenyan cleric. Salman had already issued a *fatwa* (religious ruling) calling for the death of certain Salafist scholars whom he accused of undermining jihad. "Some ask if . . . they say *Shahada* [testimony declaring belief in the oneness of Allah and Muhammad as his prophet] and pray, why kill them? I say we don't have issues with them saying the Shahada and praying; we have issues with them blocking the imposition and practicing of Sharia. They are unbelievers," he said. Friends of Abdulkadir Nur Farah Ga'amey believe it was that fatwa that led to the Salafist scholar's death.

In April 2013, the Godane camp laid the groundwork for its next step. At a lecture by Abu Salman in Nairobi, a Godane supporter reportedly asked him a question about disloyal jihadists. Other reports said Salman was responding to a letter. Either way, the cleric gave an answer with a clear message. Individuals who disobeyed their emir and sowed discord among the mujahideen, he said, could be "removed out of the way."[21]

It was the religious justification Godane needed in order to take on his high-level opponents. Burhan, Afghani, and Aweys quickly wrote to the young sheikh, asking him to clarify his statement, warning that the Amniyat would act upon it. But Salman never replied to them.

Indeed, Godane soon acted on the fatwa by issuing a notice to all his opponents.[22] He called it *"Haadaa Balaaghu Li Naas,"* or "A declaration to all people." It warned that certain individuals were working with infidels to sabotage the jihad, and conspiring against the mujahideen. It was understood by all who read it that those individuals were now in mortal danger.

Amniyat operatives began sending ominous messages to Godane's opponents. Ibrahim al-Afghani's top aide, Omar Abu Ayan, says that Afghani
would receive anonymous calls telling him he will regret "sabotaging" jihad.
He would reply to them, "Come quickly, oppressors!"—meaning do whatever you have to do.[23]

The Amniyat arrested a number of Godane's opponents in the first weeks
of June. Those detained included Zubayr Al-Muhajir, who had denounced
Godane at a mosque one Friday and accused him of deviating from Islamic
principles. One Amniyat commander reportedly advised Al-Muhajir to prepare his *karfan*, the white sheet used to cover dead bodies. The Amniyat also
arrested Ismail Samatar and put him in jail. Both had been members of the
2011 tribunal that called for Godane to step down.

Ibrahim al-Afghani remained free for the time being. He, along with
Burhan and a number of other Shabaab leaders, had relocated to the town
of Barawe, one of the group's remaining strongholds, and a beautiful beach
area to boot. Far from cowering in fear, Afghani was pursuing ambitious
plans. For months he had been working to start a jihadist school, where
elite students he personally selected would take courses in Islamic studies
and Sharia. He called it Harar Academy and planned to establish campuses
throughout the areas controlled by Al-Shabaab. He set up the first campus
in Marka. When AMISOM troops seized Marka, he moved his school to
Dinsoor.

Simultaneously, Afghani prepared a series of audio lectures and debates
about constitutions. It was a fourteen-part series, each section forty-five
minutes long, entitled "Dakharka Dilaaya Dasaatiirta" or "Killing Blows to
the Constitutions." Presenters talked about the origins of modern constitutions, how they reached Muslim countries, and their perceived deficien-
cies and contradictions. Afghani chose the lecturers and presenters—they
included his right-hand man Abu Ayan, Somali-American jihadists Ismail
Samatar and Mohamed Miski, and scholars Hassan Afrah and Abu Ridwan.
The series argued that Sharia is a complete constitution that is applicable to
any place and any time in the world.

As the Amniyat closed in, Afghani was writing a book based on the series. "He called it his greatest achievement," says Abu Ayan.[24]

A family member of Afghani confirms he seemed calm at this time. "I did not feel any fear in him," the person says. "He did not complain to me about anyone."[25]

Distracted, Afghani may have been caught unaware when a team of Amniyat operatives and Hisbah policemen descended on Barawe the evening of June 19, 2013. Their operation focused on Baghdad, a nice part of town bordered by the sea where the longtime jihadist had taken up residence. The team erected checkpoints on the roads leading into and out of the area and deployed fighters around hotels, the port, phone companies and other key buildings. The Amniyat communicated through walkie-talkies, according to a witness. Residents were not told what was going on.

Just after the evening Maghreb prayers, Afghani began walking, without a bodyguard, to a neighborhood mosque. Given the timing, he may have been late for the Maghreb prayer or was going to mosque for the Isha, the fifth and final prayer of the day. During the walk, Ayan called to inform Afghani that he had finished editing the constitution series and had saved it onto a flash drive and CDs. Afghani said that he would come by later to collect it.

Ayan says he learned what happened next from other Al-Shabaab sources. "A group of young men approached him while [he was] walking," he says. "One of them greeted him and offered to shake his hand; Afghani knew him. As he chatted with this man, a second man came from behind and fired one shot to Afghani's head."[26]

According to Ayan, Afghani fell to the ground, badly wounded but clinging to life. Moments later, a car full of armed men pulled up next to him. One gunman jumped out and shouted *"Munafiq!"*—Arabic for "hypocrite"—and shot Afghani again, finishing him off. Then, according to Ayan, "they put him in a rucksack and took his body away to an unknown location."[27]

In Islam, a *munafiq* is someone who practices the religion to conceal his true colors. Godane had previously accused Afghani of being a *munafiq* who said the correct things with Al-Shabaab but undermined jihad in other forums.

Ayan says that when he learned, soon after it happened, that there had been a shooting near the mosque, he called Afghani's phone to check on him. Afghani never allowed anyone else to answer his phone, Ayan says, but on this day another man answered the call. "The man who answered asked me who I was," Ayan says. "I immediately thought the worst and told him a false name."

That same evening, at about 7:30 p.m., Zakariye Hersi stopped by Moallim Burhan's house in Barawe. "Moallim Burhan was suffering from malaria so I visited him," he says. "While I was about five minutes in the house, we heard the shots that eventually killed Afghani. I told Burhan, 'I'm going to check what was happening.' He insisted we go together."[28]

Hersi says they exited the house but saw that the main road was closed by Amniyat operatives, who told them to go back. "We tried to take another road, but just moments later we were surrounded, arrested," he says.

According to Hersi, he and Burhan were taken to a soccer field and told to raise their hands above their heads. Without ceremony, one of the gunmen shot Burhan in the head, killing him.

The drama was not over, says Hersi. "The gunman who shot him walked towards me and tried to shoot me, but I rushed and grabbed the other side of his gun. He tried to take the gun away from my grab, but I held on to it. There was a scuffle and argument. I told him I was just visiting [Burhan]," Hersi says. He says the unit commander spoke directly to the gunman and said, "If he takes the gun away from you, I will kill both of you."[29]

The unit commander called his superiors. Hersi says he could hear the voice on the walkie-talkie but couldn't identify it, though at the time the Amniyat was run by Abdishakur Tahlil, later killed in a December 2014 US drone strike; Tahlil, in turn, was working under the guidance of Mahad Karate. The commander told his superior that there was a second man with Burhan—what should we do with him? The superior said the second man—Hersi—could go, as long as he went to his home straight away. But a suspicious Hersi asked the unit commander to escort him back to his room at the Hotel Columbus. "I wanted him to take responsibility if anything happened to me," he says.[30]

The commander did as requested and Hersi made it back to his room, where he found it impossible to sleep. "Throughout the night I was nervous, asking myself, 'When are they going to come for me?'" he says.[31]

The next morning, Al-Shabaab's governor of Lower Shabelle, Sheikh Mohamed Abu Abdalla, known as "Xiirey," visited the families of Afghani and Burhan separately. He spoke to Afghani's widow and Moallim Burhan's mother and reportedly took them to secret locations where the two men were buried. He did not explain why and how they were killed, but told them about the virtue of patience and prayed with them for Allah to give them relief. According to Moallim Burhan's widow, Al-Shabaab told her the group would take responsibility in looking after the family and raising the children.

Al-Shabaab didn't make any announcement about the killings at first, but news got out on social media June 21. Al-Shabaab confirmed their deaths ten days later. A spokesman, Abdulaziz Abu Mus'ab, didn't mention their names. In a recorded message he said, "The mujahideen forces have conducted an operation against members of the mujahideen who were found to be involved in dividing the mujahideen. Two of them, when the forces ordered them to surrender they resisted; they fought and they died. May God bless their soul and place them in heaven. The intention was not to kill them but to arrest them and put them on the Islamic trail."[32]

Hersi does not believe that. "They were killed without due process, they were killed because they were accused of destroying the jihad," he says. "That is what happens when a group commits *Inhiraf*, desertion from the true path of faith."[33]

Omar Hammami, by this time one of Godane's fiercest critics, later said of the killings: "It has nothing to do with Islam, it only has to do with propping up the division of Abu Zubeyr [Godane] and maintaining him as the leader of whatever land is still under his control."[34]

Two days after Afghani and Burhan were killed, Hassan Dahir Aweys escaped from Barawe by boat. He made it to central Somalia, where he was captured on June 26 by local forces allied with the government. He was handed over to the government three days later.

On June 22, Hersi also left Barawe, going to Qoryoley. He would evade both Al-Shabaab and the government for another eighteen months.

According to Abu Ayan, Al-Shabaab ransacked Afghani's academy, taking laptops, pistols, and a car that was parked in a garage in Bula Marer. "These belongings should have been given to his family, but the fact they didn't give them to his wife or son shows they really ruled him as an apostate," he says. "Therefore it was okay for them to confiscate as *ghanimah*."[35]

The death of Afghani closed a chapter in Al-Shabaab's history. The challenges to Godane's rule were essentially over; there was no one left of

Afghani's (or Burhan's) stature to work for changes within the group. And in a larger sense, Al-Shabaab was now cut off from its roots. Afghani had planted the seeds for jihad in Somalia and spent nearly a quarter of a century growing and shaping their violent, extremist fruit. He had been the group's chief media strategist, a teacher of jihadist ideals and war tactics, and a bridge to the clans, keeping them on Al-Shabaab's side. Without him, Al-Shabaab would be missing an important source of know-how and a voice of relative tactical pragmatism and moderation.

Of course, it might not have mattered anyway. Moderation would play no part in Al-Shabaab's future plans.

THIRTEEN

THE ROAD TO WESTGATE

LATE IN THE EVENING OF June 7, 2011, two men driving in the northern suburbs of Mogadishu were stopped at a checkpoint manned by Somali government troops. A soldier, carrying an AK-47, approached the black Toyota SUV and ordered the driver to turn the headlights off and the interior light on. "They are the elders," the driver said, in apparent hope of being waived through.

"I don't know the elders," the soldier responded.

The driver turned on the interior light. When the soldier looked in the vehicle, he saw the driver had a pistol tucked in his waistband, while the man in the passenger seat had his own AK-47, resting on his lap.

"Don't move your gun," the soldier shouted, pointing his own gun at the man with the rifle.

But the driver reached for his pistol, triggering an exchange of gunfire. The soldier, twenty-two-year-old Abdi Hassan, fired some thirty bullets into the car. When the shooting was over, Hassan was alive and the occupants of the car were dead.[1]

Such shootouts have been a fact of life in Mogadishu for years, and in line with Muslim tradition, both men's remains were buried within hours of their death. The incident rang alarm bells only when security officials examined items found in the car. The discoveries included a laptop computer, cell phones, about $40,000 in US currency, and a South African passport under the name of Daniel Robinson. Officials had the bodies exhumed and gave tissue samples to US intelligence for DNA testing. Within twenty-four hours, the United States confirmed that the man with the rifle was Fazul Abdullah Mohammed, Al-Qaeda's top leader in East Africa and the last of the three 1998 US embassy bombers operating in Somalia. Fazul, as he was generally called, was near the top of the FBI's most-wanted list and had been the subject of a $5 million bounty by the State Department since the turn of the century.

His killing was widely hailed as major blow to both Al-Qaeda and Al-Shabaab, who would now be deprived of his attack-planning skills, fundraising ability, and array of terrorist contacts across Somalia and Kenya. A senior US counterterrorism official said that Al-Qaeda "has lost one of its key figures, and while it may not be the knockout punch to militants in the region, it's certainly a strong kick in the gut."[2] Somali president Sheikh Sharif went a step farther, saying, "We have overpowered Al-Qaeda and Al-Shabaab in Somalia; they are weak and now melting away."[3]

At that moment, Sheikh Sharif was partly right; Al-Shabaab was losing ground in Mogadishu by the week. What he didn't know was that while the group was being overpowered in Somalia, it was about to become more active and dangerous in Somalia's neighbor to the south.

Almost unnoticed in the hubbub over Fazul was the death of the other militant, Muse Hussein. Hussein was not a headline-maker like Fazul, but he performed an important task for both Al-Shabaab and Al-Qaeda: attracting and facilitating support in Kenya. Kenya had become an important source of fighters and funding for Al-Shabaab starting in 2006, when a number of ethnic Somalis from Kenya came to Mogadishu to work with the Islamic Courts Union or to take part in the fights against the warlords and Ethiopians. Even before then, Al-Qaeda had drawn support from within Kenya for years and launched two major attacks in the country: the 1998 US embassy bombing and the 2002 bombing of an Israeli-owned hotel in Mombasa. "People forget that Al-Qaeda has been working in East Africa from the very beginning, [since] Osama bin Laden was in Sudan," says analyst Roland Marchal. "Very strategically, they decided to work on the coast [of Kenya]." It was an ideal area for Al-Qaeda's purposes, he says—the port cities drew people of different nationalities, many of them on the move, and many who felt marginalized by their home countries. "This was the dynamic; people were sympathizers, ready to provide logistical support," Marchal says.[4]

Kenya proved to be an even more fertile ground for Al-Shabaab. The people of Kenya's North East Province are largely ethnic Somalis who have the same religion, culture, and customs as people in Somalia. For decades, Somalis on both sides of the border conducted business and travel as if there were no boundary between them. Many of those in Kenya, however, had grievances. Some had fled Somalia after the 1991 civil war only to wind up in the congested, disease-prone Daadab refugee camps—built to hold ninety thousand, but by 2010, home to more than four hundred thousand. As a whole, the North East Province was and is one of the least developed parts of Kenya, with little in the way of paved roads, schools, sewage systems, or other basics of modern life. And many felt the ethnic Somali-majority regions—like the Ogaden in Ethiopia—could have been part of Somalia if not for colonial powers like Britain and some twists of history.

Thousands of Somalis had settled in Nairobi, primarily in the neighborhood of Eastleigh, which earned a reputation as "Little Mogadishu." Many started successful businesses, generating jobs for Kenyans. But because most Somali refugees in Kenya are in the country illegally, they became prey for corrupt police, who would arrest them on charges of lacking proper identification. To free them, relatives would have to fork over a hefty bribe.

These issues, plus alleged long-running abuses by the Kenyan military, including summary executions, created a deep animosity among many Kenyan Somalis toward the government. Al-Qaeda had exploited these feelings when it was infiltrating the coast; Al-Shabaab repeated the strategy in North East Province. *We will help you lift this oppression*, the group told Kenyan Somalis. *Just assist us in any way you can.*

Muse Hussein, also known as Muse Sambayo, started out as anything but a jihadist. In his youth, he was a soccer prodigy playing for a top-notch club in his hometown of Wajir, about one hundred kilometers south of the Somali border. "He was a midfielder and one of the best players in the team," says a childhood friend, speaking on condition of anonymity. "He was not religious, he used to chew the narcotic [khat], and his favorite hobbies were soccer and cinema."[5] But sometime after graduating from Sabunley High School in Wajir, he was radicalized. In late 2002 or early 2003, he traveled to

Somalia on a religious mission with the peaceful Tabliq movement, only to abandon the group and enter a militant camp founded by Shabaab military leader Aden Ayrow and future emir Godane. There, he attracted the attention of Al-Qaeda's East Africa leaders. They saw that Hussein could make a useful operative—he had legal travel documents, he spoke fluent English, Swahili, and Somali, and he had a knack for getting past barriers. "He knew how to bribe. [He was] a sweet-talker," the childhood friend says.[6]

Soon, Hussein was carrying money and militant fighters for Al-Qaeda across the Kenya-Somalia border. His soccer-playing days ended when he lost a leg fighting the Ethiopians in Mogadishu. But after medical treatment in Kenya, he recovered enough to resume his travels. "I believe about ten men left Wajir because of Muse Sambayo," says the childhood friend. "He used to come back and forth with them."[7]

Other Kenyan Somalis engaged in similar activities. The benignly named Muslim Youth Center (MYC) was a steady provider of funds and fighters. The group started as a religious counseling service in the Majengo area of Nairobi in late 2008, but it swiftly evolved into Al-Shabaab's main Kenyan support network under the influence of a Mombasa-based cleric, Sheikh Aboud Rogo, and his one-time student Ahmad Iman Ali. In time, the MYC would become Al-Shabaab's official affiliate in Kenya under a new name, al-Hijra. Meanwhile, Abdirahman Abdi, nicknamed Salawat, ran a hotel in Eastleigh that served as a hub for trafficking in stolen passports, travel documents, and fake IDs, helping Shabaab fighters enter and pass through Kenya. Starting in 2009, the hotel also housed wounded militant fighters who had been smuggled out of Somalia for medical treatment and recovery.

Getting recruits and members across the Kenya-Somalia border was never very difficult. Kenya lacks the resources to seal the frontier, which runs for 680 kilometers across mostly flat, dry land. Some fighters crossed using one of the many remote, dusty trails between official border crossings. Some passed through the crossings themselves. "It's often easy to bribe Kenyan police at checkpoints," says Ahmed Abdulkadir, a Somali journalist who regularly travels in Kenya.[8] Those arrested for possessing false documents, he says, can win their release by paying as little as five or ten dollars.

Al-Shabaab further encouraged East African recruitment with online videos produced by its al-Kataib media arm. Some of the videos were subtitled in Swahili for audiences in Kenya, Tanzania, and Uganda. In one, spokesman Ali Dhere ended the video by saying, "To our people in East Africa, we say, 'Welcome to Somalia, *hakuna matata*'"—the Swahili phrase meaning "no worries" that Disney borrowed for "The Lion King."[9]

Al-Shabaab found other uses for Kenya as well. In November 2008, the group kidnapped two Italian nuns employed as aid workers in El Wak, a Kenyan border town. The late militant Mohamed Toora-Toorow, who led the mission, said planning for the abduction lasted two months. "The area was militarized," he said. "There is a military barracks of about two hundred to three hundred [Kenyan] soldiers nearby. Some of the unit said we cannot face that large number of soldiers that are armed with helicopters." But Toora-Toorow insisted that with careful surveillance and preparation it could be done. The unit's first kidnapping attempt on November 4 was aborted because of distant events. "I think it was the night of the Obama election," Toora-Toorow said. "Once we got close, we realized we could not conduct the operation that night, there was too much light and noise. It was as if the whole town was awake."[10]

On the night of November 10, they tried again. The group left the Somali side at about 11 p.m. and walked several kilometers into Kenya. This time it was quiet. Toora-Toorow divided his twenty-four men into four groups— one to kidnap the nuns, one to monitor the barracks, one to hijack vehicles at a hotel, and one to secure the escape route. The first unit abducted the women from their house. Then, after Shabaab and soldiers exchanged gunfire at the barracks, all four groups opened fire. "We had to open fire in different places to look like a bigger army," Toora-Toorow said. In the confusion, the group at the hotel hijacked two pickup trucks and a Land Rover. The Shabaab team converged, piled into the vehicles with the nuns, and raced back into Somalia. Fighting muddy roads, traveling only at night to thwart Kenyan airstrikes, they reached Mogadishu two days later.

The nuns, sixty-seven-year-old Maria Teresa Olivero and sixty-year-old Caterina Giraudo, were released the following February. Toora-Toorow said he heard they were ransomed for between $1.5 and $2 million.

The kidnapping was marred only by the loss of one fighter who got lost and was left behind in Kenya. Even that problem was rectified when the man made it back into Somalia the next day and later rejoined his unit in Mogadishu. He told his friends that he had come across an unarmed Kenyan policeman in an alleyway, frantically blowing his whistle for help. The Al-Shabaab man took a shot at the officer but missed. He tried to shoot a second time, but the gun jammed. The policeman could have pounced but instead took the opportunity to run away, dropping his whistle in the process. Before making his own getaway, the Shabaab man grabbed the whistle and brought it home to show off—a tiny war trophy from Al-Shabaab's first significant operation inside Kenya.

—

Despite the kidnappings, the smuggling of money and weapons, the brazen recruitment of fighters, and the abuse of government services, Kenya resisted getting directly involved in the fight against Al-Shabaab. At the TFG's most desperate moments, when Somali leaders were virtually down on their knees, begging for help, Kenyan leaders kept their forces at home. In 2010, Kenya's then–Defense Minister Yusuf Haji told Voice of America's Somali Service that "under no circumstances shall we be intervening in Somalia."[11] The country did host political conferences for Somalia in Nairobi, but these were largely driven by powers such as the United Nations or Ethiopia, while Kenya stayed on the periphery. "In that period, up to 2010, the Kenyan state was compromising with Al-Shabaab, because there was lots of money moving, because there was kind of a gentlemen's agreement," says Roland Marchal.[12] In other words, as long as Al-Shabaab did not attack Kenya itself, and as long as border officials got their bribes, the militants could operate pretty much as they pleased.

The "agreement" began to fray, however, in part because Godane started to see Kenya as both a threat to Al-Shabaab's existence and an opportunity to expand the group's influence. In his March 5, 2010, letter to Osama bin Laden, Godane said Kenya had become "the main center for conspiracy against our jihad" by hosting anti-Shabaab foreign intelligence units and serving as a transportation hub for TFG leaders and allies. At the same time, he said, Somalis and Muslims in Kenya felt marginalized by the government, the Kenyan press was campaigning against Somali businesses, and the "brittle" coalition government had warned that the political situation could explode during the next elections. He added, "We had specific intentions to open fronts [there], so we urge you to provide us with your thoughts concerning this matter."[13]

Bin Laden's thoughts remain unknown, but Al-Shabaab's actions regarding Kenya were becoming more provocative. As early as June 2009, a Shabaab leader in Kismayo said that if Kenya came to the aid of the TFG, "We will destroy Nairobi's tall, glass buildings."[14] Several skirmishes along the Kenya-Somalia border followed, the biggest taking place on July 20, 2010, when Shabaab gunmen attacked a border patrol in Kenya's Lagdera district. The ensuing shootout left a Kenyan officer wounded and two Shabaab fighters dead.

The real countdown to warfare started in September 2011, although it wasn't by Al-Shabaab's choosing. The northeast corner of Kenya is home to beach resorts that cater to wealthy, foreign clients. The resorts generate tens of millions of dollars for Kenya's tourist industry and are generally well-protected by their operators and the military. So it sent a shock wave through government circles in Nairobi when, on September 10, gunmen attacked a middle-aged British couple, David and Judith Tebbutt, who were vacationing on a remote part of Lamu Island. David was shot and killed trying to fight off the gunmen, while Judith was kidnapped and whisked by boat into southern Somalia. British intelligence and the Kenyan government blamed Al-Shabaab. A MI6 document, dated September 13 and later leaked online, asserted there was evidence that Shabaab operatives had previously conducted surveillance in the area and that a Kenyan Somali Shabaab commander, Kahale Famau Khale, had voiced interest in kidnapping women on Lamu. The authors said Al-Shabaab's need for funding provided the motive. "We judge that the Shabaab are likely to seek ransom payments for Judith Tebbutt," said the document.[15]

Only one problem: Al-Shabaab very likely had nothing to do with the incident. Reporting by British media organizations made it clear that the kidnappers were Somali pirates. A day after the attack, Shabaab denied playing any role in the killing or the abduction. After her release in early 2012, Judith Tebbutt never blamed Shabaab or said they were involved, referring to her kidnappers as "criminals."[16]

But certain developments had been set in motion. On October 1, Somali gunmen abducted Marie Dedieu, a recovering cancer patient and paraplegic Frenchwoman, from her beachfront residence on Kenya's Manda Island. Again, Al-Shabaab was widely blamed, despite a denial from the group and a lack of evidence. Fingers pointed at Shabaab yet again on October 13, when two Spanish aid workers for Doctors Without Borders were kidnapped in the Dadaab refugee camps of northern Kenya and taken into Somali territory. To hear the Kenyan government tell it, Al-Shabaab was on a kidnapping spree aimed at destroying Kenya's tourist industry and destabilizing the country.

October 16 brought the official response. Kenya sent an estimated 2,500 troops across the border into southern Somalia for the start of "Operation Linda Nchi" or "Operation Protect the Country." Top officials portrayed the incursion as a response to the recent kidnappings. "If you are attacked by the enemy, you have the right to pursue that enemy," Defense Minister Haji told a news conference.[17] Prime Minister Raila Odinga said, "The cost of inaction will be much higher than the cost of acting now."[18]

But analysts were skeptical of the government's official statements, and rightly so. US State Department cables released through Wikileaks show that as early as November 2009, Kenyan officials were trying to get US backing for an incursion into southern Somalia. A delegation led by Kenyan Foreign Minister Moses Wetangula made an especially hard plea to US Assistant Secretary of State Johnnie Carson on the sidelines of the African Union summit in January 2010. Wetangula argued that the plan would weaken Al-Shabaab, help the TFG, and push back the threat to Kenya's border regions. Carson tried to persuade Wetangula otherwise, saying the incursion would likely be more expensive and cause more complications in both Somalia and Kenya than Kenyan officials could possibly anticipate. "I would be wrong if I suggested encouragement," Carson said.[19]

In public, Al-Shabaab played the nationalist and Islamist cards, trying to stir up Somalis' hatred of another band of invading foreigners. Hassan al-Turki took the lead this time: "I call on all Somalis to stand united against this bloodthirsty enemy that has crossed into our territories and the apostate Somali militants helping them," he said.[20] But Marchal says that in private, Shabaab leaders were somewhat perplexed, given that Kenya had given them a free hand for so many years. "When Kenya decided to send troops into Somalia ... Shabaab leadership were confused. They were saying, 'Why are you doing that?' They say, 'We are friends, we live together, you should not occupy us, we don't want to do anything bad, so why start a war that has no need to exist?'"[21]

In the first week of November, Kenyan troops and their local allies captured Qoqani and a number of other smaller towns. At the same time, Kenya was looking to secure a truce, according to Mukhtar Robow. He says Kenyan officials sent intermediaries to him three times—twice before troops entered Somalia and once after—seeking to open negotiations. Robow was open to the proposal because, he says, fighting Kenya would be an extra burden for Shabaab. Godane, always suspicious of Robow, rejected the first two Kenyan offers but accepted the third after Robow asked Al-Shabaab defense chief Farhan Kahiye to deliver the offer to the emir, who assigned political chief Hussein Dayniile to deal with it.[22]

Negotiations soon stalled, however. "He [Godane] was saying we can't make a truce with them unless they go back to their border," according to Robow. "When Kenya heard Al-Shabaab demand they go back to their border, they said we can't—we are into this with other countries, we sacrificed men and wealth. Tell us something to hold on to [as a face-saving measure]." The sides evidently couldn't agree on what that measure would be, for the Kenyans soon advanced further into Somalia and captured the town of Afmadow.[23]

Once the war was on, Al-Shabaab didn't hesitate, clashing with Kenyan troops in southern Somalia and vowing to make its new enemy pay through attacks on Kenyan territory. The first attacks took place October 24 in Nairobi, when grenades were thrown into a bar and into a bus terminal, killing at least six people. The suspect arrested by Kenyan police for the attacks admitted to being an Al-Shabaab member. After that, grenade and shooting attacks became a disquieting feature of life in Kenya, with the assailants usually targeting bus stations, churches, or nightclubs. According to a leaked report prepared by Kenya's National Intelligence Service (NIS) for top Kenyan officials, a pro-Shabaab preacher in Eastleigh, Sheikh Hassaan Mahat, was hiring criminals to throw grenades at public transport vehicles and other targets.[24] The report said that for a successful attack, Mahat paid five thousand Kenyan shillings—about $50 in 2017 dollars. Those who tried but failed still got two thousand shillings, or $20.

Sometimes, Al-Shabaab would claim responsibility for attacks, such as one on February 19, 2012, that killed a police officer in the town of Garissa, in northeastern Kenya. More often, police were left to make an educated guess, such as on July 1 when masked gunmen opened fire in two churches in Garissa, killing seventeen people and wounding sixty. Perhaps inevitably, many Kenyans began to harbor anger and suspicion against the Somali community. After a blast in November that killed at least seven people on a bus in Eastleigh, angry mobs of young Kenyans attacked and looted Somali-owned houses and businesses. Police then unleashed a wave of attacks on the community, subjecting Eastleigh residents to rape, beatings, torture, theft, and extortion. By the time the campaign died down in early 2013, thousands of people had fled the area.

In spite of the attacks and the unrest, Kenyan forces remained in Somalia, helping African Union forces drive Al-Shabaab out of the urban areas, most notably Kismayo. Kenya managed to defray some of the costs by wrapping its mission into AMISOM, effectively enabling the US and Europe to pay its troops. The mission stayed put even after Uhuru Kenyatta replaced Mwai Kibaki as president after the surprisingly peaceful March 2013 elections.

All the while, Al-Shabaab was trying to mount a large-scale terrorist attack in Kenya as a form of retaliation. The leaked Kenyan intelligence report, made public in October 2013, said that Shabaab had inserted Amniyat operatives into the country for potential attacks on a variety of targets, including the parliament building, an air base, Nyayo National Stadium, the Gulf Hotel (a frequent meeting spot for Somali intelligence agents), and various bars, bus stations, and nightclubs.[25] The NIS said it had foiled eight separate plots, the most advanced of which targeted the parliament building. That plan allegedly reached the point where the would-be assailants put on their suicide vests and loaded weapons into their car but called off the attack at the last moment for reasons not made clear.

One of the other potential targets mentioned was a popular mall in central Nairobi, known for its upscale stores, large casino, and international clientele.[26] The report warned that Shabaab operatives had already surveyed the site and were believed to be in possession of two suicide vests, two AK-47 rifles, and twelve hand grenades for the attack. But a whole year passed after the NIS told senior Kenyan officials about that particular threat, in September 2012. When the intelligence service issued new, detailed warnings about a potential attack a year later, it mentioned several likely targets, including Nairobi's Times Tower, central police station, and anti-terrorism police unit. But the reports made no further reference to the Westgate Shopping Mall.

Before Al-Shabaab could launch a major attack in Kenya, it had one thorny matter to take care of at home. Abu Mansour al-Amriki—Omar Hammami—remained on the loose and continued to agitate against Godane and his backers. In a series of tweets in January 2013, the Alabama native accused Shabaab of abusing its own members, saying it had imprisoned two "brothers" in Guantanamo-like conditions, shot another in the leg, and allowed another to almost die of thirst after "forcing to him to the border."

Al-Shabaab had heard enough, and on April 25, gunmen tried to kill Hammami. They failed, and true to form, Hammami made sure the world knew about it via Twitter. "Just been shot in neck by Shabaab assassin. not critical yet," he wrote.[27] "Sitting in tea place then 3 shots behind to left, pistol I think, they ran." The tweets were accompanied by selfies that showed blood running down his neck. The wound was evidently minor, for Hammami was well enough to throw a new jab at Godane the next day, writing "abu zubayr has gone mad. he's starting a civil war."

The drama continued four days later, when Hammami tweeted news of a shootout with more Shabaab gunmen. "We were forced to fight in self defense & killed 3 and wounded others w/no losses. The main amir who wanted 2 fight us was from the killed," he wrote. Hammami didn't give the identities of the "we" nor disclose his location, although several sources eventually learned he was being protected by members of the Rahanweyn clan and living in the Bay region—Mukhtar Robow's territory. His hideout was outside the town of Dinsoor.

By now, Hammami was a marked man in more ways than one. A month earlier, the US government had posted a reward for the Alabama native, offering up to $5 million for "information leading to his arrest or conviction."[28] The wording indicated that the United States wanted to capture Hammami alive. However, Hammami stated in various forums that he was preparing for a violent death. He had struck up Twitter relationships with a number of American counterterrorism experts and bloggers, including J. M. Berger, a Boston-based Brookings Institution researcher and analyst. In a series of tweets, Berger tried to draw out Hammami on future plans and even suggested that he could try to arrange for the Shabaab militant's safe return to the United States, although Hammami undoubtedly would have to face prosecution and jail time. Hammami would not entertain the thought. "The last card is the last round in the mag," he wrote in one tweet.[29] "No regrets. Freedom! Ha ha." To the blogger Spencer Ackerman he wrote, "I figure I can't do much but wait 4 my time."[30]

Offline, Hammami wasn't quite so ready to die and hatched an escape plan. "Elyas" is a former Shabaab militant, Amniyat member, and friend of Hammami who lives in Mogadishu. He says that Rahanweyn clan members seeking to help Hammami reached out to a human smuggler in Nairobi.[31] The smuggler agreed to help sneak Hammami out of East Africa entirely—if he could make it to Kenya. Hammami was gung ho and told his fixers he would pretend to be a Tabliq preacher if necessary. In late August, he left his hideout and headed south. He was accompanied by three Somalis and two foreign fighters, both hard-core Al-Qaeda fighters—Khattab Al-Masry of Egypt and Osama al-Britain, a British national of Pakistani origin. According to Elyas—who got an account of the trip from one of the Somali companions—the size of the group delayed and complicated the process of leaving Somalia. Hammami could have been smuggled out individually, but he insisted the entire group go with him on an envisioned journey that would take them through Kenya, South Sudan, and finally to Libya.

Al-Shabaab leaders got wind of his plans and sent gunmen after him. He avoided capture by turning off his phone and limiting his movement. He stopped coming to villages in order to avoid attracting spies. "If they needed something from the town, the Somali guys will come in and buy some food," Elyas says.[32] But Hammami, a true product of the smartphone age, couldn't stay out of contact for long. In September, he reached an area between Bardhere and Saakow. When he and his little band got a satellite signal, they posted messages on Twitter mocking Shabaab and its leadership.

Then one day, Hammami contacted Elyas and asked if he could arrange a talk with a Somali radio station. Hammami was concerned about his family in Dinsoor, who he said were being harassed by Al-Shabaab. Forget Somali radio, Elyas said—talk to Voice of America, you'll reach a larger audience. Arrangements were made and Hammami spoke to VOA's Somali Service on September 3. During the interview, broadcast later that day, he made brief mention of his two wives, whom he said Shabaab had arrested, leaving his children "motherless and fatherless." But he used most of the fifteen-minute phone call to launch a verbal fusillade against Al-Shabaab's emir. When asked why he had split with Godane, Hammami replied, "Basically, he's left the principles of our religion, and he's turned Al-Shabaab into an organization that oppresses every single Muslim in an effort to turn himself into the next Siad Barre of Somalia. He wants to be the ruler of Somalia regardless of whether he rules by Sharia or by any other laws."[33]

Hammami's voice was calm; his tone matter-of-fact. But no words could be more inflammatory to Godane and the jihadists in his corner. Al-Shabaab never mentioned the interview in any of its statements, but it seems likely that with these comments, Hammami sealed his fate or hastened his death.

Details of what happened next come from Elyas. Staying on the move, Hammami and his companions, traveling with two pack donkeys and armed with a few rifles, continued south toward Bardhere. On or about September 10, the group came upon a small reservoir near the village of Abaqbul. They approached the owner, a nomad who did not indicate he knew them. However, he let everyone drink for a fee. As they left, Khattab Al-Masry asked the man not to tell Al-Shabaab of their whereabouts—a move Elyas thinks may have been a grave mistake. On the evening of September 11, Shabaab Amniyat agents reached the same reservoir. It's not clear whether they intimidated the owner or he tipped them off willingly. But within hours Al-Shabaab had the entire area surrounded, using Amniyat, Jabhat, and Hisbah units deployed from Barawe, about thirty kilometers away.

The next morning, just after 7 a.m., Shabaab agents located Hammami and his men at Dal-Adda, a hill to the northeast of Bardhere. The ensuing shootout was relatively brief. Hammami and al-Britain were killed, al-Masry and one of the Somali fighters were wounded and captured, and the other two Somalis escaped. By 8 a.m. the operation was over, says Elyas.[34] Godane's last significant opponent in Al-Shabaab had been eliminated.

Al-Shabaab took the bodies of Hammami and al-Britain to Bardhere and buried them near the banks of the Jubba River. Word of his death leaked out within a few hours and was confirmed through a tweet that someone, presumably one of his friends, sent out on Hammami's Twitter account.[35]

⁓

Kenya's National Intelligence Service was right when it warned that Nairobi's Westgate Mall was being sized up for attack. An Al-Shabaab team led by Somali national Adan Garaar had studied the five-story, sand-colored building, taking note of entrances and exits, the layout, the security system, roads, parking lots, and other details. No doubt they noticed that the mall's security guards were unarmed and that the guards made only a casual check of incoming shoppers for metal objects. In many ways, the mall was an ideal site for a massacre.

In Garaar, Al-Shabaab could not have picked someone more suited for the task. A friend of Garaar's from the Islamic Courts Union—who asked to be identified only as "M-Arab"—says Garaar was trained at Al-Shabaab's Salahuddin camp in Mogadishu and became an Amniyat conductor of special operations, often assigned to carry out assassinations and revenge attacks. "They chose him for brutal killings because he was brutal, he was a terrorizer," M-Arab says.[36] When Al-Shabaab ejected Hizbul Islam fighters from the city of Kismayo, Garaar reportedly slit the throat of captured fighters. In a 2015 article, Kenya's *Daily Nation* said police described Garaar as a "certified psychopath, known for extreme fits of anger, which would often see him shoot haphazardly whenever he flew into tantrums."[37]

But besides being brutal, Garaar was intelligent and organized. When he helped to drive Hizbul Islam forces from Kismayo in 2009, he was rewarded and made commander of a ninety-man unit that operated along the Kenya-Somalia border. Al-Shabaab sources say this unit became a hit squad, infiltrating and ambushing Kenyan forces in the area. Taking advantage of Kenya's lax security measures, Garaar relocated to the eastern Kenyan town of Garissa in 2011 and the next year obtained a Kenyan ID. M-Arab and a relative of Garaar say he went to Garissa to organize hit-and-run attacks. It's not clear if he actually carried out that task, although assassinations and hand grenade explosions rose in the area after his arrival.

Soon afterward, he began planning an assault on Westgate, getting support and funds from Al-Shabaab's leadership. According to a Somali government intelligence official, Garaar visited Nairobi several times to personally inspect the mall. He also built a support network for acquiring necessities such as SIM cards, weapons, ammunition, and a car.[38] Then—in a sign that Shabaab had maintained its chain of command amid Godane's purge—he reported his findings to the group's intelligence chief, Abdishakur Tahlil, and external operations chief, Yusuf Dheeg. They, in turn, reported the findings to Al-Shabaab's senior operations commander, Abdirahman Sandhere, who submitted a plan of attack to Godane. The emir approved.

It was about 12:30 p.m. on September 21, 2013, when a silver Mitsubishi Lancer pulled up on Mwanzi Road, near the front entrance of Westgate. Four masked men, each one carrying an ammo pouch and an assault rifle, climbed out and with no warning began hurling grenades and firing bullets at people on the mall's outdoor terraces. One man hit by shrapnel remembered hearing a shout of *"Allahu Akhbar!"* before blacking out. Dozens of others, hearing the blasts and seeing the wounded, turned and dashed inside the mall.[39] Al-Shabaab's most painful retaliation against Kenya had begun.

Two gunmen followed the crowd inside, firing at shoppers, while two others walked up a ramp to the rooftop parking garage, shooting security guards and people trying to flee the scene in their cars. On the roof, the mall was hosting a children's cooking competition. According to witnesses, the assailants saw the tents, families, and cooking equipment and promptly tossed a grenade toward the crowd. After a deafening blast, as children wailed and dozens of people lay wounded or dying, the two men methodically shot everyone they could find. According to one witness, one gunman shouted, "In the name of Allah, the most gracious, the most merciful, we've come to kill you Christians and Kenyans for what you are doing in Somalia."

That was all within the first twenty minutes. The next hour saw all four gunmen stalking the mall corridors. Hundreds of shoppers found exits and ran outside to safety. Others huddled in shops, storerooms, and any type of space that might provide cover. When the assailants encountered someone, they would often ask: "Are you Muslim?" If the answer was yes, they would seek confirmation by asking a question such as "Who was the mother of the Prophet?" Those who could name Mohammed's mother were spared. Those who couldn't were shot dead. Police initially remained outside the mall, seemingly paralyzed by fear and disorganization, and the four men were able to converge in the mall's huge, two-story Nakumatt supermarket, where they continued to shoot people trying to hide in the aisles.

By the standards of terrorist attacks, the assault was already a success. Shabaab had spilled volumes of Kenyan blood, disrupted a major economic center, and was rapidly taking over headlines on news websites worldwide. But the group went a step further to make sure its narrative, not just its name, captured people's attention. When the assault was a few hours old, Shabaab began sending out English-language messages on its Twitter handle, HSM Press Office.[40]

> HSM has on numerous occasions warned the #Kenyan government that failure to remove its forces from Somalia would have severe consequences
>
> The Kenyan government, however, turned a deaf ear to our repeated warnings and continued to massacre innocent Muslims in Somalia #Westgate
>
> By Land, air and sea, #Kenyan forces invaded our Muslim country, killing hundreds of Muslims in the process and displacing thousands more
>
> The attack at #Westgate Mall is just a very tiny fraction of what Muslims in Somalia experience at the hands of Kenyan invaders. #Westgate
>
> The Mujahideen entered #Westgate Mall today at around noon and are still inside the mall, fighting the Kenyan Kuffar inside their own turf

Kuffar is an Arabic term meaning "disbelievers" or "infidels"—one of the most severe if overused insults in the jihadist world.

A short while later, the tweets continued:

> Since our last contact, the Mujahideen inside the mall have confirmed to #HSM Press that they killed over 100 Kenyan Kuffar and the battle is still ongoing.
>
> The attacks are just retribution for the lives of innocent Muslims shelled by Kenyan jets in Lower Jubba and in refugee camps #Westgate
>
> The message we are sending to the Kenyan govt & Public is and has always been just one: remove all your forces from our country #Westgate

Al-Shabaab's media wing, Al-Kataib, composed the tweets, based on information the attackers fed them from inside the mall. Garaar, who according to the *Daily Nation* drove from Nairobi to Mandera on the day of the attack and then snuck back into Somalia, was also "in constant communication" with the attackers and may have helped write the messages as well.

The tweets—re-sent dozens of times and reported by all major news organizations—seem to have had almost as much impact as the attack itself. Analysts instantly recognized that by communicating directly to Twitter users, Al-Shabaab had seized control of the coverage from journalists. "It was the first major terrorist attack in history in which the group that mounted the operation used Twitter to announce to the world it was responsible," wrote CNN national security analyst Peter Bergen.[41] In previous terrorist attacks like 9/11, he noted, the attackers did not have any say over actual news content. "So what we saw unfold in the attack on the mall in Kenya is something quite new: a terrorist group shaping the media coverage of the event in real time," Bergen wrote. What Bergen may not have known was that Al-Shabaab had seen this technique at least once before, when Omar Hammami live-tweeted Al-Shabaab's attempts to kill him in April.

Al-Shabaab continued to make use of Twitter over the next three days, as Kenyan forces carried out a siege of the mall but were slowed by infighting and poor communication between police and army units. When President Kenyatta suggested a woman may have been one of the Shabaab assailants, the group tweeted, "we have an adequate number of young men who are fully committed & we do not employ our sisters in such military operations."[42] When Kenyan officials announced the mall was nearly cleared, Shabaab responded: "There are countless number of dead bodies still scattered inside the mall, and the Mujahideen are still holding their ground. The Kenyan govt and FM (foreign minister) haven't the faintest idea of what's going on inside #Westgate mall."

It was not until the evening of September 24 that the building was secured. The final casualty toll was not as high as Shabaab boasted, but it was high enough: at least 67 people dead, at least 175 others wounded. It was initially unclear whether the gunmen had escaped, although an investigation by Kenyan authorities, aided by the FBI, concluded they were killed and likely buried under a section of the mall that burned and collapsed for unclear reasons during the siege. Returning store managers also found huge amounts of merchandise missing, leading many to conclude that the army and police, in the midst of hunting down armed assailants who had just murdered dozens of people, made time to do some large-scale shoplifting.

Much about the operation remains murky, and the four gunmen have never been definitely identified. In February 2015, Shabaab released an eighty-minute video on Westgate, in English and Arabic versions, that revealed little except to say the attack was the result of "meticulous planning and painstaking preparations."[43] It also included audio statements from the gunmen, recorded by phone while the attack was in progress. One said: "after lengthy reconnaissance and intelligence gathering mission Allah has granted us [success] in fighting our enemies. We have destroyed whatever we could inside and now we are waiting for the so-called counterterrorism forces which they boasted so greatly about so that we may demonstrate to them the might of Allah and the power of his soldiers."

The video also showed a masked fighter who called for lone-wolf attacks on shopping malls in the West. "If just a handful of mujahideen fighters could bring Kenya to a complete stand-still for nearly a week, just imagine what the dedicated mujahideen could do in the West to American or Jewish shopping centers across the world. What if such an attack were to occur in the Mall of America in Minnesota? Or the West Edmonton Mall in Canada? Or in London's Oxford Street?"[44]

The Somali intelligence official says Al-Shabaab rewarded Garaar with bonus money after Westgate, allowing the militant to obtain multiple wives.[45] But he didn't get to enjoy his windfall for long. On March 12, 2015, a US military drone fired missiles at a car traveling near Dinsoor. Six days later, after getting confirmation from Somali officials, the Pentagon announced that Adan Garaar was dead. The statement merely said Garaar was "connected" to the Westgate attack.[46] VOA's Somali Service, which reported on the killing first, described him more accurately as the mastermind.

Al-Shabaab would conduct many more attacks in Kenya, most notably the April 2015 massacre at Garissa University College. The attacks kept Al-Shabaab's name in the headlines and helped maintain its reputation as an organization to be feared—and loathed. But nothing had quite the same international impact as the storming of the mall, captured on security cameras and covered round-the-clock by CNN, Al Jazeera, and a dozen other international networks for four consecutive days. Part of it was the timing—after the well-publicized military losses and internal conflict for Al-Shabaab during 2011 and 2012, many observers thought the group was a spent force that would splinter and vanish like so many extremist groups before them. Westgate showed those thoughts were somewhere between premature and flat-out wrong.

The Combating Terrorism Center at West Point perhaps summed it up best: "Wracked by internal divisions . . . Al-Shabaab was in need of relief. The attack on Westgate Mall provided the group with a media triumph that catapulted it back onto the public stage."[47]

Prominence, however, carries risks as well as rewards, and Al-Shabaab's leaders were about to learn that the hazards they faced were becoming greater than ever.

FOURTEEN

NO PLACE TO HIDE

As early as 2007, less than a year after the group was founded, Al-Shabaab leaders feared death from the air. The US airstrike in the far south that wounded Aden Ayrow and other militants that January showed that the United States had the tracking ability, ground intelligence, and weaponry to deliver highly targeted attacks. Even at that stage, when the group was barely known outside Somalia, Shabaab leaders adopted tactics to keep foes from pinpointing their location. Mohamed Omer, an Islamic Courts official who worked with Ayrow, remembers that the Shabaab military chief "never spent more than forty minutes or one hour in one place. He would not drive on main roads. He would take small roads and alleyways so that he can identify which cars are following him." US missiles found Ayrow and other Shabaab leaders anyway.[1]

Al-Shabaab's worry about airstrikes grew stronger in the 2010s as US resolve to crush the group grew stronger. In June 2011, the Obama administration released a policy paper, the "National Strategy for Counterterrorism," which outlined a global plan to stop terrorist attacks and destroy the groups behind them, with a strong emphasis on Al-Qaeda. Top goals included the elimination of terrorist safe havens and the dismantling of Al-Qaeda affiliates, including Al-Shabaab. The report highlighted Al-Qaeda's role in Al-Shabaab, saying "elements" of the senior group were pushing its junior partner toward greater aggression outside Somalia. "Influenced by its Al-Qaeda elements, Al-Shabaab has used terrorist tactics in its insurgency in Somalia, and could—motivated to advance its insurgency or further its Al-Qaeda agenda or both—strike outside Somalia in East Africa, as it did in Uganda, as well as outside the region," the authors warned.[2]

The fears about attacks outside East Africa would prove to be unfounded (as of early 2018). Nevertheless, officials made it known the United States was going to exercise more muscle against the group. A senior military official told the *Washington Post*: "They [Shabaab] have become somewhat emboldened of late, and as a result we have become more focused on inhibiting their activities."[3]

The United States' first step was to turn loose the UAVs—unmanned aerial vehicles, or drones. According to the London-based Bureau of Investigative Journalism, which has done extensive reporting on post-9/11 US air attacks in Pakistan, Yemen, Iraq, and Somalia, the United States carried out only nine airborne attacks on Somali territory between 2001 and 2010, all of them using piloted aircraft or sea-launched missiles.[4] Drones were used in a surveillance capacity. But starting in 2011, the United States focused its Reaper and Predator attack drones on Al-Shabaab, using UAVs stationed at Camp Lemmonier in Djibouti; Mahe, an island in the Seychelles; the town of Arba Minch in southern Ethiopia; and not-quite-secret bases within Somalia itself, one located in a corner of Mogadishu's main airport, another set up in Kismayo. The first confirmed attack by a US drone in Somalia took place on June 23, 2011, when a Reaper fired missiles at a Shabaab base in Qandal, south of Kismayo, wounding at least two militants.[5] The main targets of the attack were later identified as British-Lebanese national Bilal Berjawi and British-Egyptian national Mohamed Sakr, considered two of the top foreign jihadists working in Somalia. It may not be a coincidence that the attack happened sixteen days after TFG soldiers captured Fazul Mohammed's laptop, which a Somali official called a "treasure trove of intelligence."[6]

Several more drone attacks were reported in Somalia by the end of the year—some confirmed by the Pentagon or independent sources, some not. Army General Carter Ham, the head of the US military's Africa Command, exulted in the torment the drones caused for Al-Shabaab's leaders. "I like it a lot that Al-Shabaab doesn't know where we are, when we're flying, what we're doing and specifically not doing," he said. "That element of doubt in the mind of a terrorist organization is helpful."[7]

The threat of attack became greater still when the US State Department dangled multi-million dollar rewards for information on the whereabouts of seven top Al-Shabaab leaders in June 2012.[8] The offers were high by any standard—up to $3 million for Shabaab media operations head Abdullahi Yare and military intelligence chief Zakariye Hersi; up to $5 million for Mukhtar Robow, Ibrahim al-Afghani, Fuad Shongole, and military commander Bashir Qorgab; and up to $7 million for Ahmed Godane. The prize for the emir was one of the highest sums available in the State Department's "Rewards for Justice" program, topped only by the money offered for Mullah Omar, Ayman al-Zawahiri, two other Al-Qaeda leaders, and the head of the Pakistani jihadist group Lashkar-e-Taiba.

To promote the offers, the department circulated a black poster headlined "FACES OF TERRORISM" in large red letters, above headshots and names of the wanted men. The poster urged anyone with information "leading to the location of these persons" to contact the nearest US embassy or consulate, write to the provided email address, or call the listed 1–800 number. The blurb promised that all messages and messengers would be kept confidential, and as further enticement, offered the possibility of relocation for sources and their families. The poster boasted the added visual touch of gold coins and a tagline that warned, "The family you save may be your own!" Shabaab leaders worried, with good reason, that bounty hunters and potential traitors within the group would take notice and volunteer their services to the Americans or Somali government intelligence.

Some tried to shrug off the threat. Shongole compared the rewards to the Quranic legend of infidels offering one hundred camels for the head of the prophet Mohammed when he was fleeing Mecca. "The dollar is the camel of today," he said. Tongue-in-cheek, he added: "Whoever informs the mujahideen fighters of the place where Obama can be found will get 10 camels, and for [Hillary] Clinton we will offer 10 roosters and 10 hens."[9]

An official in Clinton's State Department circulated a reply:

Shongole—may I call you Shongole? I must insist on a trade richer than 10 roosters and 10 hens in exchange for [Clinton], as she is far more valuable to the world, our nation, to this administration and to me personally. I have great respect and affection for her. She is very special. I therefore require 6 goats to be included in the package.[10]

Al-Shabaab countered the drone threat by trying to shoot down the machines with anti-aircraft fire and by sniffing out spies who helped guide the UAVs to their targets. Periodically, it announced it had downed a drone. Alleged shootdowns near Kismayo in October 2009 and September 2011 were never backed up by witnesses or proof. In May 2013, the group said it brought down a US surveillance drone near the village of Bulo Marer and published photos of the wreckage on Twitter with the comment "this one will no longer be able to spy on Muslims again."[11] Pentagon officials confirmed the crash of a UAV in Somalia, but they said it was "highly unlikely" that it was hit by Al-Shabaab, citing the aircraft's high altitude. Mostly, the drones flew over Somali skies unscathed.

Al-Shabaab had better luck catching spies—but only after they had done considerable damage to the group. Ibrahim Ali Abdi, also known as Anta Anta, was Shabaab's chief bomb maker. Somali intelligence sources say he also organized the terrorist attacks in Somaliland and Puntland on October 29, 2008, that killed nearly thirty people. One day short of the fifth anniversary of those attacks, in 2013, Anta Anta was driving near the town of Jilib when a US drone swooped in and fired three missiles at the car, killing him and two Shabaab military commanders. A Shabaab investigation pinned the blame for the attack on twenty-nine-year-old Mohammed Gelle, who was accused of attaching a tracking device to Anta Anta's vehicle. Gelle, along with two other alleged spies, was publicly executed by firing squad in Barawe on March 5, 2014. They were among more than ten people executed that year on charges of working with American, British, Ethiopian, Kenyan, or Somali government intelligence.

At least one spy apparently helped take out multiple Al-Shabaab figures. Ishaq Omar Hassan was a twenty-two-year-old man from Afgoye who gave an unusually detailed "confession" of committing espionage against the group. The admission came in a 2013 video released by Shabaab's own media arm, Al-Kataib, after Hassan had been captured and jailed by the Amniyat. His story was obviously told under duress and was edited and packaged into an hour-long production meant to frighten and demoralize other potential spies. But his account is worth a closer look, as a Somali intelligence official says that to the extent it can be verified, it appears to be true. It also provides fascinating insight into the tactics the United States and Somali governments have used to hunt down Al-Shabaab leaders.

In the video, a nervous-looking, T-shirted Hassan explained that he knew and sometimes helped out Bilal Berjawi and Mohamed Sakr, the two foreign jihadists who were targeted and injured in the June 2011 US drone attack in Qandal. "I was a friend of Bilal Berjawi," he said. "I used to visit his house. I also knew about his meetings with the emir of the mujahideen."[12] It was probably for that reason that he was arrested by Somali government agents during a visit to Mogadishu in early 2012 and, according to his account, blindfolded, interrogated, and tortured. He said the abuse stopped only when he agreed to work with the TFG against Al-Shabaab. He was introduced to two government intelligence officials, Muhiyadin Aw Hussein and Mohamed Yare, who in turn introduced him to a senior intelligence official identified only as Khalif. The men gave him an X-2 mobile phone, $4,000 in cash, and instructions to plant the phone in Berjawi's car. Then, when Berjawi is away from civilians, Hassan was told, the phone should be turned on.

To carry out the second directive, Hassan said he recruited Yasin Osman Ahmed, a driver for a senior Al-Shabaab leader. Ahmed, speaking in the same video as Hassan, said he needed money to start a used car parts business; he agreed to turn on the phone for $2,000. Then, Hassan explained: "One day, he [Berjawi] called me. He said he needed my help to help buy a gun. We went to the gun market, and on our return he got out of the car and went inside. I stayed behind and just hid the phone next to the seatbelt buckle"—specifically, in the gap between the front seats.

Three days later, on January 21, 2012, Ahmed's boss met with Berjawi in Siinka Dheer, a village outside Mogadishu. When they got out of their cars and walked under a tree, Ahmed snuck into Berjawi's car and turned on the phone. Guided by the signal, drones soon began flying overhead, although according to Ahmed, Berjawi did not look particularly concerned. Perhaps that is why he climbed back into his car and drove off, only to be blown apart by three missiles a few minutes later. A leaked Pentagon document that referred to al-Berjawi as "Objective Peckham" said the match with the cell phone signal took place at 10:39 a.m., and the missiles struck at 11:03.[13]

Hassan said he was called to Mogadishu, where he received a hero's welcome from the intelligence agents: "They took me to a restaurant, they ordered dhaylo [young lamb], they said I was a real man, an intelligent guy."[14] They gave him $3,000 and some new clothes. Then they gave him his next target: Mohamed Sakr. This time, Hassan was to take a tiny electronic tracking device and place it on Sakr or his driver, named Abukar. Hassan said that he agreed but while waiting for a chance to act, he kept the chip hidden outside, under a rock in a neighbor's yard, in fear that he might somehow activate it and summon the killer drone.

Hassan traveled to Marka, where Sakr lived. His first thought was to involve Yasin Ahmed again, but he said he learned from a friend that Sakr strongly suspected Ahmed of playing a role in al-Berjawi's death. However, Ahmed gave him a contact, a cousin of Sakr's driver named Abdurrahman Mohamed Osman, better known as "Arab," who agreed to get involved. Hassan said that in a face-to-face meeting he gave Arab $200, with another $800 to follow when the mission was completed. Arab promptly bought a jacket for his cousin—Sakr's driver—but before presenting it, he cut a small incision in the collar and placed the chip inside. And in the pre-dawn hours of February 24, US drones closed in on Sakr's car as he, his driver, and two others motored near the K-60 area south of Mogadishu. The men apparently heard the drones and got out of the vehicle. But since the chip was embedded in the driver's jacket, the missiles fired by the drone found their target, killing Sakr and his companions instantly.

Hassan said that a few days after the attack, he met with his TFG contacts at Tre Piano, a Mogadishu restaurant. The men were very excited. "The intelligence agents asked me about other Al-Shabaab leaders," he recalled. "They said, 'Do you know Abu Zubeyr [Godane]?' They asked me about Abu Bakr As Zayli'i [al-Afghani]. I told them I never saw them. They said don't bother with that for now, it's another issue." The agents also invited Hassan to move to Mogadishu and work with them full-time.

But he never got the chance. A short time later, Al-Shabaab officials told Hassan to report to a local headquarters and hand over his cell phone. The fact that Hassan had changed his SIM card and hidden his TFG money with

Ahmed didn't save him. He was arrested, and Shabaab agents threw Ahmed and Arab in prison as well.

Many spies in that position would never be seen nor heard from again. Hassan was. The first time was on July 21, 2012, when an impromptu, outdoor Shabaab court in Marka convicted both Hassan and Ahmed of working with the CIA.[15] On the spot, they were tied up and executed by firing squad as hundreds watched. A third accused spy was also shot dead, but it wasn't Arab; a former Al-Shabaab member believes Arab was freed by a high-ranking official who accepted a bribe.

Hassan's second reappearance came in May 2013 when Al-Shabaab's media arm released the confession video. Both the execution and the video were accompanied by vows from Al-Shabaab to "cleanse" Somalia of such spies. "For all their technological advancement, the Kuffar are still incapable of coordinating air strikes w/o relying on human intelligence," the group said in a Twitter message.[16] The comment, meant to be mocking, came across as more of a backhanded compliment; it was an admission that the CIA and other intelligence agencies, working with the TFG, had found reliable informants within Al-Shabaab.

It was no wonder Godane purged the ranks. He couldn't tell who to trust.

By this time, Godane unquestionably felt the noose tightening around his neck. The Shabaab emir had been fanatic about security for years. From 2009 on, he almost never showed his face in public and rarely talked on the phone, communicating either by text message or, when possible, in secret face-to-face meetings. Now, he frequently changed both his bodyguards and his mobile phones to frustrate any would-be trackers. For added safety, he had other men dress like him and shadow his movements to confuse potential assassins.

And yet, a Somali intelligence official who was involved in the hunt for Godane says that finding the emir was never difficult. It was simply a matter of analyzing phone records. "Whenever he changes his number, Western intelligence services had contact [information] for the people he calls, and it was easy to figure out it was him," says the official.[17]

This became especially evident in January 2014. Al-Shabaab was girding itself at the time for an AMISOM offensive on Burdhubo, a militant-controlled town of about ten thousand in the southwestern Gedo region.

Commanders sent large militias to reinforce two bases outside the town. Both Western and AMISOM intelligence learned Godane was going to the area to attend a meeting of senior Shabaab leaders. At about 6:30 p.m. on January 9, Kenyan F-5 jets bombed the meeting site in Kalabayrka junction, near the town of Birta Dheer. Kenya announced the next day that thirty militants had been killed, including several top foreigners.[18] Godane survived, but possibly only by luck. Kenyan military spokesman Emmanuel Chirchir said on his Twitter account that Godane left the scene just half an hour before the jets attacked.

After leaving Kalabayrka, Godane went to the town of Dinsoor and stayed in the area for a little more than two weeks. When a delegation of top Al-Shabaab leaders left Dinsoor on January 26, they traveled in three vehicles driving in three different directions, toward the towns of Kismayo, Saakow, and Haawaay. US intelligence found its target anyway when one of Godane's phones was turned on, in the car driving toward Haawaay. A drone closed in and fired missiles. The car was destroyed, killing Godane adviser Ahmed Abdulkadir, also known as "Iskudhuuq."[19] A source within Shabaab and sources close to AMISOM said that Iskudhuuq and Godane had a meeting before leaving Dinsoor and that Godane was supposed to travel in the vehicle that was targeted. But Godane was not inside when the missiles hit, for reasons unknown.

In spite of the near-misses, a Somali intelligence official said at the time that death was "hovering over Godane."[20] He said the United States had about forty people working on the Godane case, including informants. The official predicted that by the end of the year, Godane would be "taken off-air"—a phrase Mogadishu intelligence officials use to describe someone who is about to be killed.

—

In early June 2014, Somali media reported that Al-Shabaab had arrested the head of its Amniyat unit in Barawe, Abdurrahman al-Qannas. Officials in the group accused al-Qannas of maintaining contact with Shabaab dissidents, including Hassan Dahir Aweys and, before his death, Ibrahim al-Afghani. It was a controversial arrest, as al-Qannaas—the former Khalid Mohamud Abshir from Minneapolis—carried a good reputation in

Al-Shabaab, especially as a sharpshooter. Dozens of AMISOM and Somali government soldiers had allegedly met their deaths at the hands of al-Qannas and his rifle.

His detention sparked a dispute among the leadership. Some officials voiced their approval, including spokesman Ali Dhere and Shabaab's governor of the Lower Shabelle region, Mohamed Abu Abdalla. However, the arrest was challenged by the organization's top judge, Sheikh Abdul Haq, and a powerful Amniyat figure known as "Tooxow," both of them close relatives of al-Qannas. The dispute grew heated enough that Godane was asked to come and mediate it. According to reliable Shabaab sources, that's the reason the emir traveled to Barawe in late July. The date of his arrival is uncertain, but he was apparently there by Eid Al-Fitr, at the end of Ramadan, on July 27; witnesses reported seeing Godane pray in the city that day.

Godane then stayed in Lower Shabelle and the neighboring Middle Juba region for the next several weeks, tending to business while trying to keep a low profile. There was a lot for the emir to do. One task was to meet with members of Shabaab's Tanfid Council to discuss the ongoing offensive by AU and Somali government forces. Al-Shabaab hadn't suffered any catastrophic losses on the scale of Mogadishu or Kismayo during 2014 but continued to lose control of small and medium-sized towns across Somalia. Al-Shabaab's periodic offensive actions, including deadly assaults on Villa Somalia in January and July, the killing of a half-dozen parliament members, and several attacks aimed at retaking areas seized by AMISOM, were not enough to wrest momentum away from the pro-government side. The Tanfid Council talks likely centered on what Shabaab could do if AMISOM made a move on Barawe, whose port was one of the group's few remaining major sources of revenue.

On a different day, Godane met with Dhere, Abdalla, Haq, and Tooxow to discuss the al-Qannas matter. For once, an Al-Shabaab dispute did not end in acrimony and violence. A source in the group says Godane ordered al-Qannas to be released, and he convinced Dhere and Abdalla to drop the issue. Perhaps the men decided that Al-Shabaab could not withstand another round of internal bloodletting.

Godane also had a much more relaxed meeting during this time with Aden Onbe and Abdirahman Filow, two Shabaab officials from the Gedo region who came to see him. "Their arrival in Barawe was picked; they were known to be trusted figures of [Godane]," says a source in Al-Shabaab. The good feelings evidently continued, as Godane assured them of top positions in Gedo, with Onbe to be made head of social issues and Filow to be appointed regional intelligence commander.

While all these meetings may have kept Al-Shabaab's internal gears running smoothly, they left Godane more exposed to US and Somali government surveillance. When traveling, the Shabaab emir usually avoided hotels and private villas in favor of camps or wooden shacks; they attracted much less scrutiny. But when Godane met with Onbe and Filow, Somali government agents learned he was at the Colombo Hotel, in a northern suburb of Barawe. It was a prime example of how difficult it was for Godane to remain completely off the radar. "He was a working man, who commands a large army, managing people," says the Somali intelligence official.[21] "He does not have a regular palace so he has to travel, he has to meet people, he has to use phones." In theory, the agents could have called in US airstrikes to bomb the hotel and kill Godane right there and then. However, the US government did not want to attack terrorist targets when they were around civilians; when launching the helicopter strike that killed Saleh Nabhan in 2009, for instance, the Americans waited until the Al-Qaeda operative was on a stretch of highway outside Barawe's populated area. "[Godane's] whereabouts were known but he was in the midst of a lot of people," the Somali intelligence official says.

Amid all the meetings and a brief trip to Saakow and Jilib in the Middle Juba region, Godane stayed in the area longer than he had planned.[22] He might have stayed even longer except that on Saturday, August 30, Ugandan troops and Somali government forces captured Bulo Marer, about 60 kilometers north of Barawe. The commander of Ugandan forces, General Dick Olum, told reporters that Shabaab fighters had fled toward the coastal town and he promised to go after them. "Of course, you very well know my Barawe is my next target," Olum said.[23]

Godane and his guards had to get out of town. On the night of August 31—a night lit only by a thin crescent moon—four vehicles left Barawe around 11:30 p.m. Two headed south, on the road toward Kunyo Barrow and Kismayo, while two others drove inland toward the small town of Haawaay.

Then the vehicles switched directions, with the Kismayo-bound cars suddenly veering north toward Sablale, while the two near Haawaay turned south toward Kismayo. The twists and turns might have fooled spies on the ground but not the officials watching through drones in the sky above. "It was discussed whether all vehicles be bombed, but a decision was made to keep track of them," the Somali intelligence official says.[24]

The vehicles continued their journey, unmolested, with all passengers keeping their cell phones turned off. The following day, September 1, Godane visited a Shabaab training camp in Shanta Ameriko, a former base for an American oil company. There, he met with and lectured his commanders. He also held a meeting with local farmers and elders, urging them to stand with the mujahideen and fight the infidels. It's not known if Shabaab got any new pledges of support, but the elders were hospitable enough to give Godane and his guards a snack for the road, a fresh watermelon.

Late in the afternoon, Godane and two bodyguards climbed into their car, a Toyota Surf SUV, and started driving toward Sablale, about twenty-five kilometers away, heading inland. At around 5:30 p.m., still outside the town, they stopped by the side of the road to perform early evening prayers. According to a source close to Al-Shabaab, the three then dug into the watermelon, eating as they sat near the car.

The Somali intelligence official says that right about then, a cell phone in Godane's vicinity was switched on. The user sent a text message to a phone in Kamsuma, a village near the town of Jilib to the south.

"Did you put the kids to bed?" the message read.

"Shall I put them all of them to bed?" was the response.

"All but one," said the next text.

In Somali culture, this is a classic conversation between a husband and wife. A man will use this kind of talk to woo his wife and let her know he is coming home.

The agents tracking Godane quickly saw the cell phone was on and checked the number of the phone in Kamsuma. It matched the number they had for Godane's wife.

Immediately, they got excited. Unless this was an elaborate ruse, they had pinpointed the location of Ahmed Abdi Godane—and he wasn't near anyone except his own bodyguards.

Within minutes, the US operation was underway. According to Pentagon officials, a combination of manned and unmanned aircraft fixed on the target and launched several Hellfire missiles and laser-guided munitions. Media reports later put the number of projectiles fired between four and eleven. The resulting blast was deafening. "It jolted the entire region," said Lower Shabelle Governor Abdulkadir Mohamed Nur.[25]

The noise alerted Shabaab that something was amiss. After night fell, Shabaab members from two nearby towns moved cautiously toward the area of the blasts, fearing further attacks. They were unsure who had been targeted, as Godane told few people where he would be at any given time. But when they finally searched the area, they found the remains of Godane and his two guards, about 250 meters from the wreckage of the SUV. It was not known if the three had wandered away from the car, had tried to flee upon hearing the aircraft, or were simply tossed a long distance by the sheer force of the explosions.

In Washington, the Pentagon announced the airstrike on the morning of September 2 but could not immediately verify that Godane was dead; spokesman Rear Admiral John Kirby said there were no Americans on the ground in Lower Shabelle to provide firsthand confirmation. Three days passed before US officials, after analyzing telephone chatter and interviewing Somali officials, announced that the airstrike had killed Godane. The Pentagon statement said, "Godane's removal is a major symbolic and operational loss to the largest Al-Qaeda affiliate in Africa and reflects years of painstaking work by our intelligence, military and law enforcement professionals."[26]

The killing drew uniformly positive responses from governments in the region. Kenyan president Uhuru Kenyatta thanked the United States and said Godane's death "provides a small measure of closure" for victims of the Westgate Mall massacre.[27] Ethiopian Prime Minister Hailemariam Desalegn said the killing was "the beginning of the end for Al-Shabaab." The foreign minister of breakaway Somaliland said, "We welcome the death of the bully." And Ugandan government spokesman Ofwono Opondo said, "Uganda is happy."[28]

In Somalia itself, President Hassan Sheikh Mohamud appealed to Al-Shabaab fighters to lay down their arms. "The government is willing to offer amnesty to Al-Shabaab members who reject violence and renounce their links to Al-Shabaab and Al-Qaeda," he said. "Those who choose to remain know their fate. Al-Shabaab is collapsing. I say to the members of Al-Shabaab: Godane is dead and now is the chance for members of Al-Shabaab to embrace peace."[29]

Like the Somali president, many Somalia analysts predicted that Al-Shabaab was about to crumble, split, or at least go through a severe power struggle. The emir was only the latest in a string of top Shabaab leaders who had been killed or left the group. The militants had steadily lost territory and sources of income for the previous four years. Its parent organization seemed to be a shadow of its former self as well.

But Al-Shabaab, once again, was to defy predictions of its demise. Those who said its end was near forgot that militant groups, like weeds, can regenerate if their roots remain in the soil.

PART FOUR

RESURGENCE

FIFTEEN

ARRESTING THE DECLINE

AL-SHABAAB'S SPOKESMAN ALI DHERE WAS at a home in the central town of Galhareri on the evening of September 1 when his phone rang. His assistant answered and handed the phone to Dhere, who spoke to the caller and then told the assistant, "Leave." When the aide departed the room, Dhere came back on the line and learned the news—Godane is dead.[1] Come to Barawe at once, he was told; the Tanfid Council is to meet and choose the martyred emir's successor. Dhere understood he was to make no announcements. Godane's death was being kept hush-hush to confuse the United States and give Al-Shabaab time to plot its next move.

The next day, Dhere set out on the 400-mile (650 km) journey south to Barawe, no doubt mulling over which candidate he should support. Other members of Shabaab's executive council pondered the same question as they made their way to the meeting, though few if any had to travel as far as Dhere. Most of them were already staying in and around Barawe, Shabaab's largest remaining stronghold on the coast and its new number-one source of funding, thanks to local port fees. Barawe had great beaches too, but this meeting was not to end with a group swim. Al-Shabaab's situation was like that of a country that has suddenly lost a military dictator or president-for-life. Not only was there no succession plan, but the chances of a power struggle were very real given the high stakes, the egos of the potential heirs, and the fact that all those present were comfortable with the use of violence.

Members attending the meeting included two operations specialists with ties to the Westgate Mall attack, Abdirahman Sandhere and Mohamed Mohamud, a.k.a. Dulyadeyn. Others were allies of Godane who had supported his ruthless tactics, including senior adviser Ahmed Diriye, deputy emir Mahad Karate, financial chief Hassan Afgoye, high-ranking judge Dahir Ga'amey, longtime council member Bashir Qorgab, and Ali Dhere. One source says Mukhtar Robow was invited but Robow denies this, saying, "No, at that time they were gunning for my death."[2]

Two sources—one a current member of Al-Shabaab, the other an ex-Shabaab member who defected to the government—say the Tanfid Council discussed several candidates for emir, including Hassan Afgoye and the absent Robow. Ibrahim Al-Afghani's former top aide Abu Ayan says that Ali Dhere and Sheikh Mohamed Aala Sultan also voiced interest in the top job. But the debate soon focused on two men, Mahad Karate and Ahmed Diriye.

Karate, also known as Abu Abdirahman Mohamed Warsame, was the initial favorite. He was a diehard jihadist, had been a close friend of Godane, and was experienced at the top, having served turns as chief of the Amniyat and as head of Shabaab's "defense department," and three years as Godane's lone deputy. He had the right roots too, having fought against Ethiopian troops with AIAI during the mid-1990s in the Gedo region. Robow, who had known Karate during the early years of Al-Shabaab, says Karate went to the meeting "expecting to be crowned." But the sources say Karate's bid was weakened by personality issues; he did not get along well with everyone on the council, and some accused him of inflaming past differences between Godane and other Shabaab leaders like Robow. He also had the reputation of being good at organizing militias but avoiding the front lines.

That cleared the way for Diriye, who had support not only from Godane's allies, but also from Godane himself, who according to multiple sources had made it known he wanted Diriye to replace him if he met an untimely end. The council chose Diriye as emir, officially by unanimous decision, with Karate maintaining his post as deputy emir. Karate accepted the outcome, but supporters say he sulked for months afterward.

A Shabaab defectors' site reported the choice on September 4; official word came two days later, in a public statement addressed to Al-Qaeda chiefs Ayman al-Zawahiri and Mullah Omar. The bulk of the statement was a eulogy for Godane that veered between accurate assessment ("Decisive in action, uncompromising in belief . . ."), poetic tribute ("A mighty stem in the battlefields of Jihad he was, on whom sentiments of glory and courage hung"), and questionable personality sketch ("Humble in nature and generous in character, his was a life adorned with the cloak of bravery").[3] The real news came near the bottom, when Al-Shabaab assured its followers the group would fight on, and said Godane "has left behind a group of men . . . who will neither rest nor settle down until they govern all the corners of the earth with the Sharia of Allah." Those men, the statement said, had appointed Diriye as the group's new leader.

Diriye picked out a more jihadist name for his new position, dubbing himself Abu Ubaidah, after a companion of the prophet Mohammed.

The new emir was similar to Godane in some ways—he was in his early forties, was part of the Dir clan, and had a comparable intelligence and worldview. But Diriye/Ubaidah was no clone of his predecessor. In the early '90s, while Godane was studying in Pakistan, his future successor was already a member of AIAI. It's believed he joined around the time the group fought its initial 1991 battle in Kismayo; acquaintances say he helped to protect the families of AIAI fighters as they retreated from the town. Also, unlike Godane and many other first-generation Shabaab leaders, Ubaidah never received training from Al-Qaeda in Afghanistan nor worked with Osama bin Laden. "He may have visited Arab countries a long time ago, but otherwise he was a local man," says Zakariye Hersi.[4] After his initial experience with AIAI, the future emir had completed a training course in Dhobley, spent time stationed in Kismayo and his reported hometown of Luq, and was finally sent to Ethiopia to join AIAI's operations there.

Hersi notes another major difference between the two emirs—size. Godane stood about five feet, eight inches tall. Hersi describes Ubaidah as "very tall; a giant of a man."[5] Multiple people who've seen him in person say he towers above his associates. He could be as tall as the average NBA shooting guard—six-foot-four.

One person who knows Ubaidah well is Abdullahi Sheikh Mohamud, an Islamic scholar who taught for AIAI. He first met the future Shabaab emir in 1997 when Mohamud lectured at a workshop about Islamic law in Raskamboni. The two men stayed in touch for years afterward as Diriye/

Ubaidah taught Quran in Kismayo, got involved with the Islamic Courts Union, and began to rise in the ranks of Al-Shabaab. Mohamud says the future emir was an active fighter as Al-Shabaab seized Kismayo from government forces in 2008, and then he led the fighting to take the Bay and Bakool regions after Ethiopian troops left Somalia the following year. Al-Shabaab named him *wali* (governor) of Bay and Bakool in June 2009. Mohamud was impressed with his administrative skills. "He can remember a number he called a year ago," Mohamud says. "He is hard working, never gets tired, very generous . . . and he was good in sharing the wealth. If he asks you to do a job he will stay on top of it and make sure it gets done. He is an expert on *itisal fardi* (man management)."[6]

Abu Ayan says he got to know Ubaidah well during his time as governor of Bay and Bakool. "He is someone who likes to bring people together; very welcoming, very good at lobbying," Ayan says. "He likes discussions, and he likes to change people's perceptions. . . . When there was conflict, Godane wanted his thoughts. Diriye was doing all the outreach, lobbying. Godane used to listen to him. He was a politician, unlike Karate."[7]

Like Godane, however, Ubaidah's skills were used to advance a radical jihadist agenda. Mohamud says the new Shabaab leader, for all his abilities, is a "difficult, polarizing person who believes in Takfiri ideology," the belief system that holds that nonbelieving Muslims should be punished.[8] As governor of Bay and Bakool, Ubaidah was known for enforcing a strict, harsh version of Sharia, banning Western culture and restricting the operations of international aid agencies. The people of the regions suffered horribly during the 2011 famine. Ubaidah nevertheless maintained the trust of Godane, who eventually appointed him senior advisor and, shortly before his death, to the head of Al-Shabaab's interior maktab, overseeing the group's domestic affairs. He is also believed to have played a role in the purge of Godane's enemies, including the slaying of Omar Hammami in September 2013.

Now, as Al-Shabaab's new emir, Ubaidah was tasked with reversing its falling fortunes. The last few months of Godane's rule had been something of a disaster for the group. None of Al-Shabaab's 2014 attacks had even a fraction of the impact of the Westgate Mall assault, and on the military front, the group was losing ground almost by the day. AMISOM's troop strength now stood at more than twenty-two thousand, bolstered by contingents from Sierra Leone and Djibouti and the full-scale return of Ethiopian troops. Outnumbered at least two-to-one, Shabaab fighters mostly retreated without fighting when Ethiopian and Somali National Army (SNA) troops launched a new offensive in March 2014, capturing a string of inland towns.

On the one occasion they stood their ground, in Qoryoley, a fertile farming area, they foundered. Lower Shabelle region governor Abdulkadir Nur led troops in the March 22 Qoryoley battle. He says Al-Shabaab repulsed an initial attack using rocket-propelled grenades and machine guns, killing four SNA soldiers. But AMISOM and the SNA, cooperating effectively, sent a joint force to attack the town from the northeast. The troops broke through the Shabaab defenses by 2:30 p.m. Meanwhile, a second joint force got an assist from a dozen or so US military advisers, the men Somalis called *kabaweyne*, Somali for "big shoes." "They opened a container and removed big artillery," says Nur. "They told us to put rubbers in our ears and fired several salvos into the jungle ahead of us. It was a deafening sound. We did not hear a reply."[9] By 3:30 p.m. the second unit entered Qoryoley, and Al-Shabaab lost the town.

With no chance to win a conventional battle, Al-Shabaab leaders had fallen back again on the strategy used by outgunned armies since the beginning of time—guerilla warfare. On September 19, 2013, Somali government forces ejected Al-Shabaab from Mahaday, a town of ten thousand north of Mogadishu. But the ousted militants came back again and again. In an October 2 raid, Shabaab fighters killed several government soldiers and confiscated weapons, including two technicals. A January raid resulted in the death of another ten soldiers. In February, Shabaab was able to retake the town briefly after government troops pulled back.

Hit-and-run attacks weren't the only tactic in Al-Shabaab's playbook, as Somali National Army Colonel Abdi Mohamed Dile learned during the March 2014 offensive. Dile, the deputy commander of SNA forces in the Bakool region, expected to face a determined, strong enemy when the offensive began on March 4. Instead his men met only pockets of resistance as they marched with Ethiopian troops toward the town of Wajid. When they arrived in Wajid on March 9, they found the streets deserted. From the few stragglers left, Dile learned that Al-Shabaab had forced nearly the entire population to flee, in order to deny support to the incoming troops and prevent them from restoring any kind of normalcy.

"When we took over, we urged the people to return, and they did," Dile says. But, he adds, "Al-Shabaab immediately returned to the areas we passed through."[10] And once they came back, the militants imposed a blockade on the town. Any truck driver approaching Wajid ran a high risk of being forced to stop and having his goods either confiscated or destroyed. If he was lucky, he would be allowed to drive back to where he came from. If he wasn't, he would be executed. The blockade wasn't airtight, but it was enough to cause severe food shortages in Wajid for more than a year.

Using these tactics, Al-Shabaab also imposed crippling blockades on the towns of Bulobarde, Huddur, and El Bur. Shrewd businessmen imported goods by donkey and other means, but food and fuel prices in all three locations soared. Electric companies eventually shut down in Bulobarde, says a journalist in the town, Abdifatah Gasle, forcing people to "embrace solar power."[11] Al-Shabaab also targeted the residents who refused to leave with nighttime home invasions, murders, and beheadings. Even animals were not safe; Shabaab fighters rounded up people's donkeys at watering holes and shot them in the head.

Al-Shabaab took things a step further in El Bur. Ethiopian and Somali government forces recaptured the town on March 26, 2014, finding it empty except for about a dozen residents. The soldiers soon learned to their dismay that before leaving, Al-Shabaab had cut off the town's water supply. "They took the water well pump and the generator. They also removed and destroyed the pipes that take water to the residential areas," says journalist Mohamed Abdi, who was embedded with the Somali troops.[12]

A few days later, the soldiers learned of another well just outside the town. A unit of Ethiopian and Somali troops went to inspect it with Abdi in tow. The soldiers determined that the well needed repairs but could be fixed with equipment brought in from Mogadishu. They were driving back to El Bur when the convoy came to a sudden stop on the edge of town. "There is an Al-Shabaab flag flying in the middle of the road," Abdi explains. "The troops just passed there a few minutes ago. [We wondered,] where did Shabaab come from?"[13]

Troops dismounted and took positions. There was no movement. They cautiously approached the black flag and found words written in Somali on the ground. "You Habash infidels, you will be liberated from the land," it read.

Abdi says he got scared. Al-Shabaab was nearby.

Troops followed some tracks and entered nearby homes but there was no one to be seen. "We only saw dominoes in one of the houses but no human being," Abdi says. Al-Shabaab members reportedly play dominoes as a hobby, in the belief that the game somehow improves their decision-making skills.

But dominoes and psychological ploys don't win wars, and Shabaab forces lost control of more areas as the year dragged on. In late August, Somali and AMISOM forces advanced on Bulo Marer, an important agricultural town in the Lower Shabelle region. Regional governor Abdulkadir Nur was in the fight again, leading a unit of forty-eight soldiers. He says Al-Shabaab flooded canals along his route to the town, tried to scare him through texts and calls to his personal phone, and ambushed his men five times in an eight-hour period. Nur says he was almost killed in the second ambush, near the farm area of Golweyn-Libsoma, when a rocket-propelled grenade exploded in a field and showered him with shrapnel and sand.[14]

When AMISOM tanks rolled into Bulo Marer, Shabaab fighters targeted them with heavy machine guns mounted on top of a mosque. The multiple attacks killed six of Nur's men and caused casualties to AMISOM as well. But they didn't change the result: Al-Shabaab again lost control of a key town. The group would also lose control of its new "capital," Barawe, in early October, after abandoning a clutch of other small towns in the weeks before.

At an October 28 news conference in Mogadishu, Somali and AMISOM leaders did their best to make Al-Shabaab sound like a group ready to fold. AMISOM's commander, Ugandan Lieutenant General Silas Ntigurirwa, asserted that Somali army and AMISOM forces now controlled more than 80 percent of Somali territory.[15] President Hassan Mohamud avoided victory claims in his remarks but said more than seven hundred Shabaab militants had accepted the government's amnesty offer and turned themselves in. The former militants would get opportunities to gain skills and return to society, he said. "There will be no retribution; instead they will be given education," he said.[16]

A number of articles issued around this time suggested that Al-Shabaab, while not finished, had entered a death spiral of sorts. The former head of the UN arms embargo monitors, Matt Bryden, wrote that "steep decline" was forcing the group to reinvent itself.[17] Terrorism analyst and former FBI agent Clint Watts said combined pressure from its enemies had reduced Al-Shabaab "from the dominant entity in Somalia to a fractious force pushed to the rural interior. Losses of key cities, including a final stronghold in the port of Barawe in the fall of 2014, represented the tipping point in Al-Shabaab's collapse. Today, Al-Shabaab is a fraction of what it was at its height."[18]

And a November 2014 *New York Times* article by the paper's respected East Africa correspondent Jeffrey Gettelman and colleague Ismail Kushkush emphasized the group's falling fortunes. Even before Godane's death, they wrote, the group had begun "unraveling," shedding territory and fighters. A handful of Shabaab defectors told the reporters that Al-Shabaab offered no life and no future for Somalis. The picture they paint, said Gettelman and Kushkush, was one of Al-Shabaab getting weaker, without a captivating leader, its ranks growing thinner—a formerly powerful group now "partly defanged, although still dangerous."[19]

If 2009 represented the peak of Al-Shabaab's power in Somalia, the final months of 2014 were irrefutably its nadir.

~

But Ubaidah and top Shabaab leaders were already taking steps to effect a turnaround. One of the new emir's first steps was to "rehabilitate" critics of Godane. He increased the number of "dowro," or workshops for disaffected members and groups. Among those forced to attend were about sixty former commanders who Al-Shabaab had thrown in jail; many had mutinied after the killing of Ibrahim al-Afghani in 2013. According to a former Al-Shabaab member, their release was contingent on attending the workshops, where they heard talks on Islam, self-search, and sacrifice. "It's like ideological therapy," the former member said.[20]

Under the new management, Shabaab also increased its attacks on Kenyan soil and areas along the Kenya-Somalia border. Besides striking back at the Kenyans, the strategy had two apparent goals—winning new jihadist recruits through high-profile attacks and inflaming relations between the country's Muslim and Christian communities. In November 2014, Shabaab fighters halted a bus near the border town of Mandera. Passengers were made to disembark and lie on the ground, and then they were told to re-cite a verse from the Quran. Those who could do it were spared. Those who couldn't were shot at close range. Twenty-eight passengers were killed, all non-Muslims. The following month, Shabaab attacked a quarry camp in Mandera County and again, separated the workers by religion. Thirty-six were slain, most of them Christians. That attack prompted Kenyan President Uhuru Kenyatta to fire the country's interior minister and force the resignation of the chief of police.

For Kenya, worse was yet to come. In the early morning hours of April 2, 2015, hundreds of sleeping students at Garissa University College, a public school in east-central Kenya, were jolted awake by the sound of gunfire. Four masked gunmen, wearing fatigues and carrying AK-47s, had shot their way past the school's front gate, killing two guards and injuring two others, and were now firing on anybody they saw. They entered a classroom, where students had gathered for Christian prayer, and shot more than a dozen people. Then they made their way inside a three-story school dormitory known as Elgon B. The building became a scene out of a horror movie, as students tried to flee, only to find shooters in the hallways and school-installed security bars blocking escape through the windows. Witnesses who survived by hiding say the gunmen went from room to room calling out occupants; those perceived or identified as Christian were murdered on the spot. At one point, gunmen herded helpless students into a common room, had them lay facedown, and systematically shot them in the back of the head.

By the time police killed the assailants after a fifteen-hour siege, 148 people lay dead, nearly all of them students in their late teens and early twenties. It was the single deadliest attack Al-Shabaab had ever carried out—and it confirmed for the world that the group's tactics had not changed under the new leadership.

The assault pushed Al-Shabaab back into the headlines and deeply embarrassed the Kenyan government. Less than a week before the massacre, the new interior minister, Joseph Nkaissery, complained to the media about heightened travel alerts from Britain and Australia, saying the countries were trying to damage Kenyan tourism. After the attack, Nkaissery admitted in parliament that police had received warnings about the attack but essentially ignored them.[21] The government quickly offered a reward of about $200,000 for Dulyadeyn, who it fingered as the mastermind of the attack.

These attacks would have accomplished little had they just garnered Al-Shabaab some publicity. But it appears they helped bring in new members. In the weeks after the Garissa massacre, Al-Shabaab conducted a recruitment drive in the central Kenyan town of Isiolo. By late May, some two hundred boys were missing from the town and presumed to have joined the militants.[22]

Perhaps emboldened by Garissa, Al-Shabaab went back on the offensive in Somalia. Its first targets were Mogadishu hotels and restaurants. Al-Shabaab had attacked such establishments before, most notably in the bombing of the Hotel Shamo in 2009. But now the attacks became a core part of the group's strategy to intimidate officials, diplomats, and businessmen. The wave began with a car bomb in January 2015 outside the SYL Hotel, where a Turkish delegation was staying. Two security officers and a hotel employee were killed. A month later, Al-Shabaab assaulted the larger Central Hotel with two car bombs and a pair of gunmen who charged inside and opened fire. Twenty-five people died. Many similar attacks followed, most of them killing between ten and thirty people and doing significant damage to the buildings. A July 2015 bomb ripped off an entire side of the six-story Jazeera Palace Hotel, a city landmark that housed several foreign embassies.

Meanwhile, the AMISOM push of 2014 had stalled. Kenyan troops accompanied by Somali forces had been slated to move toward the town of Jilib in the Middle Juba region, but the KDF never got past the village of Bulogudud. Al-Shabaab's heavy presence and the thick jungles in the region may have forced KDF commanders to back off, fearing high casualties. Another setback came in December 2014 when Sierra Leone decided to remove its 850 troops from Somalia, as a massive Ebola outbreak back home made it impossible to rotate new soldiers to the force.

The real momentum shift occurred in mid-2015, as Al-Shabaab introduced a new tactic to the battlefield—sudden, *blitzkrieg*-like assaults on isolated AU bases. The first one on June 26 targeted a base held by about one hundred Burundian soldiers in the town of Leego, northwest of Mogadishu. The attack began like one of Al-Shabaab's hotel attacks, with a car bomb. But instead of sending in four or five gunmen to wreak havoc before committing suicide, Al-Shabaab deployed scores of well-armed fighters, directing intense gunfire and rocket-propelled grenades at the soldiers. Within a short time, the Burundians were overwhelmed. Shabaab fighters killed more than fifty of them; the rest fled, enabling Al-Shabaab to capture the base, raise its black flag, and steal all the military supplies. When AMISOM reinforcements approached the base two days later, the Shabaab fighters withdrew, preventing their foes from exacting revenge. Al-Shabaab would achieve similar results by storming a Ugandan base that September in Janaale and a Kenyan base in January 2016 near the town of El Adde, in the Gedo region.

The El Adde assault was especially devastating, and it also showed how Al-Shabaab's media arm, Al-Kataib, exploits such victories in its propaganda. A video released about three months later purports to show every key moment of the attack. Viewers get to meet the suicide bomber, a young, happy-looking man named Abdulqadir who is said to have "enlisted in the martyrdom brigade" after losing a leg in combat. The scene then shifts to El Adde the morning of the attack, where a thunderous blast shakes the ground in the distance. Almost immediately, dozens of Shabaab fighters dressed in green fatigues and orange headscarves open fire from rifles, bazookas, and battlewagons, the impact enhanced by a musical track of jihadist chants and a loud "swoosh" every time the video cuts to a different angle. The ramshackle base comes into view as the fighters advance through fields of dry brush and trees. Viewers see the attackers reach the base and fire over and through the low makeshift walls as Kenyan soldiers try to flee or crumple to the ground from bullet wounds.

The fifty-minute video highlights two especially gruesome moments. In one, a Shabaab fighter pumps bullets into the head of an already-fallen Kenyan soldier, shattering his skull. In the other, a Kenyan soldier emerges from the top of a smoking, immobilized tank. His helmet is off, his hands in the air. A bearded Shabaab fighter, seen from behind, steps forward and fires more than a dozen bullets at the man. After a few seconds, the soldier slumps and falls back into the tank, blood visibly oozing from his head. The video makers recognized the brutality of this moment, for when the fighter briefly turns toward the camera, his face is blurred out to prevent identification.

When the attack is done, as fighters ransack the camp's supplies, the camera scans the grounds, showing dozens of blood-spattered bodies. The number of Kenyan fatalities came to a reported 141, a fact the Kenyan government tried unsuccessfully to cover up.

These attacks highlighted a key problem faced by the African Union and the Somali government—a shortage of troops or allied militia to occupy and protect all the territory seized back from Al-Shabaab. Remote, rural areas posed the biggest challenge, as Shabaab fighters could take refuge in forests and jungles, waiting for the chance to ambush any number of targets. In those conditions, says the SNA's Colonel Dile, "It's difficult to fight against a man on the move on foot with a gun."[23]

Shabaab fighters attacked another isolated AU base in the village of Halgan in June 2016. This time, AMISOM was ready. After the initial blast, the Ethiopian soldiers manning the base repelled the assault and claimed to have killed more than one hundred Shabaab fighters. One Shabaab fighter, Mohamed Daud Mohamed, later told VOA that his unit alone lost forty-five men. "It was a difficult fight. We left behind the wounded as we didn't have a chance to evacuate them. Our cameraman was killed, foreign fighters were killed, everyone ran for their lives," he said.[24] Mohamed defected to the government eight months later.

"What we saw during the Halgan attack is they [Shabaab] are being complacent," says Bryden. "This was the fourth time they used exactly the same tactics to attack AMISOM forces, and although for the first three operations they were successful, at some stage AMISOM forces were going to learn from and anticipate this type of attack. Ethiopia clearly did."[25]

Still, by the end of 2015 the Al-Shabaab deathwatch had ended, as critics acknowledged the general upswing in the group's fortunes. Headlines tell the story. The *Daily Beast* website ran an analysis piece entitled "The Return of al-Shabaab." A similar article on the *Newsweek* site was called "Al-Shabaab's Staying Power," while the Brookings Institution wondered, "Why Are Efforts to Counter al-Shabaab Falling So Flat?" Bryden wrote an update to his earlier piece with a title that said it all: "The Decline and Fall of al-Shabaab? Think Again."[26]

It was not clear what role Abu Ubaidah played in the turnaround—the new Al-Shabaab emir, like his predecessor, maintained a low public profile and allowed no pictures of himself to circulate. He seemingly made no effort to claim personal credit for the group's successes. What was clear was that under his leadership, the group had found ways to rejuvenate itself without losing its identity. In business terms, he and other Shabaab leaders could be said to have "revitalized the brand."

Maybe that's why an outside firm—another jihadist organization with big ambitions, in fact—launched a takeover attempt.

SIXTEEN

THE ISIS INCURSION

In October 2006, just weeks after jihadists in Somalia formed Al-Shabaab, their counterparts in Iraq announced the creation of another new militant group—*ad-Dawlah al-'Irāq al-Islāmiyah*, the Islamic State of Iraq. ISI, which merged Al-Qaeda in Iraq with several allies, proclaimed that it would govern Baghdad and surrounding regions, the areas dominated by Sunni Muslims. It turned out to be an empty boast. While Al-Shabaab was taking over most of southern Somalia, ISI withered under blows from various Iraqi militias and US forces stationed in Iraq since the 2003 invasion. ISI carried out some suicide missions, but by 2010, it seemed to be on its last legs, especially after a joint US/Iraqi government raid in April that killed its top two leaders, Abu Ayyub al-Masri and Abu Omar al-Baghdadi. The head of US forces in Iraq, General Ray Odierno, said in June that 80 percent of top Al-Qaeda leaders in the country had been slain or captured, and he predicted the group would have trouble recruiting replacements or finding territory it could govern.[1]

Odierno couldn't have been more wrong. By 2014, while Al-Shabaab was struggling with the loss of leader after leader and town after town, the former ISI—now known as ISIS, the Islamic State in Iraq and Syria—was gobbling up huge swaths of territory in the two troubled countries, taking over major cities and oil fields, and imposing its harsh interpretation of Islamic law on a population of millions. The rapid rise of the group exhilarated jihadists from around the world, and thousands of young radical Muslims who might have once traveled to Pakistan, Afghanistan, Chechnya, or Somalia to fight in the name of Allah went instead to the Middle East. Significantly, ISIS pulled off its conquests in spite of a complete break with Al-Qaeda, which it now surpassed as the brightest star in the jihadist sky.

The exploits of ISIS—also referred to as ISIL, Islamic State, or the Arabic epithet Daesh, depending on one's view of the group—put Al-Shabaab in an uncomfortable position. From the beginning, from *before* the beginning, Al-Shabaab leaders had boasted close ties with Al-Qaeda. Al-Shabaab's loyalty to Al-Qaeda remained strong even as key Shabaab figures met their demise; the announcement of Ahmed Godane's death and Abu Ubaidah's appointment as emir was pointedly framed as a message to Al-Qaeda's supreme leaders. But Al-Shabaab could not ignore the new force in the jihadist world, especially after June 2014, when ISIS declared a global caliphate and named its chief Abu Bakr al-Baghdadi as the caliph, or the leader of all Muslims worldwide.

Even though few of those outside jihadist circles took the declaration seriously—UN Secretary-General Ban Ki-moon famously mocked the group as "Un-Islamic Non-State"—the rise of ISIS was earthshaking for militants in groups like Al-Shabaab.[2] ISIS, like Al-Qaeda, wants to enact its version of Sharia across the Islamic world and beyond. But its strategy for doing so is markedly different. Al-Qaeda has always focused on driving the United States out of the Islamic world so that it can topple what it sees as Western-backed regimes and replace them with "true" Islamic governments. Its preferred method of attack has been grand-scale terrorism like 9/11 or the 1998 US embassy bombings. In contrast, ISIS strives to conquer territory through military means and set up strict Islamic states immediately. It has used terrorism as more of a tactical tool, to frighten and demoralize opponents, including France, Shiite Muslims, state police and army forces, and rival militant groups like Al-Qaeda's affiliate in Syria, Jabat al-Nusra. The group has encouraged "lone wolf" attacks against the United States, like the June 2016 shootings at Orlando's Pulse nightclub that killed forty-nine people, carried out by a professed American supporter of the group. But ISIS has refrained (as of this writing) from devoting the time and resources to launching attacks on large, faraway American targets. To many Islamist militants of the mid-2010s, the ISIS strategy seemed more practical and gratifying—and in

Al-Shabaab's case, more similar to what they had attempted to do for the previous seven years.

Daniel Byman, a Middle East expert with the Brookings Institution, noted another difference between the groups while testifying before a US House of Representatives subcommittee in April 2015. "[The] Islamic State is far more successful in achieving its goals than Al-Qaeda has been," he said. "Like it or not, the Islamic State really is a 'state' in that it controls territory and governs it."[3] He warned that ISIS attacks were heightening Sunni-Shiite tensions across the Muslim world and that its military strength posed a threat to not only Iraq and Syria, but also to Libya, Egypt, Jordan, Saudi Arabia, Yemen, and Lebanon. "The Islamic State is a much bigger threat to Middle East stability than Al-Qaeda ever was," Byman said.

He could have added that ISIS threatened the stability of other jihadist groups too, none more so than one of Al-Qaeda's top affiliates, Al-Shabaab.

～

As early as 2007, Al-Shabaab forged relations with its nearest jihadist neighbor, AQAP, or Al-Qaeda in the Arabian Peninsula. An alliance between the groups was inevitable. AQAP operates in Yemen, a country that is only slightly less volatile than Somalia, is accessible by boat across the Gulf of Aden, and hosts more than a half-million Somali refugees. Al-Shabaab and AQAP never tried to merge or carry out joint attacks, but as time went on AQAP became an important ally for the Somali group. "Several top commanders who were wounded in Somalia have gone there to get better health facilities," says a source who works with Shabaab fighters in Galgala, Puntland. "They were able to access good hospitals in Yemen since they were not known by the local authorities, and this was made easier since they had connections with Somali refugees in Yemen."[4]

The groups also exchanged weapons, intelligence, and expertise, with scores, maybe hundreds, of militants moving back and forth between Yemen and Somalia. The only real obstacles in their way were international warships patrolling the Gulf of Aden for Somali pirates. On April 19, 2011, US Navy forces, acting on a tip, boarded a Somalia-bound boat in the Gulf and captured Ahmed Abdulkadir Warsame, one of Al-Shabaab's chief emissaries to AQAP. Warsame underwent two months of interrogation on a US ship and then was brought to New York, where he was indicted and eventually pleaded guilty to charges of providing material support to Al-Shabaab and AQAP. But his capture was the exception, and for the most part exchanges between the two jihadist groups continued.

However, it was this interaction that unleashed the ISIS virus in the ranks of Al-Shabaab. Yemen and AQAP served as a haven of sorts for Al-Shabaab members who had grown disillusioned with the group or Godane himself. When ISIS made its meteoric rise, these members were more than ready to cast aside Al-Qaeda and pledge allegiance to the new jihadist power. They included "Tutafika," a former Amniyat member who had stayed in Yemen after being treated there for battle injuries, and several men known as ji-hadist financiers and gun smugglers: Sharif Abdinur, Abdulwahid Bukhari, Mohamed Dhaqane, and Adam Hassan. According to militant sources in Somalia, some of these men returned to their homeland in the early months of 2014 with the goal of persuading Al-Shabaab to hop on the ISIS cara-van. Essentially, they were suggesting the group change its name and break *bay'ah*, its contract with Al-Qaeda.

Coming in the wake of ISIS's victories and Al-Shabaab's continued woes, the idea got more than a passing consideration. According to the sources, the ISIS supporters shared their views with a man they felt they could trust, Sheikh Abdulkadir Mumin, a charismatic jihadist with a beard tinted bright orange and a knack for causing friction. Formerly based in Sweden, then Britain, Mumin came to Somalia in 2010 after his jihadist views made him unwelcome in Europe. "He was always a radical cleric, nobody made him a radical," says a senior official with the US-backed Puntland Intelligence Agency (PIA). "He started radicalizing people at a [British] mosque, in-cluding many women. He created conflict between the congregation and the other clerics at the mosque. The other clerics hated him." After sneaking out of the UK, Mumin became a leading religious figure in Al-Shabaab, in charge of issuing the group's fatwas. But according to the PIA official, Mu-min remained in contact with jihadists abroad and "wanted to make Daesh official within Al-Shabaab for some time. . . . He waited until such time where there was a weakness within Al-Shabaab."[5]

It's believed Mumin voiced the ISIS proposal to some of Al-Shabaab's top leaders of the moment, including Fuad Shongole, Adan Garaar, Abdi-rahman Filow, and Hussein Abdi Gedi. They knew that merely raising the idea would likely mean conflict with Godane, an avowed Al-Qaeda admirer and loyalist. Garaar said he would go along with the change if the leadership accepted it. But Shongole and Gedi said the idea would not work, and the discussions went no further for the time being.

Godane touched on the Al-Qaeda/ISIS rivalry during a wide-ranging May 2014 speech that covered events in Syria. He did not mention ISIS by name, but he signaled where Al-Shabaab's loyalty lay when he referred to Al-Qaeda spiritual leader Mullah Omar as "leader of the believers" and called Ayman al-Zawahiri "our sheikh and emir."[6] He also urged warring jihadists in Syria and Iraq to reconcile and unite—a statement widely interpreted as a call for them to align with Al-Qaeda. However, Godane was blowing against an increasingly fierce wind. During 2014 and 2015, more than thirty jihadist groups around the globe would either pledge allegiance to ISIS or become formal affiliates. Some of the groups were small and local, but others were indisputably big fish, especially Egypt's Ansar Beit al-Maqdis—the group responsible for most of the terror attacks in the Sinai—and Nigeria's Boko Haram, which by 2014 had shot and bombed its way past Al-Shabaab, ISIS, and everyone else to become the most deadly terrorist group in the world.

In Somalia, the issue lay dormant for several months after Abu Ubaidah became Al-Shabaab's emir. But it came to the fore again in early 2015, when Tutafika and some Somali ISIS supporters in Syria began a full-court press to persuade Al-Shabaab to switch its allegiance. Mumin and Gedi were now completely on board, and the effort got a propaganda boost from Taymullah al-Somali, a blind, Somalia-born Dutch national who argued on social media (via friends) that there was no reason that Muslims shouldn't rally to ISIS's flag. "Being blind didn't stop me from coming to #Syria, what's your excuse?" he wrote.[7]

According to the militant sources in Somalia, pro-ISIS "agents" arranged phone conversations between ISIS leaders and Al-Shabaab members and visited towns around southern Somalia and northeastern Kenya, trying to drum up support. Gedi, a former ICU and Hizbul Islam member, was one of the workhorses, visiting parts of Somalia's Juba regions and northeastern Kenya, making in-person appeals to clan elders. ISIS has good governing structures, he told them; people will not be required to pay zakat, and no one will be killed unless they die in a battle. He also distributed money. In the village of Kamsuma, farmers and residents each got $50 in US bills—a characteristic move by ISIS, which had piled up large reserves of foreign cash to fund its operations.

To put a uniquely Somali spin on their pitch, the ISIS camp tried appealing to clan loyalties. When Godane was alive, there were Shabaab members who questioned why the group's attacks were concentrated in southern Somalia, leaving Somaliland relatively untouched. One rumor had it that Godane, a Hargeisa native, wanted revenge on southern clans for the havoc that Mohamed Siad Barre wreaked on the north in the 1980s. Another was that Somali intelligence had struck a gentlemen's agreement with Shabaab leaders not to attack Godane's (and al-Afghani's) home area. Neither theory was ever proven, but that didn't stop pro-ISIS agents from using them as though they were 100 percent fact. "They contacted politicians in Kismayo and Gedo and said we are working on this project to stop genocide by Godane's men against southern clans," says a Somali intelligence official in Gedo.[8]

The ISIS campaign extended into Somali mosques, where sympathizers preached that the world now had an "Islamic government" that true Muslims were obligated to support. One of Al-Shabaab's most prominent religious leaders, Kenyan cleric Abu Salman, made the same argument writ large in an audio message released in March 2015. Salman acknowledged Al-Shabaab's reluctance to leave Al-Qaeda but said, "Those jihadists who want to recognize Mullah Omar as *Amir ul Mi'min* (the emir of Muslims) are avoiding recognizing Abu Bakr al-Baghdadi instead," he said. "I see no religious grounds why a pledge to Baghdadi is not the way to go."[9]

ISIS intensified the campaign with direct appeals to Al-Shabaab members, first in an open letter ("By Allah, those who already gave *Ba'yah* to the Caliphate wonder why their brothers are late")[10] and then through Arabic-language videos posted to jihadist websites. One HD-quality production, with slick graphics and slow-motion camera techniques lifted straight from reality TV, featured Somali ISIS supporters talking to the camera, flanked by masked, rifle-toting men dressed in black. A speaker identified as Abu Hamza as-Somali asserted that the rise of the *khilafah* (caliphate) was based on the "prophetic methodology," an often-used ISIS phrase by which the group meant "the predictions of the prophet Mohammed." "If it were not, Allah would have never granted us this victory and never granted us the opening of these lands [in Syria and Iraq]," he said. "O you true mujahideen of Somalia. . . . Here is your khilafah around you and you have felt its warmth and support. So rush to your khilafah and your state."[11]

Bit by bit, the ISIS backers won over chunks of Al-Shabaab's rank-and-file. Islamic State's success had clearly excited Al-Shabaab's media arm, which extensively covered the group's advances, takeovers, and killings in Iraq, Syria, and by early 2015, Libya. ISIS videos were also shown during the weekly Shabaab screening of jihadist videos on Fridays. These developments, along with ISIS's increasing power, led many Shabaab foot soldiers to believe it was only a matter of time before the group abandoned Al-Qaeda and announced a merger with the new "caliphate."

The change appeared to be imminent on July 9, 2015 when Somali news outlet Garowe Online reported that Al-Shabaab's top leaders were discussing ISIS at a meeting in the town of Jilib. The report said emir Abu Ubaidah had "eased" his stance toward ISIS and that deputy emir Mahad Karate had agreed to pledge allegiance to the group.[12] The next day, Britain's *Daily Mail* quoted an unnamed source in Shabaab as saying, "We share many things with ISIS ideologically and we are ready to help our Muslim brothers and sisters around the globe under a united leadership with one agenda and ideology."[13]

But no actual Shabaab pledge materialized. The reasons for this remain unclear; it may be that Al-Qaeda leaders sensed that one of their key affiliates was about to slip away and engaged in some back-channel politicking to keep Al-Shabaab in the fold. Al-Qaeda chief Ayman al-Zawahiri addressed the issue directly in a message released in early September. In the message, evidently recorded some months earlier, Zawahiri expressed condolences for the death of Godane for the first time and accepted the oath of loyalty offered by Abu Ubaidah. On the issue of ISIS he said "we do not recognize this caliphate" and that al-Baghdadi was not worthy of being caliph, or ruler. He noted that Godane had disapproved of Islamic State as well.[14]

That was apparently enough for Al-Shabaab. In early September, leaders issued an internal memo aimed at silencing pro-ISIS elements. The memo said the group's policy was to continue allegiance to Al-Qaeda and warned that any attempt to create discord over this position would be dealt with according to Islamic law. It added that any speech about Shabaab policies, operations, and guidance had to be cleared with the group's media office. The leaders showed they meant business on September 30 when five foreign

jihadists who allegedly backed ISIS were detained in a raid in the town of Jamame, sixty kilometers north of Kismayo. Soon a purge was underway and
spread to the towns of Kamsuma, Mareray, and Malende; an undetermined
number of alleged ISIS sympathizers were arrested or killed.

A former member of the group's propaganda arm, speaking on condition of anonymity, says that despite the success of ISIS and the intensive
courting from the group, Al-Shabaab's leadership retained a deep loyalty
to Al-Qaeda. "Essentially, Al-Shabaab wanted to remain important in the
global jihadi arena, and Al-Qaeda gave them the brand approval, despite Al-
Shabaab having no real ties to the AQ core [as of 2015] aside from general
guidance and advice," says the man, who went into hiding after proclaiming
his support for Islamic State.[15]

At least one prominent Shabaab member in Somalia was brave or fool-
hardy enough to openly break with the group. Sheikh Abdulkadir Mumin
announced his allegiance to al-Baghdadi in an audio message released October 22. The following day it was confirmed that he led between twenty
and thirty fighters who made the switch to ISIS in Almadow, a mountainous area in the Puntland region. Jihad-watchers were less than impressed;
a Reuters reporter interviewed one of Mumin's men who said another 280
Shabaab members in the area had refused to follow the cleric's lead. But on
November 3, Al-Shabaab drew an even brighter red line for militants not to
cross. Spokesman Ali Dhere said the leadership had "agreed" to maintain
the unity of the group. Dhere did not mention ISIS by name, but his message
was clear when he said Al-Shabaab is the only "legitimate Islamic authority"
in East Africa and Somalia. Those promoting division were doing the devil's
work, he said, and divisions would not be tolerated.

The Amniyat now employed its well-honed spying and terror tactics.
Sheikh Bashir Abu Numan, a one-time AIAI fighter and friend of Robow's,
commanded a small band of fighters in the Middle Juba region who had
defected to ISIS. On November 10, six Shabaab members contacted him,
saying they wanted to join his cell. Numan reportedly welcomed them,
escorted them by motorcycle to his hideout near the town of Saakow, and
slaughtered goats for a meal. The next day, when Numan's men were relaxed
and had put their guns aside, the new arrivals repaid his hospitality with
gunfire, killing Numan and five of his followers. The gunmen had all been
fake defectors sent by the Amniyat. The world might never have learned

about the real defectors except that a few days earlier, Abu Numan had recorded a video in his hideout pledging allegiance to ISIS. The shooting that killed him occurred just moments after he handed over the video to a confidant. The friend posted it on social media several weeks later, when Numan was already dead.

Other pro-ISIS figures were slain or rooted out in short order. On November 22, Shabaab gunmen ambushed and killed Hussein Abdi Gedi. The Amniyat had tracked his communications and laid a trap for him near the village of Gududley in Middle Juba. On December 4, the Amniyat attacked a farm near Jamame and killed Mohamed Mawakki Ibrahim, a pro-ISIS Sudanese jihadist, best known for killing US development aid worker John Granville in Sudan's capital in 2008. (Ibrahim had come to Somalia and joined Al-Shabaab in 2010 after escaping prison in Khartoum.) December 7 brought news that two transplanted Americans in Al-Shabaab—Abdimalik Jones of Baltimore and Mohammed Abdullahi Hassan of Minneapolis— had surrendered to the Somali government after fleeing Shabaab because of pro-ISIS sympathies. Hassan, speaking by phone from his prison cell, told VOA's Somali Service that foreign jihadists who backed ISIS had no choice but to flee the Amniyat units assiduously hunting them down. "Some mujahideen fighters are now preferring to fall into the enemy's hands instead of meeting death in the hands of brothers," he said.[16]

One exception to that trend was Abdulkadir Mumin, still holding out in the Puntland region. On December 10, Mumin issued an audio message that taunted Al-Shabaab for killing members who pledged allegiance to Islamic State. "Your kingdom will disappear . . . caliphate will come into effect in Somalia," he warned. He challenged Al-Shabaab, saying that pledging to ISIS was in line with everything that Al-Shabaab preached.

He got his response on December 24, when Shabaab fighters attacked his little band's hideout in the village of Timirshe, near the Puntland city of Iskushuban. Residents reported hearing heavy gunfire. But the attack apparently failed, as Mumin survived and his group remained active, becoming the main ISIS cell in Somalia.

Al-Shabaab wasn't done with Mumin. On March 14, 2016, the group attempted an audacious seaborne attack on the coast of Puntland, using six repurposed fishing boats and about seven hundred men. A Somali intelligence officer says the purpose was twofold: to neutralize Mumin and to set up a Shabaab-controlled area in the Puntland region. The force left the seaside town of Hobley in two convoys, with two boats carrying 250 fighters, and four boats carrying the other 450. They sailed north for a spot on the Puntland coast between the towns of Bargaal and Elayo. But halfway to their target, anti-piracy surveillance planes made several fly-overs. According to sources within Al-Shabaab, the lead boats were concerned they had been spotted. After calling commanders on land, the first two boats were told to disembark at the Garmal village near the town of Eyl, while the second group was told to head to the nearest coastal town, Gara'ad, and stay as close as possible to the first group.

From that point on, the mission was a disaster. The men in the lead convoy landed and trekked into the strategic Suuj Valley but were attacked by Puntland government forces. The militants who landed in Gara'ad tried to slip into the jungle and make their way north to rejoin their comrades but were also ambushed by Puntland forces. The following week, officials declared victory over both groups of fighters. Casualties in the Suuj group were said to be 167 militants killed, 100 captured; in the Gara'ad group, 115 dead, 110 taken captive. And Mumin remained free, under the apparent protection of Puntland authorities. A senior Puntland military commander said that less than thirty militants escaped, including the mission's top two commanders, Moallim Janow and Duale.

For the time being, ISIS appears to have dropped or at least de-emphasized its campaign to win over Al-Shabaab. Instead, the group has focused on establishing its own toehold in Somalia. In April 2016, ISIS's media arm released a video highlighting the "Commander Sheikh Abdulkadir Mumin military camp," said to be the group's first training site in the country.[17] The word "camp" might have been an exaggeration, as the video showed no buildings, tents, or training courses, and there were only fifteen fighters seen on camera, doing push-ups and running on a scraggly, windswept plain. Mumin nevertheless appeared on camera to bless the site and reaffirm his group's allegiance to al-Baghdadi, effectively planting the ISIS flag on Somali soil. Later in the month, ISIS announced it had carried out its first attack in Somalia, saying it had bombed an African Union vehicle on the outskirts of Mogadishu, although AMISOM denied the claim.

In October 2016, the Mumin faction seized control of Qandala, a Gulf of Aden port town in northern Puntland. They held the town for five weeks before Puntland regional forces, attacking by land and sea, drove them out. The Puntland Intelligence Agency official says the soldiers seized computers, documents, and weapons during the raid. "We learned about what they are, and what they were planning," he says. "We seized explosives, readied explosives which were just waiting to be planted. . . . We seized their computers. There is very sophisticated data on them, very sophisticated training materials, and the training materials were very modern. From the data we believe they were not ready to engage in battles at this time, but were getting ready for it. They were in preoperational mode."[18] The attack on Qandala, he believes, was mainly to show their strength and attract more support and fighters. At the time of the takeover the group had no more than 150 fighters, he says, including a small number of Kenyans, fighters from Arab countries, and Somalis from the diaspora.

After Qandala, Mumin's men had setbacks, such as the defection of eight fighters, but the group explored other forms of attack. On May 23, 2017, a suicide bomber blew himself up near a hotel in Bosaso, Puntland, killing five people and wounding seventeen. The following day, ISIS's official Amaq news agency claimed responsibility on behalf of Mumin's group; it was the first ISIS suicide bombing in Somalia.

The Mumin group appears to have problems with local clans, who continuously report the fighters' movements to regional forces. But experts say Mumin is likely to stay a feared presence along the coastline and mountainous areas, as long as he has access to Yemen.

Abdi Hassan Hussein, the former director of the PIA, has criticized Puntland authorities for not destroying the Mumin group at an earlier stage. "It would have been better to destroy them when they were twenty or thirty men, before they adapted to the environment; but now the terrorists got used to the climate, they secured access to water wells, routes, and hiding places," he said in May 2016. "Now to defeat them would require the same resources and effort that was placed against Al-Shabaab."[19]

He warned that Islamic State will pose a tougher challenge for Somalia than Al-Shabaab. "Daesh is more dangerous than Al-Shabaab. They are known for committing large-scale destruction. They have more finance. They have more impact," he said.

Outside Somalia, ISIS suffered military setbacks during 2016 and 2017, most notably the losses of Fallujah and Mosul to US-backed Iraqi government forces, and it remains to be seen whether a less-successful ISIS will maintain a hold on the imaginations of Al-Shabaab members. A former Al-Shabaab media official asserted that at one point, 95 percent of Shabaab fighters were pro-ISIS. "It was only after Al-Shabaab started to ban ISIS support that members began blindly following the top leadership's decision not to switch," he said.[20] But that number sounds highly inflated, and it may have dropped even further with the losses suffered by the ISIS "caliphate."

Still, there was little doubt that as of early 2017, a significant portion of Al-Shabaab fighters still wanted to see the group bind itself to ISIS. The former Shabaab media official asserted that if the political winds change, the switchover could still happen. "To date Al-Shabaab has not provided religious justification as to why they oppose the *Khalifah* nor has Al-Qaeda," he said. "So you have now tacit supporters watching from the sidelines."

SEVENTEEN

AL-SHABAAB'S FUTURE

ON AUGUST 15, 2017, SOME forty Somali journalists who had gathered in Mogadishu's Royal Palace Hotel witnessed a sight once unimaginable: Mukhtar Robow, Al-Shabaab's co-founder and former second-in-command, sitting behind a table draped with the blue Somali national flag. The now fiftyish Islamist militant had surrendered to the government in Huddur forty-eight hours earlier, following days of clashes between his clan militia and Al-Shabaab fighters in his home Bakool region.

A bespectacled Robow, his eyes cast down, quietly read a prepared statement in which he announced he had quit Al-Shabaab more than five and a half years earlier. "I left Shabaab because of misunderstandings, and I disagreed with their beliefs, which do not serve the Islamic religion, Somalia, and its citizens," he said.[1] He thanked the Somali government for welcoming him to Mogadishu and said he would be in talks with officials, though he did not elaborate on the purpose except to say "I hope we will pursue a path of peace." He took no questions.

On the same day, to the south, a police unit patrolling a road in Kenya's Garissa County witnessed a sight that had become frighteningly familiar: Al-Shabaab gunmen ambushing their vehicle. Only one of the seven officers escaped unharmed from the attack near the small locale of Alijize. Five of them were killed, while one other was shot in the thigh. The gunmen stole the officers' weapons and set fire to their vehicle before slipping away.

It was at least the twenty-fourth time Al-Shabaab had attacked targets in Kenya since the start of the year. A Kenyan police official said security and intelligence forces would pursue the attackers, but there were no arrests announced and no indication the men were ever found.[2]

The events of the day offered starkly opposing images of the war by East African governments against Al-Shabaab. In one picture, the group was disintegrating from within. In the other, the militants were gaining strength and attacking at will. Which was correct?

Unfortunately for the Federal Government of Somalia (FGS) and its supporters, it was the scene in Garissa County that more accurately reflected the state of affairs regarding Al-Shabaab. Robow's defection was certainly a coup of sorts. But by almost any tangible measure—the sums of money collected, the swathes of territory controlled, the number of casualties inflicted, the sheer number of attacks carried out—Al-Shabaab grew stronger throughout 2017.

Observers, even the ones on the government's side, did not hide their concern. "Al-Shabaab remains a vicious threat to security in Somalia and indeed to the region," said Matthew Rycroft, Great Britain's ambassador to the United Nations, during a speech in April.[3] In May, US Director of National Intelligence Dan Coats named Al-Shabaab as one of seven terrorist groups that pose a "challenge" to the United States and its allies. The group has been weakened by the deaths of many planners, he said, but has sustained a "high pace of attacks" in Somalia and "retains the resources, manpower, influence, and operational capabilities to pose a real threat to the region, especially Kenya."[4]

The US Africa Command addressed Al-Shabaab's military strength in a June 2017 statement that made note of Al-Shabaab's success in overrunning AMISOM "forward operating bases" in Leego, Janaale, and El Adde. "Al-Shabaab has also increased its combat capability by seizing heavy weaponry, armored vehicles, explosives, small arms, ammunition, and other miscellaneous supplies during its operations overrunning [the bases]," it said.[5]

A less official but equally ominous assessment came from Tricia Bacon, a former counterterrorism analyst for the State Department. Writing in the *Washington Post*, she said she had interviewed people in Somalia and Kenya during research trips there in January and May 2017. Her finding was that

Al-Shabaab was still exploiting clan rivalries, government corruption, and general insecurity to keep itself strong. "Al-Shabaab finds ways to exploit the vacuum left by the state, tapping into a deep reservoir of grievances," she wrote. "It has become the main alternative to the government. It will not be defeated by military means alone, and the fitful progress by the Somali government may come too little, too late."[6]

If there were any doubts about the trend, they were eradicated the afternoon of October 14, 2017 in Mogadishu. The Zobe intersection (also known as K-5) was packed with cars and people when a garbage truck-sized vehicle, its cargo hidden under a red tarp, came careening down Afgoye Road, smashing into smaller vehicles in its drive to push ahead. Seconds later, the truck driver detonated an estimated 770 pounds (350 kg) of explosives in front of the upscale Safari Hotel. The deafening blast brought down the hotel and demolished or damaged dozens of nearby buildings, including the headquarters of the Somali Red Crescent, the Ministry of Planning, and the Qatari embassy. Black smoke poured into a blue sky for hours as rescue workers tried to douse the flames and find the injured among the rubble. The final death toll came to a staggering 587, with more than 300 others injured, making it the single deadliest terrorist attack not only in Somali history, but African history.

Perhaps stunned by its own brutality, Al-Shabaab did not say it carried out the attack. But there was little doubt among the public or Somali officials as to who was responsible. Tens of thousands attended pro-government, anti-Shabaab rallies four days after the blast.

Robow is also convinced of his former group's guilt. "I have no doubt about it," he says. "This has their fingerprints all over it. I was one of the people who founded this organization. I know how they sound at night, and I know their tracks by day."

The attack and its aftermath underscored an undeniable fact for Al-Shabaab. More than a decade into its violent mission, it cannot claim any type of victory. After all the offensives, all the calls to jihad, all the hundreds of millions of dollars and billions of man-hours expended to impose a form of "true" Sharia on Somalia, the group remains far, far short of its goals. Most Somalis do not live under Shabaab rule. Many who did fled elsewhere. The central government stands, albeit with lots of outside help. And Al-Shabaab itself has won relatively few hearts or minds, except when it took on what Somalis saw as an Ethiopian invasion and became a force for nationalism, with its jihadist intentions pushed to the back seat.

So that raises another question: what kind of future does Al-Shabaab have? Is there a scenario where it could regain popular backing, displace the government, and enforce the kind of Islamic law that Somalis (and others) have generally rejected as too extreme? Can it live on as a sharp, debilitating thorn in the side of Somalia's government (and others), stopping progress toward peace and stability? Or is the group destined to eventually die, the victim of too much war and too little public support?

Most experts on Al-Shabaab, both inside and outside the group, think its chances for pushing aside Somalia's government and setting up a Taliban-like state have passed—at least for the time being. "Al-Shabaab is disruptive, but it's no longer an existential threat to Somalia or the states of the region," says Matt Bryden. When asked if Al-Shabaab is Somalia's "elephant in the room"—the big problem no one wants to discuss—he rejects the analogy: "The 'elephant in the room' I would say is not Al-Shabaab, it's the failure of the government to exercise effective authority across Somalia's territory."[7] If Somalia's government could practice inclusive politics and earn the people's trust, he says, the diminished support that Al-Shabaab still finds in Somalia would dry up even further.

Former Hizbul Islam and Al-Shabaab official Mohamed Moallim Ali looks back at the Ethiopian invasion as Al-Shabaab's golden opportunity. "They built such a big military muscle," he says. "In Mogadishu about one-third of the students in school joined Al-Shabaab." But in his view, the group frittered away the public's goodwill and respect through indiscriminate violence, especially attacks like the 2009 Hotel Shamo bombing. "Displacing civilians and not showing mercy to the civilians and other acts brought bad reputation for the Islamic religion," he says. "The public has really been driven to the opposite edge by these acts."[8]

Roland Marchal believes a national Al-Shabaab government would have been doomed had it even got off the ground. "Shabaab had support to fight Ethiopia, but really at no time did you have a very strong popular constituency saying Shabaab is the solution to build a state," he says. "What you had is very [strong] popular support for the Islamic Courts Union, because the ICU were much closer to the population. . . . Shabaab were seen as strange people, very good at fighting foreigners, but they were seen as strange in the way they were enforcing Sharia, very far from what people wanted."[9]

The former director of Somalia's National Intelligence Agency, Ahmed Moallim Fiqi, says Al-Shabaab is still fundamentally at odds with most Somalis. "They don't want a government or a nation. Their goals are not to protect the Somali flag and Somali country. It's an Islamic caliphate that they want," he says. "To them, Somalia is like a wilaya, a region, like many others. They believe they are in charge of Africa or Central and East Africa on behalf of a supposed caliphate. They don't believe in the history, flag, or geographical location of Somalia. Therefore, Somalis can be overtaken by force, but they are not going to accept this."[10]

There is one thing that might render these analyses null and void—the departure of AMISOM and its twenty-two thousand troops. Despite some progress toward the creation of a strong Somali National Army (SNA), especially in the training of *Danab* ("lightning") commandos, the African Union force was as essential to the Somali government's survival in 2017 as it had been six or eight years earlier. It was AMISOM that provided the heavy security in February when Somali parliamentarians met in Mogadishu to elect a new president. It was AMISOM troops who protected all the towns over which the FGS supposedly had control.

But as AMISOM marked its tenth anniversary in Somalia, its backers seemed to be coming down with a bad case of Somalia fatigue. During 2016, officials from all the troop-contributing countries—Uganda, Burundi, Ethiopia, Kenya, and Djibouti—publicly floated the possibility of bringing home their men, and Uganda's army chief actually announced a departure date of December 2017, although that decision was rescinded. As always, money was a central issue. In March 2016, the European Union decided to cut its funding for AMISOM soldiers' salaries by 20 percent, or about $200 per soldier. This made peacekeeping in Somalia a less attractive task for these countries, whose governments have always siphoned off a chunk of EU and American funding before passing on the remainder to the troops.

Payments for the 5,400 Burundian soldiers were further complicated by international sanctions imposed on that country's government. In 2015, President Pierre Nkurunziza defied opponents and ran for a constitutionally questionable third term, setting off violence that killed dozens and prompt-ed a quarter-million Burundians to flee the country. Refusing to give money that would aid Nkurunziza, the EU and AU went several months without paying the soldiers' salaries until Burundi threatened to pull its troops from Somalia. The impasse was resolved when all parties agreed that the soldiers would be paid through a commercial bank instead of the Central Bank of Burundi, although diplomats questioned if the move would truly cordon off the government from the money.

A mounting body count also came into play. AMISOM has never public-ly revealed the number of soldiers killed and injured. However, the AU force did share partial casualty figures with the Stockholm International Peace Research Institute. That data allowed researcher Paul D. Williams, an as-sociate professor of international affairs at George Washington University, to conclude that a minimum of 1,100 AMISOM soldiers were killed in ac-tion between 2009 and 2014.[11] Fatalities have risen significantly since then, particularly since Al-Shabaab began large-scale assaults on rural AMISOM bases. In January 2017, Kenyan forces suffered their second disaster within a year—after losing at least 140 men at El Adde—when Shabaab fighters stormed a Kenyan base in the Somali town of Kulbiyow. Kenya's military said only nine soldiers were killed, but witnesses put the Kenyan death toll between forty and sixty and reported the attackers were able to loot the base before Kenyan helicopters drove them away.

In March 2018, AMISOM did a U-turn with its withdrawal plans. After a meeting in Kampala, troop-contributing countries said they will halt with-drawal and bring back troops already pulled out to deal with the continued Al-Shabaab threat. It's now expected that a full withdrawal will not hap-pen before Somalia holds elections in 2020. The timeline has slipped before and could easily do so again, given that all parties are clear about the conse-quences if AU troops leave too soon. US commanders have already warned against hasty withdrawal. "If this departure begins prior to Somalia having capable security forces, large portions of Somalia are at risk of returning to Al-Shabaab control or potentially allowing ISIS to gain a stronger foothold in the country," said the head of the US military's Africa Command, Gener-al Thomas Waldhauser, in March 2017.[12] Kenyan President Uhuru Kenyatta concurred at a London conference on Somalia two months later. "We can hurry to leave but what happens when an inadequately prepared Somali force is left to its own devices? A vacuum is left and the root of the problem will re-emerge," he said.[13]

The military chief of AMISOM at the time, General Osman Nour Soubagleh of Djibouti, summed up the situation more bluntly. "I am afraid they [the Somali army] are not ready to take over the security right now," he said. "In two years we have to prepare them. The time is very short."[14]

How to prepare capable forces is the question that still bedevils the Somali government and its supporters. Various European, African, and American entities have been trying for more than a decade to train a Somali army that can independently fend off Al-Shabaab and other threats to the government. The efforts intensified in 2017 as the African Union's self-imposed pullout date drew near; EU instructors taught combat skills to infantry, US trainers educated them on logistics, and AMISOM coached police on how to protect VIPs. AMISOM also made a show of giving the army items like mosquito nets and mobile field kitchens, while Turkey announced plans to train Somali forces at a newly opened military base in Mogadishu.

UN Secretary-General Antonio Guterres was not impressed. "The current effort involves different countries training different groups in different parts of the country with different doctrines," he told the London conference. "That is a recipe for a disaster. It is not a recipe for developing a true national army or police force. . . . Coordinated training must take place with the aim of building one army with one doctrine, capable of fighting an insurgency."[15]

Army-building was made harder still by the seemingly intractable corruption and disorder that plagues Somali politics. In an October 2016 report, UN monitors said Somali military officials had withdrawn almost $6.7 million from the country's central bank over a ten-month period to pay back salary to soldiers—but that only $3.5 million of the money could be accounted for.[16] Some units hadn't been paid in over a year.

The monitors also found it hard to tell who was and who wasn't a soldier.

> Within Mogadishu many individuals on SNA payrolls are concurrently employed by private security firms or serve FGS or [local] officials, members of parliament or the business community. Such individuals may or may not be called upon to serve in active units if needs arise. Over a quarter of the nearly

22,000 troops the FGS reports to be serving the SNA are stationed in or on the outskirts of Mogadishu yet there are—as far as the Monitoring Group can ascertain—no permanent barracks in the city, nor regular roll calls besides when salary or stipend payments are being distributed.[17]

The *Jane's* family of military/security publications gave the army a grim assessment in a July 2016 report: "The Somali armed forces are the poorest in the region in terms of training and equipment. They are currently in no position to secure all of Somalia from the Shabaab militants, let alone defend the borders of the country."[18]

In Bryden's view, the SNA is still largely a collection of clan-based units that remain undisciplined and unable to take and hold terrain or provide security for the people of Somalia. "Many of these units can only be deployed in certain areas," he says. "When they are deployed in the wrong areas they create local resentment, and that creates opportunities for Al-Shabaab. So this army is currently capable of very little. It's doing essentially what it can and that is not very much."[19]

In 2012, an internationally backed but Somali-run political process did give the country an ostensibly permanent government. The FGS, which replaced the discredited TFG, came into being with a new constitution and a new 275-member parliament. In September, MPs elected a new president, Hassan Mohamud. Significantly, the runner-up in the vote, former president Sheikh Sharif, accepted the result without protest—a rarity in any African country.

But the FGS has been weighed down by the same problems as its predecessors. Parliament and the administration remain prone to gridlock. A project to group Somalia's longstanding eighteen regions into federalized states has moved ahead in start-and-stop fashion. President Mohamud was subjected to one impeachment effort and at least two Shabaab assassination attempts. He also forced lawmakers to fire two prime ministers, with the second vote setting off a political drama that included singing, stomping, and whistle-blowing protests in parliament, accusations of bribe-taking, and a US threat to halt financial aid unless Somali leaders stopped acting like clowns.

Mohamud sought a second term in February 2017, with parliament making the choice again, after plans to hold a nationwide election fell through.

Vote-buying was rampant ahead of the poll, and a *New York Times* headline called the event a "milestone of corruption."[20] But the winner, former prime minister Mohamed Abdullahi Mohamed, a.k.a. Farmajo, was widely seen as more honest than his rivals. His presidency began on a good note, as the government began to regularly pay police and soldiers their promised salaries and made an effort to increase revenue by imposing taxes on businesses operating at Mogadishu airport.

Still, even if a reliable national army can be formed, there's no guarantee it will overpower the militants. Militarily, Al-Shabaab has bounced back strongly from its decline phase, as evidenced by its frequent attacks on Mogadishu hotels, assaults on AMISOM bases, a mid-2017 wave of roadside bombs in northern Kenya, and continued domination of the Somali countryside. Mainstream media usually say the group has between seven thousand and nine thousand fighters, but Zakariye Hersi puts the number at thirteen thousand. Also, Al-Shabaab continues to acquire large amounts of guns and ammunition, as evidenced by the weaponry captured by Ethiopian troops who repelled an attack in the town of Halgan: at least fifty rifles, eight machine guns, and more than a dozen grenade launchers plus assorted bullets and ammo clips.

Al-Shabaab still lacks tanks, aircraft, and the other hardware it would need to win a protracted battle against a professional army. But it does have the resources to deploy guerilla or "asymmetrical" warfare tactics in depth. In the Kulbiyow attack, Al-Shabaab sent not one but three car bombs speeding toward the Kenyans, helping to break down the AMISOM base's defenses.[21] It can afford all the weaponry because of successful "protection" schemes in Mogadishu, in which business owners pay fees to keep Shabaab gunmen off their property and/or merchandise.

The Amniyat, besides training men for the hotel and restaurant assaults, has shown signs of expanding its capabilities. In February 2016, Al-Shabaab claimed responsibility for sneaking a suicide attacker, armed with a laptop computer bomb, onto a Djibouti-bound Daallo Airlines flight carrying more than seventy passengers. The plot would have resulted in an epic tragedy, except that the bomber, sitting in a window seat, only blasted a man-sized hole in the fuselage and fell through it, plunging twenty thousand feet to his death. All other passengers survived, and the plane made a safe return to

Mogadishu. But the thought that Al-Shabaab was able to get the bomb past security—with the help of two workers at the Mogadishu airport, it turned out—gave aviation officials the chills.

Organizationally, Al-Shabaab has avoided the splintering and disarray that seems to befall most militant groups after a time. As of the start of 2018, the group appeared cohesive and organized, run by a twelve-man Tanfid (executive) council with Abu Ubaidah serving as emir and Mahad Karate as deputy emir. According to two sources close to Al-Shabaab and intelligence officials, the group's department heads were Ali Dhere, media and education; Hassan Afgoye, finances; Hussein Ali Fidow, politics; Mohamed Yare Moallim, judiciary and courts; Abukar Ali Aden, defense; Mohamed Abdinur Marwazi, religion; Mohamed Ala Sultan, taxes and humanitarian affairs; and Omar Matan, police. Ali Dhere and Mohamed Abdi Shiil served as senior advisers to Ubaidah, while former chief justice Dahir Ga'amey was chief adviser on "investments," meaning projects that allowed Al-Shabaab to hide money transfers. He also recently held the governor of governors position.

As always, none of the positions (except perhaps Afgoye's) were set in stone, and department heads were shifted around periodically to prevent any of them from gaining too much power. The most interesting shift was at the top; there were credible reports that Ubaidah had relinquished some of his duties due to ill health and that Karate was picking up the slack. The latter released his first-ever audio message in June, in which he attacked the "hidden and devious aggression" of the United States and Britain and urged jihadists to attack Western targets.[22] In the same month he appeared in a video eulogizing late Al-Shabaab emir Godane.[23]

Despite such threats, US involvement in Somalia shows no signs of trailing off. The greater use of armed drones since 2011 has been matched by more boots on the ground. The United States began by sending twenty advisers to Somalia in October 2013—the first official US deployment in the country in two decades. The Pentagon said the team was to play only a planning and support role to the Somali National Army. But in a classic case of "mission creep," the size and mandate of the team expanded as time and the Al-Shabaab threat went on. In 2016, US troops began accompanying SNA troops on raids. In the first attack in March, US helicopters delivered the

Somalis to their target in the small town of Awdhegle. In later raids, US soldiers took part in actual combat. Twice that September, US troops called in airstrikes to suppress Al-Shabaab gunfire, in what the Pentagon called acts of self-defense. Critics of the growing US presence pointed out there would be no need for self-defense if US troops hadn't been put on the Somali front lines in the first place.

The US role expanded again in March 2017, when President Donald Trump gave generals broader authority to launch attacks in Somalia. Another fifty Americans arrived two weeks later, and in May, a US Navy SEAL was killed during a clash with Shabaab fighters about sixty-five kilometers west of Mogadishu. The unfortunate soldier, thirty-eight-year-old Kyle Milliken, was the first US fatality in Somalia in nearly a quarter-century.

Add it all up, and it's fair to say that Somalia's prospects for peace and stability look only marginally brighter than they did on the day that AMISOM arrived on Somali soil in 2007. Matt Bryden again blames the situation as much on Somali government ineptitude as on Al-Shabaab power. "Where we still see a problem is that in Mogadishu in particular, the same tactics, techniques, and procedures continue to succeed year after year—complex attacks involving suicide bombers, suicide infantry, in much the same combination, some adaptations but not much," he says.[24] The only way to counter this, he says, is for government security forces to get stronger and more professional.

Roland Marchal thinks that when it comes to fighting Al-Shabaab, the Somali government, AMISOM, and even the United States are operating almost on autopilot. "You need to reassess a policy that has not worked, and what surprises me is how little assessment we have," he says. "The fact is, there is no deep thinking into what is happening. I still hear that, 'OK, the situation is not improving as fast as we want, but it's so much better than before.' They [the United States] kill important people and weaken the organization. But this is poor tactics, because if the organization is weakened they should not be performing. They have been performing in Somalia and in Kenya. Why an organization that has been weakened for years has been able to do much more than it was able to do two or three years ago is a mystery to me."[25]

Al-Shabaab has definitely put some thought into how it will prevail, and the strategy can be summed up in one word: tenacity. It's the belief that if the group keeps fighting, keeps overcoming obstacles, keeps striking at its foes with enough shock, force, and frequency, the foreign elements on Somali soil will grow weary of the bloodshed and go home. Then Al-Shabaab can push aside the apostate FGS and set up a state based on true Sharia—and maybe help allies in other countries do the same.

Jihadists tend to have a long-term mindset, notes former Somali intelligence director Fiqi. "The [military] ideology they practice is guerilla, which comes from the people who . . . used to do this in the mountainous areas of Afghanistan or in Tunisia or Algeria, who don't necessarily control big chunks of land," he says. "Instead they wander in the countryside, in the hinterland because they believe they are fighting for the righteous and are supposed to face this difficult struggle. They want to achieve their goals through resilience, perseverance, and patience."[26]

Indeed, Mahad Karate's June 2017 audio message was entitled "Success is Intertwined with Patience." A source close to Al-Shabaab said the group is prepared to lay low for several years if necessary, and then re-emerge in force when the military situation allows for victory. The plan was purportedly devised by Abu Yahya al-Libi, the late Al-Qaeda strategist who advised Godane to withdraw from Mogadishu in 2011 and also recommended to Islamic State that it go underground during a low ebb in 2010.

Given the frequency of its attacks, Al-Shabaab apparently saw no need to lay low in 2016 and '17—although its leaders could be excused for keeping their heads down. The list of Shabaab officials killed by US airstrikes has grown longer and longer since Hellfire missiles cut down Ahmed Godane. The slain include Amniyat bosses Tahlil Abdishakur and Yusuf Dheeq, bomb maker Ibrahim Ali Abdi, Westgate Mall attack planner Adan Garaar, Garissa College attack planner Dulyadeyn, senior official Abdirahman Sandhere, senior military commander Abdullahi Da'ud, Al-Qaeda representative Hassan Ali Dhoore, and a number of lower-ranking figures. In 2017 alone, the United States carried out more than two dozen airstrikes in Somalia—most targeting Al-Shabaab, along with a couple aimed at the ISIS faction in the north.

More airstrikes are sure to follow. As of late 2017, the State Department was offering rewards for fourteen current or former Shabaab figures, the highest being up to $6 million for information that "brings to justice" the emir, Abu Ubaidah.[27] Only six men in the world have commanded larger bounties under the US Rewards for Justice program. The number of Shabaab members wanted and the total sum offered for help in finding them—$59 million—were the highest among African groups that the US government has labeled as terrorist. The numbers were even higher before the State Department withdrew its $5 million reward offer for Robow in June, shortly before he surrendered to the Somali government.

But even if more missiles find their target, Al-Shabaab seems more than capable of taking the hits. While there's no doubt some of its fighters joined for non-religious reasons—forced recruitment, money—the group also has a backbone made up of thousands of die-hard jihadists who have kept fighting despite years of setbacks. Al-Shabaab can rely on them to fill leadership roles as needed. As the UN Monitoring Group on Somalia and Eritrea stated in its October 2015 report, "a senior regional intelligence source [said] that the ranks of Al-Shabaab's virtually unknown 'middle management' were so numerous and ideologically committed that the group was able to replace assassinated leaders with ease."[28]

Among the politicians, soldiers, diplomats, aid officials, analysts, and businesspeople who deal with Somalia, there is a consensus that politics—not war, not jihad, not outside domination or manipulation—is the only way to stabilize the country. If its people can agree on a political system, the thinking goes, Somalia will get a responsive and representative government, insurgent and militia groups will lose their appeal, the years of chronic violence will wind down, and the country can embark on a path to prosperity, perhaps paved by a combination of untapped natural resources, agricultural exports, tourism, and ports that could serve more of the thousands of cargo ships that sail through the Gulf of Aden and Somalia's Indian Ocean waters each year. Somali cities flourished in times gone by. Why can't it happen again?

Mogadishu has seen a rebound since Al-Shabaab gave up control in 2011. VOA reporter Pete Heinlein, who was based in Addis Ababa at the time, says the turnaround began almost immediately after the militants left. "I visited a week or so after the market was cleared. There was nothing in the streets but stray dogs and a few security guards. Four months later when I went back, the place was booming again," he says. "It was like the old market. Every morning you could see workmen with shovels, saying 'I'm ready.' They'd be working, and buildings were going up, with cement, mortar, loads of lumber coming. It was remarkable."[29]

Since then many, though not all, of the streets and buildings damaged over the previous twenty years have been repaired or rebuilt. The Bakara-Market and others are flourishing; Aden Adde International Airport has been modernized and sees dozens of takeoffs and landings per week. Several new hotels have opened in the last five years, and the sector could be said to be thriving if not for the fact that Al-Shabaab damages or destroys the hotels almost as fast as they are built.

In December 2015, the outgoing UN special representative to Somalia, British diplomat Nicholas Kay, asserted that Somalia had turned a corner. "I arrived full of hope, and I'm leaving not just with hope but with a very firm conviction that Somalia is now a fragile but recovering country and no longer a failed state," he said.[30] Few except President Mohamud completely agreed, given that the country continued to struggle with very high levels of corruption, poverty, infant mortality, and of course, violence. However, the United States gave the FGS a tangible vote of confidence in 2016 by appointing its first ambassador to Somalia in a quarter-century, Stephen Schwartz. Black Hawk Down is finally getting smaller in the rearview mirror.

So that raises still another key question: can the FGS and its friends make Somalia into a reasonably stable and well-governed nation? If the answer is no, the next twenty-five years in Somalia will look a lot like the twenty-five that just passed. If the answer is yes, Al-Shabaab (and ISIS) might struggle to survive, allowing a kind of normalcy to return. It will be a very Somali normalcy, with clans playing a dominant role in both local and national affairs. But if Somalis truly "buy in" to the FGS, they might be able to check into a hotel without fear that suicide bombers will prevent them from ever checking out.

The United States is certain to remain one of the pillars holding up the government. According to the State Department, the United States has given about $240 million in development aid since 2011 to help Somalia "achieve greater stability, establish a formal economy, obtain access to basic services and attain representation through a legitimate, credible governance."[31] That money pales beside the $1.5 billion the United States has provided to help the country deal with drought, famine, and refugees, or the billions more spent on various intelligence and military operations against Al-Shabaab.

At the time Ambassador Schwartz was appointed, a former Somali diplomat, Abukar Arman, said the United States must use more "soft power" if it really wants to make things better. "Dig water wells, rebuild roads, erect hospitals just like Turkey is doing in Somalia," he advised. "Offer capacity building programs, and scholarships to Somalis who are going to return and rebuild the country."[32] Drone strikes are not policy, he said, and a security-alone approach will not stabilize the country.

Whether President Donald Trump will listen to anyone regarding Al-Shabaab or Somalia remains to be seen. Trump said hardly a word about Africa during his 2016 campaign, but Somalia and Al-Shabaab edged into his comments, neither in a positive way. In December 2015, well before he clinched the Republican Party nomination, Trump called for "a total and complete shutdown of Muslims entering the United States." Within weeks, video of his comment turned up in an Al-Shabaab recruiting video that argued the United States is a racist, anti-Islamic society. When asked about the video, Trump expressed no concern, saying, "They use other people. What am I going to do? I have to say what I have to say."[33]

Then during a November 2016 stop in Minneapolis, Trump—wearing one of his red "Make America Great Again" hats—told a rally that the influx of Somali refugees into Minnesota was a "disaster" for the state. "You've seen first-hand the problems caused with faulty refugee vetting, with large numbers of Somali refugees coming into your state without your knowledge, without your support or approval, and with some of them then joining ISIS and spreading their extremist views all over our country and all over the world," he said.[34]

Despite the ensuing outcry, Trump performed better in Minnesota than any Republican presidential candidate in over thirty years, losing the usually solidly Democratic state to Hillary Clinton by less than 2 percent. As president, he designated Somalia as one of six Muslim-majority countries subject to heightened travel restrictions and also moved to cut the number of refugees admitted to the United States. Court battles kept both measures in flux, although the travel restrictions came into partial effect in late June 2017.

Nonetheless, almost from the day that Trump took office, it became harder for Somalis to come to America. Al-Shabaab could conceivably use these developments to paint the United States as anti-Somali and anti-Islam, and exploit the situation to attract more recruits in Minnesota, in Somalia, and other places around the world. As of this writing, the group has simply joined in the rampant bashing of Trump, calling him a "brainless billion-aire" and "arguably the most stupid president a country could ever have."[35]

—

Will Al-Shabaab ever be eliminated? "No, I doubt it," is the simple an-swer given by Roland Marchal.[36]

On May 1, 2010, two powerful explosions went off in a mosque run by Al-Shabaab in the Bakara Market. Al-Shabaab's chief recruiter Fuad Shongole was there lecturing the congregation when the blasts occurred. He survived but more than forty-five others died. The blasts have never been fully ex-plained, but it was widely suspected the government was involved and car-ried out the attack with the help of Al-Shabaab defectors.

According to Marchal, certain Western officials celebrated the incident and expressed hope there would be more such bombings in order to defeat Shabaab. "In Nairobi, the Western diplomats were clapping hands, saying this is good and so on," says Marchal. "I thought Shabaab at that time was about six thousand [members], so I said, 'Do you believe the solution is to kill 6,000 people?'"[37] You could kill sixty thousand people, he says, without serving any real purpose. The ideas that drive Al-Shabaab would live on.

Marchal says to truly fight Al-Shabaab, its opponents need to step back to reassess what the group is and why it has persevered for more than a decade in the face of huge losses and turmoil.

"First, it is not only a terrorist group, it is also a military organization, it's an insurgency, and also it has a cultural impact on the people," he says. "So you think you could get rid of the military component or the terrorist com-ponent without getting rid of the cultural dimension? I doubt very much because the cultural dimension addresses a number of issues that no one else is addressing—the failure of the elders, the fact that the Somali society has lost many values people believe it had before."[38]

Also, says Marchal, "Shabaab raises a very important issue—what should be the role of Islam in the Somali society?" In a broad legal sense, the matter is settled. Article 2 in Somalia's 2012 constitution says "Islam is the religion of the state," declares "no religion other than Islam can be propagated in the country," and adds that "no law which is not compliant with the general principles of Sharia can be enacted." Article 3 goes even further, stating that the constitution is the supreme law of the country after Sharia. Islam and Islamic law define the society, in other words.

An outsider might look at this and ask, "What more could a jihadist possibly want?" But of course, Al-Shabaab has as always wanted Somalia to not just be an Islamic country, but for Somalis to follow Sharia in its strictest terms. Marchal says this thinking has left an imprint on Somali culture. "You see a certain degree of intolerance in front of private behavior that you never had before in the Somali society," he says.

Somali Army Colonel Abdi Mohamed Dile is another who doubts Al-Shabaab can be completely eradicated. In his view, the public is too scared not to cooperate with the militants. "Al-Shabaab has been occupying these areas for seven years. They subjugated the civilians, they beheaded, they robbed, they terrorized people," he says. "It will be some time before people get over this trauma."[39]

"They did not come from outer space," he adds. "They are part of the society, a cancerous part, they reappear in wherever you clean them from. If we don't get a trained, strong Somali army it will be difficult to defeat them."

The Somali government continues to insist it can beat Al-Shabaab, through some combination of military power and making the group crumble from within. In a July 2016 speech, President Mohamud made a direct appeal to the militants, calling on them "to abandon this suicidal mission, to stop killing the innocent, to stop terrorizing their parents and brothers, to avoid orphaning Somali children," he said. "I urge them to cross over and come over to the government's side in order to live a normal life, and their rights will be protected."[40] Appeals like this since 2014 have persuaded a steady trickle of Shabaab members to switch sides. The government runs at least three "disengagement" camps for the defectors, one each in Kismayo and Baidoa, one at a secret site in Mogadishu. *Toronto Star* reporter Michelle Shephard, who was allowed to visit the Mogadishu camp in 2016, described it as primitive but said it houses about five hundred former Shabaab members and provides them with skills, education, and religious classes to ease their transition back into regular society.[41]

Of course, Al-Shabaab remains equally adamant that it will triumph by using what some analysts call the "long war strategy" of outlasting its foes. That strategy worked against the Ethiopians in 2007–2008 and may yet work against the countries behind AMISOM.

A cynical observer may conclude that neither side is going to win and that Somalia is past the point of recovery, locked into a vortex of war, lawlessness, poverty, and dependence. Indeed, Marchal sees scenarios in which the government and the clans may want to keep Al-Shabaab around for their own interests. "Shabaab, like Daesh, is [now] a secondary enemy for most of the military actors in Somalia or the region," he says. "The government, they have to protect themselves from Al-Shabaab, but on the other side, the very fact that Shabaab is wrong means they [the government] can do whatever they want, because the international community needs a government in Mogadishu to claim there has been progress."

As for the clans, he says, they often have competing demands, "so many clans try not to have all eggs in the same basket. [They think] 'Al-Shabaab is an option if things go bad. We could still talk to them so they could help us.' If Al-Shabaab is useful for many contenders, that means they have a long life."[42]

That would also mean Somalis have no hope of seeing a peaceful, working society and are condemned to live in a world defined by violence and clannism. It is puzzling how a people who have so much in common—a religion, a language, an ethnicity, and cultural traditions dating back hundreds of years—can still find a way to divide themselves.

If Al-Shabaab were to somehow disappear tomorrow, history would not be kind. The group built a formidable force and brought a kind of law and order to the areas where they seized control. But that order came at the expense of most freedoms and the stripping of people's wealth, mainly to fuel the group's endless cycle of war. The war itself would not be remembered fondly, either. Al-Shabaab says it is fighting to expel foreign forces from the country. But by any objective standard, the group was the primary reason those forces came into Somalia. And many of Al-Shabaab's attacks—ostensibly aimed at Ethiopians, AMISOM, the TFG, and now, the FGS—have killed and wounded thousands of civilians who have no role and no association with either the foreign troops or the governments.

Religiously, Al-Shabaab will not be remembered as jihadists who fought for Islam. More Somalis will remember their harsh, forbidding version of Sharia, which resulted in countless lives lost or ruined, and which in many people's minds distorted and tainted the Islamic faith.

Al-Shabaab arose as a result of the public uprising that brought the ICU to power; at the moment the only feasible way to defeat Al-Shabaab is by a grassroots movement that completely rejects the organization and its objectives. And a fanatic organization is unlikely to disappear in the absence of a state with popular backing and strong security organs.

It is sad to say, but for the foreseeable future the group will continue to threaten the emerging government in Somalia, the Horn of Africa as a whole, and any organization or foreign power that involves itself in the country's affairs.

After a decade and more of battle, the full story of Al-Shabaab is not yet written.

NOTES

PROLOGUE

1. Information on Dalha Ali comes from "Dhalinyarada iyo Dagaallada," or "Youth and Wars," a story aired by the Voice of America's Somali Service on December 25, 2009. Ali had been interviewed by VOA Somali Senior Editor Harun Maruf about a week earlier. The description of the mosque, the Huriwa district, and the general state of affairs in Mogadishu in May 2006 are drawn from Maruf's own familiarity with the Somali capital, the United Nations' *Report of the Secretary-General on the Situation in Somalia* of June 20, 2006, and contemporary news reports, including "Key Battle for Mogadishu Resumes," BBC News, May 12, 2006, and "Battle Intensifies for Mogadishu," BBC News, May 25, 2006.

1. JIHAD ARRIVES IN SOMALIA

1. This quote is from "The Book of Duarte Barbosa: An Account of the Countries Bordering on the Indian Ocean and Their Inhabitants," originally published in 1518 and now available online.

2. Johnson's full toast is at The American Presidency Project, http://www .presidency.ucsb.edu.

3. Thabo Mbeki, "Letter from the President," ANC Today, January 12–18, 2007.

4. The Ogaden war and ensuing internal unrest were widely reported at the time. A clear, concise overview of the situation can be found in "Somalia's Double Trouble as Client State," a November 1, 1981, article in the New York Times written by longtime NYT foreign correspondent Alan Cowell.

5. Videos of pre-civil war Mogadishu can be found on YouTube, posted by various parties. A particularly good source is the Somali news website Keydmedia Online, which as of 2016 had a playlist entitled "Mogadishu in the 80s."

6. Interview of Ambassador Bishop by Charles S. Kennedy for The Association for Diplomatic Studies and Training Foreign Affairs Oral History Project. Interview conducted in 1995, transcript published 1998.

7. Interview of al-Afghani childhood friend by Harun Maruf, 2015.

8. Ibid.

9. Interview of Jamal Guddoomiye by Maruf, 2017.

10. Ibid.

11. Ibid.

12. Interview of Abu Ayan by Maruf, 2017.

13. Interview of Guddoomiye by Maruf, 2017.

14. The background here on Abdullah Azzam is drawn from several sources, including "Who Killed Abdullah Azzam?" by Aryn Baker, Time, June 18, 2009; "Abullah Assam: The Man Before Osama bin Laden" by Steve Emerson, on the website of the International Association for Counterterrorism and Security Professionals; and "The Late Sheikh Abdullah Azzam's Books," by Youssef Abdul-Enein, a three-part series of commentaries on Azzam's writings published by the Combating Terrorism Center at West Point, 2008.

15. Interview of Guddoomiye by Maruf, 2017.

16. Interview of al-Afghani family member by Maruf, 2015.

17. Interview of Terry by Dan Joseph, 2015.

18. Details of Bishop's meeting with Siad Barre come from a diplomatic cable to Washington he sent on December 27, 1990.

19. Jane Perlez, "Fighting Subsides in Somali Capital," New York Times, January 29, 1991.

20. Interview of Scott Bobb by Joseph, 2017.

21. Interview of Mohamed Ali Sharman by Maruf, 2016.

22. Ibid.

23. Interview with Ibrahim Haji Mohamed by Maruf, 2016.

24. Accounts of the run-up to AIAI's first battle and the battle itself come from an interview with AIAI emir Sheikh Ali Warsame by Maruf, 2015; "Somalia's Islamists," International Crisis Group, December 12, 2005, p. 5; and "Al-Qaida's Misadventures in the Horn of Africa," Combating Terrorism Center at West Point, 2007, p. 35.

25. Interview of Warsame by Maruf, 2015.

26. The case was United States of America vs. Usama bin Laden et al. in US District Court, Southern Court of New York. The full 157-page indictment and related documents can be found online.

27. In the late 1990s, bin Laden gave several interviews in which he indicated that Al-Qaeda or Al-Qaeda–trained fighters played a role in the October 3–4, 1993, "Battle of Mogadishu." November 1996 interview with British journalist Abdul Bari Atwan, "My

Weekend With Osama bin Laden," The Guardian, November 11, 2001; March 1997 television interview with CNN reporter Peter Arnett, transcripts and videos of which are available online; May 1998 interview with American journalist John Miller, first aired by ABC News as "Talking With Terror's Banker" on June 9, 1998.

28. Abu Jabal video released by al-Shabaab in September 2015, translated from Somali.

29. Godane interview with al-Shabaab–run Radio Andalus, aired December 27, 2011.

30. Interview of Ayrow associate by Maruf, 2015.

31. Interview of Robow student by Maruf, 2017.

32. Interview of Mukhtar Robow by Maruf, 2017.

33. Interview of Bobb by Joseph, 2017.

34. Interview of Terry by Joseph, 2015.

2. The CIA, the Warlords, and Ethiopia

1. The note, dated September 12, 2001, reads: "We are shocked of the tragic death of innocent American citizens in the result of the attack that caused the collapse of the World Trade Center in New York and other cities, and we strongly deplore this cowardly terrorist action. Allow me Your Excellency to express on my name and on behalf of the Somali people my deepest condolence to the people of United States in general, and the families of those killed in the terrible tragedies." The Somali prime minister issued a longer statement eight days later, in which he said the Somali government had neither a direct nor indirect relationship with Osama bin Laden.

2. Donald Rumsfeld, news conference at the Pentagon, November 27, 2001. Transcripts published by CNN and the Washington Post.

3. Richard Myers, news conference in Brussels, December 19, 2001. Remark reported by Associated Press reporter Jeffrey Ulbrich.

4. Background on the CIA activities in Mogadishu comes from several sources. The International Crisis Group devoted a few paragraphs to the terrorist suspect hunting operation in a December 2005 report ("Somalia's Islamists"). But the operation first came to wider public attention a few months later as the ICU took over Mogadishu ("US Funding Warlords Intelligence Experts Say," David Morgan, Reuters, June 5, 2006; "Efforts by CIA Fail in Somalia, Officials Charge," Mark Mazzetti, New York Times, June 8, 2006). A series of articles entitled "The Secret War" by Sean Naylor, published by the Army Times in November 2011, recounts the operation in deeper detail. Naylor used the series as the basis for his subsequent book Relentless Strike: The Secret History of Joint Special Operations Command (St. Martin's Press, 2013). Mazzetti also wrote a book that covers aspects of the operation, The Way of The Knife (Penguin Press, 2013), as did journalist Jeremy Scahill, Dirty Wars: The World Is a Battlefield (Nation Books, 2013).

5. This account of the initial contact between the CIA and the warlord comes from the interview of Cawsley by Harun Maruf, 2015.

6. Ibid.

7. Ibid.

8. Interview of Warlord #4 by Maruf, 2015.

9. Interview of Cawsley by Maruf, 2015.

10. Ibid.

11. Ibid.

12. Information on Suleiman Abdullah's capture and torture comes from the January 2010 UN Human Rights Council report, "Joint Study on Global Practices in Relation to Secret Detention in the Context of Countering Terrorism," which details the brutal experiences of several men "renditioned" by US intelligence services to prisons in Afghanistan. Information on Mohammed Ali Isse comes mainly from "Nobody Is Watching," by Paul Salopek, *Chicago Tribune*, November 24, 2008.

13. Most information on Gouled Hassan Ahmed comes from his eleven-page Guantanamo detention sheet, dated September 19, 2008. Documents related to his request for release in 2016 can be accessed on the website of the US Defense Department's Periodic Review Board, www.prs.mil.

14. Interview of Warlord #4 by Maruf, 2015.

15. Ibid.

16. Interview of Cawsley by Maruf, 2015.

17. Interview of Toora-Toorow by Maruf, 2015.

18. Ibid.

19. Interview of Cawsley by Maruf, 2015.

20. Interview of Mogadishu radio journalist by Maruf, 2015.

21. The Al-Shabaab tag gained public use gradually, though at this point there was no group that had formally adopted the name. Terry, the Westerner, recalls hearing the name as early as 2003, although a later report from the International Crisis Group ("Somalia's Islamists," published December 12, 2005) included this line: "By far the smallest reformist groups are those composed of *jihadis*, such as the now-defunct *al-Itihaad al-Islaami* and the new, nameless one fronted by Aden Hashi Ayro."

22. Interview of Cawsley by Maruf, 2015.

23. Ambassador William Bellamy, diplomatic cable, February 24, 2006. The same cable contains a complete list of the warlords in the alliance and their clan affiliations.

24. Officials have issued many such denials over the years. One of the earliest, perhaps the first to be reported by a Western news agency, came from government spokesman Ali Abdu, responding to a TFG accusation that Eritrea had sent a cargo plane full of weapons to Mogadishu. ("Experts See Proxy War Underway in Somalia," Mohamed Sheikh Nor, Associated Press, July 26, 2006.) The government issued a written denial on its website, shabait.com, about one week later. The UN monitors' allegation that Eritrea was supplying arms to Islamists in Somalia dates back to its March 2003 report to the UN Security Council. That same report accused Ethiopia and Yemen of violating the arms embargo on Somalia as well, though not arming Islamist groups.

25. Interview of Bryden by Maruf, 2016.

26. Interview of former ICU fighter by Maruf, 2015.

27. Interview of Mohamed by Maruf, 2015.

28. Interview of Aden by Maruf, 2015.

29. Interview of Cawsley by Maruf, 2015.

30. Sheikh Sharif, radio broadcast, June 5, 2006.

31. Bellamy, diplomatic cable, June 2, 2006.

32. Bellamy, diplomatic cable, June 16, 2006.

33. Interview of Madobe by Maruf, 2014.

34. Arale's selection was not well publicized at the time, and he has since denied serving as Al-Shabaab's original leader. But his account has been contradicted by several people, including a former student at IIUI in Pakistan (see notes for Chapter 4), Fazul Mohammed in an autobiography he posted online in 2009, Ahmed Madobe during his interview with Maruf in 2014, and former Hizbul Islam spokesman Mohammed Aruus, speaking to Maruf in 2016.

35. Ibid.

36. Interview with Ayan by Maruf, 2017.

37. Quoted in a US diplomatic cable sent by the embassy in Addis Ababa, June 15, 2006. According to the cable, Meles made the comment during a June 13, 2006, meeting in Addis Ababa with US Charge d'Affaires Vicki Huddleston and Rear Admiral Rick Hunt, commander of the Combined Joint Task Force–Horn of Africa.

38. Interview of Omer by Maruf, 2015. Details on the fighting around Idale and Daynunay are also drawn from contemporary press reports, including Mustafa Haji Abdinur, "Somalia Fighting Escalates as Ethiopia Deploys Tanks: Residents," AFP, December 21 2006; Hassan Yare, "Ethiopian Tanks Roll in Somali Battle's Fourth Day," Reuters, December 22, 2006; Jeffrey Gettleman, "Ethiopian Warplanes Attack Somalia," *New York Times*, December 24, 2006; Salad Duhul, "Islamic Forces Retreat in Somalia," Associated Press, December 26, 2006.

39. Interview of Omer by Maruf, 2015.

40. Ibid.

41. Comments from Senator Russell Feingold in a December 4 cable from the US embassy in Addis summarizing a meeting between the senator and Prime Minister Meles on November 30. In addition, cables from US diplomats in Addis on October 14, October 26, December 8, and other dates reported Meles's threats to send forces across the border.

42. Frazer quoted by David Gollust, "US Says Al-Qaida Elements Running Islamic Movement," Voice of America, December 14, 2006.

43. Interview of Roland Marchal by Dan Joseph and Maruf, 2016.

44. Salad Duhul, "'Somalis Should Take Part in This Struggle," Associated Press, December 21, 2006; Guled Mohamed, "Somali Islamists Urge Muslims Worldwide to Join Jihad," Reuters, December 23, 2006. The ICU issued a call ahead of the battle, as documented in "Head of Somalia's ICU Calls the Mujahideen to Somalia," SITE Intelligence Group, November 26, 2006.

3. "The Real Jihad Has Just Started"

1. "Ethiopian Troops Enter Mogadishu," CNN, December 28, 2006; Jeffrey Gettleman, "Somalia Forces Retake Capital From Islamists," *New York Times*, December 29, 2006.

2. "Somali PM Announces Mogadishu Disarmament Plan," Reuters, January 1, 2007; Mohamed Olad Hassan and Elizabeth A. Kennedy, "Militants Flee Gov't Forces in Somalia," Associated Press, January 1, 2007.

3. Interview of Terry by Dan Joseph, 2015.

4. Interview of Gure by Harun Maruf, 2015.

5. Aweys interview by Al-Arabiya TV, aired June 21, 2007.

6. Interview of Marchal by Joseph and Maruf, 2016.

7. Interview of Toora-Toorow by Maruf, 2015.

8. Guled Mohamed, "Gunmen Attack Ethiopian Troops in Mogadishu," Reuters, January 7, 2007.

9. Cody Curran, "Global Ambitions: an Analysis of Al-Shabaab's Evolving Rhetoric," AEI Critical Threats, February 17, 2011.

10. Ibid.

11. Audio statement from al-Zawahiri, released online January 5, 2007.

12. Prime Minister Meles Zenawi said on December 26, 2006, that three thousand to four thousand troops had been sent across the border, and Ethiopian officials stuck with four thousand thereafter. But Peter Heinlein, the VOA correspondent in Addis starting in 2007, says Western diplomats told him the true figure was probably ten thousand, with the caveat that some of the troops may have been stationed on the border just inside Ethiopian territory, and they made day trips into Somalia as needed. The figure of twenty thousand appears to have originated from a December 2006 Reuters report that cited "military experts." It was then repeated in stories by other news outlets with no further attribution.

13. Rob Wise, "Al-Shabaab," The Center for Strategic and International Studies, July 2011, p. 5.

14. The US Treasury Department's Office of Foreign Assets Control (OFAC) added Aweys to its Specially Designated Global Terrorist (SDGT) list on November 7, 2001. The US State Department designated al-Turki as a terrorist on June 3, 2004.

15. Transcripts of the fund-raising calls initiated by Amina Ali and Halima Hassan were released in the joint exhibits to *United States of America v. Amina Ali*, tried in US District Court, District of Minnesota. The excerpts here were recorded October 26, 2008. At the end of this call, listeners pledged more than $2,000 for Al-Shabaab, although it is not known if all the money was subsequently paid.

16. Summaries and quotes from the phone conversations between Basaaly Saeed Moalin and Aden Ayrow were released in the June 28, 2013, trial memorandum for *United States of America v. Basaaly Saeed Moalin, Mohamed Mohamed Mohamud, Issa Doreh, Ahmed Nasir Taalil Mohamud*. The case was tried in US District Court, Southern District of California.

17. Initial reports were by David S. Cloud, "U.S. Strikes Suspected Al-Qaeda Target in Somalia," *New York Times,* January 8, 2007, and "U.S. Strikes in Somalia Reportedly Kill 31," CBS News, January 8, 2007. The main follow-up report came a month later: Michael R. Gorden and Mark Mazzetti, "U.S. Used Base in Ethiopia to Hunt Al-Qaeda," *New York Times,* February 23, 2007. Information from Mohamed Omer comes from an interview by Maruf in 2015. Information on Ayrow's radio address comes from an article in Uganda's *New Vision* newspaper, March 8, 2007, and "Smoldering in Somalia," a 2007 article by international analyst J. Peter Pham.

18. Jeremy Scahill, "Blowback in Somalia," *Nation,* September 7, 2011.

19. Aweys Osman Yusuf, "Car Bomb Kills Four in North Mogadishu," February 18, 2007, Shabelle Media Network; Sahal Abdulle, "Four Killed in Mogadishu Car Explosion," Reuters, February 18, 2007.

20. Guled Mohamed and Sahal Abdulle, "Mortar Blasts Rock Mogadishu," Reuters, February 20, 2007.

21. *Report of the Secretary-General on the Situation in Somalia,* February 28, 2007, paragraph 66, p. 16.

22. "Somalia Reconciliation Conference in April: President," AFP, March 1, 2007.

23. "Heavy Fighting Erupts in Mogadishu," Reuters, March 6, 2007; "Three Killed in Heavy Mogadishu Fighting," AFP, March 6, 2007.

24. "Somalia Islamists 'Fire Missiles' at Aircraft," AFP, March 9, 2007.

25. "Somalia Government Votes to Relocate to Mogadishu," AFP, March 12, 2007.

26. "Mortar Bombs Hit Somali Presidential Palace," Reuters, March 13, 2007; "Mortar Shells Hit Somali Presidential Residence," AFP, March 13, 2007.

27. Quoted in "Shell-Shocked: Civilians Under Siege in Mogadishu," by Human Rights Watch, August 2007, p. 66.

28. Interview of Mogadishu student by Maruf, 2015; Also, Sahal Abdulle, "Soldiers Corpses Dragged Through Mogadishu," Reuters, March 21, 2007.

29. Diplomatic cable sent by US Ambassador to Kenya Michael Ranneberger, March 21, 2007.

30. Ibid.

31. Ranneberger cable, March 22, 2007.

32. Ranneberger cable, March 26, 2007.

33. Interview of Toora-Toorow by Maruf, 2015.

34. Interview of Western journalist by Maruf, 2015.

35. Interview of Hersi by Maruf, 2016.

36. Ibid.

37. Interview of Gure by Maruf, 2015.

38. Xan Rice, "400 Die in Mogadishu's Worst Fighting for 15 Years," *Guardian,* April 3, 2007; "Mogadishu Clashes Killed 1,000," BBC News, April 10, 2007; Stephanie McCrummen, "Clan Says Recent Mogadishu Deaths Exceed 1000," *Washington Post,* April 11, 2007.

39. Interview of President Yusuf by VOA Somali Service, aired March 21, 2007.

40. All quotes from Ali in this section come from "Dhalinyarada iyo Dagaallada," or "Youth and Wars," by Harun Maruf, VOA Somali Service, December 25, 2009.

4. GODANE

1. Details of Arale's arrest and transfer to Guantanamo come from his detainee assessment sheet, dated August 6, 2007, later obtained by Wikileaks and released in 2011. Arale was never formally charged with any offenses, and Carol Rosenberg of the *Miami Herald* reported in December 2009 that he had been transferred back to Somalia. He apparently stayed away from militant activities thereafter and was living in Burco, Somaliland, as of 2016.

2. Accounts of the meeting come mainly from Zakariye Hersi's interviews with Harun Maruf in 2015 and 2016.

3. The US State Department announced the reward for Hersi on June 7, 2012. The news release described Hersi as Al-Shabaab's "head of intelligence"—something that Hersi has strenuously denied, insisting he was head of *military* intelligence.

4. Background on Hersi and Arale's friendship comes from a Somali man who was enrolled at IIUI at the same time as the future Al-Shaabab leaders. "Zakariye and Ismail Arale, who was also a student, were friends," says Ahmed, who asked that his last name be withheld for safety reasons. "At the time we did not know their connections with Al-Shabaab, and their frequent travels to Somalia were mysterious, but we later found out Arale was the chairman of Al-Shabaab. Zakariye graduated BC in economics, but before he started studying [for his] masters we heard money was sent by Ismail Arale and he traveled to Somalia. He never returned."

5. Interview of Hersi by Maruf, 2015.

6. Ibid.

7. Interview of Salat by Maruf, 2015.

8. Ibid.

9. Interview of Askar by Maruf, 2015.

10. Interview of Godane acquaintance at IIUI by Maruf, 2015.

11. Interview of Salat by Maruf, 2015.

12. Interview of Askar by Maruf, 2015.

13. The "Al-Qaeda Manual," p. 10. Translations of the manual, originally provided by the FBI, can be found various places online.

14. Interview of Salat by Maruf, 2015.

15. Godane's interview with Radio Andalus, aired December 27, 2011.

16. Interview of Askar by Maruf, 2015.

17. Interview of Godane acquaintance by Maruf, 2015.

18. Interview of Janaqow by Maruf, 2015.

19. Ibid.

20. Rashid M. X. Noor, "Hargeysa Judicial Court Acquits 'Hassan Dahir Aweys' of Terrorism," the *Somaliland Times*, December 9, 2006. A December 2008 UN Security Council report said both Godane and Ibrahim al-Afghani had been sentenced to death

in absentia by a Somaliland court "for their respective roles in the murders of several foreign aid workers in 2003 and 2004." But that "fact," repeated in other profiles of Godane, was incorrect. The Somaliland newspaper reported the correct twenty-five-year sentence at the time it was handed down. Note that the paper put Aweys in the headline; he was more prominent than Godane or al-Afghani prior to 2009.

21. The announcement of Godane as Al-Shabaab's new emir appeared that day in two articles without bylines: "Somalia Islamic Movement Makes New Leadership," on SomaliNet, and "Dhaqdhaqaaqa Al-Shabab oo shacciyay in uu Hoggaamiye cusub yeeshay," on the Somali-language Hiiraan Online. The SomaliNet story cited a London Arab newspaper, *Sharq Al-Aswsat,* as its source, while Hiiraan Online cited a jihadist website. Both articles referred to the new emir as Sheikh Mukhtar Rahman Abu-Zubayr. The Hiiraan Online piece also announced that Mukhtar Robow had been appointed Al-Shabaab's spokesman.

22. Interview of Hersi by Maruf, 2015.

23. Interview of Gure by Maruf, 2015.

24. Interview of Terry by Joseph, 2015.

25. Interview of Heinlein by Joseph, 2015.

26. Interview of Gure by Maruf, 2015.

27. Designation of Al-Shabaab, Office of the Coordinator for Counterterrorism, US State Department, March 18, 2008. The original designation was made by Secretary of State Condoleezza Rice on February 26.

5. Al-Shabaab Americans

1. Interview of Fadumo Hussein by Harun Maruf, 2015. All her quotes and impressions in this section come from that interview.

2. Information on Omar's movements comes from *United States of America v. Ahmed Ali Omar et al.,* 3rd superseding indictment, 2010, pp. 9–10. The case was tried in US District Court, District of Minnesota.

3. Ibid.

4. US Census Bureau, 2010. The number has likely grown since then.

5. Interview of Dr. Yusuf by Maruf for VOA, 2013.

6. Interview of Fletcher by Maruf for VOA, 2013.

7. Osman Ahmed, VOA panel discussion, Minneapolis, 2013.

8. Interview of Mohamed Abdullahi Hassan by Maruf, 2015.

9. Abdurrahman Mohamed Abdalla, VOA panel discussion, Minneapolis, 2013.

10. Salman al-Mujahir, video produced by Al-Shabaab's al-Kataib arm, released online 2015.

11. US diplomatic cable sent from the US embassy in Stockholm, July 20, 2009.

12. Ibid.; Paul Cruickshank, "Terror in Europe: Why Sweden Is in the Crosshairs," CNN, December 14, 2010.

13. Laura Yuen, "Al-Shabab Recruit Wanted to be 'Good Muslim,'" Minnesota Public Radio, October 10, 2012.

14. Ibid.

15. The testimony of the agent, Mary Boese, can be found in the complaint against Jones, accessible at https://www.justice.gov/opa/file/812381/download.

16. Hammami was the subject of many media profiles from 2010 onward. The background here is drawn from Andrea Elliott, "The Jihadist Next Door," *New York Times*, January 27, 2010; "Profile: Omar Hammami," Anti-Defamation League, February 9, 2010; Gena Somra, "Parents Despair for 'Most Wanted' Terrorist Son," CNN, June 7, 2013; and Matt Blake, "We Will Love Him Until We Die," *Daily Mail*, June 10, 2013.

17. Interview of Hammami by Maruf for VOA, September 5, 2013.

18. Al Jazeera report, aired October 2007.

19. The warrant, issued in Mobile, Alabama, can be viewed on the website of the Investigative Project on Terrorism, www.investigativeproject.com.

20. ABC News in particular paid attention to Hammami, covering each one of his "raps" like it was a new Bruno Mars release. From a review of two Hammami songs in April 2011: "In 'Send Me A Cruise,' Hammami begs to be plastered by a tank shell, a drone attack, or a cruise missile, so that he can be martyred like some of the heroes he names.... In his trademark tuneless drone, he claims 'an amazing martyrdom' is what he 'strive(s) for and adore(s)' ... Hammami opens the other track, 'Make Jihad With Me,' by slowing his voice down to a deep Barry White growl and then invites the youth of the West to make jihad with him, promising that together they will 'wipe Israel off the globe.'"

21. "Terror Charges Unsealed in Minneapolis Against Eight Men, Justice Department Announces," US Department of Justice, November 23, 2009.

22. Laura Yuen, "FBI Confirms Man Allegedly Behind Somali Bombing as Minnesota Man," Minnesota Public Radio, June 9, 2011; "FBI: Minnesota Man Was Suicide Bomber in Somalia," CNN, June 9, 2011.

23. Osman Ahmed, VOA panel discussion, Minneapolis, 2013.

6. RADICAL ORGANIZATION

1. Interview of Dhusamareb resident by Harun Maruf, 2015.

2. Information on the airstrike that killed Ayrow comes from Stephanie McCrummen and Karen DeYoung, "U.S. Airstrike Kills Somali Accused of Links to Al-Qaeda," *Washington Post*, June 2, 2008, and Eric Schmitt and Jeffrey Gettleman, "Qaeda Leader Reported Killed in Somalia," *New York Times*, June 2, 2008.

3. Godane interview with Radio Andalus, aired December 27, 2011.

4. Aden quoted by Schmitt and Gettleman, "Qaeda Leader Reported Killed in Somalia," *New York Times*, June 2, 2008.

5. Details of the fighting come from Matt Bryden, Gilbert Charles Barthe, Charles Lengalenga, Ignatius Yaw Kwanti-Mensah, *Report of the Monitoring Group on Somalia pursuant to Security Council resolution 1811*, December 10, 2008; an unclassified US diplomatic cable sent from the embassy in Kenya on August 26, 2008; and contemporary reports on the takeover of Kismayo by Reuters and AFP. The diplomatic cable, signed

by US Ambassador to Kenya Michael Ranneberger, portrayed the takeover as being the work of a "loose coalition" of clan militias, ICU remnants, and Al-Shabaab elements, while the UN monitors more accurately described it as a win for "Shabaab and its allies."

6. Tristan McConnell, "Who's Funding Al-Shabaab's War in Somalia?" Public Radio International, November 5, 2010; Rob Wise, "Al-Shabaab," Center for Strategic and International Studies Transnational Threats Project, July 2011. A senior Somali presidential advisor, Ahmed Mumin Warfa, cited the same figure in a November 18, 2010, article, "Al-Shabab Razes Somali Forests to Finance Jihad," published by the Jamestown Foundation Terrorism Monitor.

7. Mohamed Sheikh Nor, "Somali Radical Islamists Capture Port Town," Associated Press, November 16, 2008; Al-Shabaab statement of November 17, 2008, available on the website of SITE Intelligence.

8. Interview of Barawe resident by Maruf, 2015.

9. Interview of Hersi by Maruf, 2015.

10. Boko Haram captured a large chunk of northeastern Nigeria at its peak in 2013 and 2014, and its leader, Abubakar Shekau, declared a caliphate in the region. But according to numerous witnesses, Boko Haram never set up a real governing structure and ruled the population through gunfire, kidnappings, and fear. Like Al-Shabaab, Boko Haram members enforced a strict form of Sharia but seemed to take it to an even greater extreme than their Somali counterparts. According to a report by Drew Hinshaw ("Nigerian Insurgents Take a Shot at Governing," *Wall Street Journal*, December 19, 2014), Boko Haram members in the town of Gwoza ordered residents to fast even when it wasn't Ramadan. In the village of Garkidi, they taught people that the sun doesn't rise because the Earth is spinning—it rises because God commands it.

11. Godane interview with Radio Andalus, aired December 27, 2011.

12. Mukhtar Robow, on-camera interview with Al Jazeera, aired January 14, 2009.

13. Godane interview with Radio Andalus, aired December 27, 2011.

14. Information on Al-Shabaab's destruction of Sufi tombs and shrines is drawn from "Country Reports on Human Rights Practices for 2009," US State Department, p. 536.

15. Interview of Barawe resident by Maruf, 2015.

16. Interview of Quulle by Maruf, 2015.

17. Ibid.

18. Interview of former local Shabaab judge by Maruf, 2015.

19. Interview of witness to the stoning of Asha Ibrahim Dhuhulow by Maruf, 2015.

20. Ibid.

21. The FBI added Nabhan to its "Seeking Information-War on Terrorism List" on February 24, 2006. The FBI said Nabhan was wanted for questioning in connection with attacks on a hotel and an airliner in Mombasa, Kenya, in 2002. But US intelligence had been chasing after Nabhan since at least the 1998 embassy attacks in Nairobi and Dar es Salaam.

22. Interview of Jama by Maruf, 2015.

23. Interview of former Al-Shabaab commander by Maruf, 2015.

24. Interview of former Shabaab judge by Maruf, 2015.

25. Interview of former Shabaab official by Maruf, 2015.

26. Interview of second former Shabaab judge by Maruf, 2016.

27. Interview of Somali journalist by Maruf, 2015.

28. Interview of former Shabaab commander by Maruf, 2015.

29. Interview of former local Shabaab official by Maruf, 2015.

30. According to statistics kept by the piracy center of the International Maritime Bureau, Somali pirates hijacked forty-two ships in 2009 and forty-nine ships in 2010.

31. Interview with former Shabaab media official by Maruf, 2017.

32. Interview with former Somali pirate by Maruf, 2017.

33. Interview of Bryden by Maruf, 2016.

34. Meles quoted in "Stuck in Somalia," by Jason McLure, *Newsweek*, April 10, 2008.

7. "TFG IN GRAVE JEOPARDY"

1. Dalha Ali quoted by Harun Maruf, "Youth and Wars," VOA Somali Service, December 25, 2009.

2. Interview of Salat by Maruf, 2015.

3. Robow quoted in "Somali Fighters Warn Western Powers," Al Jazeera, December 20, 2008.

4. Almaqdis quoted in "Somali Fighters Warn Western Powers," Al Jazeera, December 20, 2008.

5. Estimate from *Report of the Monitoring Group on Somalia pursuant to Security Council resolution 1811*, issued December 10, 2008, p. 11.

6. Ambassador Ranneberger, diplomatic cable, December 11, 2008.

7. Interview of Terry by Dan Joseph, 2015.

8. Interview of former Al-Shabaab fighter by Maruf, 2015.

9. Interview of Aden by Maruf, 2015.

10. "Fighters Overrun Somali Town," Al Jazeera, January 27, 2009.

11. Abdulahi Hassan, "Inside Look at the Fighting Between Al-Shabab and Ahlu-Sunna Wal-Jama," Combating Terrorism Center at West Point, March 15, 2009.

12. Information on Aweys' journey to Mogadishu comes from *Report of the Monitoring Group on Somalia Pursuant to Security Council Resolution 1853*, issued March 10, 2010, p. 16.

13. Interview of Marchal by Maruf and Joseph, 2016.

14. Mareeg Online, "Ulema Make Their Recommendations," February 19, 2009.

15. Interview of Hersi by Maruf, 2016.

16. Ibid.

17. Transcripts of the fund-raising calls initiated by Amina Ali and Halima Hassan were released in the joint exhibits to *United States of America v. Amina Ali*. The excerpts from the Ali-Burhan call were recorded April 19, 2009.

18. Osama bin Laden message, "Fight on, Champions of Somalia," released March 19, 2009.

19. Final preparations began the first week in May. Information on the buildup comes from "Heavy Weapons Heading for Somali Capital—Website," BBC Monitoring, May 6, 2009, citing the Somali website Goobjoog.com; and a report from Garowe Online, May 6, 2009.

20. Ban Ki-moon, "Report of the Secretary-General on Somalia pursuant to Security Council resolution 1863," April 16, 2009.

21. The cable, sent by the embassy in Addis Ababa on May 14, 2009, quoted Mahdi Dahir Nur, an ASWJ leader who spoke to a US political officer in Addis two days earlier.

22. Interview of General Anod by Maruf, 2015.

23. Information on the first three days of battle comes from "Somali Islamists Say at Least 12 Killed in Clashes," Reuters, May 8, 2009; "Somalia: At Least Seven Dead in Mogadishu Clashes," AFP, May 9, 2009; and the diplomatic cable sent by Ambassador Ranneberger on May 11, 2009.

24. Bilal quoted by Abdi Sheikh, "Clashes Kill at Least 65 in Somalia in 3 Days," Reuters, May 10, 2009.

25. Salad Duhul, "35 Killed in Somalia Fighting Over the Weekend," Associated Press, May 10, 2009; "Mortar Shell Kills 14 at Mogadishu Mosque," AFP, May 10, 2009.

26. Ranneberger cable, May 11, 2009.

27. Ranneberger cable, May 13, 2009.

28. Ranneberger cable, May 11, 2009.

29. Ranneberger cables on May 11 and May 17, 2009.

30. Ranneberger cable, May 13, 2009.

31. Fidow quoted by Abdulkadir Khalif, "Foreigners Helping Us, Says Somali Islamist," *Daily Nation* (Kenya), May 12, 2009.

32. The warnings cited come from "Somalia: Rebels Prepared to Take Mogadishu?" Strafor, May 13, 2009; "Mogadishu Mired in Fresh Mayhem," BBC News, May 13, 2009; and Scott Baldauf, "Somali Government Encircled by Hardline Islamists," *Christian Science Monitor*, May 13, 2009.

33. Godane quoted in "Somali Insurgent Leader Vows to Fight 'Until Jerusalem Freed,'" AFP, May 13, 2009.

34. Ranneberger cable, May 13, 2009.

35. Ibid.

36. "Mogadishu Braces for Final Insurgent Assault," AFP, May 14, 2009.

37. Aweys quoted in "Hardline Somali Leader Urges President to Step Down," AFP, May 14, 2009.

38. Details on the May 14 fighting come from the AFP articles above and "Government Forces and Opposition Fight over a Key Road Not Far from Villa Somalia," Hiiraan Online, May 14, 2009; "Heavy Rains Aggravating Conditions for 'Poorest of the Poor,'" IRIN News, May 14, 2009; and Abdi Sheikh, "Clashes in Somalia Kill 139 Civilians," Reuters, May 14, 2009.

39. Interview of Aden by Maruf, 2015.

40. Ranneberger cable, sent at 10:20 UTC, May 14, 2009.

41. Ibid.

42. Ranneberger cable, sent at 13:52 UTC, May 14, 2009.

43. The US monetary help was referenced in a May 18, 2009, cable from Ranneberger: "Both Sheikh Sharif and Sharmarke, as well as Sharif Hassan and Omar Hashi, were grateful for the monetary assistance provided by the US the week of May 11."

44. A cable sent by Hillary Clinton to the US mission at the UN the evening of May 15, 2009, told the diplomats there to give the letter to the sanctions committee at the earliest opportunity. The actual content of the letter was transmitted to US embassies in Addis Ababa, Nairobi, and Kampala in a separate cable from Clinton on May 22.

45. Transcript of briefing by unidentified senior State Department official, June 26, 2009, available on the department's website, www.state.gov.

46. September 3rd letter from Acting Assistant Secretary of Legislative Affairs Michael C. Polt to Senator Russell Feingold, who had requested the information in late July.

47. Quoted in "Heavy Rains Aggravating Conditions for 'Poorest of the Poor,'" IRIN News, May 14, 2009.

8. "Send Troops . . . Within 24 Hours"

1. Details on the Carson-Omaar meeting come from a diplomatic cable sent by Secretary of State Hillary Clinton to seven US embassies in Africa on May 22, 2009.

2. Report from *Somaliland Times*, May 23, 2009.

3. Ranneberger cables on May 17 and 21, 2009; "Somali Fighters Capture Key Town," Al Jazeera, May 17, 2009.

4. UN Security Council resolution 1872, adopted on May 26, 2009.

5. UN Security Council resolution 1907, adopted December 23, 2009.

6. Patrick Worsnip, "U.N.: Little Pledged Aid Paid Up for Somali Security," Reuters, October 9, 2009.

7. Diplomatic cable from US embassy in South Africa, May 20, 2009.

8. Ranneberger cable, June 4, 2009.

9. Details on these payments comes from *Report of the Monitoring Group on Somalia Pursuant to Security Council Resolution 1853*, issued March 10, 2010, p. 23.

10. "Director of Radio Shabelle Murdered in Mogadishu," Reporters Without Borders, June 7, 2009; Ranneberger cable, June 8, 2009.

11. "Court Sentences Man in Murders of Five Somali Journalists," Committee to Protect Journalists, March 4, 2016.

12. Abdi Sheikh and Abdi Guled, "Somali Rebel Boss Aweys May Be Dead," Reuters, June 7, 2009; Ranneberger cable, June 7, 2009.

13. Ranneberger cable, June 9, 2009; Aweys interview with VOA Somali Service, June 7, 2009.

14. Ranneberger cable, June 15, 2009.

15. "Six Dead in Somali Battle," AFP, June 16, 2009; "Renewed Fighting in Mogadishu," Hiiraan Online, June 16, 2009.

16. Mohammed Ibrahim, "Police Chief Killed in Somalia Fighting," *New York Times,* June 17, 2009; Abdi Guled and Ibrahim Mohamed, "Fighting in Somali Capital Kills at Least 22," Reuters, June 17, 2009; Ranneberger cable, June 18, 2009.

17. Ranneberger cable, 11:02 UTC, June 18, 2009.

18. Ibid.

19. Mohammed Amiin Addow, "Somali Security Minister Killed," CNN, June 18, 2009; Ranneberger cable, 11:40 UTC, June 18, 2009.

20. Quote from an Al-Shabaab video released online in 2009.

21. Joint exhibits to *United States of America v. Amina Ali.* The excerpts from this Ali-Hassan call were recorded June 18, 2009.

22. Ranneberger cable, 11:40 UTC, June 18, 2009.

23. Details on the Karan district fighting come from "Fresh Fighting Restarts in Mogadishu," Shabelle Media Network, June 19, 2009; "Somali MP Killed in Mogadishu," Shabelle Media Network, June 19, 2009; "Thousands Flee from Somali Capital to Escape Fresh Fighting," AFP, June 20, 2009; and Ranneberger cable, June 22, 2009.

24. Ranneberger cable, June 22, 2009.

25. Details on the June 20 fighting come from "Thousands Flee from Somali Capital to Escape Fresh Fighting," AFP, June 20, 2009; "Fighting Restarts in Mogadishu," Shabelle Media Network, June 20, 2009; and Ranneberger cable, June 22, 2009.

26. "Somalia Seeks Emergency Military Help," VOA, June 20, 2009.

27. Ibid.

28. Nur quoted by Mustafa Haji Abdinur, "Somalia Seeks Urgent Foreign Military Aid," AFP, June 20, 2009.

29. Sharif quoted by Mareeg News, "Somalia: President Calls State of Emergency," June 21, 2009.

30. Dhere quoted in "Somalia Islamists Warn Against Foreign Intervention," AFP, June 21, 2009.

31. "Ethiopia Rejects Somalia's Request," BBC, June 21, 2009.

32. Ranneberger cable, June 22, 2009.

33. Ranneberger cable, June 23, 2009.

34. Details on the "trial" come from "Somali Islamists Order Teenagers' Hands, Legs Amputated," Reuters, June 22, 2009; "Somali 'Thieves' Face Amputation," BBC News, June 22, 2009.

35. "Somali Armed Group Al-Shabaab Should Not Carry Out Amputations," Amnesty International press release, June 22, 2009.

36. The descriptions of the amputations come from "Somali Militants Amputate Teenagers' Hands and Legs," Reuters, June 25, 2009; Xan Rice, "Somali Militia Cuts Off Right Hands and Left Feet of Teenagers Accused of Stealing," *Guardian,* June 25, 2009; and "Somali Militants Amputate Suspected Thieves Hands, Feet," VOA News, June 25, 2009.

37. Ismael Abdulle quoted by Xan Rice, "Somali Schoolboy Tells of How Islamists Cut Off His Leg and Hand," *Guardian,* October 20, 2010.

38. Xan Rice, *Guardian,* June 25, 2009.

9. Zenith and Stalemate

1. Mustafa Haji Abdinur, "Besieged Somali Leader Declares State of Emergency," AFP, June 22, 2009.

2. Scott Baldauf, "Ethiopian Troops Return to Somalia," *Christian Science Monitor*, June 22, 2009.

3. Odinga quoted by Alisha Ryu, "Kenya Undecided on Sending Troops to Somalia," VOA News, June 22, 2009; Peter Leftie, "Kenyan PM hints at Military for Somalia," *Daily Nation* (Kenya), June 22, 2009.

4. Diplomatic cable by Ambassador Michael Ranneberger, June 22, 2009.

5. Diplomatic cable by Ambassador Donald Yamamoto, June 25, 2009.

6. "Hunger Stalks Mogadishu Hospitals," IRIN News, June 22, 2009.

7. UN Office for the Coordination of Humanitarian Affairs report, June 30, 2009.

8. Ali quoted by Abdiaziz Hassan, "Somali Legislators Flee Abroad, Parliament Paralyzed," Reuters, June 24, 2009.

9. Interview of Jama by Harun Maruf, 2015.

10. Interview of Mahdi by Maruf, 2015.

11. Ibid.

12. "Shabaab Leader Tells Somalis to Prepare for Islamic State," SITE Intelligence, July 13, 2009.

13. Interview of Fiqi by Maruf, 2015.

14. Ibid.

15. Interview of Jama by Maruf, 2015.

16. Ambassador to Ethiopia John Yates, diplomatic cable, February 13, 2010.

17. Interview of Terry by Joseph, 2015.

18. Charge d'affaires Pamela Slutz, diplomatic cable, July 14, 2009.

19. Bariyge Bar Hoku, quoted in "Fighting Eases in Somalia," by Pete Heinlein, VOA, July 13, 2009.

20. Dhumaal comments reported in Ranneberger cable, July 3, 2009.

21. Information on Ali's comments around this time come from "Dhalinyarada iyo Dagaallada," or "Youth and Wars," by Harun Maruf, VOA Somali Service, December 25, 2009.

22. The friend's comments were sent via email to Maruf, 2015.

23. Secretary of State Hillary Clinton, Nairobi press conference, August 6, 2009.

24. Quotes come from "Harsh War, Harsh Peace: Abuses by Al-Shabaab, the Transitional Federal Government and AMISOM in Somalia," by Human Rights Watch, April 19, 2010.

25. Ibid.

26. Mahdi interview by Maruf, 2015.

27. Abdi Guled, "Fighting Kills 22 in Somali Capital Mogadishu," Reuters, August 21, 2009; "31 Dead in Mogadishu Battles and Bombs," Garowe Online, August 21, 2009.

28. Information on this round of fighting comes from Abdiaziz Hassan and Sahra Abdi, "Somali President Calls for Ramadan Ceasefire," Reuters, August 22, 2009;

"Dagaal mar kale saaka ka dhacay Magaalada Muqdisho," Hiiraan Online, August 21, 2009; a series of short news updates published by Al Shahid news between August 21 and 23, 2009; and a diplomatic cable sent by Ranneberger, August 22, 2009.

29. Aweys quoted by Mohamed Ahmed, "Somali Insurgents Reject Ceasefire Call," Reuters, August 23, 2009.

30. Details on the killing come from Jeffrey Gettleman and Eric Schmitt, "US Kills Top Qaeda Militant in Southern Somalia," *New York Times*, September 14, 2009; Karen DeYoung, "Special Forces Raid in Somalia Killed Terrorist with Al-Qaeda Links, U.S. Says," *Washington Post*, September 15, 2009.

31. Gettleman and Schmitt, "US Kills Top Qaeda Militant in Southern Somalia," *New York Times*, September 14, 2009.

32. Information on the attack comes from Ibrahim Mohamed, "Suicide Car Bombers Hit Main AU Base in Somalia," Reuters, September 17, 2009; "Somali Suicide Blasts Kill 14 Peacekeepers," AFP, September 17, 2009; and Ranneberger cable, September 17, 2009.

33. Mohamed Olad Hassan, "Shelling in Somali Capital Kills 24, Wounds 60," Associated Press, October 22, 2009; "Somalia President Escapes Surprise Attack," CNN, October 28, 2009; "Heavy Fighting and Shelling Kills Four, Wounds 11 Others in Mogadishu," Shabelle Media Network, October 28, 2009.

34. Interview of Fiqi by Maruf, 2015.

35. Information on the attack comes from "Deadly Suicide Blast Rips Through Hotel in Somalia," VOA News, December 3, 2009; "Somalia Graduation Ceremony Blast Kills 23," CNN, December 4, 2009; and interview of Mohamed Olad Hassan by Dan Joseph, 2016. There are also numerous videos on YouTube showing the moment of the blast and the aftermath.

36. Mohamed Olad Hassan, "Somalis Protest Bombing, Gov't Warns of New Threat," Associated Press, December 7, 2009; "Attack on Graduation Ceremony the 'Last Straw,'" IRIN, December 10, 2009.

37. The statement was signed by AMISOM, the European Union, the East African bloc IGAD, the League of Arab States, Norway, the United Nations, and the United States.

38. "Ideological Differences Split Somalia's Al-Shabaab," Garowe Online, December 20, 2009; "Al-Shabab Militants Divided Over Tactics, Foreign Control," Voice of America, December 22, 2009.

39. Ranneberger cable, December 24, 2009.

40. Ibid.

41. Ranneberger cable, January 1, 2010.

10. THE RAMADAN OFFENSIVE

1. "Somalia's Army Chief Barely Escapes Attack," Associated Press, January 7, 2010. Information on the attack itself comes from AP and "Twenty Die as Sides Exchange Shelling in Mogadishu," Xinhua, January 7, 2010.

2. Ranneberger cable, February 7, 2010.

3. Mohamed Olad Hassan and Katharine Houreld, "Delays Plague Somali Offensive Against Islamists," AP, February 7, 2010.

4. Dhere quoted by Mustafa Haji Abdinur, "Mogadishu Residents Flee Ahead of Offensive," AFP, February 10, 2010.

5. US ambassadors reported the tensions in diplomatic cables from Deputy Chief of Mission in Ethiopia Tulinabo Mushingi, December 18, 2009, and ambassador to Ethiopia John Yates, February 19, 2010.

6. Niyoyankana quoted in Yates cable, February 19, 2010.

7. Interview of Pete Heinlein by Dan Joseph, 2015.

8. Ambassador to Burundi Pamela Slutz, diplomatic cable, January 29, 2010; Elizabeth Dickinson, "For Tiny Burundi, Big Returns in Sending Peacekeepers to Somalia," *Christian Science Monitor*, December 22, 2011.

9. Ibrahim Mohamed, "Rebel Group Orders UN Food Agency to Leave Somalia," Reuters, February 28, 2010.

10. Xan Rice, "Somali Radio Stations Bow to Islamic Ban on Music," *Guardian*, April 13, 2010; Mohamed Ibrahim, "Somali Radio Stations Halt Music," *New York Times*, April 13, 2010.

11. Shugri quoted by Mohamed Ahmed, "Somalia Fighting Kills 24," Reuters, May 16, 2010.

12. Interview of Terry by Joseph, 2015.

13. Interview of General Anod by Maruf, 2015.

14. "Somali President Joins Troops on Front Lines," VOA News, July 1, 2010; "Somali President Leads Troops in Anniversary Battle," BBC News, July 1, 2010.

15. Interview of Anod by Maruf, 2015.

16. Interview of Fiqi by Maruf, 2015.

17. Dhere quoted in "New Al-Qaida Threat: Somali Group Claims Blasts," AP, July 12, 2010.

18. Godane audio message, July 14, 2010.

19. Interview of Marchal by Maruf and Joseph, 2016.

20. Interview of Olad Hassan by Joseph, 2016.

21. Ibid.

22. Ibrahim Mohamed, "Somalia's Al-Shabaab Rebels Expel Three Aid Groups," Reuters, August 9, 2010; Mohamed Olad Hassan, "Somalia's Al-Shabaab Bans Three Aid Agencies," Associated Press, August 10, 2010.

23. "A Number of People Arrested for Shaving Beard," Keydmedia.net, August 12, 2010.

24. "Foreign Militants Killed Preparing Bombs in Somalia," Reuters, August 21, 2010.

25. Wangui Kanina, "More AU Troops Arrive to Boost Somalia Peace Force," Reuters, August 23, 2010; Sarah Childress, "African Troops Aim to Quell Somali Insurgency," *Wall Street Journal*, August 23, 2010; "Uganda Deploys Another 750 Peacekeepers in Somalia," Xinhua, September 2, 2010.

26. The unidentified woman's quote is in "Harsh War, Harsh Peace," a report on Somalia by Human Rights Watch, released April 19, 2010.

27. The quote from this woman, different than the one in the note above, is in "No Place for Children," a report on Somalia by Human Rights Watch, released February 20, 2012.

28. Interview of Marchal by Maruf and Joseph, 2016.

29. Wamunyinyi quoted by Sarah Childress, "African Troops Aim to Quell Somali Insurgency," *Wall Street Journal*, August 23, 2010.

30. Interview of Robow by Maruf, 2017.

31. Details on the August 23 fighting come from "Dagaal ka dhacey Muqdishu, 30 qof oo ku dhimatey," Garowe Online, August 23, 2010; "Corpses Litter Streets Amid Mogadishu Fighting," IRIN, August 24, 2010; "Somalia Rebels Alshabab Take Over Radio Station in Mogadishu," Al Shahid News, August 24, 2010.

32. Interview of Hassan by Joseph, 2016.

33. Unidentified worker quoted in "Corpses Litter Streets Amid Mogadishu Fighting," IRIN, August 24, 2010.

34. Ibid.

35. The description of the Muna Hotel attack is drawn from "Attack at Muna Hotel," *Wall Street Journal*, August 24, 2010; Jeffrey Gettleman, "At Least 30 Killed in Somali Hotel Attack," *New York Times*, August 24, 2010; Ibrahim Mohamed and Abdi Sheikh, "Somali Militants Storm Hotel, 31 Dead Includes MPs," Reuters, August 24, 2010; Mike Pflantz, "Suicide Bombers kill 32 in Deadliest-Attack On Western-Backed Government," *Telegraph*, August 24, 2010; and "A Capital on Edge After Hotel Attack During Ramadan," Sudarsan Raghavan, *Washington Post*, August 28, 2010.

36. Information on the fighting the nights of August 24 and 25 comes from "Al Shabaab Push Toward Somali President's Palace," Reuters, August 25, 2010; Mohamed Olad Hassan, "Third Day of Fighting in Somalia's Capital Kills 8," AP, August 25, 2010; Wilifred Mulliro, "10 Civilians Killed as Rebels Try to Capture Presidential Palace," Al Shahid News, August 26, 2010; Interview of Mohamed Olad Hassan by Joseph, 2016.

37. Interview of Hassan, 2016.

38. Interview of Dhagabadan by Maruf, 2015.

39. Abu-Muscab quoted in "Mogadishu Battle Rages On After Hotel Carnage," AFP, August 25, 2010.

40. Ali quoted in "Al Shabaab Push Toward Somali President's Palace," Reuters, August 25, 2010.

41. Sudarsan Raghavan, "Somali Militants Grow," *Washington Post*, August 28, 2010.

42. Islamic State remarks reported by SITE Intelligence, August 27, 2010.

43. Interview of Anod by Maruf, 2015.

44. Ibid.

45. Interview of Hassan by Joseph, 2016.

46. Interview of Sheikh Sharif Sheikh Ahmed by Maruf, 2015.

47. Information on Dahla Ali's final attack comes from "Suicide Attack on Somalia's Government Foiled," Associated Press, September 20, 2010; "Qof isku qarxiyey gudaha Villa Somalia," Garowe Online, September 20, 2010; "Suicide Attack Takes Place at

Presidential Palace," Keydmedia.com, September 21, 2010. The photo of Ali comes from the latter source.

11. WITHDRAWAL

1. Somali government statement, "TFG Welcome UN Call for More Troops as Al-Shabab Lose Ramadan Offensive," Ministry of Information, September 17, 2010.

2. Information on the Godane/Robow rift, including details on casualties from the Ramadan Offensive and the various maneuvers and meetings afterward, comes from Abdi Mohamed, "Islamists Face Off in Deepening Rifts," Somalijournal, September 28, 2010; "Somali Militant Group Al-Shabaab Could Split," Associated Press, October 8, 2010; Adan Diini, "Serious Rift in Somalia's Al-Shabaab," SUNA Times, October 10, 2010; Hassan Abbas, "Schism in Al-Shabaab Leadership Follows Failed Ramadan Offensive," Jamestown Foundation Terrorism Monitor, October 28, 2010; and interview of Mohamed Olad Hassan by Dan Joseph, 2016.

3. Major Anthony Lukwago Mbusi quoted in "Somalia Battles Measure Success in Meters," by Jan Ferguson, CNN, September 15, 2010.

4. "Somali Militant Group Could Split," Associated Press, October 8, 2010.

5. Quoted in Somali government press release, October 4, 2010.

6. Quoted in "Abu Mansur Denies Dispute with Godane," Garowe Online, October 9, 2010.

7. Interview of Jama by Harun Maruf, 2015.

8. Interview of Mahdi by Maruf, 2015.

9. Ibid.

10. Letter from Atiyah Abd Al-Rahman to Godane dated December 11, 2010. The letter was seized by US Navy SEALS in the raid that killed Osama bin Laden at his Abottabad, Pakistan, hideout in 2011 and released in 2016 by the Office of the Director of National Intelligence.

11. Quoted in "17 Dead in Mogadishu Clashes, Aweys Praises Al-Shabab," Garowe Online, December 29, 2010.

12. Information on Farmajo's background comes from multiple VOA Somali Service articles done during his time as prime minister as well as John Leland, "After a Break to Run Somalia, Back at His Cubicle," *New York Times*, December 6, 2011.

13. Interview of Fiqi by Maruf, 2015.

14. Ibid.

15. Ibid.

16. Ibid.

17. Ibid.

18. Interview of Dhagabadan by Maruf, 2015.

19. Interview of Fiqi by Maruf, 2015.

20. Interview of Anod by Maruf, 2015.

21. Ibid.

22. Report entitled "Somalia: The Transitional Government on Life Support," by the International Crisis Group, February 21, 2011.

23. Quoted in "AU Peacekeepers in Somalia Cut Trench System, Kill 6 Foreign Fighters," Xinhua, February 21, 2011.

24. Information on the day's fighting comes from "Somali Forces in Fresh Anti-Insurgent Push," AFP, February 23, 2011; "Somali Troops Seize Rebel Bases in Mogadishu—Govt," Reuters, February 23, 2011; and "The Battle for Mogadishu," *Jane's Terrorism and Security Monitor*, April 8, 2011.

25. Interview of Fiqi by Maruf, 2015.

26. Interview of Jama by Maruf, 2015.

27. "The Battle for Mogadishu," *Jane's Terrorism and Security Monitor*, April 8, 2011.

28. Interview of Mahdi by Maruf, 2015.

29. Ibid.

30. Interview of Anod by Maruf, 2015.

31. Interview of Jama by Maruf, 2015.

32. Interview of aid worker by Maruf, 2016.

33. The accounts of Somali famine victims come from a report by Nisar Majid, Guhad Adan, Khalif Abdirahman, Jeeyon Janet Kim, and Daniel Maxwell, "Narratives of Famine Somalia 2011," published in 2016 by the Feinstein International Center at Tufts University in Somerville, Massachusetts.

34. Quoted by Ibrahim Mohamed, "Somali Rebels Say Famine Label Used for Politics," Reuters, July 21, 2011.

35. Interview of Jama by Maruf, 2015.

36. Ibid.

37. Quoted by Alshahid News, "Al Shabab Completely Withdraws from Mogadishu," August 7, 2011.

38. Interview of Hersi by Maruf, 2016.

39. Interview of Mahdi by Maruf, 2016.

40. Quoted in "Shabaab Leader Says It Is Wrong to War with Forces Armed with Tanks," Mareeg News, August 12, 2011.

41. Interview of Somali media commentator by Maruf, 2016.

42. Interview of medical worker by Maruf, 2016.

12. DIVISIONS AND PURGE

1. Interview of Hersi by Harun Maruf, 2015.

2. Interview of Marchal by Maruf and Dan Joseph, 2016.

3. Interview of Hersi by Maruf, 2015.

4. Quoted by Guled Mohamed, "Al Shabab Admit to Public Cruelty and Abuse of Power," *Star* (Nairobi), December 30, 2010.

5. Text of letter sent by Osama bin Laden to contact in Somalia, dated August 9, 2010.

6. Text of letter sent by Atiyah Abd al-Rahman to Godane, dated December 11, 2010.

7. Interview of former Shabaab commander by Maruf, 2016.

8. Interview of Hersi by Maruf, 2016.

9. Interview of Anod by Maruf, 2016.

10. Godane interview on Radio Andalus, aired December 27, 2011.

11. Text of bin Laden letter to Godane, dated August 7, 2010, released by the Combating Terrorism Center at West Point in May 2012.

12. Omar Hammami video released March 16, 2012. The back-and-forth between Hammami and Al-Shabaab around this time is well covered by Bill Roggio in "Omar Hammami's Personal Dispute with Shabaab," longwarjournal.org, January 6, 2013.

13. Ibid.

14. Audio of Aweys speech, March 30, 2012.

15. Ibid.

16. Information on the Kismayo attack comes from Abdi Sheikh, "Kenya Troops Fight on Beaches in Assault on Somali Rebel City," Reuters, September 28, 2012; Nicholas Bariyo and Idil Abshir, "Africa Troops Launch Assault on Somali Militant Bastion," Wall Street Journal, September 29, 2012; Cyrus Ombati, "Al Shabaab Stronghold Falls," Standard (Kenya), September 29, 2012.

17. Lutfi Sheriff Mohammed and Robyn Dixon, "Somali Troops Take Key Port of Kismayo After Al Shabab Rebels Retreat," Los Angeles Times, October 1, 2012.

18. Al-Shabaab tweet reported by Bill Roggio, "Shabaab Rebukes American Commander Omar Hammami," longwarjournal.org, December 18, 2012.

19. "We are not involved in any act." Aweys quoted in report by London-based Somali TV, February 16, 2013.

20. Al-Afghani, "Open Letter to Our Shaykh and Our Amir, Shaykh Ayman al-Zawahiri, may God Protect Him," April 2013.

21. Interview with Abu Ayan by Maruf, 2016 and interview with Mukhtar Robow by Maruf, 2017.

22. Godane message released in late May or early June 2013.

23. Interview of Ayan by Maruf, 2016.

24. Ibid.

25. Interview of Afghani family member by Maruf, 2015.

26. Interview of Ayan by Maruf, 2016.

27. Ibid.

28. Interview of Hersi by Maruf, 2016.

29. Ibid.

30. Ibid.

31. Ibid.

32. Statement by Mus'ab, July 1, 2013.

33. Interview of Hersi by Maruf, 2016.

34. Interview of Hammami by Maruf for VOA, September 2013.

35. Interview of Ayan by Maruf, 2016.

13. The Road to Westgate

1. Accounts of the killing of Fazul Mohammed come from Malkhadir H. Muhumed, "Young Somali Soldier: I Killed Top Al-Qaeda Operative," Associated Press, June 14, 2011, and "Al-Qaeda's East Africa Chief 'Killed in Somalia,'" AFP, June 11, 2011.

2. The official was quoted by Sudarsan Raghavan, "Alleged Architect of U.S. Embassy Bombings Killed," *Washington Post*, June 11, 2011.

3. Sheikh Sharif quoted in "Somalia Vows to Defeat Qaeda After Killing Mohammed," Reuters, June 13, 2011.

4. Interview of Marchal by Harun Maruf and Dan Joseph, 2016.

5. Interview of Sambayo childhood friend by Maruf, 2016.

6. Ibid.

7. Ibid.

8. Interview of Abdulkadir by Maruf, 2016.

9. The phrase was used in a late 2010 Al-Shabaab video, as reported by The Investigative Project on Terrorism, December 2, 2010.

10. Interview of Toora-Toorow by Maruf, 2015. Toora-Toorow's account of the two nuns' kidnapping is broadly confirmed by contemporary reports, in particular "Somali Gunmen Kidnap Two Italian Nuns," Reuters, November 10, 2008.

11. Haji quoted by VOA Somali Service, June 24, 2009.

12. Interview of Marchal by Maruf and Joseph, 2016.

13. Godane letter to bin Laden, released by the Office of the Director of National Intelligence in 2016.

14. Spokesman Sheikh Hassan Yacub Ali quoted by Scott Baldauf, "Kenya Poised to Intervene in Somalia," *Christian Science Monitor*, June 25, 2009.

15. Clayton Swisher and Will Jordan, "UK Under Pressure Over Kenya Kidnapping," Al Jazeera.com, October 21, 2015.

16. Kira Cochrane, "Judith Tebbutt: My Six Months as a Hostage Of Somali Kidnappers," *Guardian*, July 9, 2013.

17. Quoted by Nina Elbagir and David McKenzie in "Somali Militants Threaten to Enter Kenya If Troops Don't Withdraw," CNN, October 17, 2011.

18. Quoted in "Kenya, Somalia Agree on Common War Plan," Panapress, October 31, 2011.

19. Quoted in US diplomatic cable from Ambassador to Ethiopia John Yates, February 2, 2010.

20. Quoted in "Kenya Sends Troops to Attack al-Shabab," Al Jazeera, October 24, 2011.

21. Interview of Marchal by Maruf and Joseph, 2016.

22. Interview of Robow by Maruf, 2017.

23. Ibid.

24. The allegation is one of many in the thirty-two-page NIS report, entitled "Terrorism Threat in the Country," which was obtained by Al Jazeera and released in 2013.

25. Ibid.

26. Ibid.

27. This tweet and the others mentioned came from Hammami's Twitter account, abu m@abuamerican, on April 25, 26, and 30, 2013.

28. US State Department media note, March 20, 2013.

29. Hammami tweet quoted by J. M. Berger, "Omar and Me," *Foreign Policy*, September 17, 2013.

30. Hammami tweet quoted by Spencer Ackerman, "'There's No Turning Back': My Interview with a Hunted American Jihadist," *Wired*, April 4, 2013.

31. Interview of Elyas by Maruf, 2016.

32. Ibid.

33. Interview of Hammami by Maruf for VOA, September 3, 2013.

34. Interview of Elyas by Maruf, 2016.

35. Tweet from abu m @abuamerican on September 15, 2013. It read, "We confirm the martyrdom of Omar Hammami in the morning of Thur 12 2013. Shafik's family please accept our condolences."

36. Interview of M-Arab by Maruf, 2016.

37. Kenyan police quoted by Fred Mukinda, "Police 'Thwarted' Westgate-Style Al-Shabaab Attack," *Daily Nation*, March 21, 2015.

38. Interview of Somali intelligence official by Maruf, 2016.

39. This account of the Westgate attack is drawn from the blogs and articles of the *Guardian, New York Times, Daily Nation*, CNN, and other news outlets during and after the attack.

40. Al-Shabaab tweets reported in "Shabaab Siege on Westgate is Culmination of Years of Threats to Kenya," SITE Intelligence, September 21, 2013.

41. Peter Bergen, "Are Mass Murderers Using Twitter as a Tool?" CNN, September 27, 2013.

42. Ibid.

43. The video, entitled, "The Westgate Siege for Retributive Justice," can be seen on jihadology.net.

44. Translation of the masked fighter's statement is from the Site Intelligence Group, February 21, 2015.

45. Interview of Somali intelligence official by Maruf, 2016.

46. Cheryl Pellerin, "U.S. Attack Kills Key al-Shabab Operative in Somalia," Department of Defense News, March 18, 2015.

47. Christopher Anzalone, "The Nairobi Attack and al-Shabab's Media Strategy," Combating Terrorism Center at West Point, October 24, 2013.

14. No Place to Hide

1. Interview of Omer by Harun Maruf, 2015.

2. The White House, "National Strategy for Counter-Terrorism," June 2011, p. 14.

3. Greg Jaffe and Karen DeYoung, "U.S. Drone Targets Two Leaders of Somali Group Allied with al-Qaeda," *Washington Post*, June 29, 2011.

4. "Somalia: Reported Covert U.S. Actions, 2001–2016," Bureau of Investigative Journalism, first posted February 22, 2012, and periodically updated.

5. Ibid.

6. Quoted by Michelle Shepard in "Kenya Mall Attack: Training of a Terrorist," *Toronto Star*, September 24, 2013.

7. Ham quoted by Craig Whitlock, "U.S Intensifies Its Proxy Fight Against al-Shabab in Somalia," *Washington Post*, November 24, 2011.

8. State Department media note, "Rewards for Justice—al-Shabaab Leaders Reward Offers," June 7, 2012.

9. Quoted in "Somalia's Shebab Mock U.S. Bounty, Offer Camels for Obama," AFP, June 9, 2012.

10. The joke response was relayed to Hillary Clinton in an email by her assistant Huma Abedin on June 10, 2012. The email was made public by the State Department in December 2016.

11. Al-Shabaab Twitter message, May 29, 2013.

12. Hassan quoted in a one-hour video posted by Al-Shabaab to YouTube in May 2013. The video, as of December 2016, was still online at http://ia600707.us.archive.org/22/items/3d-f7dhrhm-2/SoBeware2_HQ.m4v.

13. Ryan Gallagher, "The Life and Death of Objective Peckham," *Intercept*, October 15, 2015.

14. Hassan, 2013 Shabaab video.

15. Abdi Guled, "Al-Shabab Executes 3 Members," Associated Press, July 22, 2012.

16. Al-Shabaab Twitter message, July 22, 2012, reported by longwarjournal.org.

17. Interview of Somali intelligence official by Maruf, 2016.

18. Kenya Defense Forces statement, January 10, 2014.

19. "Somali Militant Commander Killed by Missile in Suspected Drone Attack," Associated Press, January 26, 2014.

20. Interview of Somali intelligence official by Maruf, 2014.

21. Ibid.

22. This account of Godane's final days and hours is drawn largely from Maruf and Joseph, "Sources on Final Days of al-Shabab's Godane," VOA News, September 26, 2014.

23. "Of course, you very well know . . ." Olum comment aired on Bartamaha.com, August 31, 2014.

24. Interview of Somali intelligence official by Maruf, 2016.

25. Quoted by Maruf and Joseph, VOA, 2014.

26. Pentagon statement, September 5, 2014.

27. Kenyatta statement released through government of Kenya, September 6, 2014.

28. Quoted in "Uganda Gave Crucial Intel on Al-Shabaab Leader," AFP, September 6, 2014.

29. Quoted in "US Confirms al-Shabaab Leader's Death," Al Jazeera, September 6, 2014.

15: ARRESTING THE DECLINE

1. This account of Dhere's whereabouts and conversations after Godane's death comes from a Somali intelligence source.

2. The account of who attended the meeting comes from various sources, including a source within Al-Shabaab.

3. The quotes about Godane and the announcement of his successor come from "Statement of HSM Leadership," a message from Al-Shabaab released online September 5, 2014, and reported by SITE Intelligence.

4. Interview of Hersi by Harun Maruf, 2016.

5. Ibid.

6. Interview of Mohamud by Maruf, 2016.

7. Interview of Ayan by Maruf, 2016.

8. Ibid.

9. Interview of Nur by Maruf, 2016.

10. Interview of Dile by Maruf, 2016.

11. Interview of Gasle by Maruf, 2016.

12. Interview of Abdi by Maruf, 2016.

13. Ibid.

14. Interview of Nur by Maruf, 2016.

15. Ntigurirwa quoted in "Joint Security Update on Operation Indian Ocean by Somali Government and AMISOM," AMISOM News, October 29, 2014.

16. Mohamud quoted in "Joint Security Update on Operation Indian Ocean by Somali Government and AMISOM," AMISOM, October 29, 2014.

17. Matt Bryden, "The Reinvention of Al-Shabaab," The Center for Strategic and International Studies, February 2014.

18. Clint Watts, "End Game: Al-Shabab as a Model for the Islamic State's Decline," World Politics Review, March 31, 2015.

19. Ismail Kushkush and Jeffrey Gettleman, "As Power of Terror Group Declines, Once Feared Fighters Defect," New York Times, November 4, 2014.

20. Interview of former Shabaab member by Maruf, 2016.

21. "Nkaissery Admits Intelligence Was Ignored in Garissa Attack," by Jane Goin, Capital FM Kenya, April 30, 2015.

22. The figure is cited in "Kenyans Lament Al-Shabab's Recruitment of Youths," by Mohammed Yusuf, VOA, May 26, 2015.

23. Interview of Dile by Maruf, 2016.

24. Quoted in "Al-Shabab Defectors Being Rehabilitated to Re-enter Somali Society," by Harun Maruf, VOA, August 29, 2017.

25. Interview of Bryden by Maruf, 2016.

26. "The Return of Al-Shabab," Daily Beast, March 25, 2016; "Al-Shabab's Staying Power," Newsweek, May 18, 2016; "Why Are Efforts to Counter al-Shabaab Falling So Flat?" Brookings Institution, April 5, 2016; "Decline and Fall of Al-Shabab? Think Again," Matt Bryden, April 2015.

16. The ISIS Incursion

1. Department of Defense news briefing at the Pentagon, June 4, 2010. Odierno's exact words were, "In addition to that, over the last 90 days or so, we've either picked up or killed 34 out of the top 42 Al-Qaeda in Iraq leaders."

2. Transcript of UN Secretary-General remarks to "Security Council High-Level Summit on Foreign Terrorists," September 24, 2014.

3. Bynam testimony to the Subcommittee on Counterterrorism and Intelligence of the House Committee on Homeland Security, April 29, 2015.

4. Interview of Galgala source by Harun Maruf, 2016.

5. Interview of Puntland Intelligence Agency official by Maruf, 2016.

6. Godane speech of May 14, 2014, reported by SITE Intelligence and quoted by Thomas Joscelyn and Bill Roggio, "Shabaab Leader Calls for Mediation in Syria, Says Zawahiri Is our 'Sheikh and Emir,'" longwarjournal.com, May 17, 2014.

7. Al-Somali was quoted on Twitter by various supporters and often seen posing for photos with fellow militants. One picture showed him at the controls of an anti-aircraft gun, leaving unanswered the question of how he'd hit anything if he fired it.

8. Interview of Somali intelligence in Gedo by Maruf, 2016.

9. Salman audio message released online March 18, 2015.

10. The letter, released in March 2015, can be found as of this writing at https://somalianews.files.wordpress.com/2015/03/bushra.pdf

11. ISIS video released online May 21, 2015.

12. "Senior Al Shabaab officials Discussing Allegiance to ISIL," Garowe Online, July 9, 2015.

13. Mohamed Odawa, "Somalia Terror Group to 'Pledge Allegiance to ISIS' in Terrifying Expansion of Caliphate," Daily Mail, July 10, 2015.

14. The 45-minute al-Zawahiri audio message was released online September 9, 2015.

15. Interview of former Al-Shabaaab member by Maruf, 2016.

16. Interview of Hassan by Maruf for VOA's Somali Service, December 8, 2015.

17. The video, released April 14, 2016, was spotlighted 11 days later on the website of the Long War Journal, at longwarjournal.org.

18. Interview of PIA official by Maruf, 2016.

19. Interview of Hussein by Maruf for VOA, 2016.

20. Interview of former Shabaab media official by Maruf, 2016.

17. Al-Shabaab's Future

1. Information on Robow's press conference is drawn from "Former al-Shabab No. 2 Quits Militant Group," by Harun Maruf, VOA, August 15, 2017, and a video of the conference posted to somalispot.com.

2. Information on the attack is drawn from "Five Policemen Killed in IED Attack," by Cyrus Ombati, Standard, August 15, 2017, and "Al-Shabaab Kills 5 Police Officers," Xinhua, August 15, 2017;

3. Transcript of April 13, 2017, Rycroft speech at www.gov.uk.

4. Coats remark from "Worldwide Threat Assessment of the U.S. Intelligence Community," a presentation Coats made to the US Senate Select Committee on Intelligence, May 11, 2017.

5. AFRICOM statement, June 11, 2017.

6. "This is Why al-Shabaab Won't Be Going Away Anytime Soon," Tricia Bacon, *Washington Post*, July 6, 2017.

7. Interview of Bryden by Harun Maruf, 2016.

8. Interview of Ali by Maruf, 2016.

9. Interview of Marchal by Maruf and Dan Joseph, 2016.

10. Interview of Fiqi by Maruf, 2016.

11. "How Many Fatalities Has the African Union Mission in Somalia Suffered?" Paul D. Williams, IPI Global Observatory, September 10, 2015.

12. AFRICOM Posture Statement, presented by Waldhauser to US Senate Armed Services Committee, March 11, 2017.

13. Quoted in "Uhuru Concerned by Premature Focus on Somalia Troops Exit," Capital FM News in Nairobi, May 10, 2017.

14. Quoted in "In Somalia It's a Race Against Time for AFRICOM-Backed Troops," John Vandiver, *Stars and Stripes*, April 20, 2017.

15. Guterres remarks at London conference on Somalia, May 10, 2017.

16. Report of the Monitoring Group on Somalia and Eritrea pursuant to Security Council resolution 2182 (2016), p. 75.

17. Ibid., p. 74.

18. *Jane's Sentinel Security Assessment* for Somalia, December 7, 2016.

19. Interview of Bryden by Maruf, 2016.

20. "Fueled by Bribes, Somalia's Election Seen as a Milestone of Corruption," *New York Times*, February 7, 2017.

21. "Gallant Soldiers Fought to Their Last Breath to Repulse Attackers," by Nyambega Gisesa, *Daily Nation*, January 30, 2017.

22. Karate remarks from "29 Dead After Al-Shabab Attack Mogadishu Restaurants," Harun Maruf, VOA, June 15, 2017.

23. "Shabab Reveals Face of Mukhtar Abu-Zubeir in Video Biography of Former Leader," SITE Intelligence, June 26, 2017.

24. Interview of Bryden by Maruf, 2016.

25. Interview of Marchal by Maruf, 2016.

26. Interview of Fiqi by Maruf, 2016.

27. The State Department added Ubaidah to its rewards list on November 10, 2015.

28. Report of the Monitoring Group on Somalia and Eritrea pursuant to Security Council resolution 2182 (2014): Somalia, p. 27.

29. Interview of Heinlein by Dan Joseph, 2016.

30. Quoted by Maruf, "UN Envoy: Somalia Momentum Toward Peace 'Unstoppable,'" VOA News, December 30, 2015.

31. US State Department Bureau of African Affairs fact sheet, April 12, 2017.

32. Quoted by Maruf, "US Urged to Use 'Soft Power' in Somalia," VOA News, June 30, 2016.

33. Trump comment on CBS's "Face the Nation," January 3, 2016.

34. Trump quoted by Jenna Johnson and Sean Sullivan, "Why Trump Warned About 'Somali Refugees'—and Why It Could Backfire," *Washington Post*, November 7, 2016.

35. "New al-Shabab Video Calls Trump 'Brainless Billionaire,'" Abdi Guled, AP, July 24, 2017.

36. Interview of Marchal by Maruf, 2016.

37. Ibid.

38. Ibid.

39. Interview of Dile by Maruf, 2016.

40. President Mohamud speech, July 1, 2016.

41. Michelle Shepard, "Inside the Secret Rehab Camp for Former Shabab Members," *Toronto Star*, June 25, 2016.

42. Interview of Marchal by Maruf, 2016.

INDEX

popularity of, 38, 47, 268; US skepticism toward, 38–39, 44
Islamic radicalism, recruitment in US, 72–73
Islamic State (ISIS): vs. Al-Qaeda, 254–55; and Al-Shabaab, 157, 256–64; Amniyat attacks, 260–62; in Iraq and Syria, 253–54; Mumin faction 260–64; and Trump, 279; US airstrikes, 276

Jabal, Abu, 21, 24
Jabal, Ali, 193
Jabhat, 89–90
Jama, Mohamed, 89, 130, 132, 164, 171, 176
Janaqow, Abdirahman, 66–67
Jones, Malik, 76, 79, 261

Karate, Mahad: and Al-Qaeda, 21–22; as Al-Shabaab deputy emir, 194; audio message, 276; and ISIS, 259; Tanfid meeting, 193; Ubaidah selection, 242, 244; Ulema meeting, 107
Kay, Nicholas, 278
Kenya: and Al-Shabaab, 215–16, 265–66; Al-Shabaab recruitment in, 208–10; in AMISOM, 198, 208–10; El Adde attack, 251; Garissa University college attack, 249–50; Godane assassination attempts, 232; incursion into Somalia, 212–14; kidnapping of nuns, 211; Kismayo capture by, 199; Kulbiyow attack, 270; porous borders, 15, 210; US embassy bombing, 25; Westgate Mall attack, 219–24
Kenyatta, Uhuru, 216, 223, 226, 249, 270
Kismayo: and AIAI, 19–20; Al-Shabaab capture of, 82–83; AMISOM capture of, 199; defector camps, 281; drones, 226, 228; Adan Garaar, 220; Godane targeted by, 232–35; governance, 87; and ISIS, 258, 260; Islamist tensions 137–38; revenue, 69, 94; stoning, 88; and Abu Ubaidah, 243–44
Kulbiyow attack, 270, 273

Lokech, Paul, 169, 175
Luyiuma, Issa Ahmed, 149–50

Madobe, Aden 147
Madobe, Ahmed, 40, 52
Mahdi, Hassan, 130–31, 138, 164–66, 172, 177
Maktab, 83, 84–85, 86, 93, 244
Marchal, Roland: on Al-Qaeda East Africa, 208–9; on Al-Shabaab heterogeneity, 191–92; on Al-Shabaab income, 96; on Al-Shabaab in Ethiopia, 268; on AMISOM, 275; on Ethiopian invasion, 47–48; on foreign fighters, 153; on Hizbul Islam, 107; on Kenya 212, 214; on Museveni, 150; on Somalia's future, 280–82; on US-Ethiopia relations, 44
Mbeki, Thabo, 9
Me'aad, Ibrahim Haji Jama. See Al-Afghani, Ibrahim
Mogadishu: and AIAI, 19, 32; Al-Shabaab attacks on, 194–95; Al-Shabaab formed in, 40; Al-Shabaab withdrawal from, 176–78; AMISOM arrival, 49, 61; AMISOM gains, 163–64, 168, 170–71, 173, 175; August 2009 fighting, 138–39; Berjawi/Sakr killings, 229–30; chaos in, 2, 17, 26, 129–30; CIA-warlord operations, 29–32; counter-warlord operations, 33–34; defector camp, 281; drone base, 226; economic rebound, 277; and Eritrea, 36–37; Ethiopia–Al-Shabaab fighting, 68–69; Ethiopian pullout, 106; Ethiopians arrive, 43, 46; fall of Siad Barre, 17; February 2010 fighting; 144–45; first AMISOM attacks 132–33; first attacks on Americans, 21; French agents kidnapped 135–36; history, 7–10, 16; hotel attacks, 250, 273; Hotel Shamo bombing, 140–41; ICU-warlord clashes, 35–38; Islamic courts, 25; June 2009 clashes, 121–26; killing of Fazul Mohammed, 207–8; March 2007 clashes, 52–57; May 2009 clashes,

Williams, Paul D., 270
World Food Program, 94, 129, 146, 173

Yamamoto, Donald, 43, 129
Yare, Abdullahi: bounty for, 227; Tanfid
    Council, 107, 193
Yare, Asad. *See* Ali, Dalha
Yusuf Ahmed, Abdullahi: artillery use in
    civilian areas, 57, 69; defeat of AIAI in

Puntland, 20; peace conference, 53, 61;
    as president of TFG, 41, 47, 53, 104, 191;
    resignation 105–6; suicide bomb attack
    on, 41

Zakat, function of, 84, 93–95
Zobe intersection truck bomb, 267

HARUN MARUF is a senior editor in Voice of America's Somali Service who has been covering Somalia and its struggles with war, terrorism, piracy, and drought since the early 1990s. With over one hundred thousand followers, Maruf is the most followed Somali journalist on Twitter and a primary source of news to many people in the Horn of Africa. Prior to joining VOA, Maruf worked for the BBC and Associated Press as a reporter in Somalia and as a researcher for Human Rights Watch. He holds a Master of Arts in international journalism from the City University of London.

DAN JOSEPH is an editor in Voice of America's central newsroom and has headed its Africa desk since December 2005. He is a 1992 graduate of Indiana University, where he earned a bachelor's degree in journalism and political science.